Architectural Building Codes

Architectural Building Codes

A Graphic Reference

by
James G. Scott

VAN NOSTRAND REINHOLD
I(T)P® A Division of International Thomson Publishing Inc.

New York • Albany • Bonn • Boston • Detroit • London • Madrid • Melbourne
Mexico City • Paris • San Francisco • Singapore • Tokyo • Toronto

Copyright © 1997 by Van Nostrand Reinhold

I(T)P® an International Thomson Publishing Company
The ITP logo is a registered trademark used herein under license

Printed in the United States of America

For more information, contact:

Van Nostrand Reinhold
115 Fifth Avenue
New York, NY 10003

Chapman & Hall GmbH
Pappelallee 3
69469 Weinheim
Germany

Chapman & Hall
2-6 Boundary Row
London
SE1 8HN
United Kingdom

International Thomson Publishing Asia
221 Henderson Road #05-10
Henderson Building
Singapore 0315

Thomas Nelson Australia
102 Dodds Street
South Melbourne, 3205
Victoria, Australia

International Thomson Publishing Japan
Hirakawacho Kyowa Building, 3F
2-2-1 Hirakawacho
Chiyoda-ku, 102 Tokyo
Japan

Nelson Canada
1120 Birchmount Road
Scarborough, Ontario
Canada M1K 5G4

International Thomson Editores
Seneca 53
Col. Polanco
11560 Mexico D.F. Mexico

1 2 3 4 5 6 7 8 9 10 BBR 03 02 01 00 99 98 97

Library of Congress Cataloging-in-Publication Data

Scott, James G.
    Architectural building codes: a graphic reference / James G.
  Scott.
        p.   cm.
    Includes bibliographical references and index.
    ISBN 0-442-01910-6
    1. Building laws--United States.   I. Title.
  KF5701.S38   1997
  343.73'078624--dc21   97-7384
                                                           CIP

http://www.vnr.com
product discounts • free email newsletters
software demos • online resources

email: info@vnr.com

A service of I(T)P®

To Beth and Lizzie
the joys of my life
and in loving memory of
William Finley Sahlie
whose enthusiasm for my pursuits never ceased

Contents

Acknowledgments

It would have been impossible for me to complete this book without the help and support of many friends old and new. Encouragement and valuable advice was given to me by Bill Blackerby, Maurice Branscomb, Mark and Martha Burns, Clyde Buzzard, Carlos DeSaracho, Tim Doggett, Glynn Durrett, Jim Hillhouse, Ed Lamont, John Pelham, Dick and Dana Pigford, Jim and Jayne Pool, Harvey Ragland, Mary Schaffer, Steve Smith, Adele Stockham, Brett and Mary Thorstad, Rick Vognild, Mark Waldo, and Mary Wunderlich. Nap and Amy Gary provided a great deal of support, and calmed my nerves with their knowledge of publishing and their good friendship. My clients Stevan and Chris Goozee, Sheila Swain, and Rodney Winston showed remarkable patience with me during the inevitable design and construction delays that occurred whenever a book deadline approached. Valuable comments were received from Bill Hecker, Ed Kemp, Billy Manning, and Frank Setzer, all close friends who served as peer reviewers. Other friends, Dan Cahill, Bill Gilchrist, David Gregory, Clay Hickerson, Marta Salinas-Hovar, and Dick Pigford, volunteered to be peer reviewers. Their talents were never used in that capacity, but many of them contributed in other ways. Bill Tangye, Rick Vognild, Bruce Burdette, Karla Hicks, Brad Ware, and the rest of the staff at the Southern Building Code Congress International, Inc. (SBCCI) and Glen Winslow of SBCCI, PST, and ESI pulled out all of the stops and helped me immensely. A special thanks must be given to Larry and Ann Harper, and Bill Hecker. The three of them together kept my business afloat, provided me with daily encouragement, and assisted with the many tasks that made this book possible. Their support went beyond the call of duty.

Because my business is still fairly young, the process of writing this book has been a slow one, as I have had to attend to the sorts of things necessary for starting a business. Nevertheless, Jane Degenhardt and Beth Harrison of Van Nostrand Reinhold were patient with me though I know they often wondered if I would ever make a single deadline. For the record, I didn't. However, they always worked with me to help me complete my tasks, and I thank them for that. Carla Nessler had the unenviable task of dealing with me during the editing phase. I submitted late and made several changes. She was unflappable and great to work with.

My family deserves special thanks also, as they gave me the sort of support that only a family can give. My father and mother, John and June Scott, and my mother-in-law Shirley Sahlie encouraged me every step of the way. The tragic death of my father-in-law, William Sahlie, who was one of my most fervent supporters prevents me from personally being able to place a copy of this book in his hands, something that I had looked forward to for some time. I also received a great deal of support from my siblings and in-laws, especially Tom and Ann Douglass, Tommy and David Douglass, John and Barbara Scott, Bill and Mary Jo Scott, John and Ginger Virden, Clark and Cindy Sahlie, and Malcolm and Linda Patterson. Anne Sahlie's driving skills helped us to find the Fort Lauderdale Fedex office in ten minutes flat for one of my publishing submissions.

To my wife Beth goes the greatest thanks. I abandoned chores, failed to complete projects, forgot promises, and had tumultuous mood swings because of the time required for me to write and sketch. Meanwhile, she completed her residency in pediatrics, passed her boards, wed me, gave birth to our beautiful daughter, and lost her loving father during the process of writing this book. In spite of all of this, she stood behind me all the way, and remains my hero in this whole process.

Preface

I attended a boarding school just south of Birmingham, Alabama for my tenth through twelfth grades of education. Indian Springs School was full of many great institutions, but one of the most awe-inspiring was Jack, the night watchman. It was not unheard of for Jack to catch students "misbehaving" at one area of the eight-hundred-acre campus, while almost simultaneously monitoring the activities of other students at the opposite end of the campus. From this amazing ability was born the "Multiple Jack Theory." The theory held that there was more than one Jack, for Jack was everywhere. My understanding of this theory was that it was actually metaphysical in nature and not simply arithmetical. In other words, there were not lots of Jacks running around which looked and sounded alike, but rather, several Jacks constituting individual parts of a whole that was ultimately understood as "Jackness."

The more I think about it, the more I realize that construction regulations are very much like Jack. Enforcement of construction regulations can come from anywhere and at anytime. Government entities from the federal, state, and local levels all have something to say about how design and construction are implemented. There are even regulations by certain government entities of other government entities.

But this propensity to be everywhere at once is not the only characteristic construction regulations have in common with Jack. Like Jack, construction regulations are also a part of some whole which is not truly quantifiable. There are a lot of regulations out there. These regulations are updated often; there is duplicity amongst them; and they are presented in many different formats. They may be codes, standards, state and local ordinances, or even federal laws. Construction regulations are also written in a technical language that can be difficult to understand, and they incorporate a great deal of cross-references within them. All of these characteristics of construction regulations taken together help ensure a veritable "labyrinth" of information which is as confusing to government entities as it is to designers, builders, and facility management personnel.

Construction regulations are also necessary. They protect the general public from a myriad of potential problems by addressing the concerns of fire safety, health safety, structural safety, energy conservation, and accessibility for people with disabilities. They can even address aesthetic issues through zoning or historical ordinances. The difficulties faced by those who must meet construction regulations are not sufficient reasons to rid us of these regulations. Though Jack could haunt the dreams of a wayward student, we all knew his worth.

Construction regulations usually do not provide the most enjoyable reading in the world. I've never heard anyone say they didn't get to sleep until late the night before because they started reading the Building Code and just could not put it down. As a designer, I find that many books explaining construction regulations are also cumbersome to read, as their authors often assume that anyone reading their books is interested in the subject matter. This book, however, does not make that assumption. This book assumes that its readers are, for the most part, reluctant participants in the world of codes and standards. The language and the illustrations utilized in this book are intended to help an otherwise "dry" subject matter become more tolerable. After all, who needs a book about construction regulations that reads like a construction regulation?

Although, as a general rule, construction codes make for boring reading, some parts of codes are more interesting than others. And like any other technical subject, as one learns more about the subject matter, the "interest rating" of codes can increase dramatically. When a subject becomes more interesting, it is usually easier for one to understand it and remember its details. I assume that you are trying to develop enough understanding about how construction regulations "work" so that they can be used more effectively as a design tool. Then hopefully, these construction regulations will no longer be a hindrance to creative design, construction, and management of buildings, but rather a complement to these efforts.

This book is not a commentary such as the popular National Fire Protection Association's (NFPA) Life Safety Code® Handbook used in many offices around the nation. Commentaries analyze documents section by section. Though it is impossible to completely divorce this book from making observations which are "commentary-like" in nature, the primary purpose of this book is to explore building codes from a more theoretical perspective so that they can be more easily understood. Very good commentaries already exist for most of the major regulatory documents, and to duplicate these commentaries would be unnecessary.

It is hoped that you will find this book to be a helpful teaching aid, whether you are an avid reader of construction regulations, or whether you despise the ink on every page of all the codes you have ever suffered through. I also hope this book will remain an active resource for your future reference. With this in mind, an Appendix with relevant agencies and their addresses is included to help you locate the resources and documents you may need to survive in the "Code World." Before long you should be dazzling the authorities with your understanding of construction regulations, but remember: Jack is watching.

Introduction

This book looks at codes and standards from a theoretical viewpoint, and then attempts to give that theory some practical grounding, so that the book becomes a useful resource for designers, builders, or building owners when dealing with construction regulations. The information in this book is not intended as a substitute for a building code or any other code. Codes are much more thorough and detailed than this book; moreover, many of the interpretations expressed in this book reflect the author's opinion, and do not necessarily reflect the opinions of any code officials. Every effort has been made to keep from expressing interpretations that do not echo the opinions of code officials I have known and trusted. After all, no one is interested in what I think the code should say, but many may be interested in what I know code officials' opinions to be of what the code says.

As stated in the preface, this book is not a commentary. Commentaries dissect codes and standards section by section and analyze those sections. This book is more general in scope, and is more concerned with expressing the relationships of different sections to one another. Often, in order to fully convey the theory of a particular section, however, "commentary-like" analysis of that section must be made, and this book will not shy away from such commentary. Excellent commentaries for each of the codes exist and may be obtained from the model code organizations referenced in Appendix A of this book.

One will find explanations in this book for certain code sections which are not addressed in all four of the major model codes, and which may be addressed only in one of these codes. This is all the more reason not to treat this book as a substitute for a code or for a code commentary. It is my intent to expose the readers of this book to the kinds of subjects covered by codes in general, and to some very important subjects or concepts which may not be covered by all codes.

Because this book covers several construction codes, standards, and laws, the comments in this book are often general in nature. The major codes approach construction regulation with similar, though not identical philosophies, yet they each achieve their philosophical goals in a different manner. I often compare the different codes with Romance languages. To illustrate, consider the French and Italian languages which both have similar structural principles. Though their languages have similar structural principles, the French cannot understand Italian, and Italians cannot understand French, unless either is formally schooled in the other's language, of course. Similarly, many codes agree in basic structure and philosophy, but read like two different Romance languages. Their details may vary greatly. The differences in the details of the various model codes are best explained by the aforementioned commentaries on these codes.

Often two or more codes contain the same, or nearly the same requirement, but differ in where they place that requirement. For example, all three of the major building codes specify fire resistance ratings for exterior walls based on their proximity to property lines, however, each places those rating requirements in different chapters of their respective codes. The BOCA® National Building Code views these rating requirements as fire-protection-related and places them in a chapter dealing with fire protection. The Standard Building Code views these rating requirements as type-of-construction-related and places them in a chapter dealing with types of construction. The Uniform Building Code™ views these rating requirements as relating to heights and area, and places them in a chapter dealing with allowable heights and areas. Because of the variations in how different code organizations outline their texts, I have had to make some personal decisions as to where to place certain sections within this book. I have tried to place such sections where I think they will fit most logically into the designers' thought processes.

The processes used for writing codes are dynamic, ongoing processes which are in full motion even as this book is being published. Therefore, some of the regulations covered by this book may be dated. For this reason, I have tried to concentrate on the general theoretical principles which are considered timeless. In most cases, I have avoided discussion of the details which may change from year to year. Remember, however, that building design and construction is much more complicated than the theoretical principles set forth in this book.

Several terms used in this book have specific meanings in this book only. When reference is made to the "three major building codes," one should consider those codes to be the BOCA National Building Code, the Standard Building Code, and the Uniform

Building Code promulgated by the Building Officials and Code Administrators International, Inc. (BOCA), the Southern Building Code Congress International, Inc. (SBCCI), and the International Conference of Building Officials (ICBO), respectively. The "four major codes" or the "model codes" refers to these three codes and the National Fire Protection Association's (NFPA) 101® Life Safety Code®. This book does not cover any other building or fire codes unless specifically referenced. The term "code official" refers to a building official (plumbing official, mechanical official, etc. if applicable), a fire official, or their representatives. One must discern from the context of the sentence whether I am referring to the chief code official or one of his or her duly appointed representatives. To avoid excessive repetition, the term "designer" often refers to architects, interior designers, engineers, contractors, and building owners and managers. Once again, one should be able to discern to whom the discussion applies based on the context. The terms "codes" or "construction regulations" denotes building codes, standards, or local, state, and federal laws and ordinances.

The chapter organization of this book reflects the chapter organization of the three major building codes for Chapters 3 through 16 (except where the three major building codes disagree about the placement of sections applicable to all three codes, in which case I have placed the sections where I though most appropriate). Chapter 1 discusses general issues related to the application of codes and Chapter 2 discusses the administrative provisions of codes, which are usually found in the first chapters of the codes themselves. Chapter 17 covers structural foundation issues and Chapter 18 discusses those material related concerns found in many different chapters of building codes. Other codes such as plumbing and mechanical codes are discussed in chapter nineteen. Chapter 19 does not attempt to explain these codes or their theory with as much attention to detail as devoted to other subjects covered by this book, but rather attempts to acquaint designers with the types of provisions found in those codes. Finally, elevators and other conveying systems are discussed in Chapter 20, while Appendix A provides a list of resources for gathering more information related to construction regulations.

Many portions of this book are relevant to the three major building codes only and have no relevance to the NFPA 101 Life Safety Code. The NFPA 101 Life Safety Code is exclusively a fire code, and as the name implies, relates only to life safety. The three building codes are more thorough in scope, as they are fire codes, structural codes, and health codes, and as they are involved with the protection of life and property. Hence certain chapters and sections of this book, as well as much of the theory discussed in this book relate only to the three major building codes.

CHAPTER 1

Codes, Standards, and Other Regulations

*C*hapter 1 looks at the purpose for codes, standards, and other construction regulations, as well as at some of the basic theory behind such documents. The relationships of different codes to one another and the ramifications of those relationships are also discussed. This chapter closes with discussion of the processes for the writing of codes, followed by discussion of which codes are applicable in any given locale.

WHAT ARE CODES, STANDARDS, AND REGULATIONS?

Architectural building codes and standards, state and local laws and ordinances, and federal laws are used for the regulation of building construction for fire safety, structural safety, and health safety (Figure 1-1). They also address many other issues such as energy conservation and accessibility for individuals with disabilities. Of all of these different regulations, building codes are the greatest in scope. Building codes relate to all aspects of building design, and they reference standards in order to establish acceptable minimum criteria for design quality. Standards are much narrower in scope than codes are. They deal with more specific aspects of building design construction. Local ordinances supplement adopted codes and standards in order to address the unique climatological, geological, or other concerns of the areas where they apply. State regulations supplement codes, standards, and local ordinances in order to address the unique concerns of the entire state. Federal regulations supplement all other regulations in order to address national concerns.

Standards serve the purpose of establishing "thresholds" of quality for particular construction products or particular methods of construction used in building. Assume that an accessible design standard were promulgated and given the title *Accessible Design Standard X* (Figure 1-2). Assume also that the well-known *Accessible Design Standard X* specifies a maximum ramp slope of one in twelve for people who use wheel-

Figure 1-1 Typical codes and standards

Figure 1-2 X Standard

chairs. This specification would be made with the X Standard's authors knowing that many people who use wheelchairs cannot traverse a ramp with a slope as steep as one in twelve. However, a one-in-twelve ramp slope will accommodate most people who use wheelchairs, and the X Standard's authors considered a one-in-twelve ramp slope to be sufficient as a stated maximum for accessible design in the X Standard. Of course, the X Standard, like other accessible design standards would also state that a ramp must have the least slope possible, and that the one-in-twelve slope is a maximum limitation and should only be used when a lesser slope is not possible. By mandating that the least slope possible be used as a design standard, the X Standard would ensure accessibility for more people.

Because of the X Standard every designer who used the standard would know what is necessary to provide a properly sloped ramp. Also, every person who used ramps where the X Standard was required by law could be assured that ramp design and construction would be properly addressed. This is contingent, of course, on designers designing to the standard, contractors constructing to the standard, and building inspectors maintaining the standard when inspecting.

Accessible Design Standard X's requirement for a one-in-twelve maximum slope is a requirement based on specification. A maximum slope of one in twelve is a specified requirement that must be designed to, constructed to, and inspected for. *Standard X's* requirement for the least slope possible is a requirement based on performance. A performance requirement stipulates a level of performance to be achieved through design, construction, and inspection. Codes, standards, and regulations use the language of

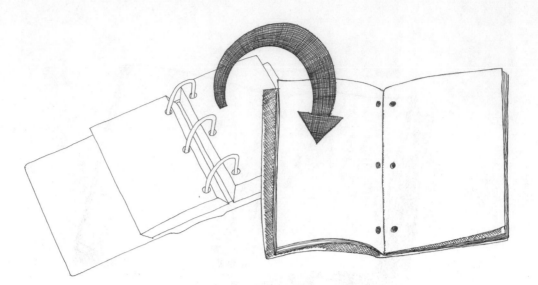

Figure 1-3 *Y Code refers to X standard*

specification requirements and performance requirements to indicate their intent. Once the *Accessible Design Standard X* is issued by its publishers, it could be referenced by local codes, local ordinances and regulations, state regulations, or federal regulations as an acceptable design standard.

Now assume that a particular building code entitled the *Y Building Code* were to reference the *Accessible Design Standard X* under the *Y Code's* chapter regulating design for people with disabilities (Figure 1-3). This *Y Code* would be much greater in scope than the *X Standard,* as accessibility would be only one of the concerns of the *Y Code.* The *Y Code* would also regulate the many fire safety, health safety, and structural safety concerns that are not related to accessibility. Many other standards would be referenced by the *Y Code* and even other codes could be referenced by the *Y Code.* The *Y Building Code,* in its adoption by many different communities, would help promote more consistent and higher quality design throughout a large geographical area. A designer working within the limitations of the *Y Code* would have to meet the requirements of the *Y Code,* the *Accessible Design Standard X,* and any other codes or standards referenced by the *Y Code.*

Government agencies adopt codes and standards for the purpose of regulating design and construction. However, those government agencies that adopt codes and standards often have other regulations of their own which supersede the requirements of their adopted codes and standards. These other regulations might come in the form of laws or ordinances, and may require more stringent or less stringent design solutions than the design solutions required by the adopted codes and standards.

The regulations of higher levels of government supersede the regulations of lower levels of government. In other words, whenever the regulations of different levels of government conflict or whenever the regulations of a higher level of government are

Figure 1-4 *A Federal Register for Title III of the ADA*

more stringent than the regulations of a lower level of government, the regulations of the higher level of government will supersede the regulations of the lower level of government. Therefore, when enforcing the codes, standards, and other regulations of different levels of government, federal regulations supersede state and local regulations, and state regulations supersede local regulations.

Assume that a federal law known as the Z Act governs building construction. Since the Z Act is a federal law, it will supersede any state or local regulations in the event of a conflict with any of the requirements of these regulations, or when the Z Act is more stringent than these regulations. Therefore, the Z Act might actually overrule some of the requirements of the state or locally adopted building codes and standards, such as the *Y Building Code* or the *X Standard*. A good illustration of a federal law which supersedes the less stringent requirements of state and local regulations would be the *Americans with Disabilities Act (ADA)* discussed in chapter eleven of this book (Figure 1-4). The ADA supersedes all state and locally referenced accessible design standards where it is more restrictive than they are, and where it directly conflicts with them. Of course, state and local regulations may also supersede locally adopted codes and standards, thus allowing state and local governments to adjust the requirements of these codes and standards in order to better fit the particular needs of the geographical area in which all of these regulations are enforced.

WHY DO WE HAVE CODES, STANDARDS, AND REGULATIONS?

We have building design and construction regulations because they are necessary for the protection of life and property. Protection of life is provided for the occupants of a building, as well as for the fire officials who must enter the building in the event of an emergency. Protection of property is provided for any specific building where an emergency might occur, as well as for any property adjacent to that building. From the designer's, builder's, or building owner's perspective, construction regulations also provide protection from liability. Although liability protection is not the specifically stated purpose of codes and standards, liability protection is a very real result of codes and standards and is often the best "policing agent" of safe building design and construction. The potential ramifications of deviating from the liability protection afforded by construction regulations often helps keep designers and builders on the straight and narrow and attentive to the requirements of codes, standards, and regulations.

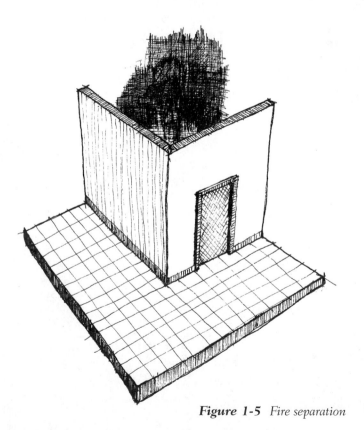

Figure 1-5 *Fire separation*

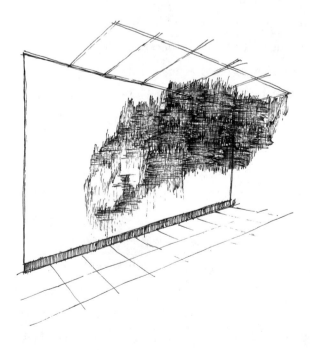

Figure 1-6 *Interior finishes*

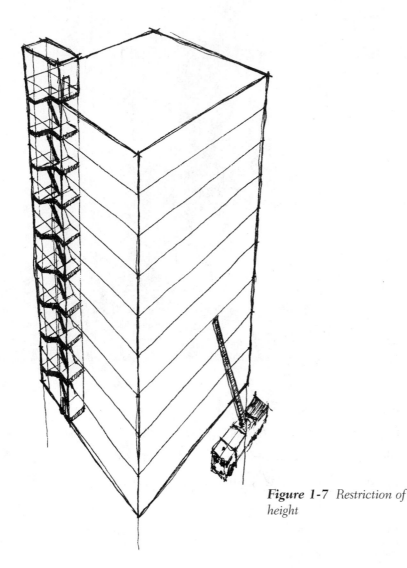

Figure 1-7 *Restriction of height*

The most important function of construction codes, standards, and regulations is the provision for construction which promotes life safety. Though it is not desirable for massive property destruction to occur as a result of a fire or a structural collapse, human life is certainly more important than any structure. Construction regulations provide for life safety in many ways, including providing for fire-rated separations (occupancy separation, tenant separation, fire protection separation, etc.), regulating interior finishes and materials, specifying heights of buildings in stories, limiting vertical openings between floors, detailing proper egress design requirements, and requiring in many instances the installation of sprinklers, standpipes, and fire alarms.

Fire-rated separations help protect lives by establishing compartmentation which restricts fire to its area of origin (Figure 1-5). The regulation of interior finishes and materials helps protect lives by minimizing a product's ability to produce smoke and to enhance the advancement of fire (Figure 1-6). Restriction of the heights in stories of buildings helps protect lives by controlling the number of stories the building occupants

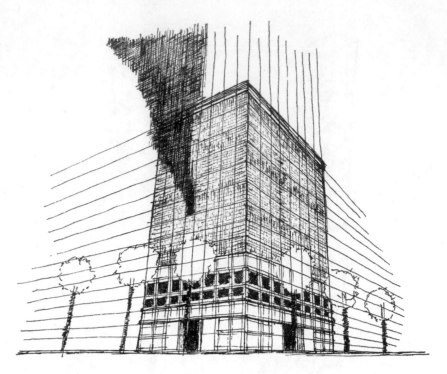

Figure 1-8 *Smoke is a real killer*

must egress from and by controlling the number of floors which can be accessed by fire officials (Figure 1-7). The limitation of vertical openings between floors helps stop the spread of smoke, as openings in floors help spread smoke throughout buildings in the event of a fire. Smoke is the real killer in most fire situations (Figure 1-8). Means of egress design considerations enable us to provide for the orderly evacuation of people from a building whenever there is an emergency, such as a fire (Figure 1-9). In the case of health care or detention and correctional facilities, proper egress design provides for

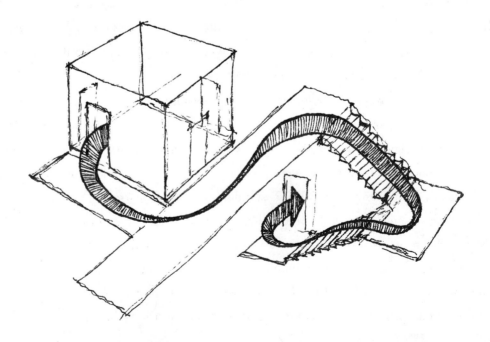

Figure 1-9 *Means of egress*

Figure 1-10 Fire alarm

the evacuation of people to safer areas of the buildings. Fire alarms, of course, provide the occupants of a building with early warning of a fire, which allows them in most cases to escape the fire before it becomes a life-threatening force (Figure 1-10). Automatic sprinkler protection and standpipes promote life safety by providing for the early extinguishing of fires (Figure 1-11).

Fire fighters often rely on life safety protection features of buildings when they enter into a building to fight a fire. Fire-resistant ratings of structural assemblies allow the structure of a building to remain in place long enough for fire officials to fight the fire from within the building without the building's collapsing on them. Firefighters can only assume that designers, builders, and inspectors have "done their part," that consequently buildings are relatively safe, and that fire officials can therefore depend on certain aspects of a particular building's design and construction when fighting a fire. The proper design and construction of buildings within the requirements of construction

Figure 1-11 *Automatic sprinkles and standpipes*

regulations can help decrease the total lives lost in the United States every year due to fires.

Many construction regulations provide property protection requirements in order to prevent the destruction of an entire building from a fire, or to limit the chance that a fire within a building will spread to an adjacent building. Major aspects of codes which help maintain property protection are those requirements regulating allowable areas of buildings, allowable heights in feet of buildings, and allowable distances between buildings.

By limiting the allowable areas of a building in square feet, building codes control the amount of fire loading that can occur in any one building (Figure 1-12a). The limitation of heights of buildings in feet also helps control the amount of fire loading within a building (Figure 1-12b). Building codes limit the area of buildings and regulate the fire resistance ratings of exterior walls, as well as the percentage of openings in those walls as a function of any building's proximity to property lines and proximity to other buildings on the same property (Figure 1-13). Building codes do this in order to reduce the chance that fire in any one building will spread to another building.

In all actuality, it is not always possible to completely separate property protection issues from life safety issues. For example, a lack of property protection features which would allow a fire to progress from one building to another building would certainly endanger the lives of those people occupying the second building. However, certain requirements in building codes can be identified as more property-protection-

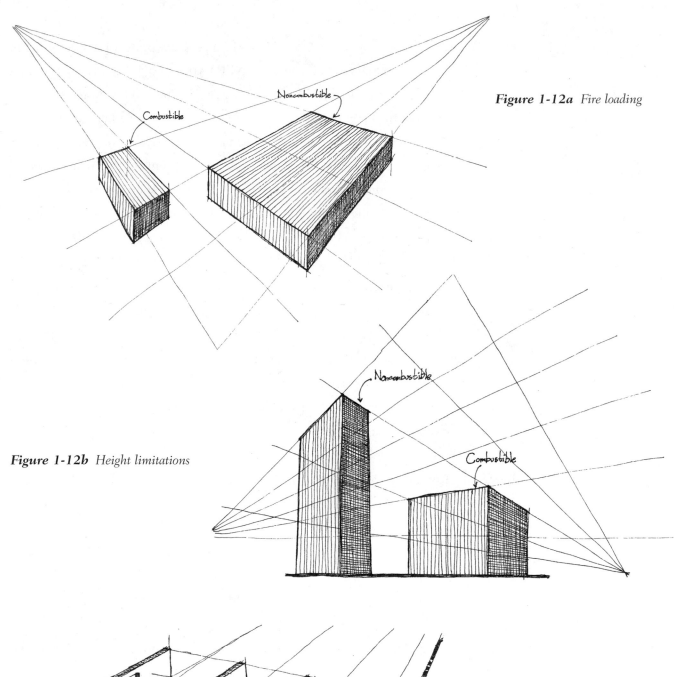

Figure 1-12a Fire loading

Figure 1-12b Height limitations

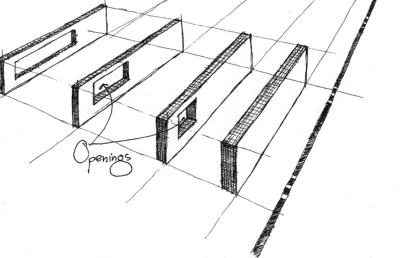

Figure 1-13 Exterior wall ratings and opening protectives

oriented than life-safety-oriented. One will not find property protection requirements in the NFPA 101 Life Safety Code, because NFPA 101 is only a life safety code.

Building design and construction regulations may provide liability protection when they are adhered to by designers and builders. Although there have been cases where designers were held to a standard of care exceeding that of locally adopted codes and standards, the general rule is that if one meets the requirements of the building codes, standards, and regulations that one is subjected to, then one should have met most of one's obligations in ensuring the safe design and construction of a building. One could always exceed the requirements of design and construction regulations in order to provide an even safer building, but one would not be required to provide such added safety measures unless perhaps the failure to provide such extra measures would result in the design or construction of a life-threatening or harmful building.

It should be noted that the more one strays from the requirements of design and construction regulations, the more one is exposed to liability. A designer may feel quite confident in using a design solution for a particular situation which is an alternative solution to the one required by a local building code. Though the designer may feel that his or her solution provides equivalent safety to the solution required by the code, the designer should consider the fact that he or she may gain increased liability exposure by straying from the code. The code official could also gain increased liability exposure by accepting the designer's "homemade" solution.

Because of the potential liability protection afforded by construction regulations, these regulations can be very beneficial to designers and builders. For example, a designer does not have to perform studies to determine what dimensions would be safe to use for stair riser heights and tread depths. Others have performed such studies and the results of those studies have affected the writing of codes. The liability incurred by designers and builders would be much greater in a world without construction regulations. Construction regulations afford liability protection by providing minimum standards and consistent standards for designers and builders to meet.

HOW ARE CODES, STANDARDS, AND REGULATIONS STRUCTURED?

Construction codes provide for the protection of life and property through their own requirements and by referencing different construction standards. Although these documents are fairly immense and complex, their requirements are mostly interpretations of ten or so basic rules (Figure 1-14).

1. Don't make buildings too large.
   Allowable Areas
   Allowable Heights

2. Build with safe materials.
   Type of Construction

3. Protect everyone from everyone else.
   Occupancy Separation
   Tenant Separation
   Exterior Wall Ratings

4. Prevent and control fires.
   Automatic Sprinkler Protection and Standpipes
   Mechanical Codes

5. Get people out of buildings in an emergency.
   Alarms
   Two Means of Egress
   Number of Exits
   Width of Exits
   Travel Distance
   Arrangement of Exits
   Exit Design
   Egress Separation

6. Make buildings strong.
   Structures
   Wind Loading
   Snow Loading
   Seismic Design

7. Design buildings for everyone.
   Accessibility

8. Design healthy environments.
   Plumbing Codes
   Ventilation

9. Keep people comfortable and dry.
   Exterior Finishes
   Roof Structures
   Mechanical Codes

Figure 1-14 Ten Construction Commandments

10. Keep creative solutions safe.

    Atriums

    Covered Malls

    High-rises

    Underground Buildings

The organization of codes varies depending on who the publisher of the code is. As of 1994, the three major building codes started using a similar format for organizing their requirements; however, their format is different from the NFPA 101 Life Safety Code.

Chapter Organization

The major building codes begin with administrative provisions which provide everything necessary for enforcing the code. These administrative provisions set up the rules for the administration of a codes department; for the provision of plans, specifications, and other construction documents by designers; for reviewing the construction documents by the codes department; for inspecting the construction progress by the codes department; and for dealing with the grievances of owners, designers, and builders. Without administrative provisions, codes cannot be enforced. Many jurisdictions write their own administrative provisions which override those administrative provisions contained within their adopted codes. The administrative requirements of construction regulations are discussed in Chapter 2 of this book.

The administration chapter in each of the major building codes is followed by a definitions chapter containing all or most of the definitions within the code, depending on the code. The definitions chapter is followed by fire safety chapters, and then by Chapter 11 which deals with accessibility for individuals with disabilities. The remaining chapters deal with structural design, requirements for the proper use of materials (e.g., wood, masonry, concrete, etc.), and miscellaneous provisions, such as light and ventilation, and elevators and other conveying systems. The NFPA 101 Life Safety Code is only a fire safety code.

The Great Organizers

I like to refer to occupancy classification and type of construction classification as the "great organizers" of building codes. Once one has determined the occupancy classification and the type of construction of a building, one can then determine such things as allowable heights and areas, egress requirements, fire protection require-

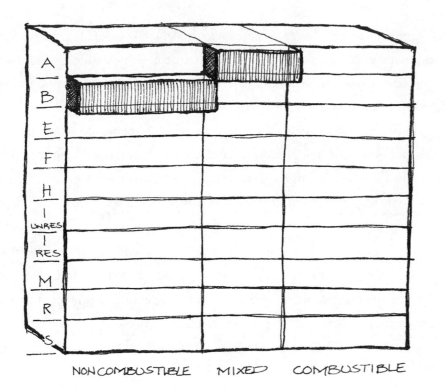

Figure 1-15 Occupancy vs. types

ments, sprinkler requirements, and other requirements for the building. Imagine a matrix with rows of occupancy classifications and columns of type of construction classifications (Figure 1-15). Now imagine one taking a relatively low hazard occupancy, such as a business occupancy, and a low hazard type of construction, such as a noncombustible type of construction, and identifying the area where those two meet on the matrix. Assume that this matrix area would contain all of the requirements in the codes for any business occupancy of a noncombustible type of construction. Those requirements would be the minimum requirements to consider a building adequately constructed for life safety and property protection. Now imagine one taking a more hazardous occupancy, such as an assembly occupancy, and a more hazardous type of construction, such as a type of construction using a mixture of noncombustible and of combustible materials, and finding the intersection area of those two on the matrix. Assume that this matrix area would contain all of the requirements in the codes for any assembly occupancy of a type of construction consisting of a mixture of noncombustible and of combustible materials. Again, this value would be equivalent to the minimum requirements to consider a building adequately constructed for life safety and property protection. In theory, one would be just as protected in the business occupancy of a low hazard type of construction as one would be in the more hazardous assembly occupancy of a more hazardous type of construction.

This would be true in theory because codes make adjustments to regulations based on the occupancy classification and the type of construction classification of the building in question. Codes make adjustments to allowable heights and areas, to fire protection requirements, and to egress requirements. Codes make adjustments to sprinkler, standpipe, and alarm system requirements. Requirements are more stringent for more hazardous combinations of occupancy classification and type of construction, and requirements are less stringent for less hazardous combinations of occupancy classification and type of construction, the result of which is a theoretically equivalent protection for all buildings. How protected is that? The best answer would probably be, "adequately protected." Perhaps this seems evasive, but safe construction is not truly quantifiable. Now, of course, because of the way codes are written, there is some variation from this theoretical principle that one building is just as protected as another. Codes are written by democratic processes which are very good processes, but because these processes rely on human input, all buildings are not equivalently protected by codes.

How to Use Codes

When confronted with a new project, it is often difficult for a designer to determine just when to incorporate codes into the design process. The proper time to incorporate codes into the design process is at the very beginning of that process. This may seem undesirable to those who worry about the technical aspects of architecture impeding the creative aspects of architecture. I don't see these two aspects as being mutually exclusive, but rather I see them as constituting what is the essence of architecture. There are two reasons for incorporating codes into the earliest phases of design. First, it allows codes to be incorporated into the design process in a gradual manner that will allow plenty of freedom for creative thought. Second, any code official will eventually incorporate codes into the design process, so the designer might as well so that he or she will retain design control, otherwise the code official will become, to some limited extent, the project designer.

Introducing codes to the design process involves working first with more general code issues, and then proceeding to more specific code issues as the design progresses. The design process itself actually dictates when certain aspects of codes can be included in design decisions. For example, program information generated from a client provides the information necessary for determining occupancy classifications, as well as heights and areas of a building. As one becomes more involved with design development, one will have to consider structural systems, and type-of-construction issues will then be incorporated into the design process. The proper type of construction will be chosen to accommodate the program heights and areas, economy of construction, potential future expansion needs, and any specific requests the client may make regarding preference for the type of materials used. As the design progresses even further, means-of-egress issues can be considered, then fire protection requirements, then more detailed requirements, and so on. Of course, the actual incorporation of codes into the design process will not necessarily be so ordered and segmented, as one will consider many code issues earlier on in the design process with each new project because of one's increasing familiarity with codes.

When buildings potentially have large occupant loads, one might consider performing a "quick and dirty" minimum occupant load calculation (see Chapter 10) during the schematic design phase just to determine the number of exits the building will ultimately require. This should be done with full knowledge that another minimum occupant load calculation will have to be executed when the building design is more refined to reflect the many changes made since the schematic design phase. The reason for an early minimum occupant load calculation is to permit the designer to control the design; if a building is going to require four exits, then the designer needs to know this in order to intentionally highlight or downplay such exits.

The following is a recipe for designing with the code as a design tool:

A. Determine Occupancy Classification(s), and Heights and Areas for the Building (see Chapters 3, 4, and 5)

   This information is derived from the building program. Height may be determined from what is necessary to accommodate the program areas on a small site,

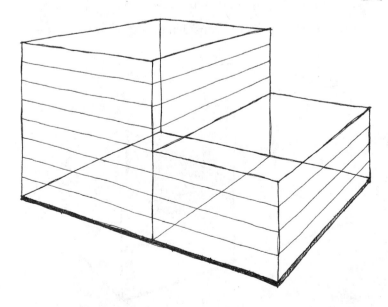

Figure 1-16 Determine occupancy, height, and area

Handwritten note in right margin: DO AN OCCUPANT LOAD CALC. EARLY TO DETERMINE THE REQUIRED # OF EXITS

or perhaps by some program issue such as tying into an existing building of a certain height (Figure 1-16).

B. Select the Type of Construction for the Building (see Chapters 5 and 6)

This decision is based on accommodating the program, future expansion needs, economy, or a client preference for a particular structural system. Designers select the type of construction after determining occupancy classifications and

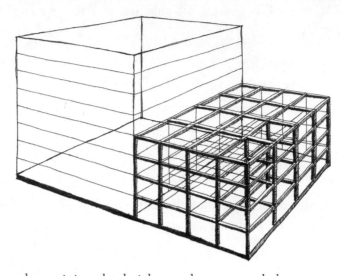

Figure 1-17 *Select type of Construction*

determining the heights and areas needed to accommodate building programs. Code officials, when performing plans reviews (see Chapter 2), may determine the occupancy classifications and the types of construction of buildings first, and then check the buildings' allowable heights and areas based on those determinations (Figure 1-17).

C. Refine Design Based on Detailed Occupancy Requirements (see Chapter 4)

Special requirements for specific occupancy classifications may affect design decisions, such as the consideration of where to locate rated fire assemblies. Malls,

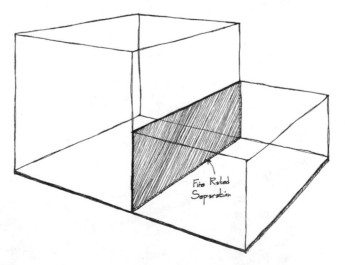

Figure 1-18 *Detailed occupancy requirements*

atriums, high-rises, and underground buildings all have special requirements in codes which must be considered before a building's design becomes too refined (Figure 1-18).

D. Incorporate Means of Egress and Accessibility Provisions into the Design (see Chapters 10 and 11)

As the design is refined, determine the numbers, capacities, and arrangements

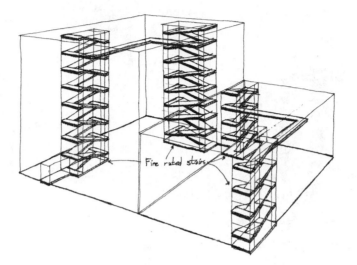

Figure 1-19 Means of egress and access

of egress components. Also, design to incorporate accessibility and egress for individuals with disabilities. Accessible design must also be considered along with those early design decisions which include the locations of buildings on sites (Figure 1-19).

E. Incorporate Fire Protection Provisions into the Design (see Chapters 7, 8, and 20)

Incorporate requirements for rated assemblies, openings in assemblies, and interior finishes. Most fire protection provisions will probably be incorporated into

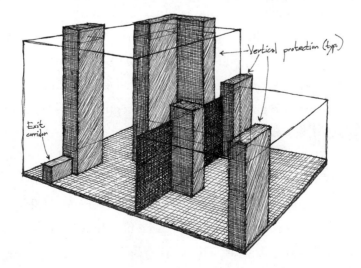

Figure 1-20 Fire protection and elevators

a design simultaneously with egress design. One should also consider elevators and other vertical shafts at this point (Figure 1-20).

F. Complete Design while Incorporating Detailed Requirements from Codes

Incorporate structural details, material related concerns, weather protection, mechanical, plumbing, and electrical concerns, and energy-related concerns into the building's final design. Some of these code concerns may actually be considered earlier in the design process (Figure 1-21).

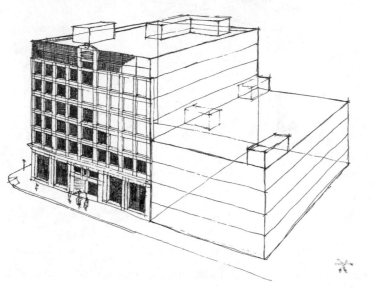

Figure 1-21 Others

HOW MANY CODES, STANDARDS, AND REGULATIONS ARE THERE?

There are many different codes published in the U.S. There are the codes promulgated by the three major building code organizations: the Building Officials Code Administrators International, Inc. (BOCA), the International Conference of Building Officials (ICBO), and the Southern Building Code Congress International, Inc. (SBCCI), which publish the National Codes, the Uniform Codes, and the Standard Codes respectively. These respective codes are used more or less on a regional basis and may include building codes, fire prevention codes, gas codes, housing codes, mechanical codes, plumbing codes, as well as others. The National Fire Protection Association (NFPA) promulgates the National Fire Codes, Standards, and Recommended Practices and Guides. These documents are used nationally by many state and local jurisdictions usually along with one of the major building codes. There are also many individual codes promulgated by certain individual states and municipalities, and some small regional areas. The three major building code organizations have also worked together to author some codes which are intended to be international in scope—the International Mechanical Code, the International Plumbing Code, and the International Private Sewage Disposal Code—and they are presently authoring the International Building Code (IBC). The IBC will be published by the year 2000 and will eventually supplant the three major building codes. The International Conference of Building Officials has already announced it will stop promulgating the Uniform Building code after 1996 in favor of the IBC.

There are many different standards promulgated by different organizations such as the American National Standards Institute (ANSI), the American Society of Testing and Materials (ASTM), BOCA, ICBO, NFPA, SBCCI, and many other organizations, as well as standards promulgated by different levels of government. Many of these standards are near-duplicates of other standards or have the same purview as other standards. For example, the federal government publishes many standards regulating the design of buildings and facilities for people with disabilities, including the Americans with Disabilities Act (ADA) and the Uniform Federal Accessibility Standard (UFAS), while the model building codes adopt ANSI A117.1 (Accessible and Usable Buildings and Facilities) as their accessibility standard. Many states also issue their own accessibility standards.

The Major Codes

The four major codes regulating building construction in the United States are the NFPA 101 Life Safety Code, and the three major building codes: the BOCA National Building Code, the Standard Building Code, and the Uniform Building Code. The NFPA 101 Life Safety Code is a life safety code only and addresses fire safety. The three major building codes are more thorough in scope and are life safety and property protection codes. They address structural safety, health safety, and fire safety. For the most part, all four of the major codes are very similar in theory as to what they require for designing and constructing for life safety, and all three of the major building codes are very similar in theory as to what they require for designing and constructing for property protection. As a general rule, the most significant differences amongst these individual codes lie in how to achieve their major theoretical goals.

Different departments and levels of government adopt different codes. The codes published by the Building Officials & Code Administrators International, Inc. (BOCA), the International Conference of Building Officials (ICBO), and the Southern Building Code Congress International, Inc. (SBCCI) are usually adopted by building departments, whereas the NFPA 101 Life Safety Code is usually adopted by fire departments.

States often adopt a model building code for all projects and NFPA 101 for certain other projects (often state-owned buildings, health care facilities, university buildings and schools, detention facilities, etc.). It is not uncommon however, for a state fire marshal to pass a "sweeping" edict that all buildings within a state will meet the NFPA 101 Life Safety Code, even though there may be no means for enforcing such an edict on a local level. Agencies of the federal government vary in their adoption of codes for projects under their purview. Many federal agencies adopt a particular code as their standard, but require their regional offices to meet the requirements of the most recognized code of that region. Frequently, designers and builders have to meet the requirements of two separate codes on the same project because of the different entities involved in the adoption and enforcement of codes and standards.

The Advantages and Disadvantages of Multiple Codes, Standards, and Regulations

The benefit of having different codes, standards, and regulations adopted and promulgated by different levels of government (local, state, and federal) is that design regulations can be customized to best "fit" a particular jurisdiction or region. For example, assume a code official enforces codes and standards in a particular mountain town in the state of Tennessee, and assume that the building code adopted by this town has a chart showing that this particular mountain town is in a zone that requires structural design for snow loads of six inches or more. If the local code official knows that snow loads of twelve inches or more are common in his or her town because of its particular location on the mountainside, the code official could ask the town leaders to pass a local ordinance requiring designers to use a snow design load of twelve inches or more when designing buildings to be located within the town. The code official could also request the lessening of that six-inch snow design load referenced in the code if for some reason this town had never received more than three inches of snow at any one time. In this case, the adjusting of the building code by a local jurisdiction helps provide for design and construction regulations that accommodate the actual needs of that jurisdiction; therefore, this adjustment leads to better local code enforcement. The local ordinances will be either more restrictive or less stringent than the adopted code, but in each case they should prove to be a more accurate reflection of the actual needs of the particular locality.

When different levels and branches of government adopt and promulgate different construction regulations, they are taking the opportunity to choose or write the legislation that will help them most effectively meet their needs in their particular jurisdictions. Adjustments can be made to "tweak" the codes and standards they adopt to make them more realistic for their jurisdictions. The clear advantages of such adjustments are that unnecessary construction expenditures need not occur if no appreciable safety can be gained by them, and if extra safe design and construction methods are necessary, they can be required. In the example given above of the snow loads, it is important to understand that the question of greater or lesser stringency is irrelevant. The Tennessee mountain town has a certain amount of snowfall each year and the design of buildings within that town needs to be based on the town's actual snowfall. The actual snowfall will dictate the correct snow design load.

There are many disadvantages to having to meet the requirements of different design and construction regulations. The main disadvantages do not come from those local and state ordinances which are promulgated in order to better adjust adopted codes and standards to the needs of particular jurisdictions or regions. The main disadvantages encountered by designers and builders alike come from having to meet two or more different codes or standards on the same project when the documents regulating the exact same design and construction situations compete. This duplication is not necessary, and it becomes a burden for designers and builders, as they already have plenty to do to design and build safe and accessible buildings without having to become familiar with two or more documents providing essentially the same requirements. When duplicate codes and standards are enforced on the same project, they pose two principal problems; researching them is confusing and overly time-consuming, and they can be impossible to apply when they disagree or conflict with one another.

Duplicate codes and standards are confusing and overly time consuming when both are enforced on the same project. It would be next to impossible for designers and builders to be intimately familiar with all of the design and construction regulations which apply to them, and to also have time to perform all of the other aspects of their jobs they must perform. In the case of the design side of the construction "equation," a small design firm would never be able to provide design services and maintain an adequate knowledge of all the construction regulations they must meet. Only the larger design firms can afford to employ someone who spends one hundred percent of their time as a codes and standards authority. However, the practice of utilizing designers with only a cursory knowledge of codes and standards and then having those designers report to an "in-house codes authority" is a questionable practice at best. Ultimately, all designers should be well familiar with the construction regulations which apply to them, so that they can provide superior design solutions, both technically and aesthetically, while eliminating the costly, inefficient use of time. Aesthetics would not be compromised for fear of not meeting the code, but instead the code would become a design tool to help achieve aesthetically superior solutions. Such an intimate understanding of codes and standards is not likely to occur in today's construction regulation environment, because designers are forced to meet too many different codes and standards.

There are other problems with having to meet nearly duplicate codes and standards on the same project. Even though these duplicate documents are likely to have similar philosophies, one must be intimately familiar with both documents in order to know where the detailed differences occur. Also, the frequency with which codes and standards change make it nearly impossible to maintain an active working knowledge of nearly duplicate documents.

Another problem comes from the subjective nature of codes and standards. Many construction regulations are very subjective, and designers and builders often receive conflicting interpretations when two different governing bodies enforce two different codes. When any two regulatory documents disagree with the level of protection required for a certain building situation, the more stringent of the two documents supersedes the other document. What does this mean? It is easy to comprehend that if a building of a particular occupancy classification and type of construction is required by one code to be no taller than three stories in height, yet is allowed by another code to be four stories in height, the code limiting the building to three stories in height is the more stringent code. In this case, the more stringent of two requirements is also the safer of the two requirements, because the building occupants will not have to egress as far and fire department personnel will have an easier time accessing the building.

But it is not always easy to determine which code requirement is the more stringent when comparing two different codes. Often the way to deal with fire safety in two different sets of regulations might encompass two different philosophies of protection which cannot be directly compared in order to determine which one is more stringent in relationship to the other. One code might allow certain lenient design "tradeoffs" if automatic sprinkler protection were added to the particular area of the building where the tradeoff occurred. Another code might allow the exact same lenient tradeoff if the area of the building in which the tradeoff occurred were protected with wall and floor-ceiling assembly fire ratings higher than those fire assembly ratings which would normally be required if the tradeoff had not been taken. How would one compare these two very different requirements in order to determine which one was the more stringent of the two? Using cost as a determinant of levels of stringency would be ludicrous. It is not the cost that is important in the building height example above, but rather safety—the more limited story height was a safer design. It could be difficult to determine which design situation was a safer design in the case of the example contrasting automatic sprinkler protection or increased fire ratings. To choose the design that costs the most would not necessarily benefit anyone. In fact, the only way to truly provide the more stringent of the two designs would be to provide both designs; that is, provide both automatic sprinkler protection and increased fire ratings of the wall and floor-ceiling assemblies. This would satisfy the requirements of each of the two different regulations, but this could also prove to be excessive regulation.

One Nation, One Code

A single national code and a single set of standards would allow designers and builders the opportunity to become very familiar with these codes and standards, thus elevating the "standard of care" of design and construction. Of course, individual localities and regions would still need to adjust the one set of codes and standards through local ordinances in order to reflect the individual needs of those particular localities and regions. However, one set of codes and standards with local adjustments would be much more easily managed than the situation we have today, four major sets of codes, and several sets of nearly identical standards with local amendments. If one wants designers to become familiar with codes, one should give those designers one code. However, if one wants to guarantee that designers not become intimately familiar with codes, one should require them to meet several duplicate codes simultaneously so that they have insufficient time to learn any one of them.

WHO WRITES CODES, STANDARDS, AND REGULATIONS?

Codes are written by processes which rely on the input of both the general public, and the code officials who enforce codes. Standards are usually written more by committees, but are often approved by large membership ballots. Other regulations are authored by federal, state, and local legislation. It is important to become familiar with the processes for the writing of codes for two reasons. First, one must understand these processes to become involved in them, and the more people become involved in code promulgation processes, the better the codes become. Second, there are many errors in codes which relate to the human element in code change processes, and an understanding of these processes helps one understand where these errors are, and therefore helps one better understand the intent of codes.

Building Codes

The beginning of a typical building code promulgation process starts with the submission of a proposed code change form (Figure 1-22). The code change form provides an area for one to identify the code section one wants to change, as well as an area for the code change proponent to print the code section to be changed. The proponent of the code change would identify the material to be added, or the material he or she wanted to delete. One could also substitute an entirely new section or delete an entire section. Then the proponent of the code change would give the reason for the code change. Without the reason for the code change it is difficult for a code official to understand why a change is necessary. Therefore, a good reason can often help a code change make it successfully through the code change process. The code change proponent would then submit the proposed code change to the building code organization. Once the proposed code changes were received, they would be printed in a booklet and distributed for public perusal.

After studying the proposed code changes, individuals could attend hearings to argue for or against any proposed code change (Figure 1-23). Several hundred people attend these hearings each year to argue for or against proposed code changes. One would not actually have to attend these in order to voice their opinion for or against a proposed code change; one could simply write a letter to the applicable committee in charge of the code being promulgated. The committee would consider the contents of the letter when acting on the proposed code change.

After reviewing and listening to comments, the committee would then discuss each proposed code change and would rule one of four ways. They could either approve it, approve it as revised, disapprove it, or recommend it for further study. If the committee were to recommend a particular code change for further study, an ad hoc committee would look at the proposed code change in the following year. The ad hoc committee would then make recommendations concerning the further studied proposed code change item, and would resubmit the proposed code change as modified by the ad hoc committee in the following year's code change cycle. Another action which can occur at those Code Promulgation Hearings is the withdrawal of a proposed code change by its proponents. Often a proponent will withdraw a code change when it is discovered that someone else submitted a better worded code change on the same subject, or when the proponent discovers an error in his or her proposed code change wording.

After these initial code promulgation hearings were concluded, all of the code change committee's actions would be printed and distributed again for public perusal.

Southern Building Code Congress International, Inc.

SBCCI

900 MONTCLAIR ROAD   BIRMINGHAM, ALABAMA 35213-1206   205/591-1853

ITEM NO. _____ SHEET _____ OF _____ STANDARD _____ CODE

PROPONENT _____ DATE _____

ADDRESS _____ PHONE _____ / _____

CHECK ONE ☐ Revise section to read as follows: ☐ Delete section and substitute the following:
          ☐ Add new section to read as follows: ☐ Delete section without substitution:

~~LINE THROUGH MATERIAL TO BE DELETED~~   UNDERLINE MATERIAL TO BE ADDED

Y N
☐ ☐ Will this proposal add to the cost of construction?
If "yes," explain total economic impact in REASON, including compensating savings, if any.

REASON:

Proposed Code Changes Become SBCCI Property for Publication In Copyrighted Documents

Provide release if copyrighted material is used in this proposal. Proponent is responsible for providing copyright release from copyright holder where copyrighted material is used in a code change proposal.

FOLLOW DIRECTIONS ON BACK

Figure 1-22 Typical Code Change Form

The public could then decide whether or not they needed to express their opinion to the code change committee on any particular proposed code changes by writing a letter to the code change committee or by attending the conference where the final voting occurs for all of the proposed code changes. At this conference, delegates rather than individual code change committees vote on proposed code changes. The delegates represent government entities (state and local governments, and agencies thereof). The delegates vote to either accept or reject each individual code change committee's rec-

Figure 1-23 Code
Promulgation Hearings.
Photo courtesy of the
Southern Building Code
Congress International, Inc.

ommendation from the previous hearings. If, for example, the code change committee
recommended that a particular item be approved, the delegates could vote to overturn
this recommendation if they felt the committee's recommendation was not justified.
One would then have to make a new motion such as disapproval, and the motion would
have to be seconded, and then voted on by the delegates. The voting procedures at code
change hearings and conferences are conducted in accordance with *Robert's Rules of
Order*. Those items that are approved or approved as revised by the delegates become
the newest edition of the code.

The National Fire Protection Association uses a code promulgation process which
relies more on committee action, and then allows their entire membership to vote. The
advantage of this process is that it allows for more thorough code section writing, but
the disadvantage is that it allows voting by members who may have a vested interest in
the outcome of the vote.

Potential Problems with the Language of Codes, Standards, and Regulations

I often hear complaints about construction regulations from architects, builders,
and code officials alike. The main complaints I hear are that construction regulations
are too immense, their organization is too complex, their language is very difficult to
understand, and there are too many of them. All of these complaints are legitimate, but

some of these limitations are unavoidable. For example, it would be possible to eliminate many construction regulations without impeding life safety and property protection because of the unnecessary duplication of several regulatory documents. However, it would be next to impossible to create a safe and flexible set of construction regulations that was not somewhat cumbersome in size and complex in organization, and which did not use a precise regulatory language. These latter three limitations are simply the "nature of the beast" with regards to construction regulations, and by trying to simplify them, one could very easily lose the flexibility within those regulations to permit many different affordable approaches to design and construction problems.

There are several reasons why construction codes are often immense and complex in organization. One, codes are immense and complex in order to accommodate the many desires of building owners and designers. Two, codes are immense and complex in order to thwart the tactics of those who try to circumvent the intent of these codes. And three, codes are immense and complex because they must respond to certain previously unforeseen potential hazards that may occur as a result of the design and construction of buildings. As unavoidable as they may be, these three reasons create documents which are cumbersome for designers and builders to use.

Codes are immense and complex in order to accommodate the many desires of building owners and designers. If one wanted to, one could write a very lean building code that would also be very easy to understand. It might say something like:

1. All buildings are to be concrete with all assemblies to be fire-rated four hours;

2. No building will have any openings between floors except for fire-rated stairs;

3. All buildings will be fully sprinklered;

4. Egress design will be provided in every building for an occupant load of one person for every three square feet; and

5. No building will be taller than one story nor greater than 5,000 square feet in building area, etc.

This lean code would help ensure the safest of buildings and the greatest of construction costs. However, the construction industry requests more flexibility with design and construction regulations in order to provide adequate life safety and property protection while maintaining affordable construction. The right to choose different construction materials is requested so that affordably priced building materials can be used when it is safe to use them. Different occupancy classifications are requested as a means of reflecting that some building uses are less hazardous than others, and that the less hazardous building uses need not be regulated as heavily as the more hazardous ones. Exceptions to the provision of automatic sprinkler protection in buildings are requested if certain safe designs do not mandate the installation of automatic sprinkler protection in such buildings. As more design flexibility is requested, construction regulations become more voluminous and more complex. This increase in size and complexity of design and construction regulations comes as a result of these regulations having to detail the many different options provided in the name of flexibility.

Not only do the many individual requirements of a flexible regulatory document increase the size and complexity of the document, but also the relationships of these individual requirements to one another. When one designs a building of several different occupancy classifications, for example, one must deal not only with the constraints of each individual occupancy classification, but also with the ramifications of mixing occupancy classifications within a single building. Which occupancy classification determines the allowable area of the building in square feet? Which occupancy classification should be used to determine the fire protection issues of the entire building, or should each individual occupancy classification area be treated as a separate building? Many questions are generated by codes' allowing for multiple building occupancy classifications to be located within a single building. Therefore, design and construction regulations become thicker and more complex in an attempt to provide more flexibility and affordability.

Codes are immense and complex in order to thwart the tactics of those who try to circumvent the intent of the code. I have often heard designers, builders, and even code officials argue the meaning of the "letter" of a particular code section when it was obvious that the intent of that code section had a different meaning altogether from its literal meaning. These construction professionals became "master grammarians," trying to manipulate the language of construction regulations in order to gain some backing for their design and construction opinions. Such attempts at circumventing the intent of codes have a cause-and-effect relationship which results in thicker and more complex regulations. Designers, builders, and code officials alike must propose more changes to codes in order to clarify the intent of debated requirements.

Codes are thick and complex because they must respond to certain previously unforeseen potential hazards that may occur as a result of the design and construction of buildings. Many of the requirements within codes were submitted in response to particular tragedies: a fire on the upper level of a school building killing many children and causing us to think about the wisdom of locating younger children on upper floors of school buildings, a deadly theater fire convincing us to swing doors in the direction of egress travel, numerous New York chimney fires proving that wood chimneys are not good design, and so on. When a situation "cries out" for more construction regulations in order to protect life, one can hardly ignore the cries, so construction regulations are adapted to include new requirements which address particular design and construction problems that have been encountered. New technology can also contribute to the thickness and complexity of construction regulations. The technology which led to the increased use of high-rise design (more advanced structural frames and the development of elevators), eventually led to a need for codes to address egress concerns within high-rises. These new requirements consequently thicken construction regulations and make them more complex.

Codes, standards, and other design and construction regulations use concise language to convey their intent. The language we use in day-to-day communication is usually not so concise, as we may use colloquial expressions and slang reflecting our regional vernacular. Many of us are often unfamiliar and uncomfortable with the type of language employed by regulatory documents. Construction regulations cannot be so casual in their approach to language. It is necessary for construction regulations to be concise so that two or more people involved in the same construction process will garner the same meaning from them.

This is not to say that the language of codes could not be improved. Many inconsistencies in building codes are mainly a result of the process of writing codes. Often authors of code changes are not concise enough in their use of language, and they may therefore substitute new terminology for existing accepted terminology. The new terminology may not have an equivalent meaning to the old terminology, resulting in confusion for those who must actually use the code. It becomes difficult for such code users to ascertain exactly what the code requires when two or more different terms are used to describe the same situation. They may assume that the code is actually differentiating between two separate situations.

WHICH CODES, STANDARDS, AND REGULATIONS DO WE USE?

It is important for designers to realize that they must use the proper code in any particular jurisdiction (Figure 1-24). Some states adopt a particular code for the entire state, while other states allow local government entities to adopt their own code. If a particular jurisdiction adopted the 1991 Standard Building Code, the designer should not use the 1994 Standard Building Code when designing buildings in that jurisdiction.

Figure 1-24 *Standard codes with and without revisions*

The 1994 Standard Building Code will be more stringent in certain areas and less stringent in other areas than the 1991 Standard Building Code, but stringency is irrelevant, as the edition of the code adopted by a particular community is the law of that community. No edition of a code preceding that adopted edition nor any edition of a code published after that adopted edition are the law of that community. Designers must keep all of their old code editions, because it is almost certain that in any large geographical area, such as some states or regions, one will find up to twenty years of difference in codes enforcement based on the community in which they are designing. One must use the codes and standards that are adopted by law for the jurisdiction where they are designing.

If two sets of building regulations, each from a different level of government, conflict with one another, the regulations adopted by the higher level of government will supersede the regulations adopted by the lower level of government. This concept works in theory, but as a practical matter, the representatives of the lower level of government may not be very familiar with the regulations adopted by the higher level of government, and these representatives may not care to familiarize themselves with those regulations. They may then try to force the designer to design by their local standard, causing the designer to violate the higher level of government's standard. A good example of this would be the conflicts that have constantly arisen in states with strong laws regulating the design of buildings and facilities for people with disabilities. One state has a very aggressive accessibility design standard which was at one time in direct conflict with the Americans with Disabilities Act. Instead of deferring to the federal law, many of this state's code officials were telling designers to meet their state's accessibility standard or the designers' clients would not be able to receive building permits. The result was that the state was requiring designers to violate a federal civil rights law. I cannot think of a better example of irresponsible governing. In this case, the designer was "caught between a rock and a hard place," because those who were enforcing the law were not taking responsibility for their actions.

Administration

Chapter 2 covers the administrative items that provide for the implementation and enforcement of codes and standards. This chapter begins with discussion of sections that define the purview of codes, and continues with discussion about a code official's responsibilities. The chapter then covers many of the processes for enforcing codes and standards, as well as the grievance procedures for private sector individuals who disagree with a code official's rulings. Finally, the relationship between code officials and the private sector is addressed.

Administration chapters of codes are the chapters which give codes power as regulatory documents. They define the title, purpose, scope, and applicability of codes. Administration chapters describe the code departments that enforce the codes and detail the duties and powers of the code officials who administer those code departments. The process of enforcing codes is established through requirements for plans review and permitting, inspections, and the issuing of certificates of occupancy. Administration chapters in codes also discuss violations of codes and the penalties associated with such violations. The means of appealing code administrators' decisions when private sector individuals disagree with them are also detailed by codes. Without administration chapters to provide for their implementation, codes would have no legal authority.

TITLE, PURPOSE, SCOPE, AND APPLICABILITY

Sections of codes dealing with the title, purpose, scope, and applicability of codes are charged with defining the general limitations of codes. These limitations are expressed in terms of what codes cover, as well as to how they relate to federal, state, and local laws and ordinances. Without such limitations, designers would not know when to apply the requirements of any one particular code in question.

There are so many loosely defined and subjective requirements within codes that it is often necessary for designers, builders, owners, and enforcers of codes to determine the intent of various code requirements. The section entitled "purpose" helps one determine intent by stating that the very reason for a construction code's existence is to protect life, health, and property. By considering this standard of protection when determining the intent of a "gray" area of a code, one can often generate a superior solution to the requirement in question.

Scope or applicability sections under the administration chapters of codes define those situations where codes are to be applied. Typical applicability parameters include: new construction, additions, alterations, repair, and demolition or removal of existing buildings, the location of either new or existing buildings, and the occupancy and maintenance of all buildings and structures. In some cases, applicability provisions require the upgrading of existing buildings not already slated for any improvements. Such retroactive code enforcement is not common. The change of occupancy classification of a building can obligate one to meet the requirements of the latest adopted codes and standards.

The scope of some codes is limited primarily to new construction, while other codes are retroactive in nature and apply to existing buildings. Even those codes applying to new construction usually have provisions which increase their scope to include existing construction whenever that existing construction presents a health or life safety hazard. Retroactive codes and standards regulating existing structures usually provide a lower "standard of care" than would be provided by codes and standards regulating new construction, additions, alterations, repairs, or change of occupancy.

CODE OFFICIAL AND CODE DEPARTMENT

Duties

One of the tasks of administration chapters of building codes is to establish the requirements for code officials and code departments, as well as to define their duties and responsibilities. Some codes are fairly explicit in defining what is necessary for one to become a code official, specifying their professional and educational background, their years of experience, and perhaps some certification requirements. Other codes remain silent on this subject, allowing building departments to set their own employee qualification requirements.

The code official is responsible for managing a department that receives construction documents submitted by designers for plans review. The department then reviews those construction documents and issues construction permits based on the approval of the construction documents, inspects the ensuing construction as a result of the issuance of construction permits, and issues certificates of occupancy at the conclusion of construction, if the construction is performed in accordance with all applicable locally adopted construction regulations. Code officials may also become involved with the permitting and inspection of buildings by other means than someone's application for a permit. A public complaint or a code department's own investigation of an unsafe structure can lead to permitting and inspection procedures.

Right of Entry

Right of entry guarantees the code official or the code official's deputized inspectors the right to enter a structure when deemed necessary in order to protect its occupants from the potential harm created by that structure (Figure 2-1). The code official may need to enter the structure in order to determine whether it is life-threatening because of violations with locally adopted codes or because of deterioration of the structure. Administration chapters of codes usually contain a right-of-entry section, which states that the code official must give adequate warning before inspecting a

Figure 2-1 *Unsafe structure*

structure. The code official would then need to inspect the structure during reasonable hours, and he or she would need to be prepared to show proper credentials, as well as some proof of why the inspection was necessary. The occupant or owner of the structure must permit an inspection to occur when the code official follows proper procedures.

Consider a situation in which someone were to take an old house and convert it into a boarding home without notifying the code official. In many communities, because of a limited number of inspectors employed by those communities, such a conversion could occur without inspectors' ever knowing that the conversion took place. The alterations might be entirely indoors and the construction materials might be brought in through a rear entry. Assume that the department of codes and inspections were then informed by some source that a structure which was formerly a single family residence was now being operated as a multi-family boarding house. One could imagine that the code officials would be uneasy about the conversion of this former single family residence into a boarding house. The conversion may not address the potential life safety problems encountered because of a probable lack-of-proper-egress design, and other potential problems such as inadequate tenant separation, and a lack of upgraded smoke detector and alarm systems, as well as other concerns. Using the right-of-entry section within a building code, the code official could then secure entry to the structure in order to determine whether or not proper improvements had been made to the structure. Proper improvements would include upgrading the structure to the present locally adopted codes and standards for a multi-family boarding house. If these updated code requirements had not been followed when converting the structure to a new use, the code official would then have the right to require the structure to be upgraded to meet the requirements of the present codes and standards in force, or the code official could require the occupants of the structure to abandon the improper use of the structure as a boarding house.

It is a sensitive situation when government officials enter private property to enforce government regulations, so code officials need to be very cautious when using the powers of right of entry. Every step in the right-of-entry process should be well documented, and every opportunity should be taken to work with the owner of a structure before demanding entry. If the potential problems of a structure could be remedied without using right of entry, then all parties would be best served by such a solution.

Stop Work Order

As with the imposition of right of entry, the imposition of stop work orders is another sensitive area of codes enforcement (Figure 2-2). Stop work orders provide for the

STOP WORK

____
JURISDICTION

OFFICE OF BUILDING OFFICIAL

NOTICE

This building has been inspected and

- ☐ General Construction
- ☐ Concrete, Masonry and Finish Cement Work
- ☐ Lathing
- ☐ Plastering
- ☐ Elevators
- ☐ Plumbing
- ☐ Mechanical Work
- ☐ Electric Wiring
- ☐ Gas Piping

IS NOT ACCEPTED

Please correct as noted below before any further work is done.

— NOTE —

____

Date Inspector

Do Not Remove This Notice

- -

DETACH and Bring this Portion of Card With You.

Location: ______________________________

Date ______________________________

____
JURISDICTION

FORM 400.7

B-9

____
INSPECTOR

***Figure* 2-2** *Stop work order*

stoppage of work when a code official determines that improper construction methods are being used on a construction site. To illustrate their use, assume that the digging of a deep trench for a plumbing service entry had been in progress on a construction site when a code official noticed that the walls of the trench were not properly shored, and that there was therefore a chance that the walls would collapse, possibly resulting in the injury or death of the construction workers digging the ditch. The code official would probably issue a stop work order requiring the work to stop until proper shoring of the ditch had been undertaken. Contractors do not like to have their work stopped, so code officials need to be very careful when issuing a stop work order. Code officials should not use stop work orders casually in order to establish authority, but instead code officials should use stop work orders only when they are truly warranted, such as in situation affecting life safety. Code officials need to document completely every phase of issuing and enacting a stop work order.

Unsafe Buildings, Structures, or Equipment

Often it becomes necessary for a codes department to inspect buildings where no construction is occurring at all. This need usually arises from some condition within a building which is creating a hazard to life by impeding the structural safety or the fire safety of the building. In this case, codes provide a means for code officials to enter the structures through right of entry (discussed in this chapter), and then provide them with a means to determine whether or not the building is safe. If the code official deems particular structures to be unsafe, then the code official can require such structures to be repaired, altered, or demolished. The unsafe building section is another way that codes help code officials provide for life and health safety, and for the public welfare.

Revocation of Permits

Revocation of permits grants a code official the ability to revoke a permit when it has been determined that the applicant for the permit has misrepresented him or herself. The permit applicant might, for example, begin construction work in an area of a building that was not specifically permitted for construction by the local codes enforcement agency. Permits can also be revoked if there are violations of code provisions, or if the permits are for altering unsafe buildings or structures and corrections are being made without correcting the problems which made the buildings unsafe. Revocation of permits can occur for any reason that may cause concern for the code official as to the public safety, or health and general welfare provided by the construction or renovation of a particular project.

Alternate Materials and Methods of Construction

Alternate materials and methods of construction sections within codes give code officials the power to accept new construction materials or methods of construction previously unknown to them, should the code officials feel that these alternate materials or methods of construction are safe to use. New construction products and new methods of construction are constantly being developed. These products or methods may encompass some idea or some innovation never before seen in construction, or they may simply be a refinement of some product or method already in use. Code sections dealing with alternate materials and methods of construction give a code official the right to accept new products and construction methods even though they may not be specifically referenced in codes. Code officials do not want to deny the use of new construction innovations which can be used safely within the parameters of building codes and regulations.

Most code officials do not have time to research all the new products and methods of construction that become available each year, as the other requirements of their jobs already demand all of their time. In one process available to code officials, a third party actually investigates new materials and methods of construction so that code officials can simply read the reports of this third party and quickly garner enough information to feel more comfortable with approving their use. These reports are known as evaluation reports, and all three of the major building code organizations issue them. The evaluation report process utilizes staff members of the model code organizations to write reports on new products, materials, or methods of construction, and to investigate the validity of claims being made by the product or material manufacturers and by the developers of new construction methods. These reports are then reviewed by code officials for correctness. After the reports are reviewed, they are mailed to code officials throughout an entire region, so that they can quickly gain some insight into determining whether or not a new product or method of construction is safe to use.

To illustrate how evaluation reports work, assume a company developed a new type of roofing shingle with good fire resistance and which was made of some combination of affordable materials never before used for roofing. Naturally, that company would want to get their new product into the marketplace as quickly as possible. For code officials to accept these new roofing shingles, the manufacturer would have to have these roofing shingles tested by a recognized testing organization in accordance with the standard ASTM E 108, Method for Fire Tests of Roof Coverings (or some equivalent standard based on the code for the area in which the new shingles are being used) in order to determine the fire classification of the shingles—Class A, B, or C. ASTM E 108, Method for Fire Tests of Roof Coverings is a standard commonly referenced by codes and standards for determining the classification of roof systems. Of course, the manufacturer would want the best classification possible in order to increase the market value of their product, so the manufacturer would hope that their shingles would exceed the test requirements for Class A roof finishes in accordance with ASTM E 108. A Class A roof finish could be used in more locations than Class B or Class C roof finishes because of its higher resistance to the spread of fire.

If the manufacturer of these newly developed roof shingles were then to market different communities with their roofing product, well-documented test results that showed their roofing product carried a Class A fire rating in accordance with ASTM E 108 would convince many code officials to accept the new product as being safe to use as a Class A roof finish within their jurisdictions. However, many code officials would be somewhat apprehensive about approving or disapproving this new product for use within their jurisdiction. They may not trust the test literature to be legitimate, or they may feel that they do not have time to validate test results. This is not an uncommon occurrence.

The manufacturer of the new roof shingles could then retain the services of one of the model code organizations to write an evaluation report on their new product (Figure 2-3). Of course, the manufacturer would retain the services of that particular model code agency that promulgated the code for the region where the manufacturer is having trouble getting their product accepted. The manufacturer would submit test data and any other pertinent information on their roofing product to the model code organization writing the report. They would also inform the model code organization which testing laboratory performed the tests. The model code organization would then either except the testing laboratory as a legitimate testing laboratory, or it would require the testing laboratory to submit documentation about staffing, equipment, procedures, and third-party inspection in order to prove that they were a reputable testing laboratory.

Once the model code organization accepted the testing laboratory as legitimate, a staff member of the model code organization would then write a report describing the new roofing shingles, documenting the testing of the new roofing shingles, and discussing the results of those tests. The report would include limitations to the use of the roofing shingles based on their test results. For example, if the manufacturer's product was tested at a three-in-twelve maximum slope, then the product would not be granted a Class A finish for a four-in-twelve slope, as fire will move more rapidly across a more steeply sloped roof. If the manufacturer had not tested their roof shingles for the

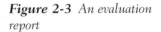

Figure 2-3 *An evaluation report*

more steeply sloped pitch, then their shingles could not have received the Class A classification at that greater pitch. Therefore, the report author would write that the product was safe and was a Class A finish at slopes not exceeding three in twelve. Of course, the test results by the recognized testing laboratory and the resulting listing of the roofing product would also state that the maximum slope allowed for the roofing product to maintain a Class A fire rating would be three in twelve. At certain periods of time all the new evaluation reports written by any particular model code organization would be gathered and mailed to a committee of code officials who would review these reports and make comments on them when necessary. These comments would then be addressed in the rewriting of the report. Once the reports were accepted by the committee of code officials, the reports would be mailed to other code officials throughout an entire region so that they could utilize these reports to make decisions about whether the new roofing shingle was safe for use in their jurisdiction. Code officials who are initially nervous about the use of new materials and methods of construction in their jurisdiction would receive these evaluation reports, and would hopefully gain the confidence they need to allow the safe use of the materials and methods of construction discussed in the reports.

It is very important to understand that the evaluation report process is not an approval process. The model code organizations are not approving materials and methods of construction; rather, they are describing the materials and methods of construction, and determining that these have been tested by recognized testing organizations in accordance with acceptable testing standards. The model code organizations then prescribe how the materials and methods of construction can be used properly within the parameters of their respective model codes, while listing any limitations on how those materials and methods of construction should be used.

Liability

Administration chapters of codes usually attempt to limit the liability of code officials and their employees. The philosophy of these sections is that code officials are responsible for checking the designs of architects, engineers, and other designers, in addition to being responsible for inspecting the construction process. The ultimate responsibility for proper design and construction within the code however, falls on the shoulders of the designers and builders. As of the writing of this book, it is proving fairly difficult to successfully sue code officials or their representatives for errors and omissions in relationship to their reviewing plans and inspecting construction. This does not necessarily mean that the liability sections of codes extend protection. This liability protection is contingent, of course, on code officials acting in an official capacity only, and does not protect them from mistakes made with their own personal designs and construction. Some codes regulate the amount of personal design and construction activity employees of a code and inspections department can perform.

PLANS REVIEW AND PERMITS

Whenever a structure is required to meet design and construction codes and standards, the code official is incorporated into the process of overseeing the design and construction of that structure by the permitting process. The code official checks the design of that structure in order to help ensure its compliance with local codes and standards through the plans review process, and checks the construction of that structure through permitting and inspections.

Permit Application

Codes dictate what sorts of alterations and new construction require permitting. An application for permit form is filled out by the owner or the owner's representative (often the contractor), and a fee is paid to help pay for the permitting process. The code also dictates who must submit the permit application. The permit application is received by the code official along with required construction documents.

Figure 2-4 *Construction documents*

Drawings and Specifications

Usually a code official requires two sets of plans and specifications, and any other documentation necessary to prove that a project's design is in accordance with all applicable locally adopted codes, standards, and regulations (Figure 2-4). The code official may require additional drawings, additional engineering details, or even test results or reports of products or methods of construction in order to ensure compliance. The code official requires two sets of documents so that one set can remain at the codes enforcement office as a matter of record, and another set can be left at the job site so that the contractor builds by an approved set of construction documents.

Plans Review

Once the code official has received all of the documentation that he or she requires in order to check a structure for compliance with all locally adopted codes and standards, that code official then submits the construction documents to the plans review process. The code official or a member of his or her staff reviews the construction documents, and checks them to make sure that they comply with whatever local codes and standards are adopted by the code official's particular locality. Good plans reviewers use a thorough checklist to ensure that they do not overlook any particular section within a code (Figure 2-5a,b,c). Some code departments are not well organized and use either inadequate checklists or no checklists at all. By not using some sort of checklist, code officials can virtually guarantee difficulties for designers and builders, because inconsistencies will occur between the plans review and the

PLAN REVIEW WORKSHEET

PROJECT: _____ PLAN REVIEW NO. _____

BUILDING DESCRIPTION: _____

CODE EDITION: _____ FIRE DISTRICT: □ IN □ OUT

NUMBER OF BUILDINGS OR AREAS SEPARATED BY FIREWALLS: _____

SBCCI
900 Montclair
Birmingham, AL 35213

HEIGHT AND AREA - CHAPTER 4

ALLOWABLE AREA

Occupancy group(s) _____ if mixed occupancy, Principal Use _____ Minimum Construction Type _____ if allowable area (Column F) ≥ Building Area (Column A); and allowable height ≥ actual height; then minimum construction type O.K. For mixed occupancies compare the allowable building area for the principal use to the total building area, then evaluate the allowable building area for each secondary occupancy to the actual area occupied by that occupancy.

Story No.	Description and Use	(A) Building Area Per Story On Plans	Table 400 Areas[1]		(D) Open Space Increase[1, 2] (%) x (B)	(E) Special Increase[1, 3] (%) x (B)	(F) Allowable Area (B)+(D)+(E) or (C)+(D)+(E) or Unlimited[4]
			(B) Unspk	(C) Spk			

[1] If Table 400 area ≥ proposed building area then increases are not applicable.
[2] Open space area increases from Section 402.3.2 are computed thus:

    a. Perimeter   = _____ = (F)
    b. Total Building Perimeter   = _____ = (P)
    c. Ratio (F ÷ P)   = _____ = (F/P)
    d. Percent of Increase
         I=4/3 (100% (F/P -.25))   = _____ = (%)
    e. The percentage increase is multiplied by the unsprinklered area (Column B) and entered in Column D above.
[3] Special increases may be applicable to A & E occupancies. For percentage and conditions see Sections 402.4.4, 4.6 and 4.7.
[4] Unlimited area applicable under conditions of sections: Group B, F, M, S (402.4.1); Group E (402.4.2); Group A (402.4.3); (Participation Sports (402.4.5); and Malls (507)).
[5] Table 400 areas are replaced by individual tables for open parking garages (412.6) and HPM facilities (511.2.1).

SBCCI © Rev. 7/91
C-2

Page 1 of 4

PLAN REVIEW REPORT

PROJECT: _____ PLAN REVIEW NO. _____

JURISDICTION _____ DATE _____

BUILDING DESCRIPTION: _____

CODE EDITION: _____ FIRE DISTRICT: □ IN □ OUT

CONSTRUCTION TYPE _____ OCCUPANCY GROUP _____

SBCCI
900 Montclair Road
Birmingham, AL 35213

Documentation Submitted		Name of Architect or Engineer Sealed by	Registration State No.
Site Plan: Date:	Sheets ___ thru ___		
Building Design Plans Date:	Sheets ___ thru ___		
Building Design Plans (Structural): Date:	Sheets ___ thru ___		
Mechanical Plans: Date:	Sheets ___ thru ___		
Plumbing Plans: Date:	Sheets ___ thru ___		
Electrical Plans: Date:	Sheets ___ thru ___		
Specifications: Date:	Pages ___ thru ___		
Structural Calcs: Date:	Pages ___ thru ___		
Soils Report: Date:	Pages ___ thru ___		
Sprinkler Plans □ NA Date:	Sheets ___ thru ___		
Sprinkler Calculations □ NA Date:	Pages ___ thru ___		
Energy Conservation Calcs □ NA Date:	Pages ___ thru ___		
Existing Building Plans □ NA Date:	Sheets ___ thru ___		

Instructions
A. A complete plan review (all Standard Codes) requires the submittal of all applicable documents listed above.
B. Each sheet of plans shall be sealed by a registered Architect and/or Engineer.
C. Specifications, calculations and soil reports should have at least the front page, cover sheet, or signature block sealed by the Architect or Engineer.

SBCCI © Rev. 7/91
C-3

Page 1 of ___

PLAN REVIEW
ASSEMBLY OCCUPANCY REQUIREMENTS

PLAN REVIEW NO. _____
JURISDICTION _____ DATE _____
BUILDING DESCRIPTION _____

SBCCI
900 Montclair Road
Birmingham, AL 35213

□ LARGE ASSEMBLY   □ SMALL ASSEMBLY   □ W/ □ W/O WORKING STAGE

SPECIFIC REQUIREMENTS

CODE SECTION	ITEM	O.K. COMMENT OR N/A	CODE SECTION	ITEM	O.K. COMMENT OR N/A
T.400	Building Height & Area		404.12	Amusement Park Buildings	
402.2	Height Modifications		503	Grandstands and Bleachers	
402.2.5	Group A Basement		513	Special Amusement Buildings	
402.3.2	Open Space Increase		T.600 Ftnote M	Rated Floors in Type V Unprotected Construction	
402.4	OCCUPANCY AREA MODIFICATION	□ N/A	704.3	INTERIOR FINISH REQUIREMENTS	
402.4.3	Unlimited Area		704.7	Carpeting in Corridors & Exits	
402.4.4	50% Area Increase		901	SPRINKLERS WHERE REQUIRED	□ N/A
402.4.5	Unlimited Area		901.5(1.)	Basement > 2500 sq.ft. or Used as Lounge or Nightclub any size	
402.4.6	33 1/3% Area Increase		901.5(2.)	Buildings Without Access (703.2)	
403.1	Mixed Occupancy		901.7.2	Large Assembly	
403.2	Accessory Occupancies		T.400	For Height or Area Increases	
403.3	Special Occupancy Separation		402.4.3	Unlimited Area	
403.4	Tenant Separation		513.3	Special Amusement Buildings	
404.1.3	Main Exit Fronts on a Public Place		T.600 Note L	Reduction of Hourly Ratings in Type I Construction	
404.3 1103.2	Occupancy Capacity Sign		702.2.2.3	Partition Exception (Type IV)	
404.5	Interior Finishes		704.3	Interior Finish Modifications	
404.7	Stages and Platforms Construction		903.1.2	Omission of Manual Fire Alarm	
404.8	STAGES	□ N/A	T.1104	Exit Travel > 200 ft.	
404.8.1	Construction		901.2	Sprinkler Standard NFiPA 13	
404.8.2	Accessory Rooms		901.8	Supervisory Facilities	
404.8.3	Vents		902.3	STANDPIPES WHERE REQUIRED	□ N/A
404.8.4	Proscenium Walls		902.3.1	Bldgs > 3 Stories or 50 ft. high	
404.8.5	Gridirons, Fly Galleries & Pinrails		902.3.4	Large Assembly w/Legit stage	
404.9	Flame Retardant Requirements		902.1	Standpipe Standard NFiPA 14	
404.10	Projection Rooms		902.7	Supervisory Facilities	
404.11	Tents for Assembly		903	Fire Alarm System	

SBCCI © Rev. 7/91 C-4A

Page ___ of ___

Figure 2-5a,b,c *Plans review forms*

inspection process, leading to expensive and time-consuming changes at job sites. Should a plans reviewer encounter areas in the construction documents that do not seem to be in compliance with locally adopted codes and standards, he or she will then need to discuss these potentially noncompliant areas with the designer so that they can work out a mutually agreeable solution.

There are many "gray" areas in construction codes. Some gray areas in construction codes are there because of poorly written code sections, but many others exist because the grayness creates flexibility for designers and builders, and even for code officials. Obviously, whenever a gray code section occurs, a determination has to be made by the code official as to what is required for any particular building or structure. The private sector and the public sector meet together to come to some sort of mutual consensus when gray areas are encountered.

Once construction documents have been approved, they are labeled as such by the codes department in charge of the plans review process, and one set of construction documents will be kept by the codes department, while the other set of construction documents will be kept at the job site. The construction documents at the job site will be made available for the use of the code official or his or her staff. In most construction projects an architect's or engineer's seal will be required on the construction documents in order for a code official to proceed with a plans review. This is based on the size of the project, the cost of the project, the story height of the project, or other requirements, as referenced in codes or by state laws. Different states have different requirements regarding who must sign and seal construction documents.

Issuing Permits

After construction documents are approved by the codes department, permits are issued for the construction of the building described in the approved construction documents (Figure 2-6a,b,c,d). A construction project can be permitted in phases. For example, a project may receive a permit for foundation work only, and another permit for the superstructure of the building. The permitting of a project may be phased where a particular phase of construction receives one permit and another phase of construction receives a second permit. It must be noted, however, that if a building is permitted in phases, the issuance of a permit for an early phase of construction does not obligate the code official to the permitting of a latter phase of construction. To illustrate this point, if one were to permit the construction of the foundation for an office building separately from the rest of the construction and problems arose while that foundation was being built, the code official would not be required to permit

BUILDING PERMIT 1

Jurisdiction of ______________

Applicant to complete numbered spaces only.

JOB ADDRESS

1 LEGAL DESCR. | LOT NUMBER | BLK | TRACT | (☐ SEE ATTACHED SHEET)

2 OWNER | MAIL ADDRESS | ZIP | PHONE

3 CONTRACTOR | MAIL ADDRESS | PHONE | REGISTRATION NO.

4 ARCHITECT OR DESIGNER | MAIL ADDRESS | PHONE | REGISTRATION NO.

5 ENGINEER | MAIL ADDRESS | PHONE | REGISTRATION NO.

6 LENDER | MAIL ADDRESS | BRANCH

7 USE OF BUILDING

8 Class of work: ☐NEW ☐ADDITION ☐ALTERATION ☐REPAIR ☐MOVE ☐REMOVE

9 Describe work:

10 Valuation of work: $

SPECIAL CONDITIONS:

APPLICATION ACCEPTED BY: | PLANS CHECKED BY: | APPROVED FOR ISSUANCE BY:

OWNER | JOB ADDRESS

PLAN CHECK FEE		PERMIT FEE
Type of Const.	Occupancy Group	Division
Size of Bldg. (Total) Sq. Ft.	No. of Stories	Max. Occ. Load
Fire Zone	Use Zone	Fire Sprinklers Required ☐ Yes ☐ No
No. of Dwelling Units	OFFSTREET PARKING SPACES Covered	Uncovered

Special Approvals	Required	Received	Not Required
ZONING			
HEALTH DEPT.			
FIRE DEPT.			
SOIL REPORT			
OTHER (Specify)			

NOTICE

SEPARATE PERMITS ARE REQUIRED FOR ELECTRICAL, PLUMBING, HEATING, VENTILATING OR AIR CONDITIONING.
THIS PERMIT BECOMES NULL AND VOID IF WORK OR CONSTRUCTION AUTHORIZED IS NOT COMMENCED WITHIN 6 MONTHS, OR IF CONSTRUCTION OR WORK IS SUSPENDED OR ABANDONED FOR A PERIOD OF 6 MONTHS AT ANY TIME AFTER WORK IS COMMENCED.

I HEREBY CERTIFY THAT I HAVE READ AND EXAMINED THIS APPLICATION AND KNOW THE SAME TO BE TRUE AND CORRECT. ALL PROVISIONS OF LAWS AND ORDINANCES GOVERNING THIS TYPE OF WORK WILL BE COMPLIED WITH WHETHER SPECIFIED HEREIN OR NOT. THE GRANTING OF A PERMIT DOES NOT PRESUME TO GIVE AUTHORITY TO VIOLATE OR CANCEL THE PROVISIONS OF ANY OTHER STATE OR LOCAL LAW REGULATING CONSTRUCTION OR THE PERFORMANCE OF CONSTRUCTION.

SIGNATURE OF CONTRACTOR OR AUTHORIZED AGENT (DATE)

SIGNATURE OF OWNER (IF OWNER BUILDER) (DATE)

WHEN PROPERLY VALIDATED (IN THIS SPACE) THIS IS YOUR PERMIT

PLAN CHECK VALIDATION CK. M.O. CASH PERMIT VALIDATION CK. M.O. CASH

A-1

Figure 2-6a *Building permit*

PLUMBING PERMIT 2

Jurisdiction of ______________

Applicant to complete numbered spaces only.

JOB ADDRESS

1 LEGAL DESCR. | LOT NUMBER | BLK | TRACT | (☐ SEE ATTACHED SHEET)

2 OWNER | MAIL ADDRESS | ZIP | PHONE

3 CONTRACTOR | MAIL ADDRESS | PHONE | LICENSE NO.

4 ARCHITECT OR DESIGNER | MAIL ADDRESS | PHONE | REGISTRATION NO.

5 ENGINEER | MAIL ADDRESS | PHONE | REGISTRATION NO.

6 USE OF BUILDING

7 Class of work: ☐ NEW ☐ ADDITION ☐ ALTERATION ☐ REPAIR

8 Describe work

9

APPROVED BY:

SPECIAL CONDITIONS:

APPLICATION ACCEPTED BY: | PLANS CHECKED BY: | APPROVED FOR ISSUANCE BY:

OWNER | JOB ADDRESS

PERMIT FEES

No.	Type of Fixture or Item	Fee
	WATER CLOSET (TOILET)	$
	BATHTUB	
	LAVATORY (WASH BASIN)	
	SHOWER	
	KITCHEN SINK AND DISP.	
	DISHWASHER	
	LAUNDRY TRAY	
	CLOTHES WASHER	
	WATER HEATER	
	URINAL	
	DRINKING FOUNTAIN	
	FLOOR SINK OR DRAIN	
	SLOP SINK	
	GAS SYSTEMS: NO. OUTLETS	
	WATER PIPING AND TREATING EQUIP.	
	WASTE INTERCEPTOR	
	VACUUM BREAKERS	
	LAWN SPINKLER SYSTEM	
	SEWER	
	CESSPOOL	
	SEPTIC TANK & PIT	
	PERMIT	$
	TOTAL FEE	$

NOTICE

THIS PERMIT BECOMES NULL AND VOID IF WORK OR CONSTRUCTION AUTHORIZED IS NOT COMMENCED WITHIN 6 MONTHS, OR IF CONSTRUCTION OR WORK IS SUSPENDED OR ABANDONED FOR A PERIOD OF 6 MONTHS AT ANY TIME AFTER WORK IS COMMENCED.

I HEREBY CERTIFY THAT I HAVE READ AND EXAMINED THIS APPLICATION AND KNOW THE SAME TO BE TRUE AND CORRECT. ALL PROVISIONS OF LAWS AND ORDINANCES GOVERNING THIS TYPE OF WORK WILL BE COMPLIED WITH WHETHER SPECIFIED HEREIN OR NOT. THE GRANTING OF A PERMIT DOES NOT PRESUME TO GIVE AUTHORITY TO VIOLATE OR CANCEL THE PROVISIONS OF ANY OTHER STATE OR LOCAL LAW REGULATING CONSTRUCTION OR THE PERFORMANCE OF CONSTRUCTION.

SIGNATURE OF CONTRACTOR OR AUTHORIZED AGENT (DATE)

SIGNATURE OF OWNER (IF OWNER BUILDER) (DATE)

WHEN PROPERLY VALIDATED (IN THIS SPACE) THIS IS YOUR PERMIT

PLAN CHECK VALIDATION CK. M.O. CASH PERMIT VALIDATION CK. M.O. CASH

A-2

Figure 2-6b *Plumbing permit*

ELECTRICAL PERMIT 3

Jurisdiction of ______________

Applicant to complete numbered spaces only.

JOB ADDRESS

1 LEGAL DESCR. | LOT NUMBER | BLK | TRACT | (☐ SEE ATTACHED SHEET)

2 OWNER | MAIL ADDRESS | ZIP | PHONE

3 CONTRACTOR | MAIL ADDRESS | PHONE | REGISTRATION NO.

4 ARCHITECT OR DESIGNER | MAIL ADDRESS | PHONE | REGISTRATION NO.

5 ENGINEER | MAIL ADDRESS | PHONE | REGISTRATION NO.

6 LENDER | MAIL ADDRESS | BRANCH

7 USE OF BUILDING

8 Class of work: ☐NEW ☐ADDITION ☐ALTERATION ☐REPAIR

9 Describe work:

SPECIAL CONDITIONS:

APPLICATION ACCEPTED BY: | PLANS CHECKED BY: | APPROVED FOR ISSUANCE BY:

OWNER | JOB ADDRESS

PERMIT FEES

		No.	Each	Fee
RECEPTACLE / LIGHT / SWITCH	Total Outlets			
LIGHTING FIXTURES	Total Fixtures			
RANGES CLO. DRYER WTR. HTR.				
GABAGE DISP. STA. COOK TOP				
DISH WASH. CLOTHES WASH.				
SPACE HTR. STA. APPL. 1/2 H.P. MAX.				
MOTORS:	H.P.			
SIGNS	NO. TRANS.			
	NO. LAMPS			
TEMP POWER ☐POLE ☐UNDGD.				
SEVICE	0-200A			
	201-400A			
☐NEW	401-600A			
☐CHANGE	OVER 600A			
PERMIT ISSUING FEE			$	
TOTAL FEE				$

NOTICE

THIS PERMIT BECOMES NULL AND VOID IF WORK OR CONSTRUCTION AUTHORIZED IS NOT COMMENCED WITHIN 6 MONTHS, OR IF CONSTRUCTION OR WORK IS SUSPENDED OR ABANDONED FOR A PERIOD OF 6 MONTHS AT ANY TIME AFTER WORK IS COMMENCED.

I HEREBY CERTIFY THAT I HAVE READ AND EXAMINED THIS APPLICATION AND KNOW THE SAME TO BE TRUE AND CORRECT. ALL PROVISIONS OF LAWS AND ORDINANCES GOVERNING THIS TYPE OF WORK WILL BE COMPLIED WITH WHETHER SPECIFIED HEREIN OR NOT. THE GRANTING OF A PERMIT DOES NOT PRESUME TO GIVE AUTHORITY TO VIOLATE OR CANCEL THE PROVISIONS OF ANY OTHER STATE OR LOCAL LAW REGULATING CONSTRUCTION OR THE PERFORMANCE OF CONSTRUCTION.

SIGNATURE OF CONTRACTOR OR AUTHORIZED AGENT (DATE)

SIGNATURE OF OWNER (IF OWNER BUILDER) (DATE)

WHEN PROPERLY VALIDATED (IN THIS SPACE) THIS IS YOUR PERMIT

PLAN CHECK VALIDATION CK. M.O. CASH PERMIT VALIDATION CK. M.O. CASH

A-3

Figure 2-6c *Electrical permit*

MECHANICAL PERMIT 4

Jurisdiction of ______________

Applicant to complete numbered spaces only.

JOB ADDRESS

1 LEGAL DESCR. | LOT NUMBER | BLK | TRACT | (☐ SEE ATTACHED SHEET)

2 OWNER | MAIL ADDRESS | ZIP | PHONE

3 CONTRACTOR | MAIL ADDRESS | PHONE | REGISTRATION NO.

4 ARCHITECT OR DESIGNER | MAIL ADDRESS | PHONE | REGISTRATION NO.

5 ENGINEER | MAIL ADDRESS | PHONE | REGISTRATION NO.

6 LENDER | MAIL ADDRESS | BRANCH

7 USE OF BUILDING

8 Class of work: ☐ NEW ☐ADDITION ☐ALTERATION ☐REPAIR

9 Describe work:

SPECIAL CONDITIONS:

APPLICATION ACCEPTED BY: | PLANS CHECKED BY: | APPROVED FOR ISSUANCE BY:

OWNER | JOB ADDRESS

Type of Fuel: Oil ☐ Nat. Gas ☐ L.P.G. ☐

PERMIT FEES

No.	Type of Fixture or Item	Fee
	Air Cond. Units—H.P. Ea.	$
	Refrigeration Units—H.P. Ea.	
	Boilers—H.P. Ea.	
	Gas Fired A.C. Units—Tonnage Ea.	
	Forced Air Systems—B.T.U. M Ea.	
	Gravity Systems—B.T.U. M Ea.	
	Floor Furnaces—B.T.U. M	
	Wall Heaters—B.T.U. M	
	Unit Heaters—B.T.U. M	
	Evaporative Coolers	
	Clothes Dryers	
	Ventilation Fan	
	Range Hood	
	Air Handling Unit— C.F.M.	
	Incinerator	
	PERMIT	$
	TOTAL FEE	$

NOTICE

THIS PERMIT BECOMES NULL AND VOID IF WORK OR CONSTRUCTION AUTHORIZED IS NOT COMMENCED WITHIN 6 MONTHS, OR IF CONSTRUCTION OR WORK IS SUSPENDED OR ABANDONED FOR A PERIOD OF 6 MONTHS AT ANY TIME AFTER WORK IS COMMENCED.

I HEREBY CERTIFY THAT I HAVE READ AND EXAMINED THIS APPLICATION AND KNOW THE SAME TO BE TRUE AND CORRECT. ALL PROVISIONS OF LAWS AND ORDINANCES GOVERNING THIS TYPE OF WORK WILL BE COMPLIED WITH WHETHER SPECIFIED HEREIN OR NOT. THE GRANTING OF A PERMIT DOES NOT PRESUME TO GIVE AUTHORITY TO VIOLATE OR CANCEL THE PROVISIONS OF ANY OTHER STATE OR LOCAL LAW REGULATING CONSTRUCTION OR THE PERFORMANCE OF CONSTRUCTION.

SIGNATURE OF CONTRACTOR OR AUTHORIZED AGENT (DATE)

SIGNATURE OF OWNER (IF OWNER BUILDER) (DATE)

WHEN PROPERLY VALIDATED (IN THIS SPACE) THIS IS YOUR PERMIT

PLAN CHECK VALIDATION CK. M.O. CASH PERMIT VALIDATION CK. M.O. CASH

A-4

Figure 2-6d *Mechanical permit*

other phases of construction until the foundation problems were rectified. Code officials must enforce the principles for designing and constructing safe buildings.

INSPECTIONS

After permits have been issued and construction has begun, inspectors from the codes department visit the construction site from time to time to inspect the construction for compliance with the approved construction documents and for proper implementation in accordance with any special knowledge that the inspectors have regarding proper construction methods (Figure 2-7). Administration chapters of building codes specify that the code official has the right to require as many construction inspections as the code official deems necessary in order to ensure proper compliance with codes and standards. These administration chapters usually suggest certain logical times for inspections to occur. For example, most codes specify that when providing building inspections, there should be a foundation inspection after all forms for foundations have been erected and after all trenches to receive foundations have been excavated. This would be followed by a framing inspection. The framing inspection occurs after the building is "dried-in," that is after the roof, framing, fireblocking, and bracing are all in place, and after all building systems such as wiring, plumbing pipes, gas pipes, chimney ducts, vents, and any other mechanical systems are completed but not concealed. A third and final inspection would occur after the building is completed and ready to

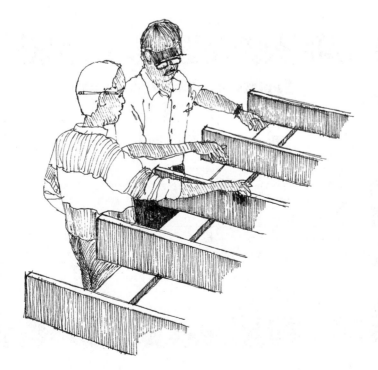

Figure 2-7 Inspection

be occupied. Often code officials require other inspections in addition to these routine inspections, if they feel this would be necessary to ensure compliance with all locally adopted construction regulations.

Each building discipline is subject to inspections by inspectors familiar with that particular discipline. For example, an electrical inspector should be somebody with a great deal of experience in electrical construction, and with a great deal of knowledge about what to look for when inspecting electrical systems within a building. The plumbing inspector is often a former plumber, someone familiar with plumbing installation and the proper construction of plumbing systems. This is true for mechanical inspectors, gas inspectors, and building inspectors as well. All inspectors should be intimately familiar with the area of construction they are inspecting. Inspectors do not usually inspect for aesthetic issues, as the quality of construction is not important to inspectors as far as it relates to the beauty of the structure, but rather as it relates to the structural, health, or fire safety of the structure. Of course, certain zoning or historical issues may obligate codes departments or zoning departments to inspect certain buildings for issues that are primarily aesthetic in nature.

CERTIFICATES OF OCCUPANCY

Once the construction of a project has been completed, and the code official and his or her staff have determined that the construction project was built in accordance with

Figure 2-8 *Certificate of occupancy*

all locally enforced construction regulations, as well as with acceptable construction practices, the code official can issue a certificate of occupancy (Figure 2-8). Once the certificate of occupancy has been issued, it is lawful for people to inhabit the building and use the building for the purposes for which it was designed to be used. Often the certificate of occupancy is the building official's "trump card" in the codes enforcement process. If one were to refuse to correct a violation cited by a code official, the code official could then refuse to issue a certificate of occupancy, therefore making it illegal to occupy the structure.

TESTS

Often a code official requires tests or test reports from an approved testing organization before accepting a particular product or method of construction. The code official may require tests because of his or her unfamiliarity with the product or method, or because of the nature of the product or method called for by the design. For new products or methods of construction, code officials may rely on evaluation reports (discussed in this chapter under alternate materials and methods of construction), or they may demand their own requirements for testing be met. When tests are required by a code official, the test results become part of the construction documents.

CONSTRUCTION BOARD OF ADJUSTMENT AND APPEALS

If a private sector individual such as a designer has a grievance with a code official's interpretation of a specific section of the code, that individual has a means for presenting his or her argument to a board of appeals. The board of appeals can ultimately overrule the code official. The designer should first try to meet with the code official in order to arrive at some sort of mutual consensus as to how to interpret the code section in question. If no progress can be made through meeting with the code official and the designer still feels strongly about his or her own interpretation of the section, the designer can present an argument to the board of appeals. A board of appeals can grant the authority to the designer to proceed with the design in the manner he or she feels is appropriate. However, should a board of appeals side with the code official, then the designer would have to abide by the board's decision, or take his or her argument to a court of law.

It is not uncommon for a code official to support a designer's interpretation of a particular code section, while maintaining some "apprehension" about issuing "blanket" approval of the interpretation because of the potential liability that would be incurred by the code official. Therefore, the code official might require the designer to have his or her interpretation of the code section approved by the board of appeals, while the code official shows support for the designer in front of the board of appeals. By doing this, the code official helps the designer, but does not carelessly subject his or her department to extreme liability exposure.

SEVERABILITY

When enforcing codes and standards, there is always a possibility that in a given instance, a particular section in a code will be proven invalid, illegal, or void in a court of law. To protect the entire document from becoming invalid in this case, codes rely on a concept called validity or severability. The concept of validity or severability establishes that in the case of a particular code section's being declared illegal or void, the rest of the code would be considered valid and could be enforced in its entirety. One can only imagine the chaos that would ensue if an entire code document were made invalid because of one voided portion. Without the concept of validity or severability, if someone did not want to meet the guidelines of a particular building code, then one would have to prove only that a single section of that building code were illegal or invalid. This would probably not be that difficult to do.

VIOLATIONS AND PENALTIES

Whenever someone constructs, alters, extends, repairs, removes, demolishes, occupies, or moves a building or a structure in violation of the code, that person has committed an unlawful act. Codes give code officials the power to act on such a violation of the law. The code official should consult with the attorney for the local jurisdiction and determine how to proceed in regards to such a violation (Figure 2-9). The violator must correct the violation and may have to pay fines. The code official might use this opportunity to issue a stop work order until the violation is corrected.

RELATIONSHIP WITH CODE OFFICIALS

The relationship between an architect, builder or owner, and a code official has a direct bearing on the efficiency of a construction project. Most anyone would find it difficult to work with someone who was constantly belligerent. Designers, builders, and code officials should all be considered as part of a team of professionals, charged with the

CODE VIOLATION

Type of Inspection _____

Date _____

_____
Inspector   Permit Number

Figure 2-9 *Violation notice*

responsibility of producing safe, high-quality buildings and structures. I believe in involving code officials early in the design development process so that they know that their opinions are valid to me. Many code officials are wary of the construction documents in front of them when they see the project for the first time after the entire project has already been designed. A code official involved in the early phases of the project can help point the designer towards potential problems that may hinder the project's outcome. This, in turn, enables the designer to correct the problem in the most cost-effective manner. Treating the code official in a professional manner virtually guarantees that the code official will treat the designer in a professional manner.

In many localities designers have to deal with two sets of code officials—those representing the building official's office and those representing the fire official's office. This can become very complicated as the two sets of code officials might disagree with one another, and may enforce two different codes. The building official's office will probably enforce one of the building codes and the fire official's office will probably enforce the NFPA 101 Life Safety Code. In some cities, the building official and fire marshal are the same person. This is a wonderful situation for designers in that all codes enforcement comes from one direction. There are also many cities where the building official and the fire official work very closely together in order to streamline the process for designers, and to help designers get through the multiplicity of codes to which they must design.

A city in Alabama used to have Thursday review sessions (Figure 2-10). Every Thursday, representatives of the fire department and the building department were available for scheduled review sessions of potential construction projects. They could help the designer locate potential code-related design problems early so that the design problems could be avoided. These sessions also provided an opportunity for simultane-

Figure 2-10 *Thursday group*

ous review and comment by both code enforcement authorities having jurisdiction in that city (the building official and the fire official), thus ensuring savings of time for the designer and the client. The Thursday review sessions proved to be very valuable to the designers that utilized them.

Many cities have implemented a system of one-stop permitting. This is a process where construction documents are delivered to one location, the building department perhaps, and are then routed to all of the areas of the city where they must be reviewed and approved. This process keeps the designer from having to schedule appointments at several different departments, therefore wasting valuable time. Some government entities even have full-time employees whose job it is to see that construction documents are routed properly and expeditiously. For example, one might stop by the building department and leave two sets of construction documents. The employee in charge of routing these documents would deliver them to zoning, planning, engineering, and the building department, as well as to any other agency responsible for looking over these documents. The designer would only have to return if violations were found, or to receive permits after the construction documents had been approved. This is an example of code officials trying to provide better service by expediting a process which can be fairly cumbersome. This sort of public service and "working relationship" attitude exemplifies the very best that a codes department can offer through their administration of codes, standards, and other regulations.

CHAPTER 3

Use or Occupancy

*C*hapter 3 begins with a discussion of the reasons for separate occupancy classifications, along with a discussion of what makes one occupancy classification different from another. The chapter then looks at each occupancy classification in more detail, including what codes require in general for each classification. A discussion about choosing the proper occupancy classifications when designing concludes the chapter.

WHY DO WE HAVE DIFFERENT OCCUPANCIES?

As discussed in Chapter 1, building codes could be very lean indeed if society did not desire flexible regulation. We desire flexible regulation so that buildings that are more fire resistant will not be required to meet the same expensive design parameters as buildings that are less fire resistant. Of course, codes could just state that all buildings are of one occupancy classification, and that all buildings must meet the most stringent requirements that we presently assign to any occupancy classification. Rather than taking such a strict approach, codes allow us some flexibility, realizing that not every building is used in the same way as every other building, and therefore that some buildings can be allowed certain liberties in design that other buildings cannot.

OCCUPANCY CLASSIFICATION CONCEPTS

Once one asks for flexible construction regulations which incorporate different occupancy classifications, some decisions must be made about why one particular occupancy group is safer than another. Different occupancy classifications are applied to different buildings to recognize the differences amongst these buildings in content-related characteristics and human behavior characteristics. These differing occupancy classifications recognize that all buildings uses are not alike. People behave differently in one occupancy classification than they do in another; also, one occupancy classification has different amounts of fire loading and different amounts of toxins within it than another occupancy classification.

Content-Related Characteristics

Content-related characteristics deal with the relative differences amongst buildings in the amounts of fire loading, and the amounts of toxic contents within different buildings. The amount of fireloading and the amount of toxic contents within a building are related to how the building is used. Every building has fireloading, as one can learn from the many fire officials who have had to fight fires in "noncombustible" buildings. Similarly, most buildings contain toxic contents. However, code officials are more interested in the relative differences in the amounts of fireloading and toxic contents amongst separate occupancies, so that code officials can determine which occupancy is safer than another. The fact that one building may be built of a more combustible type of construction than another building is not a fireloading concern in regards to occupancy classification. The relative combustibility of a building's structure is a concern of type of construction, and is covered under Chapter 6 of this book.

Combustible Contents

One of the major content-related differences amongst separate occupancy classifications is the amount of combustible contents typically found within each different occupancy group (Figure 3-1). The relative differences in the amounts of combustible contents within buildings of separate occupancy classifications help code officials establish rules governing those buildings. As mentioned earlier, all buildings have combustible contents within them: furniture, carpet, draperies, office products, etc. Codes do not treat all occupancies equally in regards to combustible contents, however, because some occupancies, such as storage or factory industrial facilities, have greater amounts of combustible contents than do typical businesses or residences. It may cause great concern to some people to trivialize the danger of the many combustible contents usually found within a business or residence, but codes do not ignore these

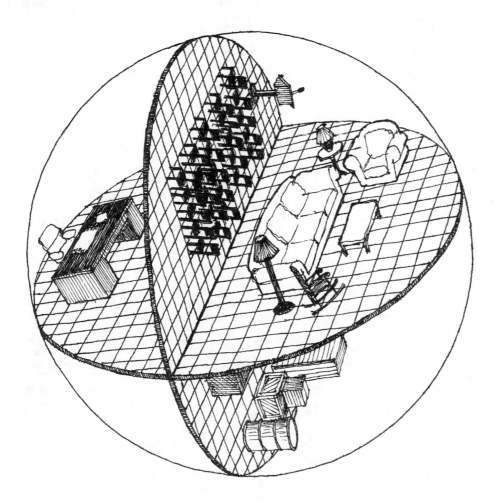

Figure 3-1 Combustible contents

businesses or residences. Indeed, businesses and residences are regulated by codes with concern to combustible contents mainly through limitations of heights in feet and areas in square feet. They are just not as strictly regulated as storage or factory industrial facilities. The key word is "relative"; code officials are looking for relative differences.

Explosive or Toxic Contents

The relative differences amongst buildings of separate occupancy classifications with respect to the amount of explosive or toxic contents utilized or stored within these buildings also leads to differentiation within codes amongst separate occupancy classifications (Figure 3-2). Once again, one is looking for relative differences, and while recognizing that all occupancies have some explosive or toxic contents within them, one must discern which occupancies are particularly hazardous and which occupancies are relatively low in hazard as far as the use and storage of explosive or toxic contents is concerned. As with combustible contents, the risk leaders for explosive or toxic contents tend to be storage and factory industrial facilities. Often these two occupancies are reclassified as hazardous occupancies because of their excessive storage or use of explosive or toxic contents. It must be noted, however, that many factory industrial facilities and storage facilities are actually low hazards with regards to explosive or toxic contents.

Human Behavior Characteristics

How people behave in buildings during emergency situations is of great concern to code officials. An otherwise routine building evacuation can go awry if the occupants of that building do not egress in an orderly manner. If a building is crowded with people, there is a real potential for panic due to the way people behave in crowds. Lack of familiarity with a building's layout can also create a hazardous panic situation, especially if the building is filled with smoke from a fire, and visibility is therefore limited. Sleeping occupants must be alerted to the fact that an emergency situation exists before they can even begin to react to that situation. Many people need other peoples' help when egressing a building. These people may be attached to life-preserving medical equipment, or they may be inmates in a correctional facility. As with content-related characteristics, human behavior characteristics vary from occupancy classification to occupancy classification. Therefore, we can say that one occupancy classification is more hazardous than another in the way that its building occupants are likely to behave in the event of an emergency.

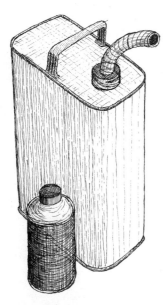

Figure 3-2 *Toxic or explosive contents*

Number of People per Square Foot

When using human behavior characteristics to discern the differences amongst separate occupancy classifications, the particular human behavior characteristic dealing with number of people per square foot is often called "potential for panic." The more people per square foot within a building or area, the greater the hazard, because of the likelihood that a panic situation will ensue due to the crowded conditions (Figure 3-3). Codes try to alleviate the problem of panic in buildings where there are a great number of people per square foot by requiring those particular occupancies to meet more stringent egress requirements. If people in a crowded building perceive the egress scheme to be adequate and safe, there is not as great a likelihood that panic will ensue in the event of an emergency. Therefore, codes provide stricter egress control in occupancies with a large number of people per square foot.

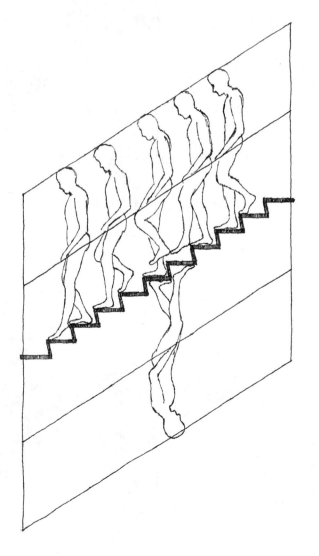

Figure 3-3 *Occupant density*

Assembly occupancies are the highest hazard of all occupancies in relation to the number of people per square foot. For this reason, assembly occupancies are heavily regulated by egress chapters of building codes. In addition to meeting the "standard" sorts of requirements that all occupancy groups must meet for the size and number of exits, assembly occupancies must also meet other egress requirements, such as those specifying a certain amount of egress capacity at a main exit and at peripheral exits (see Chapter 10). These additional egress requirements are there to help ensure that assembly occupancy exits and exit access are adequate in number and size, and are spaced in such a manner that the inhabitants of the building can easily egress the building no matter where the fire hazard occurs. Also, the inhabitants of an assembly occupancy will hopefully recognize in the event of an emergency, that the egress scheme is adequate, and they will therefore be less inclined to panic.

Familiarity with the Building

How familiar the building occupants are with a particular building they use is of great concern to code officials. Confusion can result from one's lack of knowledge of a building's layout, especially when the building is filled with smoke and one is crawling on one's hands and knees trying to find an exit (Figure 3-4). Many may feel, for example, that they know how to exit from their favorite, frequently visited movie theater complex, but if the main entrance to that complex which they invariably use is blocked by fire, they will have to rely on good building code design in order to egress the com-

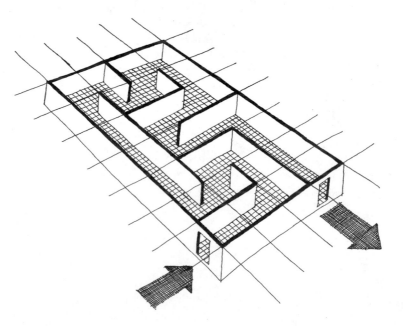

Figure 3-4 *Familiarity with the building*

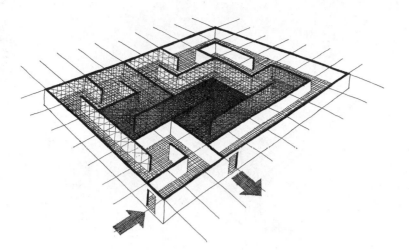

Figure **3-5** *Smoke in facility*

plex. We tend to be much more familiar with our own residences than we are with assembly occupancies, health care occupancies, or certain other occupancy groups.

An architect friend of mine in Dallas, Texas is the construction manager for a medium-size firm that designs fairly large projects. He once told me about an opportunity he had to participate in a fire official's smoke testing of a building. My friend has a good sense of direction and "reads" cities and buildings very well, and is therefore able to find his way around a town or within a building with relative ease. Being construction manager on this project, he told me he was in and out of this building most every day for three years and was intimately familiar with it. However, he said when the smoke bombs were detonated and the building was filled with smoke, he became so disoriented that he had no idea where he was within the building. He had to rely on others in order to egress the building. We must realize that in a fire situation, because of the smoke production from a fire, that often a building we are intimately familiar with can become unfamiliar (Figure 3-5).

Familiarity with the building can become even further complicated by the fact that in many buildings, visitors are barely familiar with them, and therefore, when an emergency situation occurs and the building is full of smoke, the visitors are doubly confused. Within certain occupancy groups, there can be a great variation in the differences of hazard associated with one's familiarity with buildings. For example, many companies conduct their business primarily by phone or mail; therefore, these business occupancies are inhabited mostly by the employees who work at these companies and are therefore very familiar with their particular building. Many companies also conduct business with clients who actually visit the companies' facilities. In these cases, their buildings are occupied with people who are not intimately familiar with the facilities. Thus, in the case of business occupancies, there are many low-hazard and high-hazard situations concerning the occupants' familiarity with the building.

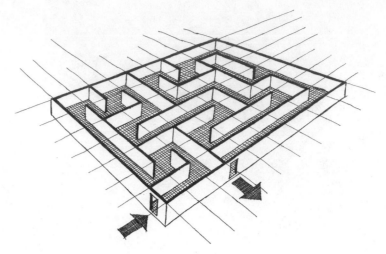

Figure 3-6 *Size of facility*

The size of a facility can also affect one's familiarity with a building (Figure 3-6). If a building is very large, it stands to reason that the occupants of that building will not be as familiar with it as they would be if the building were smaller. A large building can be more complex in its layout and it occupants may tend to memorize particular routes to get them to the services that they need within the building, instead of becoming acquainted with the layout of the entire building. These occupants may have to traverse an unfamiliar area of the building in the event of an emergency because their familiar route may be blocked by the emergency condition. In this case, lack of familiarity with the building can be a real hazard to them.

Assembly occupancies, health care occupancies, and detention and correctional occupancies tend to be very high hazards for lack of familiarity with a building. Once again, residential occupancies are considered very safe. Another example of a safe occupancy due to building familiarity would be a factory industrial occupancy where few outsiders enter the space. This creates an environment where most of the occupants of the building are intimately familiar with the building.

One way codes deal with the problem of building occupants' lack of familiarity with a building is by requiring signs identifying exits and the routes to these exits. In some cases, codes even require main exits to be positioned in a certain manner so that the location of those main exits are obvious to building occupants.

Alertness of Occupants

Have you ever awakened in the middle of the night to answer a phone call only to find yourself making incoherent statements that seemed perfectly logical to you at the time? Herein lies the problem with sleep as it relates to fire safety (Figure 3-7). Not only does one need to be awakened from a deep sleep in the event of a fire, but one needs to act quickly and rationally. This is why codes require the installation of smoke

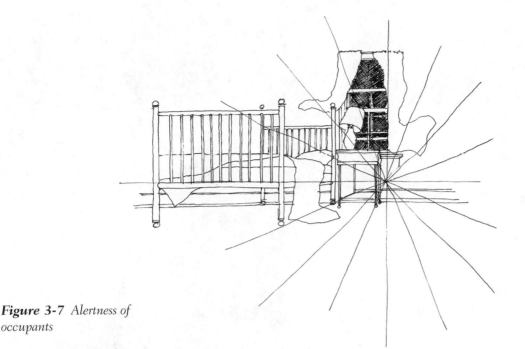

Figure 3-7 *Alertness of occupants*

detectors adjacent to sleeping areas. Their primary purpose is to alert people in sleeping areas in order to let them know that it is time to leave the building when smoke is generated from a fire. One should condition oneself to egress without thinking when the smoke detector sounds its alarm. Alertness of occupants deals with the fact that when people are in a deep sleep, they will not react as quickly in the event of an emergency as would somebody who is wide awake.

In different buildings, our level of alertness changes. Once again we must consider these differences when comparing separate occupancy groups. Obviously, residential, health care, and detention and correctional facilities would have the highest level of hazard associated with alertness of occupants. All other occupancies would be somewhat lower in hazard due to the alertness of occupants.

Mobility of Occupants

The category of mobility of occupants is based on the question, "Do the people within a particular building need someone else's help in order to egress the building, or in order to egress to a safer place within that building?" In hospitals, many of the patients are not able to egress themselves, because of the medical treatment they are receiving, or because of being connected to medical equipment which immobilizes them. These patients rely on hospital staff to egress them from fire areas to safer areas of buildings. In hospital nurseries and in nursing homes, infants and the elderly also rely on medical staff in order to egress a building (Figures 3-8 and 3-9). If so, how many of the building's occupants need this help in egressing? Inmates in detention and cor-

Figures 3-8 and 3-9
Mobility of occupants—Health Care

rectional facilities can egress only when the staff at these facilities open the locked doors that confine them (Figure 3-10). In health care occupancies and in detention and correctional occupancies, codes approach egress differently than they do in other occupancies. Usually these two institutional occupancy classifications egress their occupants to a different area of the facility, rather than to a public way as is done in other occupancy classifications; after all, inmates must remain incarcerated and patients must receive medical attention. This compartmentalization guarantees that there are safe areas of buildings where the occupants can egress to in the event of an emergency condition such as a fire.

The people we worry about when considering the mobility of occupants besides inmates and patients are small children and the elderly. Odd though it may seen, most occupancy classifications do not consider people with disabilities when considering the category of mobility of occupants. The reason they do not is that once again, codes are looking for relative differences amongst occupancies, and supposedly most occupancy classifications should have the same percentage of people with disabilities within them. This is especially true with the "mainstreaming" effect that the Americans with Disabilities Act will foster. That is not to say that people with disabilities will not require specific consideration in codes and standards, but rather that if essentially the same percentage of people with disabilities use all occupancy groups, then those people with disabilities are not a good determinant of the differ-

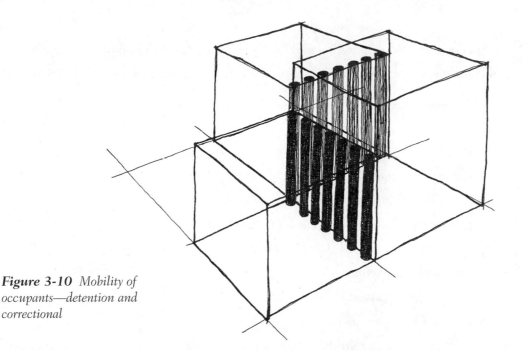

Figure 3-10 *Mobility of occupants—detention and correctional*

ences amongst occupancy classifications. Institutional occupancies (health care and detention and correctional) present the greatest hazard associated with mobility of occupants.

Ignition Sources

I have seen lists of determinants of occupancy classification that are much more extensive than the six-item list I have just covered. However, these six items sufficiently explain the types of things looked for when classifying occupancy groups. Another important consideration has to do with the number and location of ignition sources. Fireloading characteristics are not nearly as much a concern if there are not many ignition sources available. Examples of ignition sources might be people smoking, open flames, or perhaps the arcing of electrical equipment. There are adjustments in codes within specific occupancy groups to account for the varying threat of ignition sources.

INDIVIDUAL OCCUPANCY GROUPS

After having looked at the six basic determinants of the differences amongst occupancy classifications, one can see that codes have good reasons for adjusting requirements based on the occupancy classifications of buildings. The three major building codes and the NFPA 101 Life Safety Code share the same basic occupancy classifications. Nonetheless, there are differences amongst these four codes in the titles of the separate occupancy classifications, and differences in the titles and numbers of occupancy subclassifications within each of those codes. The basic occupancy classifications are:

- *Assembly Occupancy*
- *Business Occupancy*
- *Educational Occupancy*
- *Factory Industrial Occupancy*
- *Hazardous Occupancy (Hazard of Contents)*
- *Institutional Unrestrained (Health Care) Occupancy*
- *Institutional Restrained (Detention and Correctional) Occupancy*
- *Mercantile Occupancy*
- *Residential Occupancy*
- *Storage Occupancy and*
- *Utility Occupancy (Utility occupancy is not recognized as a specific occupancy classification in all four major codes)*

Assembly Occupancy

Assembly occupancies are occupancies where a building or a portion of a building is used for the gathering together of persons for social or religious functions, for recreation, for food or drink consumption, for deliberations, or for awaiting transportation. Code officials are so concerned about the number of people within assembly occupancies that the definitions of assembly occupancy classifications and subclassifications, in most codes, are based on the number of people within that room or space. These codes state a minimum number of people that "trigger" each individual subclassification of an assembly occupancy.

Examples of assembly occupancies include amusement park buildings, assembly halls, auditoriums, churches, conference rooms, courtrooms, dance halls, drinking establishments, exhibition halls, certain gymnasiums, motion picture theaters, museums, passenger depots, recreation halls, restaurants, skating rinks, stadiums and grandstands, and theaters (Figure 3-11). This is not an exhaustive list.

As already stated, two of the most important characteristics of assembly occupancies are the number of people per square foot within these occupancies, and the lack of familiarity with these occupancies by the occupants of these facilities. The number of people per square foot within assembly occupancies causes concern for code officials because of the potential for panic in an emergency situation due to crowd behavior. Lack of familiarity with an assembly occupancy by its occupants concerns code officials, because of the potential difficulty in egressing experienced by people not familiar

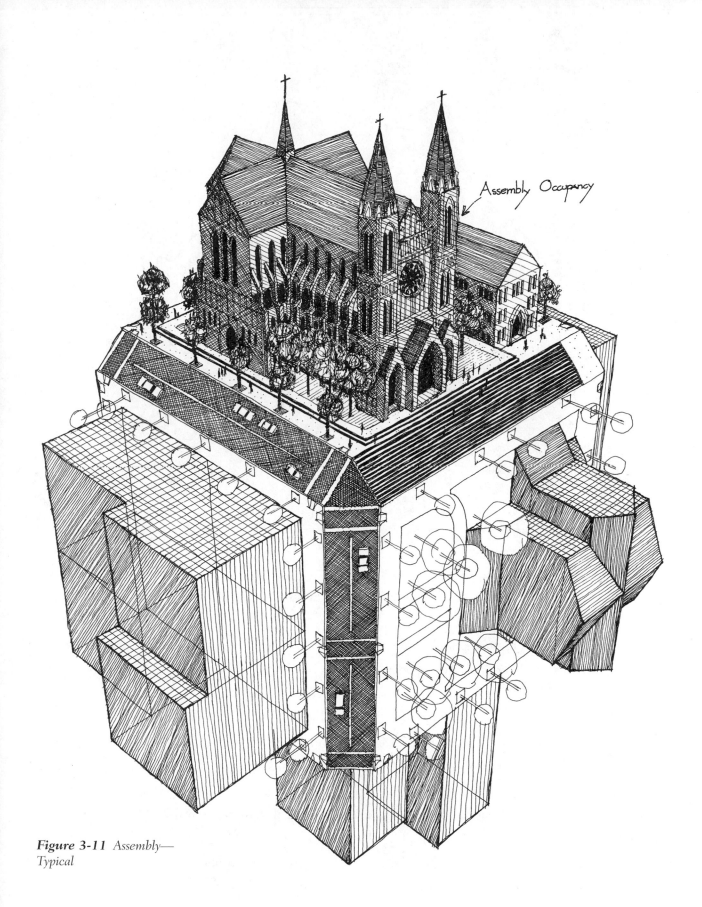

Assembly Occupancy

Figure 3-11 *Assembly—Typical*

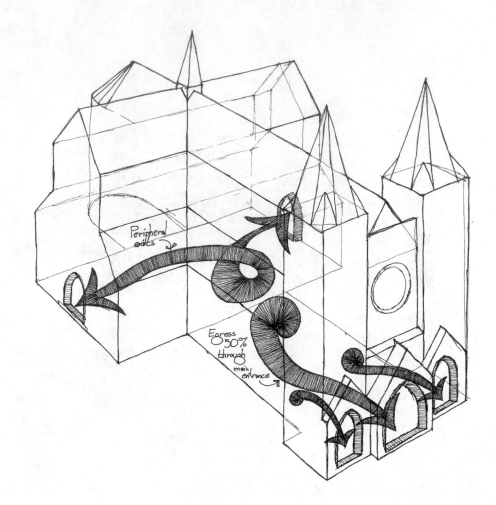

Within the image: Peripheral exits; Egress 50% through main entrance

Figure 3-12 Assembly—
Characteristics

with a building. Codes address these two concerns by requiring assembly occupancies to provide specific amounts of egress capacity at main exits and at other peripheral exits (see Chapter 10).

In the cases of assembly occupancies with large stages, code officials are concerned with the "mixed occupancy" situations which often occur, because the auditorium areas and the stage resemble two separate occupancy classifications. The stages causing concerns for code officials are those in which the curtains, drops, leg drops, scenery, lightning devices and other stage effects are retractable horizontally or suspended overhead. These stages (legitimate or working stages) are therefore stages where fairly major theater productions can occur, and not usually the typical raised platforms located at the end of many high school gymnasiums. The obvious concern with a legitimate stage is the potential amount of combustible materials used for curtains and scenery, and the potential ignition sources created by lighting fixtures and other electrical equipment associated with the operation and use of a legitimate stage. Often legitimate stages might even have workshops adjacent to them loaded with great amounts of combustible materials. Because of the concern with the fireloading and ignition sources often associated with legitimate stages, assembly occupancies containing legitimate stages are considered more hazardous than those assembly occupancies which do not have legitimate stages. Most codes allow more area for assembly occupancies not associated with legitimate stages than they do for assembly occupancies associated with legitimate stages. Codes usually require some sort of protection between stages and the auditorium portions of assembly occupancies. This protection is provided by a proscenium curtain which drops and maintains a fire rated separation in the event of a fire, or by a system of sprinklers which deluge the proscenium opening. The four major codes are inconsistent in defining assembly classifications and subclassifications, so one has to be careful when designing or constructing a structure incorporating a legitimate stage, especially if one has to meet the requirements of two different codes.

In the case of auditoriums and theaters, motion picture projection rooms create another concern for fire officials in that many of the films utilized in these facilities are very flammable. Requirements are established in order to ensure that should a film ignite, the people in the seating area will be protected from that fire. These requirements specify separations between projection rooms and assembly spaces, as well as limit allowable openings between projection rooms and assembly spaces. Of course, projection rooms require some openings in order to project film images onto screens in assembly spaces.

Business Occupancy

Business occupancy is defined as a building or portion of a building used for office, professional, or service-type transactions, including normal accessory storage and the keeping of records and accounts. A typical business occupancy has incidental storage areas dispersed throughout the building. The total area of all of these storage areas combined is usually small enough that it would not concern a code official, or cause a code official to reclassify the storage areas as a separate occupancy. A special concern that is often related to business occupancies is the concern of high-rise buildings (Figure 3-13). High-rise buildings are discussed in Chapter 5 of this book.

Typical businesses include animal hospitals, kennels and pounds, automobile and other motor vehicle showrooms, automobile or other service stations, banks, barber shops, beauty shops, car washes, specific administration buildings such as city halls, classroom buildings above the twelfth grade such as college classrooms and vocational schools, dentist's offices, doctor's offices, dry-cleaning establishments, electrical data processing areas, florists and nurseries, general offices, laboratories incorporating non-hazardous testing and research, laundries, outpatient clinics, police stations, post

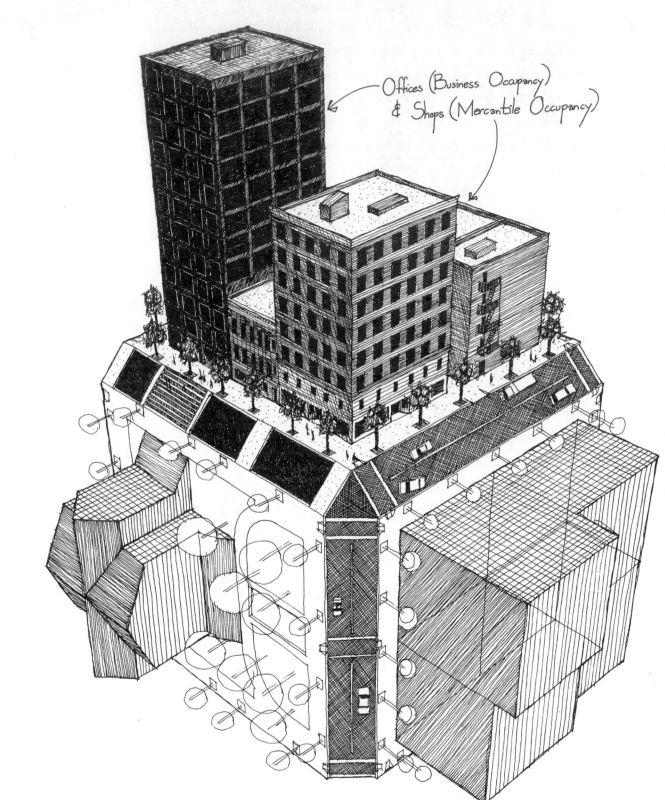

Offices (Business Occupancy)
& Shops (Mercantile Occupancy)

Figure 3-13 Business—Typical

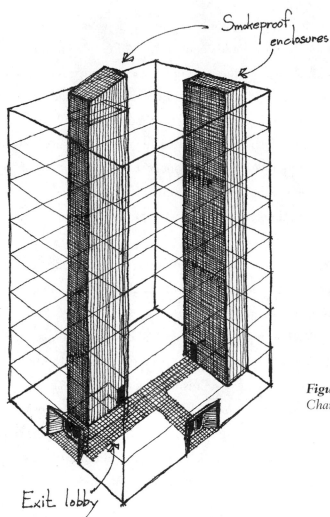

Figure 3-14 *Business—*
Characteristics

offices, printing shops, professional service buildings of architects, attorneys, dentists, physicians, engineers, etc., and radio and television stations. This list is not exhaustive.

As a whole, business occupancies are relatively safe occupancies. In most cases there are not significant amounts of combustible, explosive, or toxic contents. People are usually very familiar with the building except in the cases where a great many of the people occupying the building are visiting clients and are therefore not familiar with the building. The number of people per square foot is usually very low, except for example in the case of a restaurant with too few people to be classified as an assembly occupancy. People are usually very alert in business occupancies and are very mobile, not requiring the help of others in order to egress the building. Because business occupancies are so safe codes are fairly lenient when regulating business occupancies. Many business occupancies are located in high-rise buildings and must meet code requirements for high rises (Figure 3-14).

One special business occupancy type is automotive service stations. It should be noted that not all codes classify automotive service stations as business occupancies; some codes classify them as mercantile occupancies. Of course, in order to remain a low-hazard occupancy such as a business occupancy, automotive service stations have to meet standards regulating the dispensation of combustible liquids, and the storage of flammable and combustible liquids. When gasoline and other hazardous products are stored in a properly listed fashion, automotive service stations are considered safe. Codes further regulate automotive service stations by restricting the use of combustible products in the construction of the canopies covering the areas where cars are refueled. Codes also have many requirements dealing with pumps, and how and when their devices are activated, as well as how close the hose of a pump can extend towards the building. All of these requirements regarding automotive service station design and construction help designers and builders avoid having to classify these buildings as a more hazardous occupancy classification.

Many codes reference bowling alleys as a special business occupancy. The reason for codes to even mention bowling alleys as a special concern is the potential hazard associated with bowling pin finishing or refinishing operations. These operations can be extremely hazardous and may need to be conducted in a properly designed finishing room which is separated with fire-rated construction from the area of the building containing the bowling lanes. Bowling pin finishing facilities are not usually incorporated in the design of bowling alleys; usually finishing and refinishing is done at a separate facility. However, the finishing and refinishing of bowling pins can be a hazardous enough process that code officials feel the need to regulate facilities designed for this process. The failure to meet codes and standards' requirements concerning bowling pin finishing rooms would of course result in the reclassification of the building as a more hazardous occupancy.

Educational Occupancies

Educational occupancies are buildings or portions of buildings used by persons for educational purposes through the twelfth grade. Codes specify the minimum number of people that "trigger" the educational occupancy classification. Classrooms used by students above the twelfth grade are considered business occupancies unless the occupant load of the classroom is such that the classification of assembly occupancy would be more appropriate. Younger school children concern code officials in that they do not have the motor skills of adults when egressing a building. The design parameters for educational occupancies are actually based on children from kindergarten through middle school age, therefore the students in high schools receive the benefits of an extra

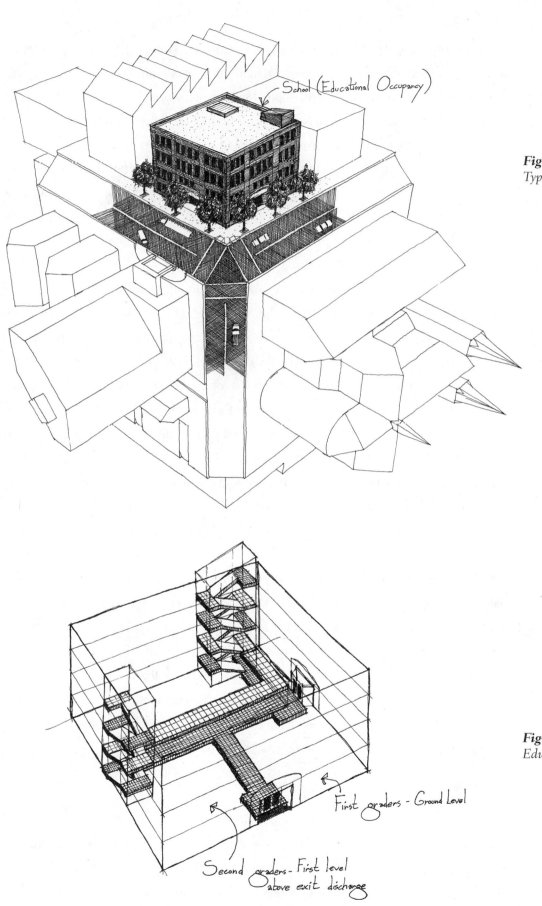

Figure 3-15 Education—Typical

School (Educational Occupancy)

Figure 3-16
Educational—Characteristics

First graders - Ground Level

Second graders - First level
above exit discharge

safe building due to over design. Classroom buildings used by college-age or vocational students are treated as the occupancy which these classroom buildings most closely approximate. A classroom for thirty people, for example, would be treated as a business occupancy if that classroom were set up for traditional classroom seating. On the other hand, a much larger classroom would be treated as an assembly occupancy. A wood shop which served as an instructional space for students above the twelfth grade may be classified as a factory industrial occupancy or perhaps even a hazardous occupancy.

Typical educational occupancy buildings include academies, kindergartens, nursery schools, elementary schools, middle schools, and high schools (Figure 3-15). Within educational occupancies, the students may or may not be familiar with the building based on the size of the school. Codes regulate the number of stories above the level of exit discharge that can be used for the youngest school children (Figure 3-16). Educational occupancies may or may not contain a large number of people per square foot depending on the school. However, the designer should consider the potential hazard associated with the fact that in large schools, often all of the students change classes at the same time, resulting in congestion in the school corridors. Should a building emergency occur during a class-changing period, panic could ensue due to the crowded corridor conditions. In kindergartens, there is often a concern with the mobility of the occupants, as many of the occupants will require assistance when egressing.

Educational occupancies are traditionally a low hazard regarding combustible, explosive, or toxic contents. One might be alarmed at the idea that schools are not traditionally considered to be at great risk because of these contents, as well can all remember the many supplies, pencils, paper, paints, and other combustibles, or potentially toxic or explosive contents within the schools of our youth. However, it is important for us to understand that for the basis of comparing occupancies, the contents within educational occupancies present a relatively low hazard. The warehouse where these papers and pencils and combustible, or explosive or toxic, contents came from might be a moderate or high hazard in relation to educational occupancies. It is also important to understand that educational occupancies can often have more hazardous areas, such as wood shops, chemistry labs, kitchens, etc.

Factory Industrial Occupancy

Factory industrial occupancies include buildings or portions of buildings that are used for assembling or disassembling, repairing, fabricating, finishing, manufacturing, packaging, or processing operations. Certain codes may further divide factory industrial occupancies into two subclassifications, low hazard and moderate hazard.

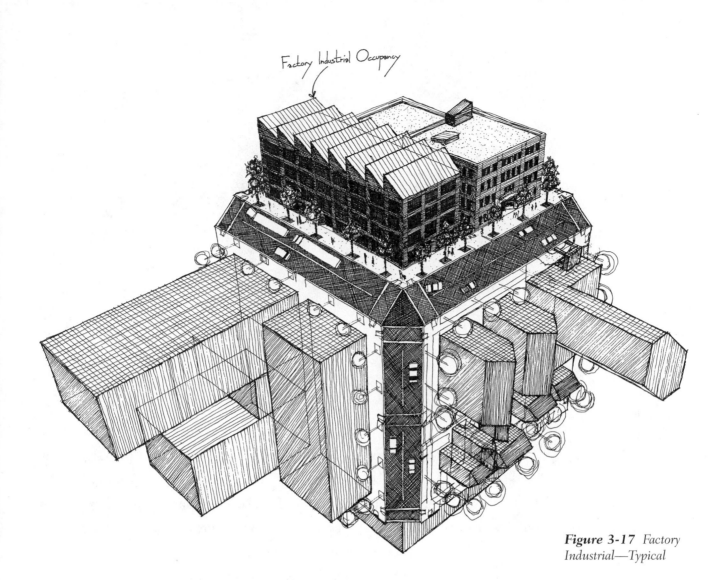

Factory Industrial Occupancy

Figure 3-17 *Factory Industrial—Typical*

Typical factory industrial occupancies include assembly plants, dry-cleaning plants, factories, laundries, manufacturing plants, mills, power plants, and processing plants (Figure 3-17). This list is not exhaustive. In most cases, factory industrial occupancies have very few people per square foot because the very nature of the business conducted at a typical factory industrial occupancy would prohibit the facility from being too densely populated. There are exceptions to these cases as some factory industrial occupancies are relatively densely populated. The designer must design the factory industrial occupancy for the most appropriate occupant load.

Familiarity with the building is usually not a major concern in factory industrial occupancies. Because of insurance requirements and security risks associated with most factory industrial occupancies, the general public usually is not allowed to enter these occupancies except perhaps for tours. Therefore, most of the people who inhabit factory industrial occupancies are intimately familiar with the building in which they work.

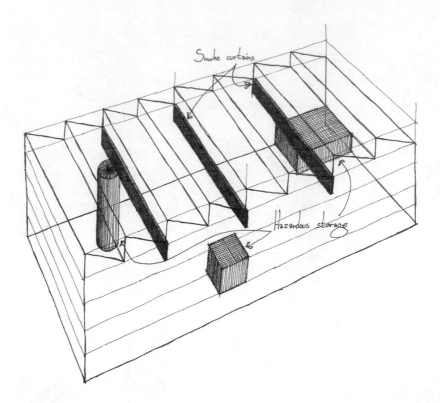

Figure 3-18 *Factory*
Industrial—Characteristics

The potential amount of combustible contents, and toxic or explosive contents within factory industrial occupancies causes code officials significant concern (Figure 3-18). These products are often either stored or used in a manner which is hazardous. When a factory industrial occupancy contains great amounts of combustible, explosive, or toxic contents, or when it incorporates extremely hazardous processes, this factory industrial occupancy may be reclassified as a hazardous occupancy. To avoid such an expensive reclassification of occupancy, factory industrial buildings are often designed to store and use hazardous products in smaller, more manageable amounts.

When discussing factory industrial occupancies in my seminars, I have often found that designers are not able to receive adequate code interpretations from state or local code officials regarding their factory industrial designs. This is of course contingent on where the factory will ultimately be located. In these cases, the complexity of the processes within the factories intimidate the code authorities as their training may not be adequate to address such concerns. Usually the insurance underwriters for the client become the only code authority when state and local jurisdictions refrain from code enforcement.

Hazardous Occupancy

A hazardous occupancy is any building where an overabundance of combustible, explosive, or toxic materials are stored, manufactured, or used for manufacturing or other processes. Hazardous occupancies are usually storage facilities and factory indus-trial facilities which have exceeded certain limitations for storing and processing haz-ardous materials, and have therefore become classified as hazardous occupancies. Each of the codes define the limitations for storage and use of hazardous materials which "trigger" the hazardous occupancy classification.

The three major building codes have an individual occupancy classification known as hazardous occupancy. The NFPA 101 Life Safety Code chooses to classify areas of buildings as hazard of content areas rather than create an actual occupancy classification for potentially hazardous situations. In all actuality the difference between building codes and NFPA 101 when treating hazardous material areas is more of a difference in outline than a difference in philosophy. They all address the design of buildings where hazardous materials are used. The theory of the building codes is that any occupancy becomes a hazardous occupancy once it houses the stor-age, production, or use of certain amounts of hazardous products. The NFPA 101 Life Safety Code treats the storage, production, or use of certain amounts of haz-ardous products as areas within other occupancies which must be treated different-ly than other areas and which must be separated from those other areas with fire-rated construction. The three major building codes would require one to classify an explosives factory as a hazardous occupancy, which would in turn subject one to the design requirements of a hazardous occupancy, including the requirements for sepa-ration of the hazardous occupancy from other factory industrial buildings on the site. The NFPA 101 Life Safety Code would treat an explosives factory as a hazard of con-tents area, and would then subject that factory to many requirements for hazard of contents areas, which would be very similar to the building code requirements for hazardous occupancies. Once again, the actual difference in what these codes would require is not that great.

Hazardous occupancies are often subdivided into other subclassifications in recog-nition of the fact that materials need to be treated differently based on the different threats that these materials pose. Threats may come from detonation, deflagration, combustion, physical, or health hazards. The materials may be explosives and blasting agents, highly toxic and toxic compressed gases, flammable and combustible liquids, flammable solids, liquid and solid oxidizers, organic peroxides, pyrophoric materials, unstable reactive materials, water reactive materials, cryogenic fluids, highly toxic and toxic solids and liquids, corrosives, irritants, sensitizers, dry-cleaning solvents, or other health hazard solids, liquids, and gases. Codes provide information about these materi-als and their safe storage and use in order to help designers discern the differences amongst these materials, so that the occupancies of the buildings where these materials are stored, produced, and used will be properly classified. The appropriate classification inevitably dictates the height and area limitations of the building, as well as many other code requirements for the building. Those hazardous occupancy subclassifications which are more hazardous than other hazardous occupancy subclassifications will be regulated more stringently by codes.

Hazardous occupancies usually consist of factory industrial occupancies and storage occupancies, which, because of the nature and amount of materials contained within them, are reclassified as hazardous occupancies (Figure 3-19).

It is desirable to maintain the least hazardous occupancy classification that one can when designing or constructing a building because of the great expense of constructing buildings for the more hazardous subclassifications and because of the greater limitations on their heights and areas (Figure 3-20). Often the easiest way to achieve this is to divide highly combustible, explosive or toxic materials into smaller, more manageable

Figure 3-19
Hazardous—Typical

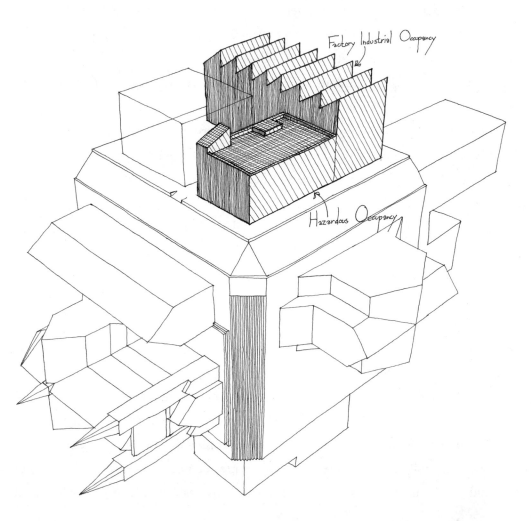

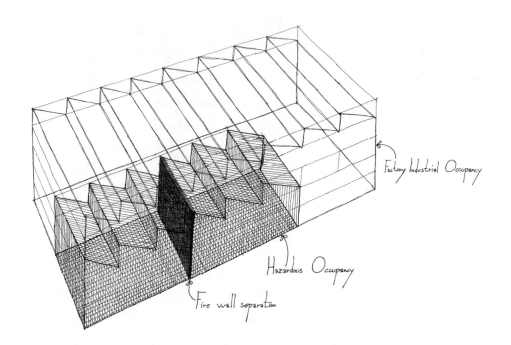

Figure 3-20
Hazardous—Characteristics

quantities, which are separated from one another either physically or with fire-rated construction.

These materials would then have to be stored and protected in a manner specified by any codes or standards relative to them. Hazardous occupancies provide protection by the use of sprinkler systems, explosion venting, or explosion suppression, separation of spaces into storage and dispensing areas, spill control, drainage and containment, ventilation, and whatever means necessary to ensure safe buildings.

Another major hazardous occupancy concern is the design of hazardous production material facilities (HPMs). Hazardous production material facilities are facilities where research, development, and fabrication of hazardous materials occur. So codes regulate buildings that store and utilize hazardous materials, as well as those in which those hazardous materials are produced.

Hazardous occupancies are very complex. Much of the language used for regulating hazardous occupancy design and construction within building codes is foreign to most designers. I find that most designers are not very knowledgeable about the design of hazardous occupancies, and that only those designers who deal directly with the design and construction of hazardous occupancies are very knowledgeable about these areas of codes and standards. This latter group is usually only knowledgeable about the particular types of facilities they have designed. The same generalization can be made about code enforcers in many cases. It is not uncommon for me to have a hazardous occupancy designer in one of my classes who complains that they do not receive enough code enforcement from a local code official because the code official is intimidated by the highly technical nature of hazardous occupancies. Often a local code official will defer hazardous occupancy regulation authority to the state fire marshal or the state building commissioner. Then often when the architect calls the state code official, that state code official will defer authority back to the local code official. The end result is that factory industrial occupancies and hazardous occupancies are frequently regulated by insurance underwriters. Insurance underwriters possess a great deal of knowledge of the design of buildings for the storage, production, and use of hazardous materials.

If a designer has a problem understanding the nature of the materials he or she is dealing with, and what hazards are presented by those materials, the designer should seek the advice of someone who understands those materials—either a consultant, an insurance underwriter, or a fire official. Many fire officials undergo comprehensive training about the properties of hazardous materials and how to handle them in an emergency. Ultimately, if a fire occurs, it is the fire official who has to deal with the hazardous materials and therefore, they are often trained to understand these materials and how they react under different conditions.

Institutional Unrestrained (Health Care) Occupancy

Health care occupancies are those where many of the occupants are ill or injured, or are very elderly, or are very young, and where the occupants may need the help of others when egressing a fire area. The people served by health care occupancies need the help of others when egressing a fire area, because they may be connected to some sort of medical equipment which is prolonging their life or maintaining their health, or they may be in traction or in a body cast, or they may not have good motor skills because of their age. Health care occupancies are defined as buildings or portions of buildings where people go for medical, surgical, psychiatric, nursing, or custodial care and where the people are not capable or mostly not capable of self-preservation.

Codes often further divide health care occupancies into occupancy subclassifications in order to address the unique concerns of the different types of health care occupancies. Usually, some distinction is made between ambulatory health care occupancies and nonambulatory health care occupancies. Ambulatory health care occupancies are those occupancies which are often referred to as outpatient clinics. The obvious difference between an ambulatory health care occupancy and other health care occupancies is that the occupants of the ambulatory health care occupancies are not in need of twenty-four-hour care and therefore do not stay overnight at the outpatient clinic.

Typical health care occupancies are detoxification facilities, hospitals, limited care

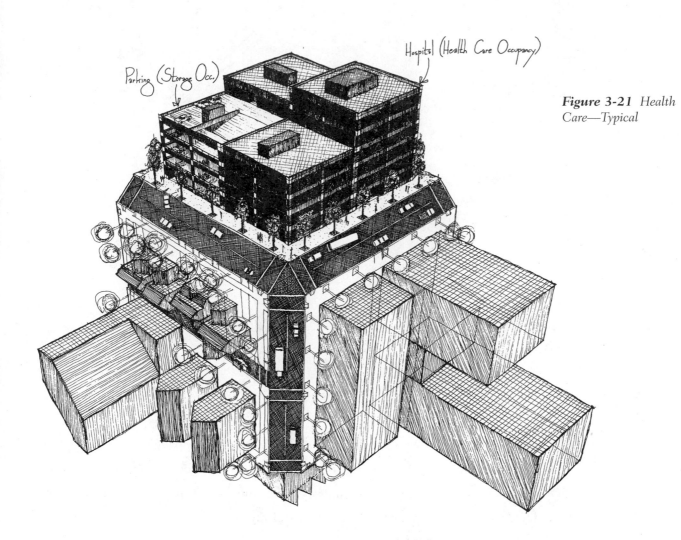

Parking (Storage Occ.)

Hospital (Health Care Occupancy)

Figure 3-21 Health Care—Typical

facilities, mental hospitals, and nursing homes. Some codes classify child care facilities which house very young children as health care occupancies (Figure 3-21).

It is typical of health care occupancies to be in a constant state of change and growth as they respond to increased needs and allow for innovations in medical technology. Because of this state of constant change and growth, the layout of health care occupancies is often extremely disorienting, leading to the confusion of the building occupants when egressing. Health care occupancies are therefore considered to be a relatively high hazard concerning the occupants' lack of familiarity with the building.

Although health care occupancies have a large number of occupants, they also have a great amount of square footage, so health care occupancies are not considered a high hazard based on number of people per square foot. Health care occupancies are a high hazard for alertness of occupants, because many of their occupants sleep overnight, except in the case of ambulatory health care occupancies.

The mobility of occupants can be very limited in health care occupancies, as many of the occupants are not mobile, and need help in evacuating from a fire or

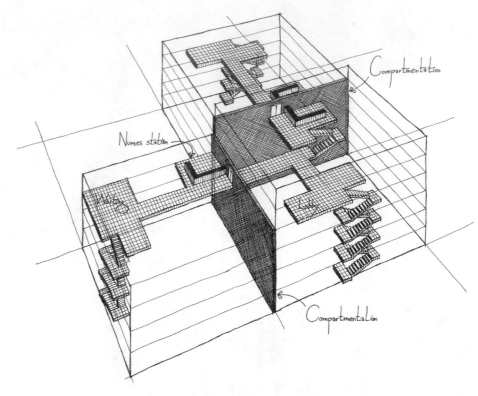

Figure 3-22 *Health Care—Characteristics*

emergency area. Because health care occupancies are occupancies where people are aided in egressing to safer areas of buildings by trained personnel, there is a great reliance on compartmentation and sprinkler control within these occupancies. In fact, health care occupancies are almost always provided with automatic sprinkler protection throughout. Health care occupancies are also divided into at least two separate areas. Codes specify the maximum amount of area within each compartment, thus creating more than two compartments in larger hospitals. These compartments are a means of providing the non-fire areas with smoke protection from the fire areas, so that patients can be moved from unsafe areas to safer areas (Figure 3-22). These separations allow the fire officials the time to extinguish fires before the non-fire areas are affected. Of course, when patients are moved from one compartment to another, there are not always enough patient rooms in the safe compartment to house the new influx of patients. For this reason, codes require health care occupancies to have enough area in corridors to accommodate the beds of the newly egressed patients. Codes regulate the design and construction of the fire-rated walls that provide compartmentation, as well as regulate the types of doors that can be used in these fire rated assemblies.

Health care occupancies often have a need for nursing stations which are adjacent and open to corridors in order for these health care occupancies to function properly. As a rule, code officials do not allow egress corridors to be used for anything but circu-

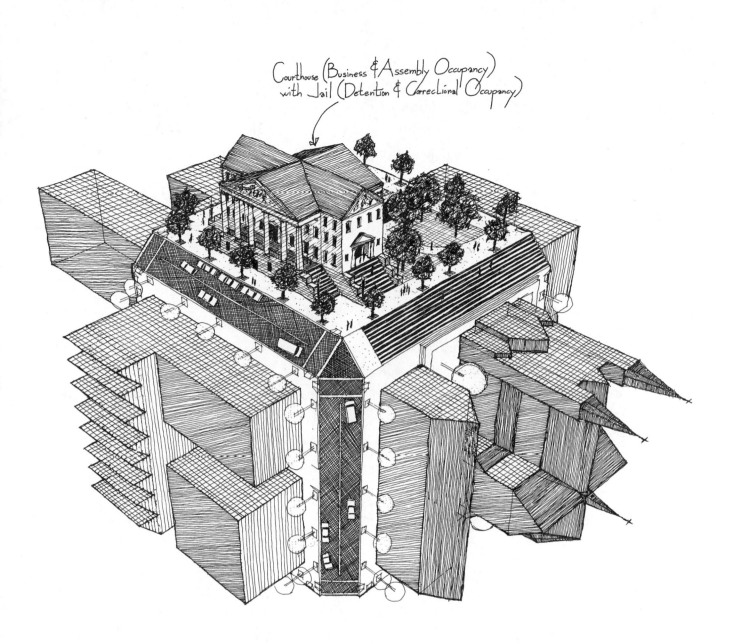

Courthouse (Business & Assembly Occupancy)
with Jail (Detention & Correctional Occupancy)

lation because of the fire-loading potential incurred when a corridor is used for activities other than egress. Codes make some exceptions for nursing stations within health care occupancies, however, as these nursing stations are monitored by trained staff.

Health care occupancies must provide separation between hazardous areas and other areas. Hazardous areas in health care occupancies include certain storage rooms, kitchens, boiler rooms, and laundry rooms.

Institutional Restrained (Detention and Correctional) Occupancy

Institutional restrained (detention and correctional) occupancies are those occupancies where people are incarcerated due to either extreme mental illness or because they are offenders of public law. These occupancies are defined as occupancies where

Figure 3-23 *Detention and Correctional—Typical*

the building occupants are under some degree of restraint or security, and therefore are incapable of self-preservation due to the security measures that are not under the occupants' control. Codes further divide detention and correctional occupancies into individual use conditions which differ in the amount of free circulation the occupants of these facilities have.

Detention and correctional or institutional restrained occupancies include community residential centers, correctional institutions, juvenile detention facilities, juvenile training schools, detention centers, jails, work camps, and reformatories (Figure 3-23).

The number of people per square foot should not be a great concern within detention and correctional occupancies. Obviously many of us are familiar with media accounts of overcrowding in state and local correctional facilities. These overcrowded conditions are not in accordance with codes, but are in fact code violations by the state and local government entities. The design parameters of detention and correctional occupancies as detailed in codes and standards are based on buildings with a great amount of square footage per person.

Detention and correctional occupancies pose a high hazard concerning the occupants' familiarity with the building due to the restraint imposed upon their incarcerated occupants. Detention and correctional occupancies are also considered a high hazard regarding the alertness of occupants in that their occupants sleep overnight within these facilities.

Detention and correctional occupancies are a very high hazard for mobility of occupants. Because of the security restraints placed on the occupants, they need assistance in egressing a building. Detention and correctional occupancies are divided into use groups which reflect the different degrees of restraint that can be imposed on the inmate population. An example of a lower hazard system of restraint might be a complex where free movement is allowed from sleeping areas and other spaces to a restrained exterior space, whereas an example of a higher hazard system of restraint might be a complex where manual operation of doors by staff is necessary for one to egress from sleeping areas. These different use conditions directly relate to egress requirements in that the amount of restriction of the movement of prisoners relates directly to their ability to egress from the building.

Content-related characteristics such as combustible contents, or explosive or toxic contents are usually considered a low hazard within detention and correctional occupancies. Some exceptions to this can occur when certain areas of detention and correctional occupancies contain workshops where inmates are involved in processes that would use combustible or flammable materials. For example, some prisons have furniture refinishing shops where the furniture, as well as the solvents used for refinishing the furniture create a fire hazard. These shop buildings may be required to provide fire-rated separation between them and the buildings housing prisoners in order to avoid classifying the entire correctional facility as a hazardous occupancy, which could in turn, prove to be prohibitively expensive.

The proper design of detention and correctional occupancies utilizes a system much like that of health care occupancies. Design of egress is based on the premise that the inmates will require assistance when egressing. Inmates will be moved to a safer area of the building. Sprinkler systems will be employed to extinguish fires in most buildings, and then fire departments will be notified quickly in order for them to respond to the fire emergency.

It is a concern of code officials whenever different floor levels of any occupancy classification communicate with each other because of the possibility of the passage of smoke from floor to floor in the event of a fire. However, in detention and correctional occupancies it is beneficial to the staff overseeing the facility that communication between floors exist so that fewer people can manage many of the detained simultane-

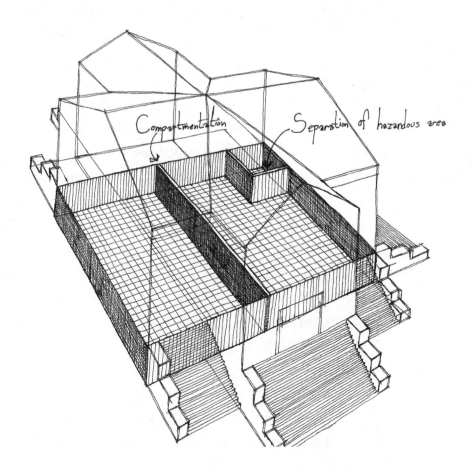

Figure 3-24 *Detention and Correctional— Characteristics*

ously. Codes allow this communication to exist between floors in detention and correctional occupancies when the facilities meet certain stringent requirements which provide for additional safety.

As in health care occupancies, detention and correctional occupancies utilize fire-rated separations to provide compartmentation in buildings so that inmates can egress from an unsafe area of a building to a safer area of the building (Figure 3-24). A proper amount of square footage needs to be provided on each side of the fire-rated separations in order to ensure that there is enough room on either side to accommodate the potential occupant load in the event of an emergency. Openings in these fire rated separations must also be properly rated.

Another concern for detention and correctional occupancies is that of windowless buildings. If windowless buildings occur, then smoke vents must be provided in order to provide a means for smoke to escape in the event of a fire emergency. Obviously, smoke cannot escape a building without windows or vents.

Mercantile Occupancy

Mercantile occupancies are defined as buildings or structures for the display and sale of merchandise, and involving stocks of goods, wares, or merchandise incidental to such purposes and accessible to the public. Mercantile occupancies often are occupied with more people than the minimum number of people used to classify buildings as assembly occupancies, but codes do not reclassify mercantile occupancies based on population. Oddly enough, some code officials would classify a restaurant serving one hundred people which is located within a large department store as an assembly occupancy, but the same code officials would not classify that department store as an assembly occupancy even though it may be inhabited with a thousand people or more.

Mercantile occupancies include auction rooms, department stores, drug stores, markets, retail stores, sales rooms, shopping centers, and wholesale stores. Some codes classify automotive service stations as mercantile occupancies, whereas other codes classify automotive service stations as business occupancies. Mercantile occupancies are occupancies where people go to shop (Figure 3-25).

The number of people per square foot within mercantile occupancies is usually a relatively low hazard, but during holiday shopping seasons this number often increases greatly, resulting in many mercantile occupancies' becoming a higher hazard for the number of people per square foot. For a period of time beginning before Thanksgiving Day and ending several weeks after New Year's Day, most mercantile occupancies are quite full and have a great number of people per square foot, which can create an egress hazard. Egress from mercantile occupancies needs to be sized to accommodate these maximum holiday occupant loads.

Familiarity with the building is often a high hazard with mercantile occupancies. Many mercantile occupancies are very open, with merchandise displayed in the center of the stores at no higher than eye level. Many other mercantile occupancies, however, have merchandise throughout the stores displayed very high, creating a sort of labyrinth which makes it difficult for the building occupants to see the exits (Figure 3-26). If the mercantile occupancy were full of smoke from a fire, this could be a serious problem. If a mercantile occupancy is large in area, the volume of the space can potentially contribute to the dilution of smoke to a point where the occupants can egress before the smoke density reaches dangerous levels.

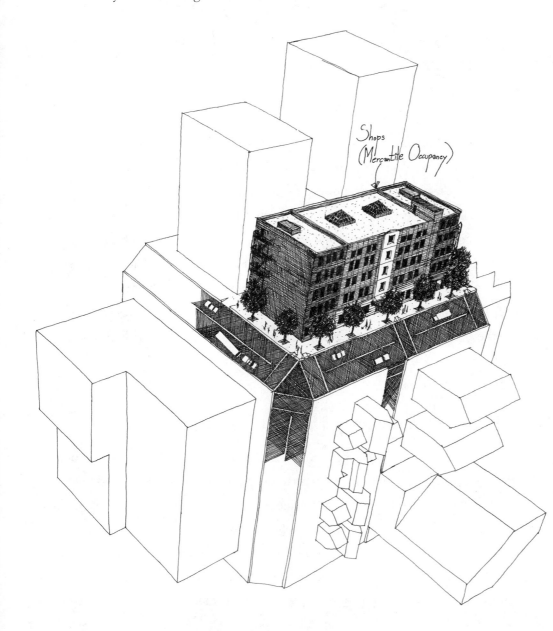

Shops
(Mercantile Occupancy)

Figure 3-25
Mercantile—Typical

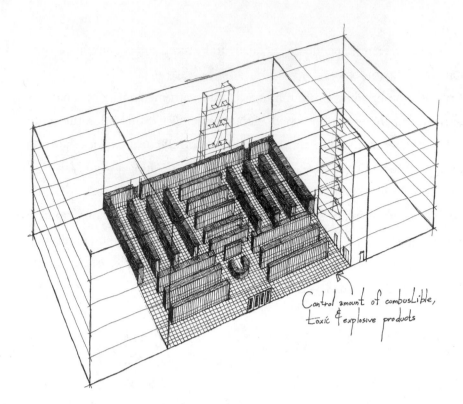

Control amount of combustible, toxic & explosive products

Figure 3-26 *Mercantile—*
Characteristics

Mercantile occupancies can be a relatively high hazard for combustible contents and toxic contents because of the merchandise displayed within the them and the products used to package that merchandise. The larger the mercantile occupancy, the more likely it will increase in hazard for content related characteristics. Codes address the concern of combustible contents, and explosive or toxic contents within mercantile occupancies by regulating the square footage of mercantile occupancies. The NFPA 101 Life Safety Code does not limit the square footage of buildings for all occupancies, however it assigns different subclassifications to mercantile occupancies based on the area of the mercantile occupancies and the highest level above exit discharge of the mercantile occupancies. NFPA 101 places more stringent requirements on the larger mercantile occupancies.

Residential Occupancy

Residential occupancies are defined as occupancies in which sleeping accommodations are provided for normal residential sleeping purposes. Often codes classify buildings with very few occupants as residential occupancies when these buildings would otherwise have been classified as health care occupancies or detention and correctional occupancies if their occupant load had been greater. For example, if a building which would normally be classified as a health care occupancy contained sleeping accommodations for only two people at one time, that building would be considered a

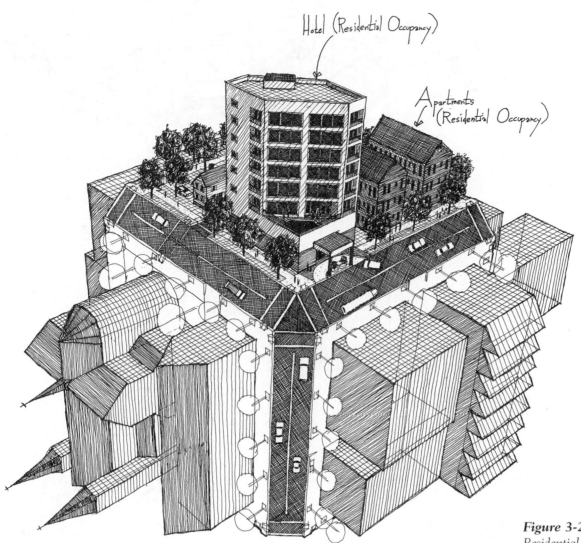

Hotel (Residential Occupancy)

Apartments (Residential Occupancy)

Figure 3-27
Residential—Typical

residential occupancy within most codes. Many codes divide multifamily residential occupancies into subclassifications which recognize the differences between residential occupancies where the occupants are primarily transient in nature such as hotels and motels, and residential occupancies where the occupants are not primarily transient in nature such as apartment buildings. Codes also treat single-family dwellings and duplexes differently from multifamily residences.

Residential occupancies include such buildings as transient boarding houses, hotels, motels, apartments, convents, fraternities and sororities, monasteries, rectories, dormitory facilities, duplexes, and single-family dwellings. Often, child care facilities which accommodate small numbers of children for any period of time are classified as residential occupancies (Figure 3-27).

Residential occupancies are a very high hazard for alertness of occupants because people sleep within residential occupancies. Codes require the use of smoke detectors

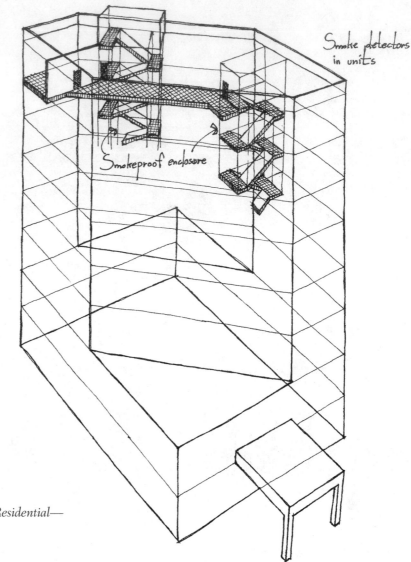

Smoke detectors in units

Smokeproof enclosure

Figure 3-28 *Residential—Characteristics*

adjacent to sleeping areas to alleviate the potential problem of building occupants' not being aware of a fire emergency for being asleep (Figure 3-28). Single-family dwellings, duplexes, and multifamily dwellings serve people who primarily are not transient in nature (people who stay for short periods of time) and are low hazards when considering the occupants' familiarity with the building. Obviously, the occupants live there and are therefore intimately familiar with their building. Multifamily dwellings serving people who are primarily transient in nature are a high hazard when considering the occupants' familiarity with the building.

Residential occupancies are not considered to be a high hazard concerning the amount of combustible contents, and toxic and explosive contents. Many code officials are uncomfortable with this premise, because they know that residential occupancies have many combustible, toxic, and explosive contents. However, relative to other occupancy classifications such as storage occupancies or factory industrial occupancies, residential occupancies do not have a great amount of combustible, toxic, and explosive contents.

Storage Occupancies

Storage occupancies are occupancies in which goods are stored, and which are not classified as hazardous occupancies. They are defined as buildings or structures utilized primarily for the storage or sheltering of goods, merchandise, products, vehicles, or animals. Of course, when determining whether the storage of certain products causes a building to be classified as a hazardous occupancy versus a storage occupancy, one should consult with fire officials or other experts knowledgeable about the storage of those products. Storage occupancies are divided into distinct subclassifications which recognize the different relative hazards of these storage occupancies based on what is being stored within them.

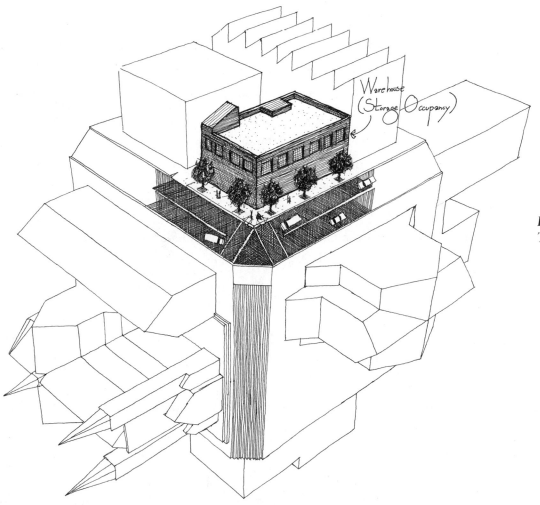
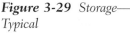

Warehouse (Storage Occupancy)

Figure 3-29 *Storage—Typical*

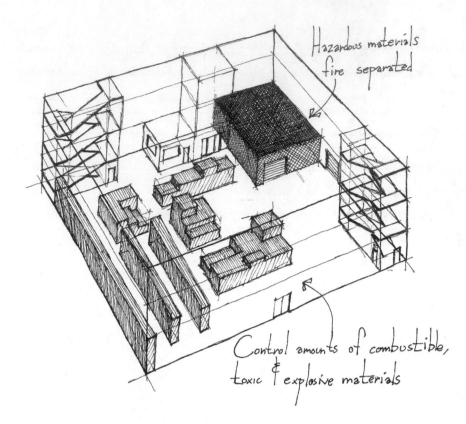

Hazardous materials fire separated

Control amounts of combustible, toxic & explosive materials

Figure 3-30 Storage—
Characteristics

Storage occupancies include barns, bulk oil storage, coal storage, freight terminals, grain elevators, hangars (For storage only), parking structures, stables, truck and marine terminals, and warehouses. The types of products stored in storage occupancies include beer or wine, cement in bags, electrical motors, empty cans, fresh fruit and vegetables in nonplastic trays or containers, dairy products, dry cell batteries, dry insecticides, electric coils, electric insulators, meats, metal cabinets, metal desks, metal parts, mirrors, foods, frozen foods, glass bottles, gypsum board, and inert pigments (Figure 3-29). This list is not exhaustive.

Storage occupancies can be low, moderate, or high hazards concerning the storage of combustible contents, and toxic or explosive contents (Figure 3-30). When determining the relative hazard of a particular storage occupancy, one would not only need to consider the hazard of the materials or products being stored, but also the hazard of how these products or materials are stored, as well as the hazard associated with their packaging. It is not uncommon for the combustibility of the packaging to increase the hazard associated with the storage of certain products and materials.

One of the chief concerns for code officials regarding storage occupancies is the propensity for many people who own or lease storage occupancies to change the use of the building without the code officials' knowing the change has occurred. For example, it is not uncommon to drive by a mini-warehouse complex only to find that a warehouse door is open, and a renter is selling some sort of goods, therefore converting the warehouse to a mercantile occupancy. In most codes, this mixing of storage occupancy and mercantile occupancy would require some sort of fire-rated separation between the two different occupancy classifications.

Many types of storage occupancies create special concerns for codes officials. One of those types is automobile parking structures. Automobile parking structures are usually divided into two types of structures, open parking structures and enclosed parking garages. Open parking structures are not as great of a concern as are enclosed parking garages, because of their ability to vent smoke through their open sides, thus reducing the threat of smoke inhalation to their occupants. At one time, many code officials were leery of all parking structures for fear of automobiles exploding, and the subsequent chain reactions of explosions that would ensue if any automobiles exploded. Burning automobiles igniting other automobiles is an uncommon occurrence, and the American Iron and Steel Institute helped prove this point by igniting an automobile in an open parking structure adjacent to another automobile. The test illustrated that an automobile fire in an open parking structure, is a low hazard fire, and would probably be extinguished before any adjacent automobiles were ignited. It also illustrated that the heat generated from an automobile fire in an open parking structure does not significantly affect the structural system. This film was circulated around the nation and went a long way towards easing the fears of code officials regarding automobiles exploding within buildings. The prevalent concern with most open parking structures now is not that of fire, but rather of crime. Therefore, codes have relaxed some requirements for parking structures, such as allowing wired glass in steel frames to be utilized in stair shafts instead of requiring fire-rated opaque walls, so that high visibility can be maintained for security.

Other special concerns involving storage occupancies include aircraft hangars and residential aircraft hangars. Within aircraft hangars many of the requirements in codes dealing with these special structures relate to concerns with fuel spillage, such as requirements for the use of noncombustible floor construction. Repair garages are also storage occupancies of special concern to code officials. Repair garages are regulated as to the amount of combustible materials used in their construction and where those materials can be used, such as in the construction of the floor surface of the repair garage. The placement of heating equipment is also regulated, as heating equipment provides a potential ignition source for vapors from automobile gasoline tanks. Therefore, heating equipment is raised above the floor and not placed in the areas where the vapors are likely to remain. Continuous ventilation must be provided for in the design and construction of repair garages.

Utility Occupancy

The classification of utility occupancy is not common to all four of the major model codes. This classification deals with such structures as fences over six feet high, tanks and towers, private garages, carports, sheds, and agricultural buildings. These types of structures are addressed in all four codes, though they are not always addressed as a separate occupancy classification.

Choosing the Proper Occupancy Classifications

Often occupancy classifications can be highly subjective, as it is not always easy to determine whether a particular building is of one occupancy classification or another. Because of the subjective nature of some occupancy classifications, code officials should be involved in determining the occupancy classifications of buildings as early in the design process as is possible. The opinion of a code official eventually will determine the actual occupancy classification of a particular building unless that opinion is overridden by a board of appeals or a court of law. It makes no sense to proceed with the design of a project without knowing how a code official is going to classify the occupancy of that project, especially if the project involves a highly subjective occupancy classification or a mixed occupancy classification. The early involvement of the code official in a project will help the designer avoid costly surprises in the final stages of the project.

Although all of the four major codes use fairly similar occupancy classifications, in some cases there are discrepancies amongst two or more of the codes when classifying occupancies. For example, automotive service stations are classified as mercantile occupancy under one code and as business occupancy under another code. When a designer must design by two or more competing codes, the designer should involve the authorities having jurisdiction over each of these codes to give their opinions as to occupancy classification as early in the design of a project as is possible. The headaches associated with the subjective nature of occupancy classifications can become magnified very quickly when dealing with two or more similar, but different codes. By involving all of the governing authorities early in a project's design, the designer can avoid having to make unforeseen costly adjustments during the late stages of a project. When two or more occupancy classifications exist within the same building, the result is a mixed occupancy. Chapter 5 of this book discusses mixed occupancies in detail.

CHAPTER 4

Special Occupancy

*C*hapter 4 covers special occupancy concerns relating to different occupancy classifications. The special occupancy concerns covered by this chapter are atriums, malls, high-rises, and underground buildings.

Atriums, covered malls, high-rise buildings, and underground buildings present potential problems for firefighters, as well as unique opportunities for designers. The regulation of these special types of buildings by building codes creates opportunities for designers to provide buildings which are aesthetically pleasing and highly functional, yet also safe. A designer must be cautious when designing atriums, covered malls, high-rises, and underground buildings because of the potential hazards that these special building situations pose.

Atriums act potentially as multistory smokestacks through which smoke from a fire on one floor of a building can traverse to other floors of the building, creating a threat to life on many floors other than the floor of fire origin. Covered malls are buildings in which several different tenant spaces are open to central mall corridors. A fire in one of the tenant spaces can create smoke which spreads to the other tenant spaces. High-rise buildings present a unique problem, because it is very difficult for fire officials to extinguish fires in upper floors of high-rises, due to the height limitations of firefighting vehicles. Also, the occupants of high rises must egress through stair shafts, and this vertical egress is not nearly as easily managed by human beings as is horizontal egress along corridors or through doors. Underground buildings create a problem in that limited openings and limited access make it very difficult to fight fires within these buildings. There are many reasons why designers, owners, and building managers want to incorporate atriums, covered malls, high-rises, and underground buildings into their design concepts, be it for aesthetics, marketing purposes, energy efficiency, or economy. Rather than disallowing these special types of buildings because they have potential hazards associated with them, building codes recognize their design importance and prescribe rules in which they can be safely designed. In this case, codes allow one to make adjustments to designs in order to help ensure that these special design situations are not hazardous. Such adjustments may include altering egress capacity, providing automatic sprinklers, and constructing rated assemblies (including occupancy separation and tenant separation), as well as providing other safety measures.

ATRIUMS

Atriums are often a powerful aesthetic tool for the designer. Atriums can be delightful, exciting spaces, full of visual energy in which people can observe activity above, below, and around them. They are a popular design feature within hotel and office building lobby designs, and if properly proportioned, atriums are often the visual "highlight" of a building. Atriums provide the architect a means of varying the form and shape of a space vertically, as well as horizontally (Figure 4-1). However, there is a potential problem with atriums. Atriums become for all practical purposes a chimney in the event of a fire. A fire on the lower floor of a building creates smoke and releases unburned gases that can traverse through the atrium to other floors of the building, perhaps resulting in injuries or even death on these other floors. Therefore, code officials are very concerned about atriums, and utilize codes to provide regulations which help advance the design of safe atriums.

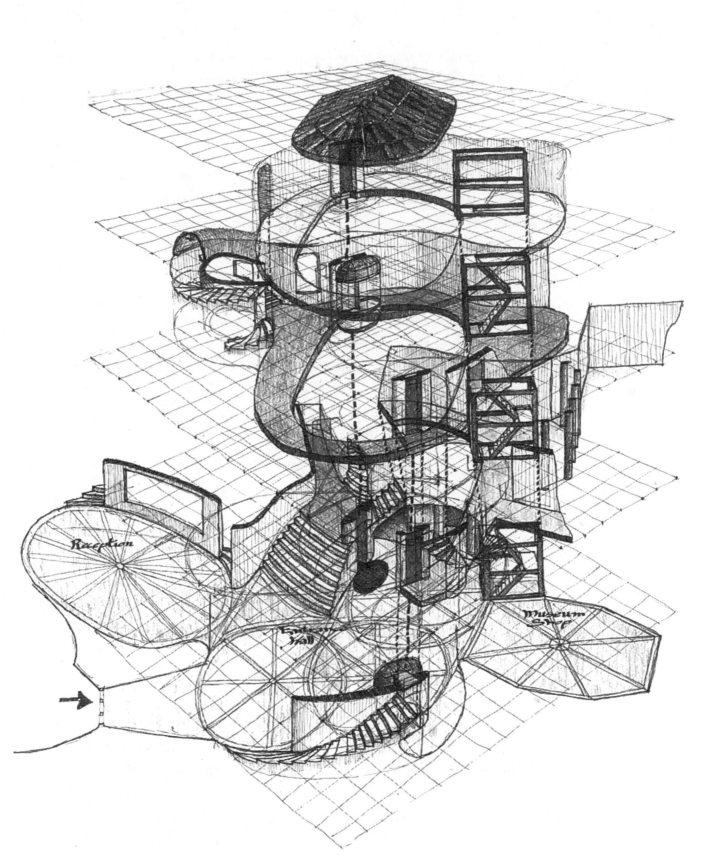

Reception

Exhibition Hall

Museum Shop

Figure 4-1 *Atriums*

The rules for proper atrium design vary from code to code, but some atrium design rules are common to all of the four major codes. For instance, the four major codes differ as to the amount of egress, the length of travel distances, and the types of egress allowed through atriums. The designer must review the appropriate code when designing atriums.

Codes typically require that buildings incorporating atriums in their design be provided with automatic sprinkler protection for the entire building. Some codes allow the sprinkler protection to be dropped in certain areas of the building, based on the ceiling height of the atrium, and based on whether or not the atrium is separated from adjacent spaces with fire rated assemblies of at least two hours.

Engineered smoke control systems are used to exhaust atriums in the event of a fire. This exhausting is achieved by shutting down the supply of air to the fire floor and by shutting down the return air on all other floors, then by providing an exhaust system that changes the volume of air in the atrium a specified number of times per hour. If an atrium is polluted with smoke from a fire, the atrium exhaust system will exhaust the polluted air to the outside of the building, thus decreasing the chance that the smoke density levels within the atrium will be hazardous.

Codes address atrium separation issues by requiring designers to provide positive separation between the atrium and adjacent spaces. This required separation is one-hour rated, and in many codes there is an exception allowing glazing to be used in this one-hour wall if the glazing is sprinklered on both sides with sprinkler heads designed and installed in such a manner that the glazing will be washed with water in the event a fire emergency. The separation between atrium spaces and other spaces helps minimize the possibility that smoke generated from a fire on any one floor of the building will pollute the entire building by traveling through the atrium.

COVERED MALLS

Covered malls attract shoppers from large geographical areas and provide a means for shoppers to walk in an air conditioned and dry environment, as well as to shop at a great variety of stores. It is key to most merchandisers, who own or lease spaces in covered malls, that their store fronts remain open enough to attract shoppers to the merchandise they sell. Covered malls provide an added attraction to shoppers in that they house not only mercantile occupancies but often some business, assembly, and educational occupancies. One can shop, eat, bank, check out a book from a library, or maybe even buy insurance in a covered mall without ever leaving the building (Figure 4-2).

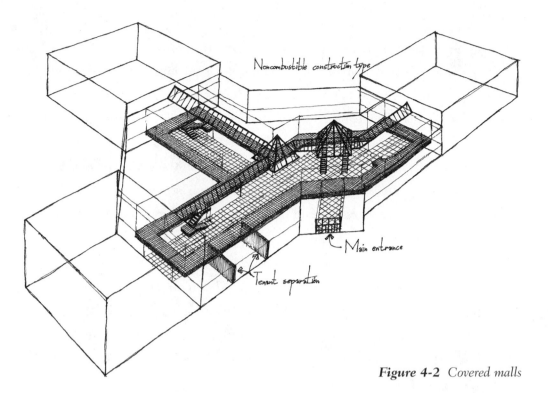

Figure 4-2 *Covered malls*

The concern amongst code officials regarding covered malls is that a fire in one store can pollute the entire mall, exposing all of the building occupants to the risk of smoke inhalation. Code officials are also concerned that because covered malls are so large, they contain an immense amount of fire loading, and the potential exists that a fire could burn for a long period of time because of this immense fire loading. Designing covered malls within the requirements of codes helps lessen the fears of code officials about the potential hazards of covered malls.

Codes utilize the strengths of covered malls when regulating their design. One of the strengths inherent to covered malls which is utilized by codes is the great potential for the dilution of smoke to a safe and tolerable level. For example, if a fire were to occur in one of the stores within a covered mall, the very volume of the area that the smoke from that fire can exhaust to is so large that significant smoke dilution occurs. This dilution of smoke lessens the risk that the mall occupants will be injured or killed because of smoke inhalation.

I once had an opportunity to view a mall immediately after an evacuation due to a fire. The doors were locked and I could not enter, but as I looked through the glass doors, I could not help but notice that the smoke within the mall was so thin that one could walk freely throughout the building without having to wear any sort of breathing apparatus. Some of the people gazing through the glass doors with me informed me that they had been inside the mall when the fire had occurred, but had been outside of the mall for only a matter of minutes. I concluded from this information that egress from the mall was quick, and that the mall volume provided impressive smoke dilution. Codes require covered malls to provide wide pathways and many entrances so that the occupants of the malls can egress the mall quickly in the event of a fire emergency.

One-hour fire separation is provided between tenant spaces to keep fire from spreading from store to store. Code officials want to stop the spread of fire, but they recognize that it is unlikely that fire will spread from store to store via the mall entrances to these stores. Consequently, stores are separated from one another, but are not separated from the mall corridors.

Codes require substantial egress to be provided in covered malls to ensure that people have many ways of exiting the mall building. Other requirements help ensure that the total required mall egress width is evenly dispersed amongst these different ways out. Mall egress provisions ensure that the occupants of the mall building have fairly short travel distances and wide egress paths to traverse when exiting. These egress provisions also limit the dead end length of malls, so that occupants will not find themselves trying to egress to an area with no exits. Covered mall provisions require that all the tenants within the mall have at least one or more exits through the rear of their stores which lead directly outside or directly to an exit corridor.

Covered mall sections in building codes place strict requirements on the use of certain construction materials within malls. The type of construction of malls is controlled in order to help ensure that there is little chance of the destruction of an entire mall due to a fire. Interior finishes are also controlled, especially storefront sign finishes. Limits are placed on the use of plastic signs, because plastics potentially produce very toxic smoke in the event of a fire.

Covered malls are classified as mercantile occupancies. The percentage of a covered mall which can be occupied with other, non-mercantile occupancies (assembly, business, and educational) is generally limited by covered mall sections within building codes. If an assembly occupancy with a large occupant content such as a theater is located within a covered mall, that assembly occupancy will be required to be located adjacent to a major mall entrance.

Malls are outfitted with automatic sprinkler protection to help ensure early suppression of a fire in the event that one occurs. As a deterrent to the risk of smoke pollution, malls are also outfitted with smoke control systems to help restrict smoke to the fire area, thus creating safer means of egress from the mall. The installation of hose connections throughout malls helps provide fire fighters with sufficient means to extinguish mall fires quickly.

HIGH-RISE BUILDINGS

High-rise buildings are defined as buildings which are 75 feet or more above the lowest level of fire department vehicular access (Figure 4-3). One concern of code officials regarding high-rises is that it is very difficult for fire departments to fight fires on upper levels of high-rise buildings. Many floors in high-rises are higher than the highest access point of the ladder trucks of fire departments, but even if the floors were within reach of the ladder trucks, it would be a slow process to use a ladder to "pick" people out of a building in order to rescue them. Another concern of code officials regarding high-rises is that it can be cumbersome for occupants of high-rise buildings to egress in the

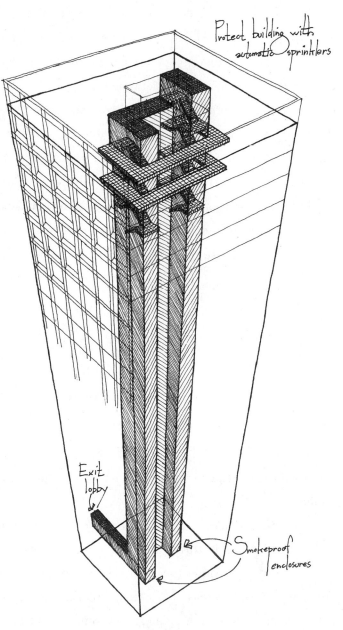

Figure 4-3 *High-rise buildings*

event of an emergency. People who are on upper floors of high-rise buildings must egress to a lower floor or to a floor above the fire area, and vertical passage by building occupants up or down stairs is much more slow and difficult than horizontal passage along corridors or through doors.

Good high-rise design depends on many different systems to ensure the safety of the occupants within the building. These systems include automatic sprinkler protection, smoke alarms, emergency lighting, standby power, detection systems, and communication systems. The most desirable result in high-rise fire protection design is the early suppression or control of a fire before it becomes life-threatening. Should suppression or control of a fire not occur, however, fire-rated separation from fire and smoke are necessary to ensure life safety. Strict adherence to codes and standards is absolutely pertinent in high-rise design in order to design and build safe high-rises.

Codes differ in their treatment of high-rise design requirements for fire safety. Most codes require automatic sprinkler protection in high-rises. Some codes allow an option, either automatic sprinkler protection, or compartmentation. Compartmentation is an option in which the building is divided into two or more compartments by a fire-rated wall so that people can egress towards a "safe" compartment from an "unsafe" compartment on any given floor of a building whenever a fire occurs.

High-rise provisions of building codes require smoke detection in specific locations so that early warning of a fire will occur as will activation of all smoke control equipment. Locations for smoke detectors in high-rise buildings may include:

1. Rooms housing mechanical, electrical, or telephone equipment, rooms housing elevator machinery or transformers, and similar rooms,

2. Elevator lobbies,

3. Recirculating air systems serving more than one floor, and

4. Each connection to a return air duct or riser serving a recirculating air system of more than one story.

The actual required locations of smoke detectors may be more limited or more extensive than the previous list depending on which of the four major codes is being applied.

The smoke detection system (when required) will trigger the voice alarm signaling system, which will in turn warn building occupants of a fire condition and instruct them as to the procedures they should follow to egress safely. The voice alarm messages are sent to specific areas of a building in order to help ensure that all building occupants are alerted to the fire emergency. Smoke control systems are utilized to remove the products of combustion from fire floors, and elevator lobbies are designed so that the elevators do not become a pathway for smoke to pollute the entire building.

High-rise buildings are required to have fire command stations. These stations are areas where fire officials can coordinate their efforts to control and extinguish a fire, as well as coordinate the egressing of those building occupants who need assistance. Codes specify what types of control and monitoring equipment must be installed at the fire command station.

The electrical systems and the mechanical systems used for controlling fires and smoke in high-rise buildings must remain in operation for certain specified amounts of time in the event of an emergency. These systems are required to be maintained by a standby power source.

Egress stairs in high rise buildings are usually required to be smoke-proof enclosures. Smoke-proof enclosures ensure vertical egress routes which are virtually free of smoke. Smokeproof enclosures are discussed further in Chapter 10 of this book.

UNDERGROUND BUILDINGS

Like high-rise buildings, underground buildings concern code officials because of the potential hazards associated with floors that are difficult to access by fire personnel, and by the fact that the occupants of underground buildings must egress vertically through stairwells, a process which is slower than egressing horizontally through corridors and doorways (Figure 4-4). Underground buildings are usually defined as buildings where at least one floor used for human occupancy is located more than 30 feet below the lowest level of exit discharge. Codes treat underground buildings much like high-rise buildings when establishing requirements for fire safety. Systems such as automatic sprinkler protection, smoke exhaust systems, voice communication, and standby power are utilized in conjunction with compartmentation and limitations for allowable types of construction.

Underground buildings are required to be built of noncombustible types of construction. This is not dissimilar to the requirements for high-rise buildings. As buildings become taller, their structural components must maintain more fire resistance integrity. The stringent requirements for type of construction of underground buildings also helps ensure that the structure will be more resistant to fire, and will remain in place long enough for the building occupants to egress at the level of exit discharge should a fire occur.

Some codes require underground buildings to be divided into at least two com-

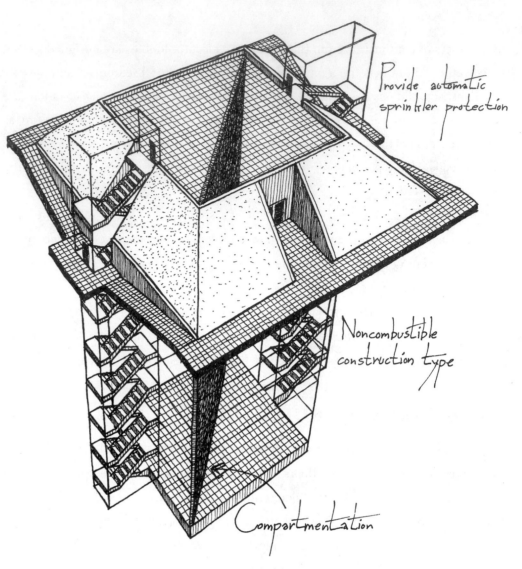

Provide automatic
sprinkler protection

Noncombustible
construction type

Compartmentation

Figure 4-4 *Underground buildings*

partments of approximately equal size. This compartmentation, formed by one-hour fire-rated partitions, provides a safe area of refuge for the occupants of any one underground floor level. The occupants would egress from the compartment of fire origin to the compartment which is free of any fire, and then the occupants would egress through the stairwells serving the fire-free compartment.

Underground buildings are usually required to be protected with automatic sprinkler protection. Of course, the purpose of the automatic sprinkler protection is to provide early extinguishing of any fire that would occur within the underground building.

Underground buildings may be required by building codes to be provided with smoke detection in specific locations so that early warning of a fire will occur as will activation of all smoke control equipment. Locations for smoke detectors in underground buildings (when required) are usually the same locations required for smoke detectors in high rise buildings and may include:

1. Rooms housing mechanical, electrical, or telephone equipment, rooms housing elevator machinery or transformers, and similar rooms,

2. Elevator lobbies,

3. Recirculating air systems serving more than one floor, and

4. Each connection to a return air duct or riser serving a recirculating air system of more than one story.

The actual required locations of smoke detectors may be more limited or more extensive than the previous list depending on which code is being applied. Compartmentation of underground buildings may necessitate the use of additional smoke detectors.

The smoke detection system (when required) triggers the voice alarm signaling system, which will in turn warn building occupants of a fire condition and instruct them of procedures they should follow to egress safely. The voice alarm messages are sent to specific areas of a building in order to help ensure that all building occupants are alerted to the fire emergency. Smoke control systems are utilized to remove the products of combustion from fire floors, and elevator lobbies are designed so that the elevators do not become a pathway for smoke to pollute the entire building.

The electrical systems and the mechanical systems used for controlling fires and smoke in underground buildings must remain in operation for certain specified amounts of time in the event of an emergency. These systems are required to be maintained by a standby power source.

General Building Limitations

Chapter 5 discusses the relationships of occupancy classifications and types of construction to allowable building heights and areas. This chapter also expands on how allowable heights and areas are affected by buildings of multiple occupancy classifications and of mixed types of construction. The chapter concludes with a discussion of typical allowable height and area increases permitted by codes, and with discussion of fire districts.

Buildings are limited in height and area based on the occupancy classifications within the buildings and the types of construction of the buildings (Figure 5-1). These varying limitations recognize that each combination of occupancy group and type of construction has inherent characteristics that make it less hazardous or more hazardous than another combination of occupancy group and type of construction. Codes provide separate occupancy classifications and separate types of construction so that each building can be regulated in the most appropriate manner in order to ensure a proper balance of economy, life safety, and property protection. The different occupancy classifications reflect the different ways in which people use buildings. The different construction types reflect the differences in combustibility and fire resistance of structural and nonstructural assemblies of different buildings. Heights and areas are governed by combinations of occupancy classification and types of construction. The relationship of occu-

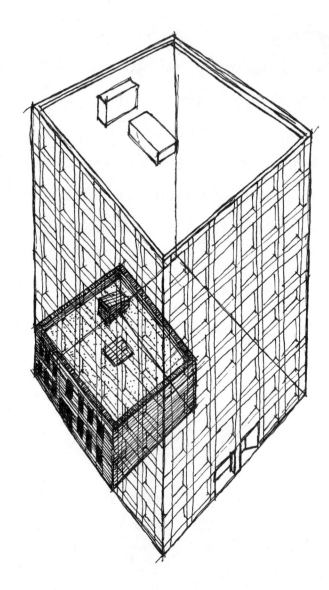

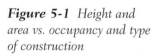

Figure 5-1 *Height and area vs. occupancy and type of construction*

pancy classification and type of construction go far beyond heights and areas, however; fire protection requirements, egress requirements, and many other code requirements are also contingent on the occupancy classifications and on the types of construction of buildings. For more discussion on occupancy classifications, see Chapter 3 of this book, and for more discussion on types of construction, see Chapter 6.

HEIGHT AND AREA

If a building contains low hazard occupancy groups and is constructed of a type of construction of high fire-resistance integrity, then that building will be allowed to be large in area and tall in height. If a building contains high hazard occupancy groups and is constructed of a type of construction of low fire-resistance integrity, then that building will not be allowed to be as large in area nor as tall in height. Each combination of occupancy group and type of construction affects the height and area of buildings; the safer a building's use and construction, the larger that building can be.

All four of the major codes regulate the heights of buildings in stories based on the buildings' uses and types of construction, as height in stories is considered a life safety concern. Height in stories is considered a life-safety concern, because the taller a building becomes in stories, the more difficult it becomes for the occupants of that building to egress, and the more difficult it becomes for fire fighters to control the fire in that building. The three building codes also regulate the heights of buildings in feet and the areas of buildings in square feet based on their uses and types of construction. These are property protection concerns, as the height of a building in feet and the area of a building in square feet defines a volume which is subject to certain pounds per square foot of fire loading based on the building's use and the type of construction. Because the limitation of building heights in feet and the limitation of building areas in square feet are generally viewed as property protection concerns, the NFPA 101 Life Safety Code, in most cases, does not regulate heights of buildings in feet nor does it regulate areas of buildings in square feet.

Each of the three major building codes refers to a table within their chapter on general building limitations which limits the allowable heights and areas for buildings based on the occupancy classifications within the buildings and the types of construction of the buildings. These tables limit the area of buildings in square feet, and the heights of buildings in feet and in stories. NFPA 101 lists only the allowable heights of buildings in stories within each of the individual occupancy chapters. In many of NFPA 101's occupancy classification chapters, type of construction is not applicable, and

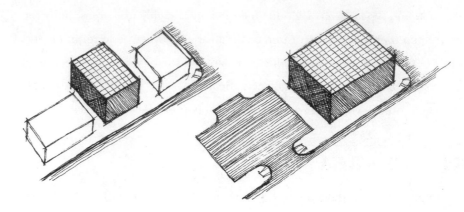

Figure 5-2 *Area increases*

therefore there are no limitations of height in stories for those particular occupancy classifications. The three major building codes provide for general height and area limitations and then for modifications to those height and area limitations. Increases to the heights and areas of buildings are allowed when buildings are equipped throughout with automatic sprinkler protection. Increases to areas of buildings are also allowed in many cases where the buildings are surrounded with a certain amounts of open space (Figure 5-2), thus decreasing the risk that these buildings will be greatly affected by fires in neighboring buildings. There are many other situations where building codes allow increases to the allowable heights or areas of buildings based on the inclusion of certain fire safe features in the buildings' designs. These special features might include, but certainly would not be limited to a low hazard occupancy classification, a low hazard type of construction, exits at grade, compartmentation, and so on.

All of the three major building codes regulate basic allowable height and area limitations based on buildings' occupancy classifications and types of construction, all allow some height and area limitation increases if buildings are sprinklered, and all allow some height and area limitation increases based on the provision of certain other safe features in the designs of the building. However, each of the three major building codes differs in how to implement allowable height and area limitations of buildings and the subsequent increases of those allowable height and area limitations. For example, under a single table, the Standard Building Code lists the allowable height and area limitations of buildings in square feet per story and their subsequent increases if the buildings are provided with automatic sprinkler protection. On the other hand, the Uniform Building Code (UBC) and the BOCA National Building Code (NBC) each list the allowable height and area limitations of buildings under a table (the UBC in allowable square feet per building and the NBC in allowable square feet per story for a one- or two-story building), but modify those allowable height and area limitations based on automatic sprinkler protection within the text of their chapters dealing with general building limitations. The actual allowable heights and areas and their subsequent increases vary from code to code. Though the philosophies of the three codes are similar regarding heights and areas, the means for implementing the principles of those philosophies vary from code to code.

MULTIPLE OCCUPANCIES

Determining heights and areas of buildings becomes more complicated when buildings house more than one occupancy classification within them. Within buildings of mixed occupancy classification, one must determine which occupancy group dictates the allowable heights and areas for the entire building. If codes compensate low hazard occupancy classifications by allowing more heights and areas than would be allowed for higher hazard occupancy classifications, what sort of height and area limitations should be imposed when combining two or more occupancy classifications within the same building? Building codes could require that the allowable heights and areas of multiple occupancy buildings be governed by the requirements of the most stringent occupancy group of the occupancy groups in question, but building codes do not require such a stringent approach. Codes are flexible in their approach to multiple occupancy buildings, and their attempt to give designers different options to choose from when designing multiple occupancy buildings.

The three major building codes actually provide up to three options for dealing with a building containing two or more different occupancy classifications. First, separate each occupancy classification with a fire wall or area separation wall and treat each occupancy classification as a separate building. Second, provide no occupancy separation and follow the very stringent rules for treating multiple occupancy classifications as a single occupancy classification. Third, provide occupancy separation and treat the building as a building of mixed occupancy classification. Each of the three major building codes provides these three options, though they differ in how they establish the determination of allowable heights and areas of buildings of mixed occupancy classification.

Separate Buildings

The first option for dealing with a building containing two or more occupancy classifications within the same building would be to separate each occupancy classification with a fire wall or area separation wall and treat each occupancy classification as a separate building (Figure 5-3). If an assembly occupancy were separated with a fire wall

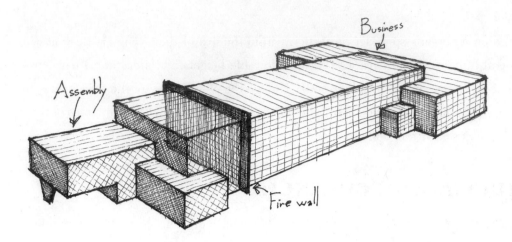

Figure 5-3 *Separate buildings*

from a related business occupancy then there would be two buildings—a building of assembly occupancy and a building of business occupancy. Each separate building would be subject to its own height and area requirements, independent of the other building. There would be no mixed occupancies in reality, because a fire wall defines separate buildings as far as building codes are concerned.

A Single Occupancy

A second option allowed by building codes for dealing with a building containing two or more occupancy classifications would be to provide no occupancy separation and follow the rules for treating multiple occupancy classifications as a single occupancy (Figure 5-4). One could consider a building containing different occupancy classifications as being a single occupancy classification if one were to follow several stringent requirements. One would have to use the more restrictive of the occupancy classifications for determining the height and area of the entire building. One would have to use the more restrictive of the occupancy classifications for determining sprinkler, standpipe, and alarm requirements for the entire building, and, depending on the code,

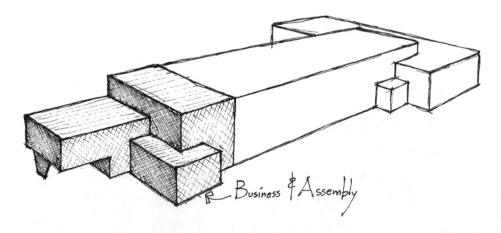

Figure 5-4 *Single occupancy*

one would have to use the more restrictive of the occupancy classifications for determining fire protection requirements for the entire building. All other requirements of the codes would be based on the individual occupancy classifications. Under option two, if an assembly occupancy and a business occupancy shared the same building, the building could be classified as a single occupancy if the allowable height and area of the building were based on assembly occupancy, which would have more stringent height and area requirements than a business occupancy. The fire protection requirements, and the sprinkler, standpipe, and alarm requirements would be assessed individually and would be designed in accordance with whichever of the two occupancies, assembly or business, had the more stringent requirements. Egress provisions and all other provisions would be based on the occupancy in which they occurred. For example, when determining minimum egress loads (see Chapter 10), the assembly portion of the building would utilize egress design loads associated with assembly occupancies, and the business portion of the building would utilize egress design loads associated with business occupancies. If any of the egress scheme were shared by both occupancies, one would use the more stringent egress design loads of the two occupancies within the shared areas. The height and area requirements under this second option are extremely stringent and many people wonder why anyone would ever choose this option. An example of why one might choose this option is that the program for the building may not call for a very large building, and the building may not need as much allowable height and area as permitted by the more stringent of the two occupancies, and therefore a great deal of savings could possibly be realized by not having to provide occupancy separation between the two adjacent occupancies.

Mixing Occupancies

The third option for dealing with two or more occupancy classifications within the same building would be to provide occupancy separation and treat the building as a building of mixed occupancy classification (Figure 5-5). In this case one must determine the height and area requirements based on the occupancies involved. The BOCA National Building Code and the Uniform Building Code utilize a formula involving ratios to determine the allowable heights and areas of these buildings. To work this formula, one would take the actual areas for each of the separate occupancies and divide those by the total allowable area for each of the separate occupancies respectively, and then add these ratios together. The added ratios could not exceed the number one. When using this formula, if one occupancy increases in area, the other must decrease in area, and therefore some control of fire loading is maintained. Remember once again

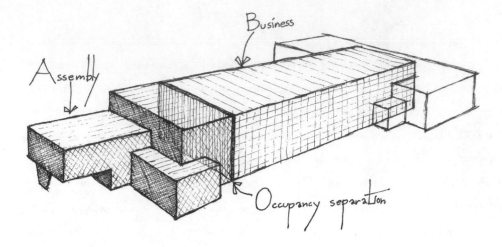

Figure 5-5 *Mixing occupancies*

that allowable height in feet and allowable areas in square feet are fire-loading concerns. The Uniform Building Code does have a section that states that any occupancy classification which is more than ninety percent of the area of any building would govern the allowable height and area of that building.

The Standard Building Code requires one to determine the principal intended use of the building in order to determine the allowable height and area of the entire building. Principal intended use is a very subjective term and is determined by code officials using their own knowledge and intuition. They may consider the relative hazards of the occupancies, the amount of time each occupancy is used daily by its occupants, the number of people using each occupancy, the area of each occupancy, and any other relevant concerns. The principal intended use will govern the height and area of the entire building. All of the other occupancy groups within the building will be considered accessory uses and must meet their own individual height and area limitations.

It is important to note that for allowable height, the Standard Building Code applies the principal intended use concept to determine the allowable height. The other two model codes allow the individual occupancies to meet their individual height requirements as long as the separation walls between those occupancies are detailed properly. As a final note on mixed occupancies, it should be noted that NFPA 101 Life Safety Code states that when there are two or more adjacent occupancies of different classifications and they are arranged so that it is not practicable to provide separate means of egress or fire protection or other safeguards, then the most restrictive life safety requirements of the individual occupancy will govern the entire building.

MIXING TYPES OF CONSTRUCTION

When one separates a building into two or more compartments using fire walls or area separation walls, each compartment becomes a separate building. Therefore, if a structure is divided by a fire wall or area separation wall, and one side of the structure is constructed with a combustible type of construction of light framing, while the other side of the structure is constructed with a noncombustible type of construction, then that building is considered to be two separate buildings, each of a different construction type (Figure 5-6). One of the buildings is allowed to be as large in area and as tall in height as prescribed by the code for the combustible type of construction of light framing to which it corresponds, and the other building is allowed to be as large in area and as tall in height as prescribed by the code for the noncombustible type of construction to which it corresponds. The allowable height and area of either building is not affected by the adjacent building, because the fire wall or area separation wall has created two separate buildings.

When no fire wall or area separation wall separates a building constructed in accordance with two or more different types of construction, the height and area requirements allowed by the most stringent type of construction classification represented in the building governs the allowable height and area of the entire building (Figure 5-7). If one-half of a building were constructed in accordance with a combustible type of construction of light framing and the other half of the building were constructed of a noncombustible type of construction, the height and area requirements of the combustible type of construction would govern the height and area of the entire building, as these requirements would be more stringent than those of the noncombustible type

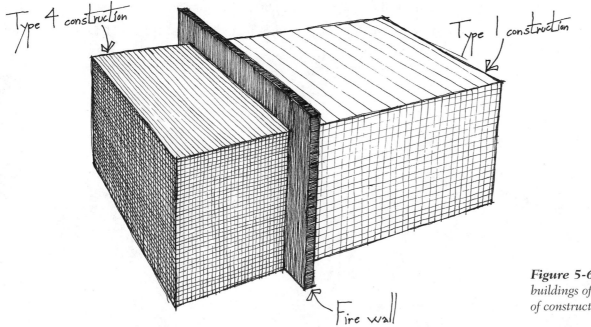

Figure 5-6 *Two different buildings of different types of construction*

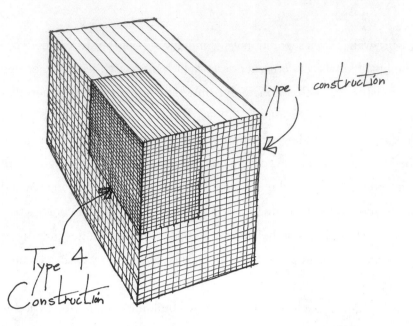

Figure 5-7 *Two different types of construction*

of construction. Unlike mixed occupancies, when types of construction are mixed, no separation is required between them, but also unlike mixed occupancies, when types of construction are mixed the most stringent height and area requirements always apply.

HEIGHT MODIFICATIONS

All of the codes provide different means for modifying allowable heights. As mentioned previously, allowable height modifications are given for buildings with automatic sprinkler protection. Some codes allow basements to avoid being classified as a story of allowable height if they meet certain physical requirements for location below grade (Figure 5-8). All of the four major codes, including the NFPA 101 Life Safety Code

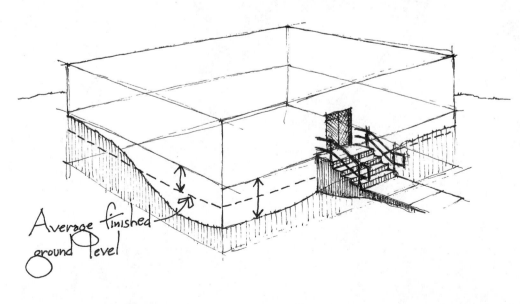

Figure 5-8 *Basements*

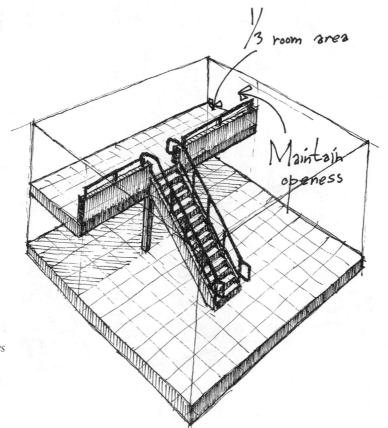

Figure 5-9 *Mezzanines*

allow increases to height in stories for mezzanines that meet the particular mezzanine requirements detailed within each of the individual codes (Figure 5-9). In order for a mezzanine to avoid being counted as a story in height, it cannot occupy more than one-third of the area of the room or space in which it is located, and the mezzanine must remain substantially open to the room or space in which it is located. Other requirements within each of the codes detail how to design the egress from a mezzanine, as well as detail when exceptions to the "openness" rule occur.

Whenever a height modification is granted, one must pay particular attention to what sort of modification is being granted. For example, when mezzanine sections tell designers that they need not count certain mezzanines as allowable stories of height, these sections are excepting height in stories, not height in feet. The building must still maintain a maximum height in feet as prescribed by each of the building codes. It is also important to note that these exceptions are not exemptions from such mezzanines' being considered actual stories in height for other aspects of the code. For example, most codes require that stairwells four stories or more in height must be separated from the rest of the building with two-hour-rated assemblies, instead of the one hour separation required for stairwells three stories or less in height. If a stairwell serves three full

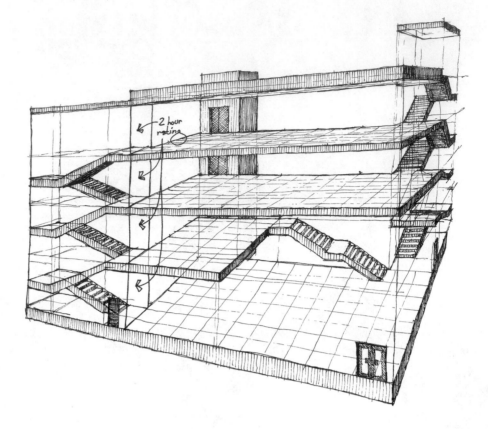

Figure 5-10 *Stair serving three floors and mezzanine*

floors and a mezzanine, that stairwell would be considered as serving four floors, and would have to be separated from the rest of the building with two hour rated assemblies (Figure 5-10). The mezzanine rule simply states that the mezzanine need not count as a story in height when determining the allowable height of the building. The rule does not exempt the mezzanine from actually being a story but rather it allows an additional story over what would normally be allowed.

AREA MODIFICATIONS

Once again, the NFPA 101 Life Safety Code, as a general rule, does not regulate allowable areas in square feet for buildings because NFPA 101 considers the limitation of allowable areas in square feet as a property protection issue, and NFPA 101 is a life safety code. In some specific cases, NFPA 101 does regulate allowable areas of buildings. However, the three building codes see property protection issues as relevant to their purview; therefore, they do regulate the allowable areas of buildings in square feet. When these three codes refer to allowable areas of a building, they are limiting what is known as building area or floor area, depending on which code one is using. The definitions are essentially the same. It is easiest to define building or floor area by contrasting it with net, and gross area. Net area is all of the square footage of a building within the thickness of the exterior walls, exclusive of spaces not usually occupied, such as corridors, rest rooms, closets, mechanical rooms, and so on (Figure 5-11). Gross area is all of the square footage of a building within the thickness of the exterior walls, inclusive of all interior spaces (Figure 5-12). Building area (Floor area) includes everything within the drip line of a building. Building area includes overhangs, balconies, eaves, decks, or any other sort of projection from the building (Figure 5-13), though many code officials may not include eaves when determining building area. Building areas or floor areas are the types of areas referenced under the three major building codes when discussing allowable areas of buildings.

The three major building codes allow an increase of allowable area for buildings equipped with automatic sprinkler protection. Other allowable area increases can be gained by providing certain specified safe design features in buildings or by locating buildings on their sites in a manner that provides a great deal of open space around the buildings. There are actually many special exceptions within building codes which deal with allowable area increases, some of which even allow unlimited area. Of course, buildings that are allowed to be unlimited in area must meet all the other requirements in codes, such as those requirements dealing with travel distances under each code's egress chapter.

All three of the major building codes allow increases in allowable area for buildings with specific amounts of open space around them. The theory behind permitting allowable area limitation increases for providing open space around a building's perimeter is a simple one. If one's building is close to a neighboring building, the chance that fire can spread from one building to the other is great (Figure 5-14). On the other hand, if one's building is not close to a neighboring building, the chance that fire can spread from one building to the other is not as great. A burning building can emit enough radiant heat to ignite combustible surfaces of adjacent buildings; the greater the distance between two buildings, the less radiant heat the non-fire building will receive. Therefore, building codes permit the greatest area increases for those buildings that are located the greatest distances from other buildings. Each code has a different formula for determining how much area increase is allowed due to maintaining some distance from property lines or from other buildings, and each code has a different idea as to what is considered as enough distance from a property line or from another building to warrant some sort of allowable area increase. But in each code, a substantial amount of open space around the perimeter of a building will allow a designer to apply a substantial increase to the allowable area limitations of the building.

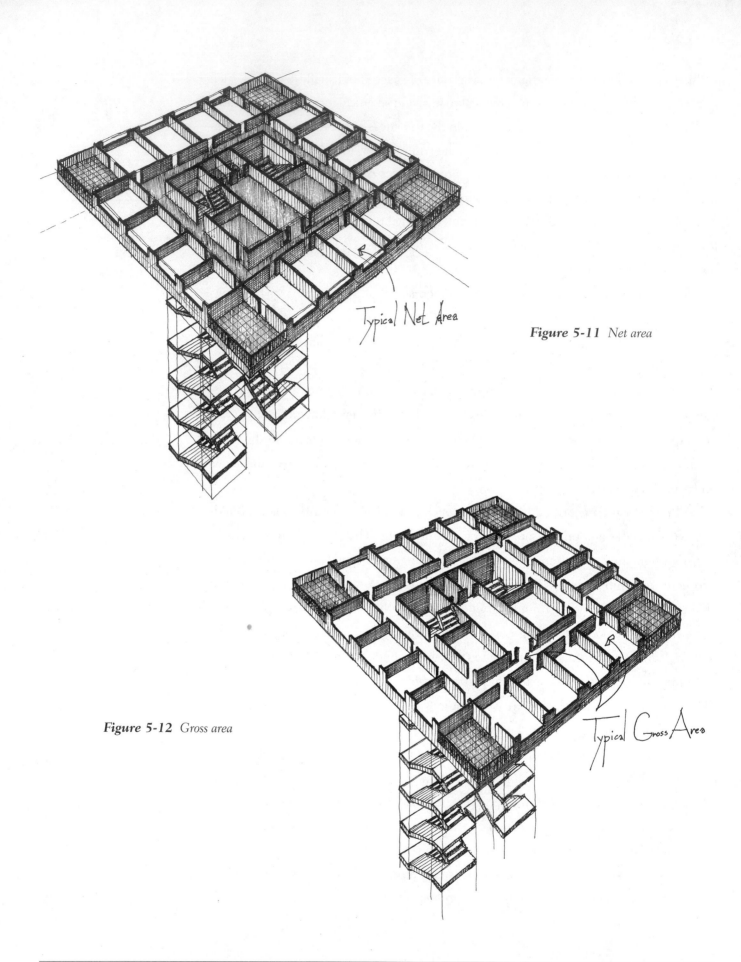

Typical Net Area

Figure 5-11 Net area

Figure 5-12 Gross area

Typical Gross Area

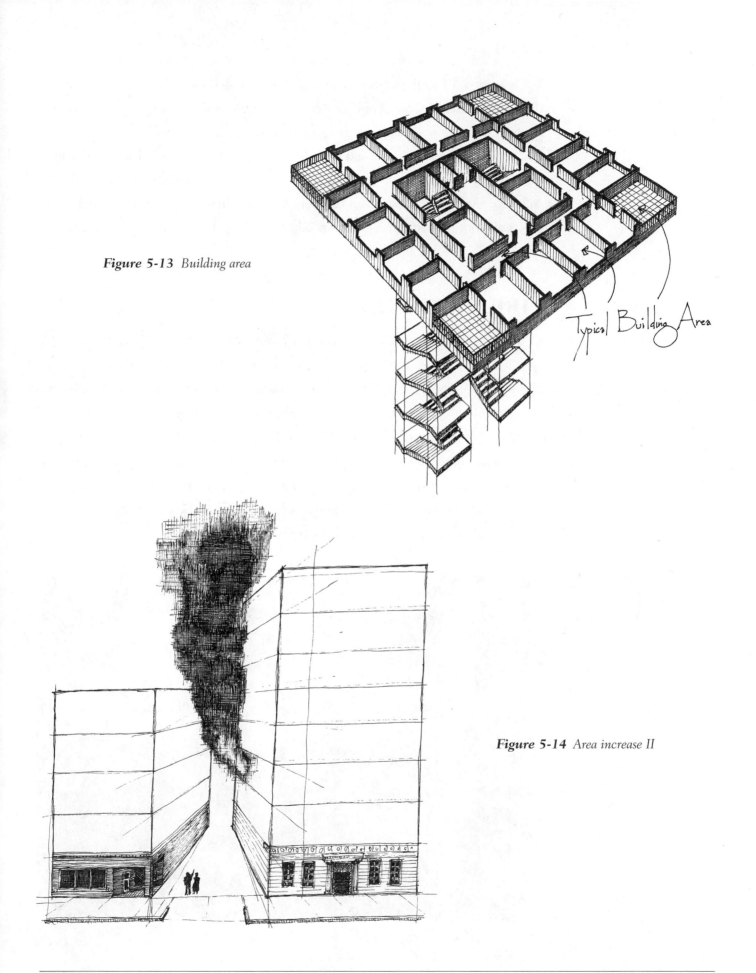

Figure 5-13 Building area

Typical Building Area

Figure 5-14 Area increase II

Years ago, I found that many codes officials and designers alike did not know that these area increase sections of codes existed, and therefore building owners were paying for expensive fire walls or area separation walls that were not actually required. I find now that most designers and most code enforcers are very familiar with the open area increase sections of the building codes. Keep in mind that other sections of codes will have something to say about exterior walls and their treatment based on how far they are from property lines, or from other buildings located on the same site (see Chapter 7).

FIRE DISTRICTS

In dense urban areas, there is a potential problem that a fire in one building could spread rapidly to adjacent buildings, resulting in the destruction of an entire area (Figure 5-15). The conditions which contribute to this potential problem are the close proximity of buildings to one another in urban areas, the combustible construction used in older buildings in urban areas, and the fact that many buildings in urban areas predate existing fire codes in their design and construction. In these urban areas (primarily central business districts) codes can establish fire districts in order to prohibit certain occupancy groups such as hazardous occupancies from being constructed in these fire districts. Certain less fire-resistant types of construction can also be prohibited,

Figure 5-15 *Fire district*

such as light wood framing. Fire district provisions may also regulate the types of roof coverings that can be used within the fire district. Not all codes endorse the concept of fire districts, but one can see that by establishing certain safe zones within cities, the potential spread of fire can be deterred more effectively.

Type of Construction

Chapter 6 discusses type of construction and those components which define the different types of construction—materials and assembly ratings. How codes treat buildings with two or more areas built in accordance with different types of construction is also addressed by this chapter.

As already stated in this book, codes could be promulgated that are very lean and easy to use, but such codes would be overly restrictive and provide for very costly construction. Therefore, codes are thick and complex because the construction industry desires flexible codes and standards which recognize that there are appropriate uses for affordable construction of low fire resistance, as well as appropriate uses for less affordable construction of greater fire resistance. One may wish to construct a building of an affordable combustible type of construction, though that building will be subjected by codes to very strict height and area requirements because of the combustibility of the construction type (Figure 6-1a). One may also choose to construct a building of a more expensive noncombustible type of construction in order for the building to be allowed greater heights and areas by codes (Figure 6-1b). Codes establish different types of construction in recognition of the fact that there are different ways of constructing buildings and some ways are more fire-resistant than others. Construction types are defined by the materials they employ and the fire ratings of their structural assemblies. Those types of construction which are noncombustible and which have the highest structural assembly fire ratings are allowed by codes to be larger in height and area than those types of construction which are combustible and which have lower structural assembly fire ratings.

MATERIALS

The major concern with materials when defining construction types is whether the materials are combustible, noncombustible, or a combination of combustible and non-

Figures 6-1a and b
Combustible and Non-combustible construction vs. height and area

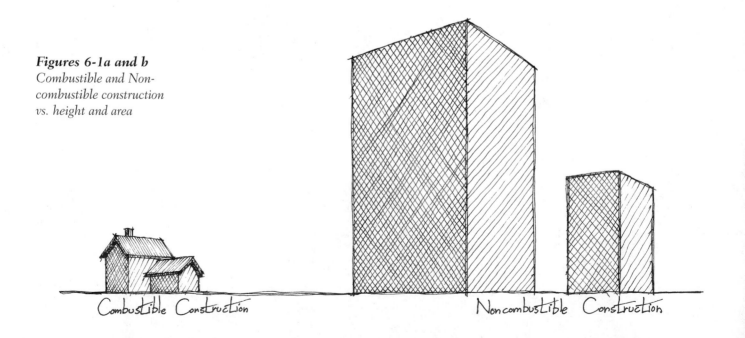

Combustible Construction   Noncombustible Construction

combustible. A type of construction using combustible materials burns more quickly than a noncombustible type of construction, and therefore most combustible types of construction are more limited by codes than are noncombustible types of construction. Buildings of noncombustible construction types are usually allowed by codes to be greater in height and area than buildings of combustible construction types. Codes establish combustible construction types, noncombustible construction types, and construction types that combine noncombustible materials and combustible materials. These latter types are construction types where the exterior walls are noncombustible and all roof framing, and interior structural elements are combustible. Combustible construction types include heavy timber construction and light wood frame construction.

A typical standard for determining whether or not a material is combustible is the American Society for Testing and Material's ASTM E 136, Test Methods for Fire Tests of Building Construction and Materials (Figure 6-2). In this test, the material is exposed to a furnace of approximately 1400°. The material must meet three requirements during the test in order to be considered noncombustible. First, the material cannot increase the temperature of the furnace 54° Fahrenheit over the initial temperature of the furnace. Second, the material can not propagate its own flame after 30 seconds exposure to the furnace. And third, the material cannot increase the initial temperature of the furnace if the material loses more than 50 percent of its own weight over the test period. This description of ASTM E 136 is grossly oversimplified. The actual standard should be consulted by those who want to become more familiar with the test.

ASSEMBLIES

Codes give several different choices of types of construction—those employing non-combustible materials, those employing combustible materials, and those employing a combination of the two. These choices differ in the assembly ratings applied to each structural assembly. Assemblies are tested in accordance with a fire resistance standard by a recognized testing organization, and the assembly is consequently listed in a fire resistance directory. For more discussion of these fire resistance tests and directories, see Chapter 7 of this book. Not all structural assemblies are required by all types of construction to carry some fire resistance rating. Some assemblies are simply required to be noncombustible, and others may have no material or fire rating requirements whatsoever. When comparing construction types of similar materials requirements, the construction types with the higher assembly fire resistance ratings are allowed to be larger in height and area than the construction types with lower assembly fire resistance ratings (Figure 6-3).

Figure 6-3 *Assembly ratings vs. height and area*

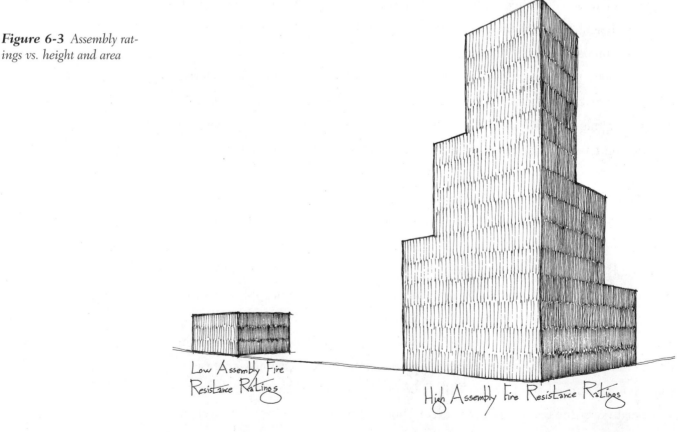

Low Assembly Fire Resistance Ratings

High Assembly Fire Resistance Ratings

NONSTRUCTURAL PARTITIONS

Nonstructural partitions are regulated by codes as to their allowable material content for each type of construction within codes. Code officials do not want the composition of nonstructural partitions to be inconsistent with the fire resistance integrity established by structural partitions within any particular type of construction. Inevitably, noncombustible types of construction maintain the higher fire resistance standards regarding nonstructural partitions when compared with combustible types of construction. This is another reason noncombustible types of construction are usually allowed greater heights and areas.

COMPARING TYPES OF CONSTRUCTION

Each of the three major building codes and NFPA 220, Standard on Types of Building Construction, have different types of construction. NFPA 220 is a standard for defining types of construction, and is referenced by the NFPA 101 Life Safety Code. Though there are a great number of similarities amongst the four codes' types of construction, each uses different titles for each of the types of construction. The BOCA National Building Code and NFPA 220 have five noncombustible types of construction, two types of construction employing a combination of combustible and noncombustible materials, and three combustible types of construction including one type of construction of heavy timber materials. The Standard Building Code and the Uniform Building Code have four noncombustible types of construction, two types of construction employing a combination of combustible and noncombustible materials, and three combustible types of construction including one type of construction of heavy timber materials. One cannot actually make direct comparisons amongst the different codes' types of construction, as each one makes unique adjustments to each type of construction. The result of these adjustments is that a particular type of construction in one code can only be compared loosely to a supposedly equivalent type of construction in another code.

MIXING TYPES OF CONSTRUCTION

I see more problems dealing with mixed types of construction occurring with the design of medical facilities than perhaps any other type of facility. Hospitals, being what they are, constantly change and expand. It is not uncommon for a hospital addition to be planned which will increase the area of the hospital over the allowable area permitted for the existing hospital by the applicable code. Complications usually arise when the existing hospital is already constructed with a "hodgepodge" of types of construction without any fire walls or area separation walls between the different types of construction. In order to increase the area of the hospital, one would have to separate the new construction from the old construction with a fire wall or area separation wall. If the hospital is a high-rise, and many of them are, then detailing this fire separation could be a nightmare.

The reason this mixing of construction types is a problem is that the height and area of the entire building must not exceed the height and area limitations prescribed by the applicable code for whichever one of the types of construction within the building would allow the least height and area. Buildings of mixed types of construction are governed by the most restrictive height and area requirements, as well as the most restrictive of any other requirements related to types of construction, for the types of construction within them (Figure 6-4a). The only way to avoid the most restrictive type construction's governing the height and area of a building of mixed types of construction is to separate each area of differing type of construction from the other areas with fire walls or area separation walls (Figure 6-4b). In this case, one will have created two separate buildings.

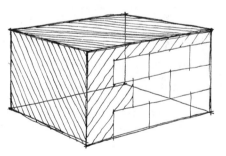

Figure 6-4a *Mixed types—no separation*

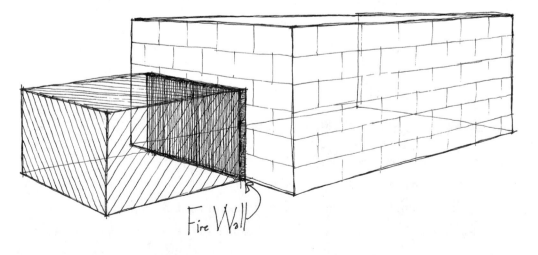

Figure 6-4b *Mixed types—fire wall separation*

SELECTING TYPES OF CONSTRUCTION

The future use of a building should be considered when the designer selects the type of construction for that building. If the designer knows that a building owner wants to expand his or her building in the future, the designer should choose a type of construction to accommodate that expansion, or at least the designer should weigh the costs of providing fire wall separation or area wall separation versus the costs of upgrading the building to a more fire resistant type of construction. If the designer knows of future expansion plans for the building, the designer may select a more expensive type of construction that would accommodate all future expansion needs. The designer should indicate to the code official the intended type of construction classification for any project. If the code official were not aware of the designer's reasons for selecting a more expensive type of construction, the code official might mistakenly review the construction documents as a lesser type of construction, thinking that he or she were helping the designer to save construction costs. Designation of the desired type of construction on the construction documents would help prevent such a good-willed mistake from occurring.

Fire-Resistant Materials and Construction

*C*hapter 7 discusses the requirements for both fire-rated and nonrated construction assemblies. These requirements include the proper termination of such assemblies, as well as the ratings required of many of them. The required ratings of exterior walls based on their distances from property lines are also discussed as are the requirements for allowable openings in those walls. Chapter 7 discusses required methods to use when penetrating interior walls and partitions, exterior walls, and floor/ceiling and roof/ceiling assemblies. Vertical shafts are discussed, along with other protection methods, including requirements for doors in rated assemblies. This chapter includes some discussion of the proper resources used for determining the fire resistance ratings of assemblies.

Chapters in codes dealing with fire-resistant materials and construction serve the purpose of describing what materials and products are appropriate for fire-resistant construction, as well as detailing how these materials and products should be used. Many of the requirements of these fire protection chapters are based on the occupancy classifications and the types of construction of buildings. Therefore, it is necessary to have determined the occupancy classification and the type of construction of any building before investigating thoroughly the requirements for fire resistant materials and construction. This chapter will be concerned with materials utilized for fire resistance, the testing and listing of those materials, the proper construction of rated construction assemblies incorporating those materials, and the penetrations of rated and nonrated construction assemblies.

MATERIALS FOR FIRE RESISTANCE

Materials utilized in building construction must meet certain standards regulating the quality of the materials, as well as how the materials can be used safely. When building materials are used for the purposes of fire separation, they must meet fire resistance standards applicable to their fire resistance, as well as structural standards applicable to their structural integrity. The fire resistance standards regulate the quality and use of

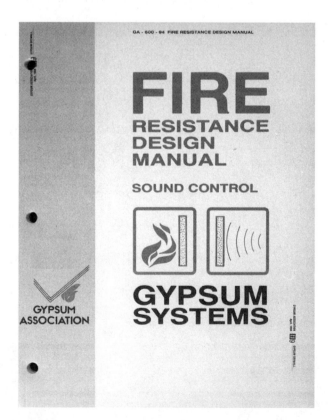

Figure 7-1 *Fire Resistance Directory*

materials to help ensure that they provide adequate fire separation. Typical materials utilized for fire resistance include brick, clay or shale tile, gypsum, gypsum lathe, wall board and sheathing board, metal or wire lathe, concrete block, vermiculite, perlite, and glass block. As a designer it is not necessary for one to be intimately familiar with all of the standards governing these materials, but it is important for the designer to make sure that his or her construction documents reference all applicable standards required by codes for whatever material is being used (Figure 7-1). The designer should then verify on the job site that the construction materials are identified in some manner as having met their applicable governing standards. The proof of a building material's having been tested in accordance with an approved standard might be in the form of a grade stamp on the material itself, in the form of documentation submitted with the material, or by some other method. If a building product is appropriate for a specific construction use, it will almost certainly have been tested in accordance with all standards for its production and use as referenced within building codes.

FIRE-RESISTANT SEPARATIONS

There are many reasons within codes to provide fire-resistant separations (Figure 7-2). Fire-resistant construction is used to provide for protection of structural assemblies, for

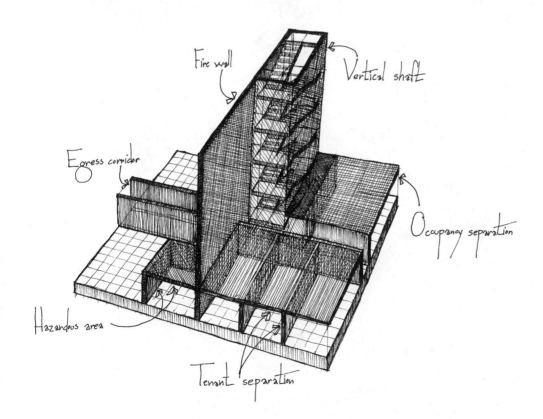

Figure 7-2 *Different reasons for separation*

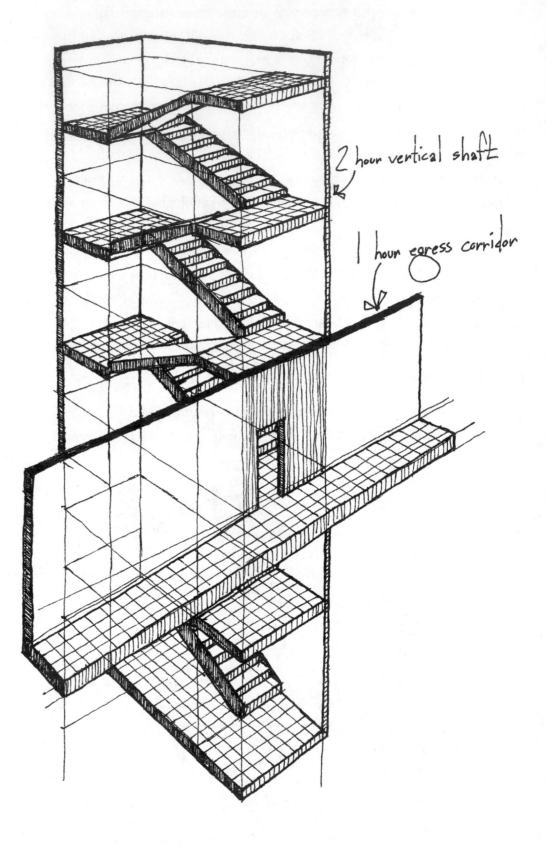

2 hour vertical shaft

1 hour egress corridor

Figure 7-3 *Higher rating controls*

occupancy separation, for tenant separation, for separation of egress elements, and for other reasons. Often, a single fire-resistant assembly addresses several of these concerns simultaneously. A fire-rated wall providing a protected egress path along one side of an exit access corridor might also provide part of a required occupancy separation within the building, as well as provide some protection of a structural assembly. Whenever one particular fire rated assembly meets the requirements of several different fire-rated concerns, the higher required rating of each of the concerns, when compared, dictates the ultimate fire rating of that assembly (Figure 7-3). For example, a wall required to have a one-hour fire resistance as part of an exit access corridor and required to have a two-hour fire resistance as part of required occupancy separation would have to be designed and constructed for the requirements of a two-hour fire resistant assembly.

INTERIOR WALLS

Occupancy Separation

Chapters 3 and 5 of this book discuss the mixing of occupancies and the ramifications thereof. Whenever two or more different occupancy classifications exist within the same building, that are not separated by a fire wall or an area separation wall, a mixed occupancy occurs. Because the adjacent occupancies have different life safety requirements in codes based on how they are used and because codes have different requirements for the height and area of each occupancy classification, it is necessary to provide some fire-rated separation between them. The fire-rated separation is determined by comparing adjacent occupancies and basing their separation on the more hazardous of the two (Figure 7-4).

If there were an assembly occupancy adjacent to a business occupancy tenant in a strip shopping center which was regarded as a single building, the two tenants' spaces would be separated with fire-resistant construction unless the building complied with a particular exception allowing that separation to be of non-fire-rated construction (Figure 7-5). The separation would be based on the assembly occupancy which is potentially more hazardous than the business occupancy. Occupancy separation buys time for the inhabitants of adjacent occupancies to respond appropriately to an emergency condition.

Codes often exempt occupancy separation requirements when the adjacency of any two or more particular different occupancies does not create a situation hazardous enough to warrant the use of fire-resistant separation. All buildings require some storage

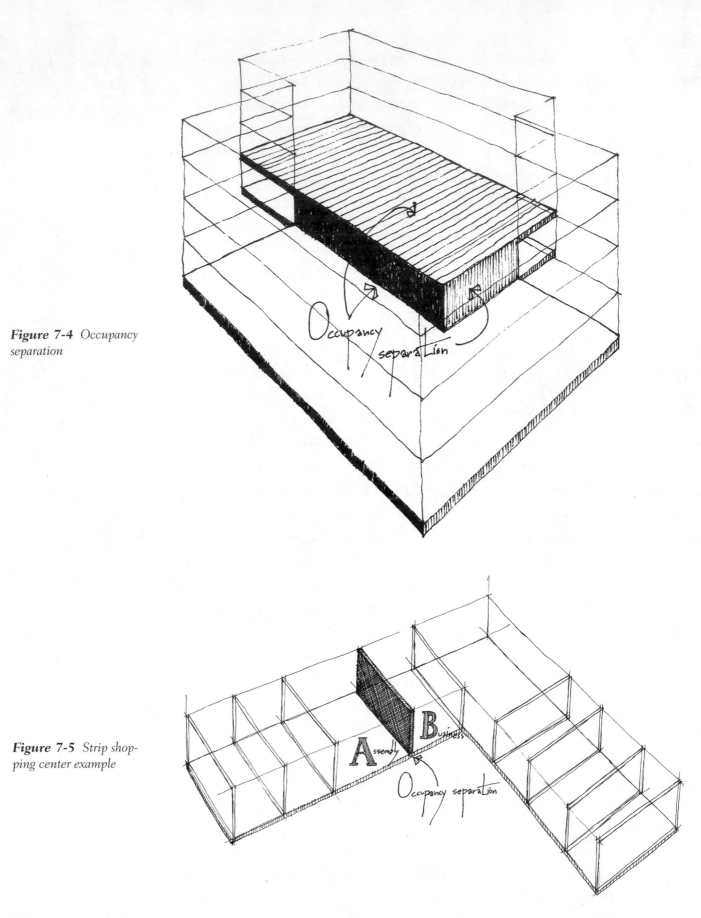

Figure 7-4 *Occupancy separation*

Figure 7-5 *Strip shopping center example*

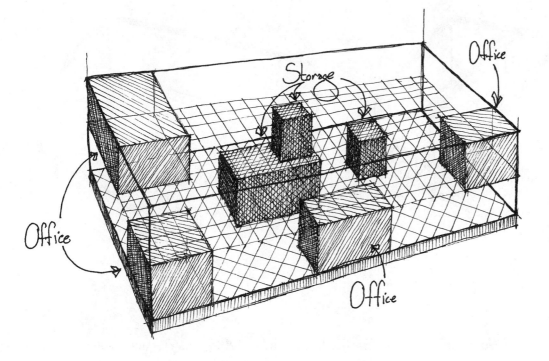

Figure 7-6 *Accessory occupancy*

and most buildings require offices in order to conduct the business of the major occupancy located within these buildings. Incidental offices and incidental storage areas are usually not required to be separated from the major occupancy with rated construction because they are not seen as a great enough hazard to require that separation. Of course, in order for fire-resistant separation to be exempted between storage and office areas and the major occupancy, they must be incidental in use and they must not exceed certain minimum square footages of area prescribed in each of the codes (Figure 7-6).

Depending on the code, other fire-rated separations between two or more areas of the same building may exist. Codes may actually require special occupancy like separation for areas of buildings which are considered to present a special hazard as well. For example, boiler rooms or furnace rooms occasionally are required to be separated from other areas of a building depending on the Btu capacity size of the boiler or furnace.

Tenant Fire Separation

Whenever a building or a portion of a building of a single occupancy classification contains different tenants adjacent to one another, some codes as a general rule require fire separation between these different tenants (Figures 7-7a & b). Each code is different in its application of tenant separation requirements. The purpose of tenant separation is to provide protection for each tenant from the threat of a fire in an adjacent tenant space. Tenant fire separation is usually fairly minimal, recognizing the fact that each

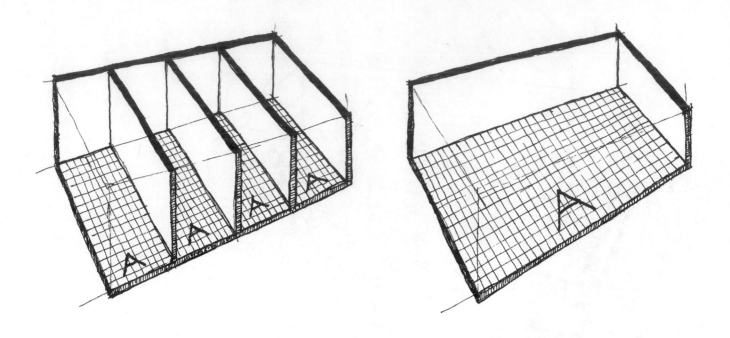

Figures 7-7a&b *Tenant separation and single tenant*

adjacent tenant is of the same occupancy and therefore, each tenant is subjected to the same content-related characteristics and the same human behavior characteristics as its neighbor. Some codes exempt fire-rated separation between adjacent tenants when the adjacent tenants are of the same low hazard occupancy classification, and when their tenant spaces are fairly small in area.

Interior Wall and Partition Fire Separation Requirements

With the exception of shaft partitions, exit passageway partitions, and partitions that separate fire areas (depending on the code being implemented), all fire-rated partitions can terminate against a roof deck or floor deck above, or against a roof-ceiling assembly or floor-ceiling assembly above if that assembly above is of a fire rating at least equal to that of the fire-rated partition (Figure 7-8). If a two-hour partition that is not a shaft partition or a partition that separates a fire area terminates against a two hour roof-ceiling or floor-ceiling assembly, and is secured tightly to that assembly so that the connection is smoke-tight, then the partition does not need to extend to the roof deck or floor deck above. The smoke tightness of the junction of the horizontal and vertical planes is critical, because fire-rated partitions also serve as smoke partitions which should prevent the passage of smoke.

It is not uncommon for codes to allow one-hour rated corridor partitions to contain some glass, so that one can view through these partitions (Figure 7-9). The glass within these partitions is usually restricted to one-quarter-inch thick wired glass in a steel frame, glass block, or glazing which is part of a three-quarter-hour assembly depending on the code used. Codes specify the maximum percentage of a tenant space wall adja-

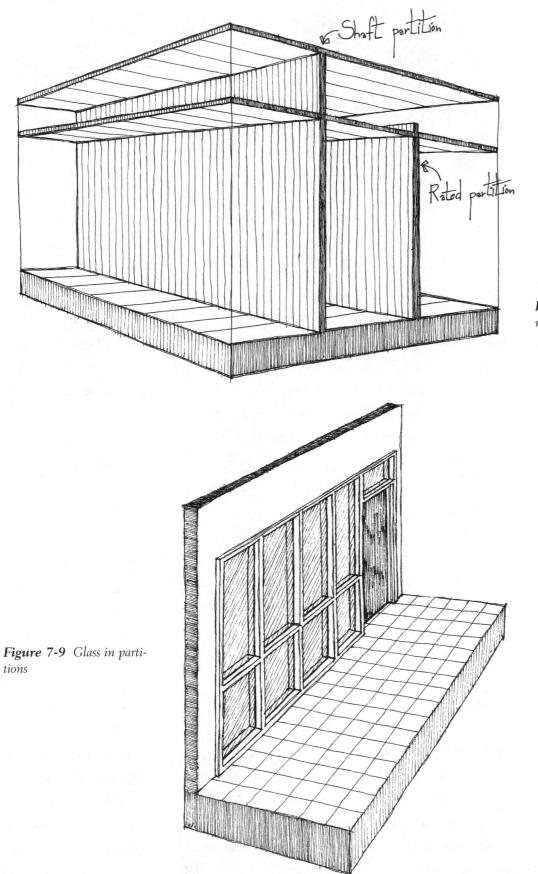

Figure 7-8 Partition termination

Figure 7-9 Glass in partitions

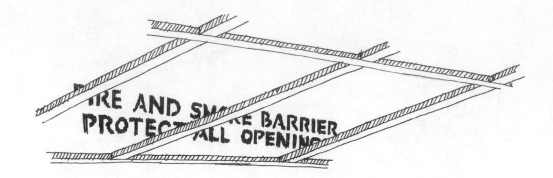

Figure 7-10 *Identifying rated partitions*

cent to a corridor which can contain this glass. The maximum size of individual wired glass panels or glass block panels is also restricted to reduce the risk of a fire's deforming the panels to the breaking point.

Codes are playing a probability game by allowing nonrated glass within one-hour-rated corridor partitions. The glass areas represent a weak point in the one-hour protection, but such glazing areas are limited in area with the understanding that as long as most of the corridor wall maintains a one-hour fire resistance, then the chance of the spread of fire through that wall will be significantly reduced. Of course, if one used a one-hour fire-rated glass assembly within a one-hour rated corridor partition, then the entire partition could be of glass as long as the glass were installed in accordance with its listing, and as long as other requirements of the code were adhered to, such as the requirement for smoke tightness.

I have often heard of code officials' allowing designers to put unlimited amounts of glass block, wired glass in steel frames, or glazing which is part of a three-quarter-hour assembly within one-hour corridor partitions if the designers provided for sprinkler protection on each side of that glass in a manner that would wash the glass and keep it cool in the event of a fire. The code officials were usually using the atrium section of their code as precedence in order to allow this unlimited sprinklered glass area. It is important to remember that each of the codes vary some in their requirements for glazing in corridor walls.

When rated partitions are installed in buildings, codes require that these partitions be labeled (Figure 7-10). The wording might be as that suggested in the Standard Building Code for example: "Fire and Smoke Barrier Protect all Openings" (Southern Building Code Congress International, Inc. 1994). This labeling is required so that when contractors and subcontractors penetrate a rated wall during the course of a construction project, they are alerted to the fact that the wall must be penetrated in a listed fashion. When they run plumbing, duct work, and wiring through the wall, they must protect those penetrations in an acceptable manner as listed under all applicable codes and standards.

Partition Requirements by Occupancy

The unique content-related characteristics and human behavior characteristics of each occupancy classification warrants variation in the way codes and standards treat each individual occupancy. This is true also when establishing requirements for interior partitions. Often codes provide for a great deal of flexibility concerning interior partition requirements when those partitions are located in a building of a low hazard occupancy or when a building is sprinklered. For example, many codes allow partitions forming exit access corridors to be nonrated when those partitions are located within a single tenant space of a business occupancy that is fully sprinklered. Each code will vary as to what it requires of partitions within each respective occupancy classification.

EXTERIOR WALLS

Distance from Property Lines

One of the concerns of the three major building codes is that of the potential spread of fire from one building to another building. When a building is burning and is in close proximity to another building, then there is a chance that the radiant heat or flames from the burning building will ignite a fire in the adjacent building (Figure 7-

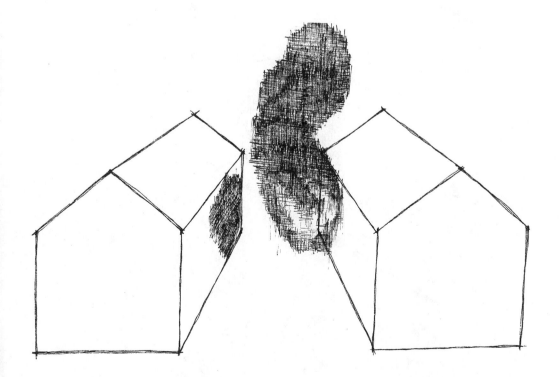

Figure 7-11 *Radiant heat—exterior walls*

11). The closer a burning building is to another building, the greater the risk of conflagration due to the radiant heat emitted from the burning building. There are methods available to help control this potential conflagration hazard. Codes require exterior walls to maintain specific fire resistant ratings and limit the openings in these walls based on the exterior walls' distances from property lines or distances from other buildings on commonly owned property. The regulation of exterior walls based on proximity to other buildings is considered to be a property protection issue. The NFPA 101 Life Safety Code does not contain requirements for rating exterior walls and limiting their openings based on proximity to property lines because the Life Safety Code is not a property protection code.

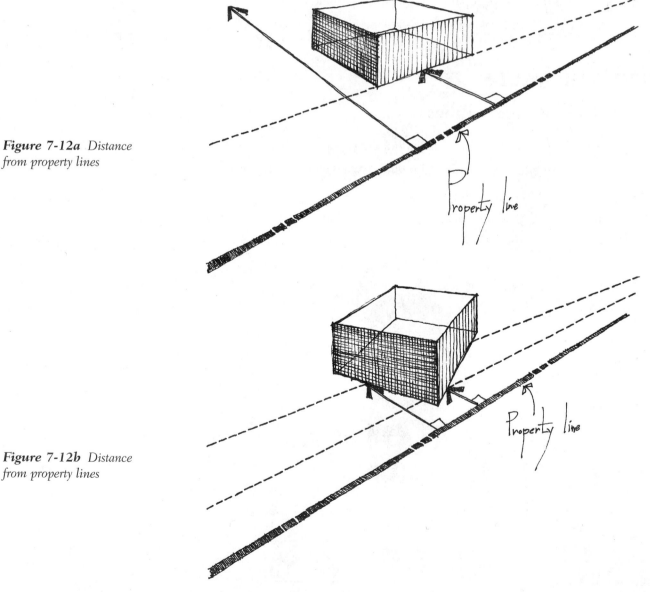

Figure 7-12a *Distance from property lines*

Figure 7-12b *Distance from property lines*

Under the three major building codes, the closer the wall is constructed to a property line or to another building on commonly owned property, the more the fire resistance rating of an exterior wall is increased (Figures 7-12a & b). These codes also decrease the allowable area of exterior wall openings the closer an exterior wall is constructed to a property line or to another building on commonly owned property. The percentage of exterior wall openings allowed in these codes is a percentage of wall opening per floor.

Though all three of the major building codes regulate exterior walls and openings in this manner, they each differ in their opinions about where to provide for these requirements in their respective codes. One code sees exterior wall exposure requirements as a fire protection issue and addresses these concerns under its fire protection chapter. Another code sees exterior wall exposure requirements as a type of construction issue and addresses these concerns under its type of construction chapter. The third code sees exterior wall exposure requirements as a height and area concern and addresses these concerns under its height and area chapter. These differences amongst the three major building codes illustrate once again more of a difference in philosophy of how to outline a code than an actual difference in philosophy as to what a code should require. However, the Standard Building Code is the only one of the three major building codes that does not modify exterior wall exposure requirements based on occupancy classification, a departure in philosophy from the other two building codes.

Buildings Located on the Same Lot

The location of more than one building on an individual lot potentially creates a situation in which fire moves from one building to another, resulting in a great amount of property loss. The three major building codes address this potential problem by requiring the establishment of assumed property lines between buildings on the same lot. The exterior walls facing assumed property lines would then meet the same requirements for fire resistance and for percentage of openings that walls facing actual deeded property lines would have to meet based on the walls' distances from property lines (Figure 7-13a). The NFPA 101 Life Safety Code does not address assumed property lines as this concept is viewed as a property protection issue and NFPA 101 is a life safety code only.

The location of an assumed property line can be anywhere between the two adjacent buildings in question, but must be consistent for both buildings. In other words, once the assumed property line is located, it must remain in that location for both buildings. As the assumed property line moves closer to one building that building is

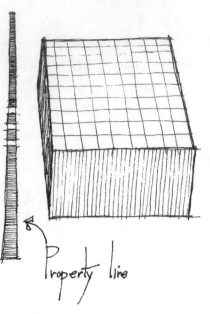
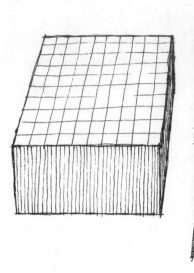

Figure 7-13a *Assumed property lines*

Property line

Figure 7-13b *No assumed property lines*

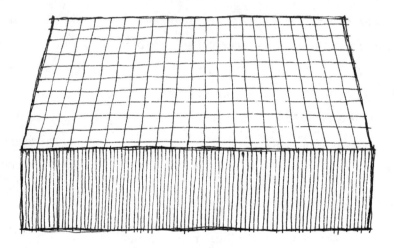

subjected to higher required fire resistance ratings and is allowed a smaller percentage of openings, while the other building is subjected to lower required fire resistance ratings and is allowed a larger percentage of openings.

When one wants to construct a new building adjacent to an existing building, determining the location of the assumed property line between the two buildings may become a difficult task. One would have to know the type of construction of the existing building and the rating of the existing exterior wall, as well as the percentage of openings per floor of the wall facing the new building (and depending on the code, maybe even the occupancy classification of the building) before determining how close an assumed property line could be located to the existing building. An assumed property line can always be located directly adjacent to the exterior wall of a new building and the exterior wall and its openings can be designed accordingly based on the new building's type of construction. However, with an existing building, the type of construction and the exterior wall ratings and openings are predetermined, and as a consequence the assumed property line location must respond to these existing conditions.

Some codes do not require adjacent buildings on the same lot to assume property lines between them if the total area of these buildings together is not greater than the total allowable area within codes for a single building (Figure 7-13b). If the adjacent buildings were of different occupancy classifications or of different types of construction, one would have to consider the rules of mixing either of these when determining the allowable area for a single building in order to receive this exception to establishing assumed property lines. By not assuming a property line between two buildings on the same lot and consequently not rating the exterior walls and limiting their openings, a designer might create a situation in which future expansion of either building might require a fire wall or area separation wall. If no property line were assumed between two adjacent buildings, then those buildings would be considered as one building, and would have to be treated as such within codes for allowable areas.

If a fire wall or area separation wall is employed to divide a building into two buildings on the same lot, then that wall becomes the assumed property line. Fire walls or area separation walls can have openings in them, but these openings have very stringent protection requirements. Nevertheless, these openings do allow passage from one side of the building to the other through the fire wall or area separation wall.

Parapet Walls

Whenever exterior walls are required to be fire-rated, the termination of those exterior walls at the roof surface must be accomplished in a manner that ensures proper fire separation is maintained. Codes, therefore, require parapet walls where the roof slope permits the use of a parapet wall and where a parapet wall adds protection to a fire-resistant wall (Figure 7-14). Parapet walls extend the fire resistance of a wall beyond the roof surface, which in turn provides more protection by protecting the roof surface from exposure to fire and radiant heat. There is variation amongst the codes as to what is required of a parapet wall, as well as when one is required.

FIRE WALLS (AREA SEPARATION WALLS)

The three major building codes have a means of separating a building into two or more buildings, each building subject to its own code requirements and independent of the other building. Each separated area would therefore be subject to its own height and

Figure 7-14 *Parapet walls*

area requirements, its own type of construction requirements, its own fire protection and egress requirements, and so on. The actual separation would be a rated wall with stringent requirements for allowable openings, and for termination against exterior walls and roof-ceiling construction. Depending on the building code one is using, this wall would be referred to as a fire wall or an area separation wall. For the purposes of this section, this book will use the term fire wall to represent a fire wall or an area separation wall. The NFPA 101 Life Safety Code does not utilize fire walls, as fire walls are viewed as property protection elements, and NFPA 101 is a life safety code only.

Fire walls must separate a building completely (Figure 7-15), and they often penetrate exterior wall planes and roof-ceiling planes in order to provide that "complete" separation. Each code provides for a means of building a fire wall which does not completely penetrate exterior walls and roof-ceiling construction, but even in these cases, total separation is provided. These walls allow buildings to do a great deal, including doubling their size in area, changing their occupancy classification, changing their type of construction, etc., so it is extremely important that they provide total separation in order to ensure that the areas on either side of fire walls act as independent buildings.

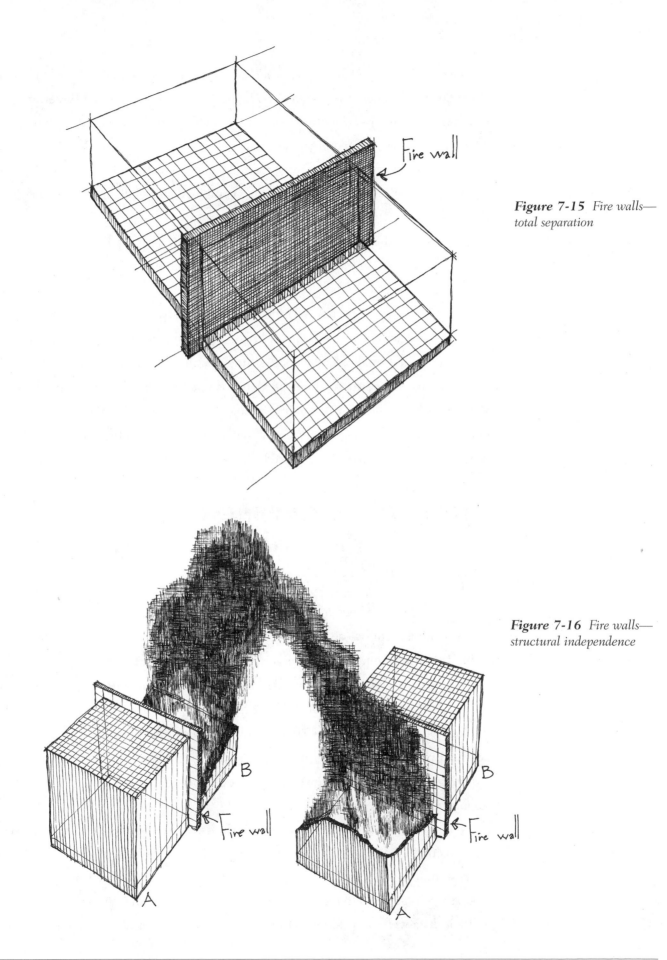

Figure 7-15 Fire walls—
total separation

Figure 7-16 Fire walls—
structural independence

Fire walls are rated either four hours, three hours, or two hours depending on the situation and the code (the Standard Building Code does not consider three-hour rated walls and two-hour rated walls to be fire walls). One also has to look at each individual code to determine the requirements for penetrations of fire walls. Restrictions in the various codes apply to one or more of the following: the nature of the openings, the rating of the openings, and the total allowable combined area of all of the openings in one fire wall.

Some of the model codes have requirements for the structural independence of fire walls (Figure 7-16). In these codes, fire walls are required to remain in place if the construction on one or the other side of the fire wall is destroyed by fire. This is not to say that fire walls cannot be load-bearing walls, but simply that if they are load-bearing walls then the designer should employ break-away connections or some other means of ensuring the structural independence of the fire wall. It is important to understand that the requirement for structural independence is not a requirement that the wall remain standing if both sides of the building are destroyed by fire. The purpose of structural independence is to ensure that the wall maintains its required fire separation after the construction on one side has collapsed.

PROTECTION OF OPENINGS

Protection of Wall Openings

Exterior Walls

When an opening occurs in an exterior wall, there is a potential for spread of fire if it is located within close proximity to, and above or below another opening in that wall. Fire within a building could actually move from one of the openings to one of the other openings. The resulting spread of fire from one opening to another could make it difficult if not impossible for the local fire department to extinguish the fire before the total building was destroyed. Codes address this problem by regulating the exterior finish materials when wall openings are in close proximity to one another or by requiring a horizontal projections, such as ledges, between vertically adjacent windows (Figure 7-17).

When walls are close to the property lines, as we have mentioned earlier the walls must maintain a certain minimum fire rating and the percentage of openings per floor must be minimized in order to reduce the risk of the spread of fire from one building to another. In addition to regulating the percentage of openings in exterior walls based on their distance from exterior walls to property lines, codes also require that some of

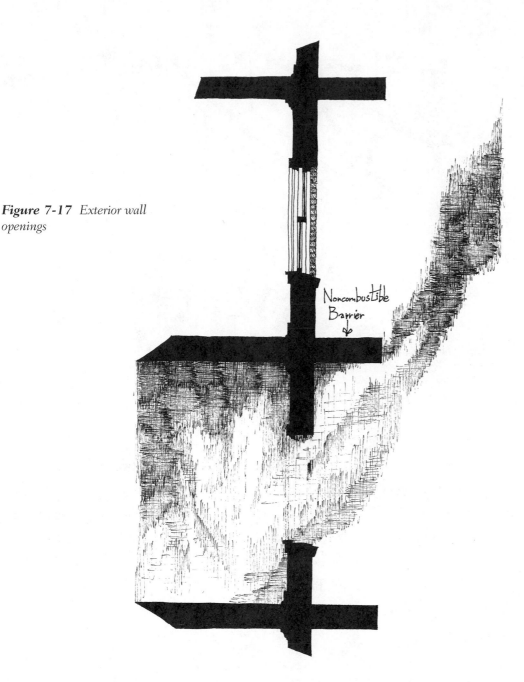

Figure 7-17 *Exterior wall openings*

Noncombustible Barrier

these openings be protected with fire shutters or some other approved opening protectives. Whether or not these opening protectives are required is also based on the distance of exterior wall openings from property lines (Figure 7-18).

Interior Walls

When interior fire-rated partitions are constructed, openings in these partitions reduce the fire separation capabilities of the partitions. Therefore, codes require some means of protecting openings in fire-rated interior partitions. Openings are necessary for the passage of HVAC ducts, plumbing, wiring, and other building services, but

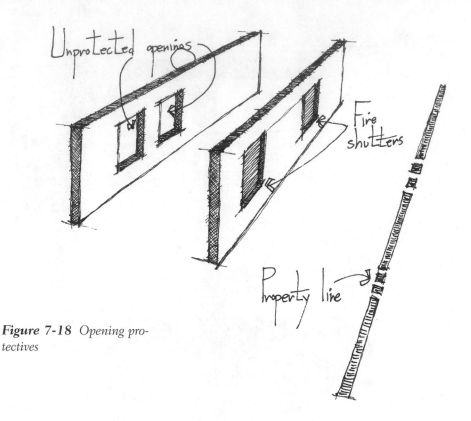

Figure 7-18 *Opening protectives*

openings must be protected to ensure the fire-resistance integrity of rated partitions.

The protection methods prescribed by codes for openings in interior fire-rated partitions serve two purposes; they prevent the passage of smoke and the passage of heat and flames. In most cases, fire dampers are used to close the wall opening at the point where the duct penetrates the wall. The provision of fire dampers often proves to be an expensive proposition. Indeed, fire-rated walls are not always expensive to construct, but those with many fire-dampered duct penetrations can be very expensive to construct.

Approved Types of Fire Windows, Doors, and Shutters

When fire-rated walls require a door opening within them, the doors must also maintain a certain fire resistance rating unless a specific exemption to this requirement is allowed by a code. The door rating in hours is almost always less than the wall rating in hours, because doors are not structural elements. Typical door ratings are three hours, one-and-a-half hours, one hour, three-quarters hour, thirty minutes, or twenty minutes. Walls required to be fire-rated only for structural protection by type of construction requirements may contain unprotected openings if those openings do not reduce the walls' structural fire resistance.

Doors that are required to be rated are tested in accordance with NFPA 252, Fire

Tests of Door Assemblies. NFPA 252 assigns a fire rating to each type of door tested based on each door's performance during the test. Under NFPA 252, doors are subjected to laboratory furnace conditions which are calibrated to approximate an average actual fire condition. The schedule for this calibration of furnace temperatures is known as the "Time-Temperature Curve." This time-temperature curve is used in many different fire tests. After a door has been exposed to varying furnace temperatures, the door is subjected to a hose stream as prescribed by NFPA 252. The door is then assigned a fire rating dependent upon how the door performed after exposure to the furnace and the hose stream (Figure 7-19).

Fire-rated doors are also regulated for the amount of wired glass in a steel frame allowed within the door. For example, doors in stairwells can have no more than one hundred total square inches of wired glass with each glass panel having a maximum height dimension of thirty-three inches and a maximum width dimension of twelve inches. A three-hour door in a four-hour fire wall, on the other hand, is not allowed to have any glass in it. NFPA 252 does not provide for the regulation of glazing in doors, as such glazing requirements are not determined by the results of the test, but rather by the location in which doors are intended to be used.

Figure 7-19 *Typical door label*

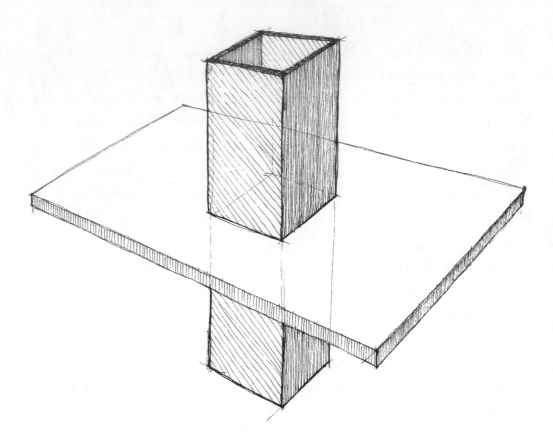

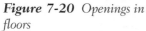

Figure 7-20 *Openings in floors*

Some codes require doors used in stairwells to meet additional requirements which limit the rise of temperature on the unexposed side of the door in the event of a fire, the unexposed side being the side of the door opposite of the fire. These codes require that doors located in stairwells have a temperature developed on the unexposed side which does not exceed 450° Fahrenheit (232°C) at the end of thirty minutes of standard fire test exposure. The temperature rise of stairwell doors is limited because of the potential problems from radiant heat generated by a door if that door is adjacent to the fire area.

Protection of Floor Openings

Whenever floor-ceiling assemblies are penetrated, there is a potential for vertical communication between floors which could result in a chimney effect if a fire were to occur. Smoke and unburned gases escaping through such a vertical opening could prove to be fatal to the occupants of the uppermost communicating level even though the fire may actually be on the lowest of the communicating levels. Fire can also move through any available vertical openings, no matter how small the openings are, as fire will seek oxygen. It is necessary, therefore, to provide some protection of floor openings in order to prevent vertical communication between floors (Figure 7-20). Typical examples of penetrations of floor-ceiling assemblies include but are not limited to stairwells, atriums, plumbing penetrations, penetrations for electrical wiring, and duct penetrations. Each one of these types of floor-ceiling penetrations are treated differently by codes, but all of these penetrations are regulated by them.

Shaft Enclosures

Many penetrations of floor-ceiling assemblies, such as exit stairwells and elevators, are required by codes to be contained in vertical shafts. Vertical shafts provide a means to protect the inhabitants of a building from the potential danger of fire and smoke moving from floor to floor should a fire occur. The concept of a vertical shaft is to create a container-like element which does not allow the passage of smoke into the shaft or out of the shaft.

Vertical shafts are formed by partitions which run from floor to floor, as well as by horizontal planes formed by floor-ceiling assemblies and roof-ceiling assemblies (Figure 7-21). Unlike other rated partitions, shaft partitions must go from floor to floor or from floor to roof and cannot terminate against the ceiling surface of an equivalently rated floor-ceiling or roof-ceiling assembly. The termination of these partitions must be smoke-tight. This creates a situation where there are no interstitial spaces communicating with a vertical shaft. Interstitial spaces are the spaces between the ceilings and

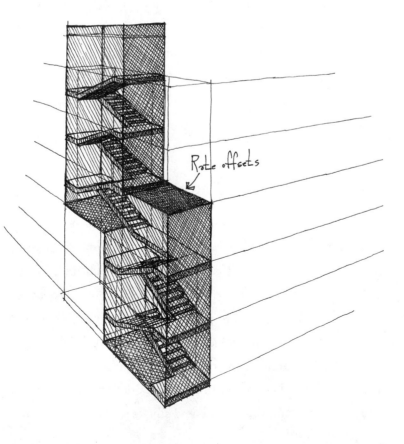

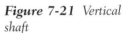

Figure 7-21 *Vertical shaft*

the floors of floor-ceiling assemblies and the spaces between the ceilings and the roofs of roof-ceiling assemblies. These interstitial spaces can potentially form passageways that allow smoke to travel throughout buildings, and therefore their separation from vertical shafts is mandatory for life safety.

Whenever a vertical shaft does not terminate above the roof of a building, the vertical shaft must have its own roof-ceiling assembly which has the same rating as the partitions forming the walls of the vertical shaft. Whenever a vertical shaft does not terminate at the bottom of a building or a structure, the vertical shaft must have its own floor-ceiling assembly which has the same rating as the partitions forming the walls of the vertical shaft. Offsets in a vertical shaft must also be rated equivalently to the shaft's vertical partitions. This total separation of shafts from other spaces maintains the desired "separate container" effect.

Special Provisions for Refuse and Laundry Chutes

Refuse and laundry chutes pose potential fire-related problems in that they are vertical shafts which may allow the passage of flames and smoke to more than one level of a building. They also pose some fire risk by terminating in rooms that receive the refuse or laundry emitted from the shaft. This refuse or laundry represents potential fire loading. Codes require protection of the openings of refuse and laundry chutes in order to maintain their effectiveness as separated shafts. Codes also establish requirements governing the separation of refuse and laundry chute termination rooms, so that there is positive separation between these fire loaded shaft areas and other areas of buildings. As a final guard against flame passage through refuse or laundry chutes they are required to contain some automatic sprinkler protection (Figure 7-22).

Fireblocking and Draftstopping

The interstitial spaces between wall surfaces and between ceilings and the floors or roofs above act as hidden pathways that can allow the passage of fire and smoke without anyone's knowledge that a fire has even occurred. Fireblocking and draftstopping are means of containing both fire and smoke, respectively, within interstitial spaces. Fireblocking is used to prevent the communication of vertical interstitial wall spaces with horizontal interstitial floor-ceiling or roof-ceiling spaces. Draftstopping is used to compartmentalize interstitial floor-ceiling, roof-ceiling, or cove spaces when they are constructed of combustible construction, thus inhibiting the buildup of drafts that can aid the rapid travel of fire and smoke.

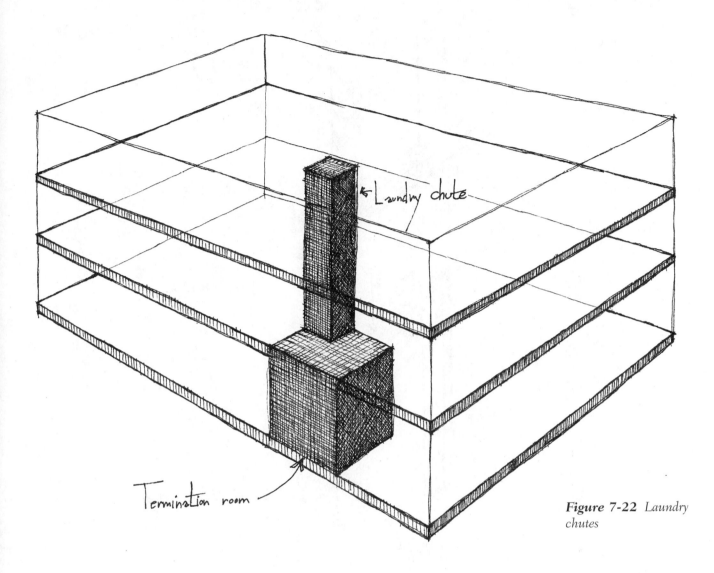

Laundry chute

Termination room

Figure 7-22 *Laundry chutes*

Fireblocking is used at the junction of partition assemblies and floor-ceiling and roof-ceiling assemblies to separate the vertical interstitial spaces formed by the studs within the partitions from the horizontal interstitial spaces formed by floor joists or roof trusses. Fireblocking usually consists of two inch nominal thickness lumber. If a fire were to start in a wall, fireblocking would prevent the passage of that fire to horizontal interstitial spaces or even other vertical interstitial spaces. A lack of fireblocking would create a situation where a fire could move throughout the structure of a building, and become very involved before anyone knew of the fire's existence (Figure 7-23).

Draftstopping is used in closed attic and floor spaces of combustible construction, and interstitial cove spaces created by exterior trim of combustible construction and attached to a building. Draftstopping is often created with gypsum board or plywood. Draftstopping compartmentalizes these spaces to help prevent the rapid passage of fire and smoke due to draft buildup. This is achieved by dividing the spaces into small

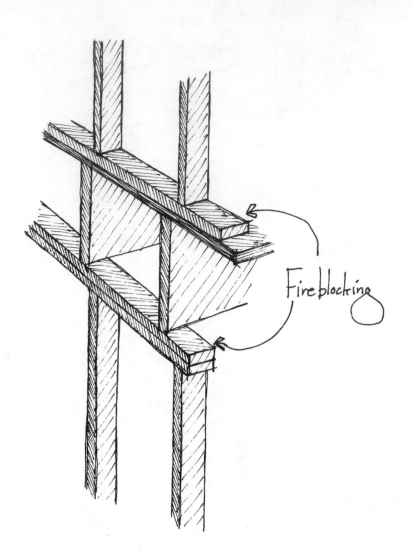

Figure 7-23 *Fireblocking*

enough areas so that it is unlikely that a draft will cause the fire to spread. The actual detailed requirements for draftstopping are usually covered in the portions of codes which deal with combustible framing construction (Figure 7-24).

Penetrations of Fire-Resistant Assemblies

When rated assemblies are penetrated with pipes, tubes, conduits, wires, cables, and vents, the fire resistance integrity of the rated assemblies is potentially impeded. Therefore, it is necessary to protect such penetrations in a proper manner so that the rated assemblies which are penetrated can continue to resist fire and smoke as they were initially designed to do. There are several methods available for protecting penetrations of rated assemblies. One can protect these penetrations by the use of vertical shafts, listed dampers in ducts, tested and approved through penetration firestop systems, and by protecting the annular space around the penetrating item in an approved manner. Whenever building elements such as cabinets, bathroom and kitchen compo-

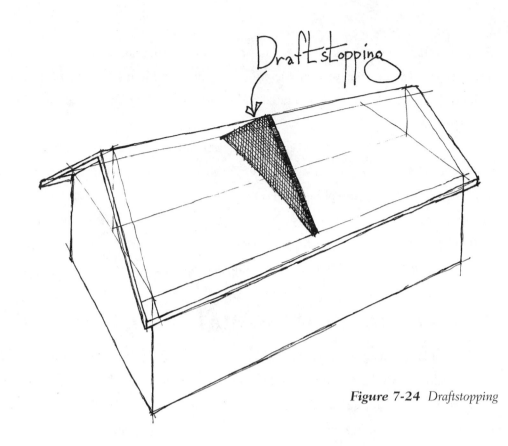

Figure 7-24 *Draftstopping*

nents, lighting fixtures, plumbing fixtures, and other fixtures are attached to rated construction assemblies, they must be installed so that the fire resistance of the rated assembly is not reduced.

COMBUSTIBLES IN FIRE-RATED ASSEMBLIES AND CONCEALED SPACES

When fire-rated assemblies are tested, the results of the tests are applicable only to the products included in the assemblies at the time of the tests for fire resistance. When combustible products are added to a fire-rated assembly, these products can affect the performance of the rated assembly, and should not be introduced unless they were specifically tested as part of the listed fire-rated assembly. Combustible products can propagate their own flame because of the radiant heat load encountered when they are located in a partition subjected to a fire. Also, if combustible products penetrate fire-rated assemblies, the resulting void created by the loss of the combustible products to combustion would create weak points in the rated assemblies. Of course, if the manufacturer of a combustible product can show proof through other tests that the inclusion of their particular product within a fire-rated assembly will not adversely affect the performance of that assembly, then it would be acceptable to use that manufacturer's product if approved by the code official. Occasionally, combustible materials and products are allowed by codes to be placed in rated assemblies depending on the building's type of construction.

Similarly, combustibles located in plenums and in concealed spaces of noncombustible types of construction provide a potential weakness that exceeds the limitations of the design of plenums and of buildings of noncombustible types of construction. Fire adjacent to these hidden combustibles can cause them to ignite, thus creating hidden fires that are not easily discovered or controlled. Codes stipulate when and where combustible materials can be utilized in concealed spaces.

THERMAL INSULATING MATERIALS

Thermal insulating materials may prove to be hazardous as they may be combustible or able to produce highly toxic smoke as a product of combustion. Therefore codes and standards intentionally regulate thermal insulating materials. In addition to thermal insulating materials' having to meet certain flamespread ratings and smoke developed ratings, codes may also require that thermal insulating materials be separated from usable spaces by other construction materials depending on where the insulation is applied. One should be careful when installing thermal insulating materials within fire-rated assemblies, as the insulation may trap heat which could cause the fire rated assembly to fail prematurely. If one wishes to install thermal insulating materials within a fire-rated assembly, then one should look for a listed assembly that includes insulation in its listing. Because of the importance of thermal insulating materials, codes try to establish safe means for incorporating their use.

APPROVED FIRE-RATED ASSEMBLIES
Testing and Listing

When construction assemblies are required to be fire rated, they are tested for fire resistance and then listed in a fire resistance directory (see Figure 7-1). The listing will prescribe how the assemblies must be constructed in order to maintain their fire resistance rating, and the listing will also detail any limitations which could adversely affect the fire resistance rating of the construction assembly. In many codes, rated assemblies are listed in accordance with ASTM E119, Test Methods for Fire Tests of Building Construction and Materials published by the American Society for Testing and

Materials. It is important to understand that there are many different standards organizations, and that often several standards organizations will have a standard which is concerned with the same subject area. For example, the National Fire Protection Association and the International Conference of Building Officials each have standards which are similar to ASTM E119. Designers should use the standards referenced by the particular codes that the designer is following.

One of the biggest headaches that I know of in architecture, construction, and inspection is trying to find assemblies which meet the rating requirements of building codes. There are not many fire resistance directories available, and many of them are difficult to use, or reference archaic materials for the construction of fire-rated assemblies. Those directories that are easier to use tend not to be as thorough as the directories which are more difficult to use. Any fire resistance directory published by a recognized testing organization should be acceptable for use. If a manufacturer has a product for a fire-rated assembly tested by a recognized testing organization in accordance with a fire resistance test such as ASTM E119, the assembly will be listed in a fire resistance directory if it passes the test. A designer could then cite the listed assembly in his or her construction documents, and the assembly would be constructed in accordance with its listing. The code official would then inspect to ensure the construction of the assembly was indeed carried out as called for in its listing.

Designers frequently ask me how they can gain a fire resistance rating from a particular assembly which has an aesthetic quality they desire. Unfortunately, the answer is usually that their particular assembly is not a listed fire-resistant assembly. This answer is often greeted with a response somewhat like, "Well, they don't give you many options within these fire resistance directories." I suppose the major problem here is that there just are not that many materials and assemblies that are fire-resistant. Generally these materials are going to be cementitious, ceramic, or masonry products. Even gypsum board is a cementitious product, as it utilizes gypsum to provide its fire resistance. Gypsum retains water in its manufacturing process and when exposed to fire releases this water slowly thus enabling it to provide proper fire resistance. Brick, concrete block, and certain tiles are other very common fire resistance materials. The options for determining the fire resistance of assemblies include utilizing the many available listings of recognized testing organizations or using calculated fire resistance.

When using fire resistance directories, designers should become familiar with the directories' nomenclature. For example, the term "proprietary" indicates a specific product from a specific manufacturer, and supposed equivalent products by other manufacturers should not be substituted. The use of another manufacturer's product would void the listing of the assembly.

Calculated Fire Resistance

Some codes employ the concept of calculated fire resistance for creating fire-rated assemblies. Calculated fire resistance is a method of assigning ratings to different building products and assembling these products together to achieve a particular rating. This is a conservative method which could prove to be very costly within a building, and should really be used in most cases only as a last resort.

To illustrate what I mean by conservative, a typical calculated fire resistance table would assign a value of 40 minutes of fire exposure to a ⅝ inch type X gypsum wall board product. The same calculated fire resistance table might assign 20 minutes in value to wood studs at 16 inches on center. Therefore if one put ⅝ inch type X gypsum board on each side of wood studs at 16 inches on center, one would receive one-hour fire rating (40 minutes plus 20 minutes) for each side of the wall assembly (Figure 7-25a). One would not add 40 minutes plus 20 minutes plus 40 minutes, because once the studs are gone the wall is gone, as the gypsum board requires the studs for support. Most fire resistance directories list this assembly and assign a one-

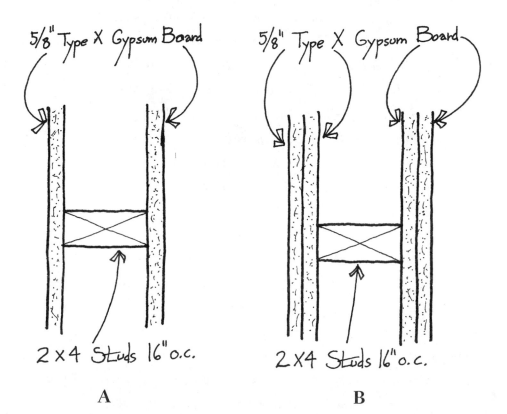

Figures 7-25a and b
Calculated fire resistance.
Courtesy of Gypsum
Association, Washington, DC

hour fire rating to it. If one went to most fire resistance directories and researched a wall constructed of two layers of ⅝ inch type X gypsum board on each side of wood studs at 16 inches on center, one would inevitably find that the wall was listed as a two-hour rated wall. However, using calculated fire resistance, the same assembly would net 40 minutes plus 40 minutes plus 20 minutes for one hour and 40 minutes, which would garner one no more than a one-and-a-half hour rating (Figure 7-25b). Using calculated fire resistance would require one to have three layers of type X ⅝ inch gypsum board on each side of wood studs at 16 inches on center in order to achieve at least two hours of rating. A building utilizing calculated fire resistance instead of a fire resistance directory would, in this case, use 50 percent more gypsum board in all two-hour walls. Of course, this example is somewhat ludicrous, because it is very easy to find this two-hour fire-rated assembly within fire resistance directories; however, this example proves my point that in many cases calculated fire resistance can be very restrictive. There is a need to be extremely conservative when using the calculated fire resistance method of adding materials together in order to create fire-rated assemblies because the nature and spacing of fasteners is not controlled as in fire resistance directories.

Existing Buildings

Probably one of the greatest sources of consternation for designers that I know of is trying to identify the fire resistance of construction assemblies within existing buildings. The identifying of the ratings for existing roof-ceiling assemblies, floor-ceiling assemblies, column assemblies, beam assemblies, or wall assemblies should be performed on site with the code official. I have utilized this partnership method before when working on the renovation of an historical building for a new use. In the case of that building, the code official walked through the building with me and helped me determine the type of construction of the building, as well as the fire resistance of certain wall assemblies. Basically, the code official looked at certain assemblies and stated that they were extremely similar to what he had seen in other buildings that were constructed with listed fire ratings. He said that he would consider the walls in my building to be equivalent in fire rating to the walls in those other buildings. This helped us determine the type of construction of the historical building so that we could progress with the building design.

This building was a mercantile type building with two-foot thick masonry walls and heavy timber construction throughout the interior. It was very easy to classify this building for type of construction; however, it is not always so easy to identify the fire resistance of construction assemblies within an existing building. Some documents available assign ratings to historical building assemblies. One such document is published by the Historical American Building Survey (HABS). Some model code organizations also have existing building codes that publish some of these historical fire-rated assemblies.

Interior Finishes

Chapter 8 discusses interior finishes and what codes have to say about testing those finishes. The discussion includes wall finishes, floor finishes, and ceiling finishes. The use of foam plastics as trim is also discussed.

Interior finishes can pose a great hazard in a fire situation by contributing to the spread of fire as well as contributing to the generation of toxic smoke. Codes therefore restrict the surface burning characteristics and the smoke development characteristics of interior finishes. These restrictions vary based on the occupancy classification of the building. Codes establish different means of restricting interior finishes depending on whether the interior finish in question is attached to a vertical surface such as a partition, or attached to a horizontal surface such as a floor or ceiling. Codes intentionally regulate finishes within buildings. Burning buildings often trap smoke and fire inside, and therefore the production of flame and smoke must be minimized in order to promote life safety for the building occupants (Figure 8-1).

WALL FINISHES

Two characteristics of interior wall finishes concern codes officials. One of these characteristics is the flame spread of the finish; that is, how quickly the flame moves across the finish and spreads throughout the fire area. The other concern is the smoke developed rating. A smoke-developed rating is assigned to a material's finish based on the density of smoke produced by the interior finish in a fire situation.

Wall finishes are divided into three classifications, a Class A finish with a flame spread rating of zero to 25, a Class B finish with a flame spread rating of 26 to 75, and a Class C finish with a flame spread rating of 76 to 200. Codes reference tests to deter-

Figure 8-1 Smoke trapped inside

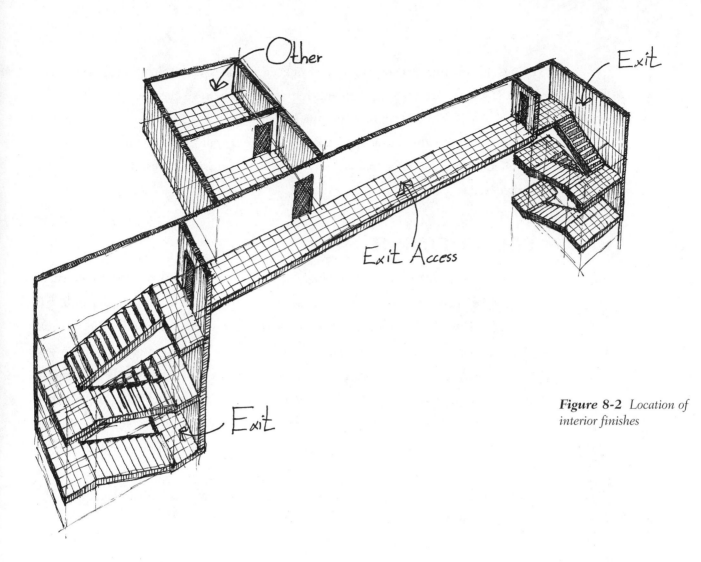

Figure 8-2 *Location of interior finishes*

mine the surface burning characteristics of materials. These tests measure the surface burning characteristics of building materials when the materials are installed in a furnace and a flame is applied to their finish. As the flame moves across the material, technicians chart the distance the flame travels over time. This movement of flame over time is compared with the movement of flame over time of certain materials such as gypsum which is given a flame spread rating of zero, and oak which is given a flame spread rating of one hundred. Depending on how quickly the flame moves across the finish of the material, a flame spread classification is assigned to the material. It should be noted that all interior wall finishes allowed within buildings have a smoke-developed rating of 450 or less whether they are Class A materials, Class B materials, or Class C materials. Any wall material with a flame spread rating greater than 200 (exceeding a Class C finish rating) is not permitted by codes for use within buildings.

Interior wall finish restrictions vary according to the occupancy classification of the area in question and according to whether the building is sprinklered or not. Interior wall finish restrictions also vary as a function of the type of space where the finish occurs, be it within exit spaces, within exit access spaces, or within other spaces (Figure 8-2). The most stringent requirements for interior wall finish classifications occur within exit spaces, the next most stringent occur within exit access spaces, and the least stringent occur within other spaces. More stringent wall finish classifications are also required within buildings that are unsprinklered than within those buildings that are sprinklered.

FLOOR FINISH

Codes often restrict the use of combustible flooring within noncombustible construction, while specifying how these floor surfaces can be used within combustible construction. The floor finish that usually causes the most concern for code officials is carpet. Codes reference nationally recognized standards for testing carpet. These tests help ensure that carpet can withstand a certain amount of radiant heat before igniting, and that carpet will therefore help maintain a safe environment within the buildings where it is used. Neither the designer nor the contractor is responsible for testing carpet, but they should verify that any carpet they use has been properly tested. The test results will be listed on the label applied to the carpet. If a carpet manufacturer has paid for these tests, one can be well assured that the manufacturer will adequately publish the results of the tests.

ACOUSTICAL CEILING SYSTEMS

When acoustical ceiling systems are part of a fire-resistant assembly, these systems must be installed in accordance with the listing for the assembly. Some precaution must be taken to ensure that these panels stay in place. Codes usually require these panels to remain in place with a certain minimal upward force applied to the panel. This can be achieved in the design of the panel, or by providing some sort of wire backing which holds the panel in place. If a ceiling panel dislocates from its framing then the fire-resistant assembly is voided in that area.

CARPET ON WALLS AND CEILINGS

Code officials are concerned about the use of carpet on walls and ceilings. Fires burns up and out, and therefore wall and ceiling finishes are subjected to a more extreme fire exposure than are floor finishes. When a finish material, such as carpet, is installed on a wall or a ceiling, the material must meet all applicable requirements within codes for wall finishes or ceiling finishes, respectively. Therefore, when carpet is used on walls the flame spread rating and the smoke-developed rating of that carpet must be taken into account, regardless of the fact that carpet is often considered a floor finish. When a designer creates a situation in which carpet is applied to walls, that designer will need to verify that the carpet has been tested and listed in accordance with the applicable standards referenced by the codes he or she is following.

FOAM PLASTICS

Foam plastics are not allowed to be used as interior finishes with some certain exceptions for trim items such as picture molds, chair rails, baseboards, hand rails, ceiling bins, beams, door trim, and window trim. In order to be used in construction these trim items must be constructed of a foam of a density and thickness allowed by codes. Foam plastics are potentially hazardous because they may be highly combustible and they may produce very toxic smoke. Therefore, codes usually require foam plastics to be concealed behind other building materials. The exceptions for trim recognize that there are many foam plastic products, which if used in small amounts and constructed of the proper density and thickness, can be used safely within buildings.

CHAPTER 9

Fire Protection Systems

*C*hapter 9 discusses what building codes have to say about automatic sprinkler protection, standpipes, and fire alarms. The discussion includes various classifications of and typical code requirements for these different types of fire protection systems.

Automatic sprinkler protection is used to control fires when they occur within buildings or structures. Fire alarm systems serve the purpose of providing early warning for the occupants of a building when a fire occurs. Fire officials use standpipes to help in fighting fires within buildings.

SPRINKLERS

Sprinkler systems provide outstanding life safety protection for the occupants of buildings. They are very efficient and usually extinguish a fire before a fire ever becomes life threatening. Unfortunately, sprinkler systems are often expensive to install. Codes try to encourage the use of sprinkler systems by providing substantial tradeoffs for the incorporation of these systems into building design and construction. The three major building codes allow larger areas and larger heights in feet for buildings equipped with automatic sprinkler protection (Figure 9-1). All four major codes including the NFPA 101 Life Safety Code allow greater heights in stories for buildings equipped with automatic sprinkler protection. There are many other exceptions within codes which provide for more flexible design regulation based on the provision of automatic sprinkler protection. There are also certain combinations of occupancy classifications and types of construction which must be provided with automatic sprinkler protection no matter what their area and their height.

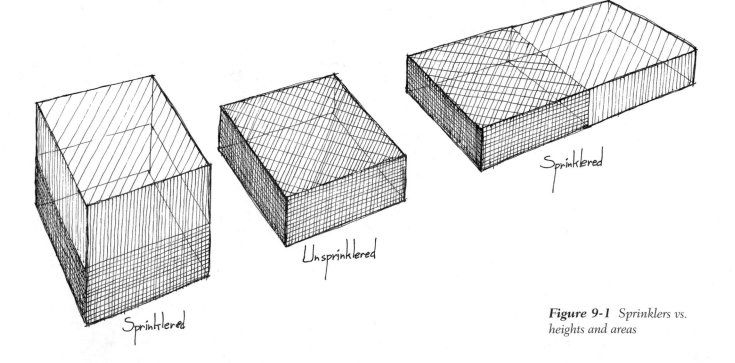

Figure 9-1 Sprinklers vs. heights and areas

There are different types of sprinkler systems and the proper system must be chosen for the particular design situation. For example, one would not install a residential sprinkler system designed for one- and two-family dwellings within a commercial building. There are certain building uses where the use of water will exacerbate a harmful fire situation rather than alleviate it, so sprinkler systems which utilize chemicals for fire suppression are used instead of those systems which utilize water. One should always use the most appropriate sprinkler system for the given situation.

STANDPIPES

Standpipes provide water to different areas of buildings in order for fire officials or others to fight the fire within these buildings. Based on the classification of the standpipe system, standpipes may be designed for use by fire officials or by trained building personnel. NFPA 14, Standard for the Installation of Standpipe and Hose Systems, lists three classifications of standpipes as follows:

Class 1 systems, 2½-inch hose connections to supply water for use by fire departments and those trained in handling heavy fire streams,

Class 2 systems, 1½-inch hose stations to supply water for use primarily by building occupants or by fire department during initial response, and

Class 3 systems, 1½-inch hose stations to supply water for use by building occupants and 2½-inch hose connections to supply a larger volume of water for use by fire departments and those trained in handling heavy fire streams. (National Fire Protection Association, 1996).

One should consult NFPA Standard 14 in order acquaint oneself with the specific requirements for and the exceptions to each of these standpipe classifications. Standpipes are either wet or dry systems. Wet standpipes have water pressure maintained at all times. Dry standpipes admit water into their system upon activation of the system. Some dry standpipes automatically admit water when a hose valve is opened. Other dry standpipes admit water upon the activation of remote control devices located at each of the hose stations. Standpipes are required in those buildings where code officials have particular concerns about the fighting of fires (Figure 9-2). For example, they are required in certain multistory buildings, in covered malls, and on the sides of stages that are of a certain square footage in area.

Codes specify the type of standpipes that should be used in any given situation, which classification of standpipes should be used, whether they should be dry or wet

Figure 9-2 *Photo of standpipe*

systems, and if they are dry systems, which types of dry systems should be used. Codes specify the location for hose connections. There are usually requirements for the use of standpipes during construction. Often standpipes are required during construction to be operable within one floor of the highest point of construction which has secured decking or flooring. Codes also require adequate water supply for standpipes. If an inadequate water supply is provided for a standpipe system, then obviously the standpipe cannot do the task which it has been designed to do. Usually standpipes are required to have some sort of link with an alarm system which will be triggered upon the opening of a standpipe valve.

ALARMS

There are two principal types of fire alarms—manual fire alarm systems and automatic fire detection. Manual fire alarm systems involve a pull station or many pull stations throughout buildings in which people activate the alarms by manually pulling the fire alarm controls. Automatic fire detection systems are smoke detectors. Both of these systems serve the purpose of alerting the occupants of a building when a fire situation occurs, and in many cases these systems also alert local fire personnel.

Manual fire alarm systems are required to be built in accordance with NFPA 72, Installation, Maintenance and Use of Protective Signaling Systems and NFPA 72E, Automatic Fire Detectors. Codes require manual fire alarm pull stations within different occupancies when the presence of certain potentially hazardous circumstances

Figure 9-3 *Fire alarm*

exist. Often the circumstances that cause concern are related to the occupant load or to the height of the building in stories above the level of exit discharge. Codes also require that manual fire alarm systems be tested after their installation.

Automatic fire detection systems should be installed in accordance with NFPA 74, Household Fire Warning Equipment. If the smoke detectors are connected to a fire protective signaling alarm system, they are required to be installed also in accordance with NFPA 72 and 72E. Most of us are fairly familiar with smoke detectors, as they have become a very common household item. They are required to be within any dwelling unit by codes.

When smoke detectors first started to be used with some frequency, it was not uncommon for people to install them in kitchens, thinking perhaps that kitchens were the most likely places for fires to start. One of the main purposes of smoke detectors is to wake building occupants when fires occur; therefore, smoke detectors are placed outside of sleeping areas in order to provide such a "wake-up call." If there are changes of levels within a residence smoke detectors should be placed at those changes of levels. The proper location of smoke detectors is detailed in their listings, which are often found on the smoke detectors themselves.

Smoke detectors can be battery operated or hard-wired into an electrical system, or both. Codes stipulate where each type of smoke detector is required or permitted. Some code officials prefer hard-wired detectors, so that the detectors will have no batteries capable of losing power. Other code officials argue that hard-wired detectors are deactivated by power failures and therefore that battery operated detectors should be used.

Accessibility concerns need to be considered when designing and installing fire alarm systems. Fire alarm pull stations need to be located within accessible reach for people with physical disabilities. If the alarm projects too far from the wall, accessibility standards require that the alarm be located at a height where it will not harm those with limited or no vision (Figure 9-3). When manual fire alarms are provided, buildings should have both audible and visible signals so that all of the building occupants will be alerted to the fire emergency even if they are hard of hearing or deaf. The Americans with Disabilities Act requires a visible signal of 75 candela, a signal which is much more powerful than the signal required by many codes in the past.

Means of Egress

Chapter 10 discusses means of egress. The chapter begins with the concepts used to design an egress scheme (minimum occupant load, minimum number of exits, capacity of exits, and arrangement of exits), and then moves on to a discussion about the number of people that an egress scheme can actually accommodate (maximum occupant content). The chapter follows with a discussion of individual egress components, and the requirements for their design.

Means of egress provisions in building codes are essential for the protection of lives from fire and other emergencies. Means of egress is the means by which people exit from buildings in the event of an emergency, or in some buildings the means by which people exit to safer portions of the buildings in the event of an emergency (Figure 10-1). Means of egress is comprised of exit access, exits, and public way. An exit access leads to an exit which in turn leads to a public way. Means of egress is a continuous and unobstructed path, and is not allowed to traverse through adjacent tenant spaces, kitchens, closets, rest rooms, or other similar areas (depending on the code being applied).

Public ways are the ultimate destination of the means of egress system when exiting people from a building. A public way is an outdoor area, separate from the building and safe from a fire or other emergency condition within the building. Once one has exited to the public way, one should be considered as having reached a "safe haven."

Exits are comprised of exit doors, exit stairways, horizontal exits, and exit passageways. Exits lead to a public way. Enclosed exits such as exit stairways and exit passageways, are protected paths which are used only for the purposes of exiting, and which lead directly to a public way (with few exceptions) once they are entered. Indeed one is considered to be very safe once one has entered an exit.

Exit access is comprised of all the spaces leading to an exit. Exit access may or may not be protected. Exit access is often a corridor, but sometimes exit access is an intervening room or space between a room and an exit, such as a reception space or an open office space (Figure 10-2). Exit access corridors are usually constructed of one-hour fire-resistant construction, but many codes allow them to be nonrated in certain occupancies when automatic sprinkler protection is provided.

In order to design a proper egress scheme for a building, a designer must first determine the minimum occupant load of the building, that is the number of people likely to use the building. The designer must then determine the proper number of exits and the minimum width of the exits based on the minimum occupant load. Finally, the exits must be arranged to minimize the possibility that any two exits will be blocked by a single emergency condition, and so that they are within certain maximum travel distances of any area of the building.

OCCUPANT LOAD

The first step in designing a proper egress scheme for a building involves the determination of how many people will actually be using the building, and therefore how many

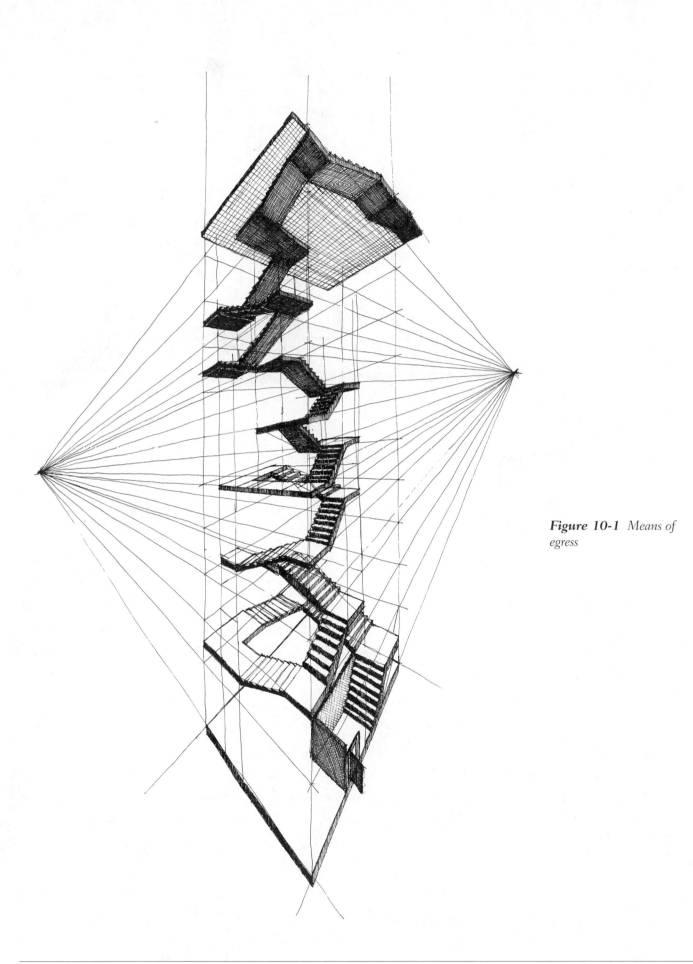

Figure 10-1 *Means of egress*

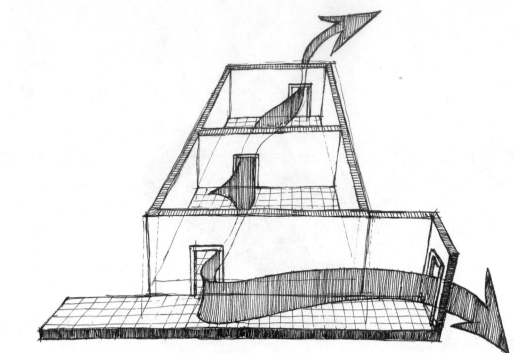

Figure 10-2 *Exit access*

people it will be necessary to egress in the event of an emergency. This number is arrived at by using the minimum occupant load factors listed in codes, by querying the building owner as to how a building or space within a building will be used, and by employing any special knowledge one has as to how similar buildings or spaces are usually used. The minimum occupant load is the number of people for which the designer must provide exits. It is a design load which must not be reduced, even if a client feels that it is an excessive load.

Codes usually express minimum occupant loads in number of net square feet per person or in number of gross square feet per person. Net square footage is the area of a building or space deducting ancillary spaces such as corridors, toilet rooms, storage rooms, mechanical rooms, and so on. Gross square footage is the area of a building inclusive of all interior spaces. Net square footage helps determine the actual probable population of a given space based on the use of that space, whereas gross square footage helps to determine a reasonable average occupant load within a building type that may vary somewhat based on the specific utilization of that building type. Often, it is necessary for a designer to use both net square foot factors and gross square foot factors together when determining the minimum occupant design load for a particular building (Figure 10-3).

It is not unusual for the designer's client to possess some special knowledge of how a space will be used, the use of which will increase the minimum occupant load for that

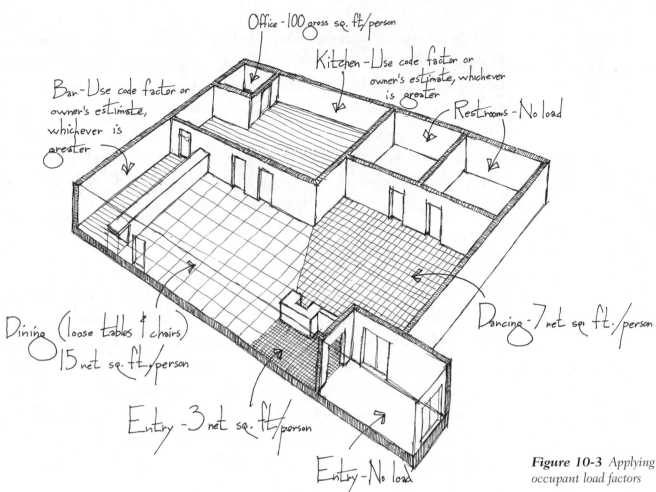

Office - 100 gross sq. ft/person

Kitchen - Use code factor or owner's estimate, whichever is greater

Bar - Use code factor or owner's estimate, whichever is greater

Restrooms - No load

Dining (loose tables & chairs) 15 net sq. ft/person

Dancing - 7 net sq. ft/person

Entry - 3 net sq. ft/person

Entry - No load

Figure 10-3 *Applying occupant load factors*

space. Remember that the designer cannot allow the minimum occupant load factors within codes to be reduced, but rather the designer can add to those loads based on the knowledge of how the space will be used. It is also not unusual for an occupant load to be increased by a code official because of that code official's personal belief that the building or space in question will be used by greater numbers of people than codes' minimum occupant load factors might otherwise suggest. A good example of this variation in required minimum occupant load by a code official would be that of a high school gymnasium designed for basketball and volleyball with no spectator seating. The code official might suspect that the gymnasium will be used for dances or perhaps a graduation ceremony, and therefore the code official might require that the gymnasium's minimum occupant load be based on the design factors for assembly spaces even though no spectators will witness the games played there. The eventual administrators of the school are not likely to know that it would be a code violation to use the gymnasium as an assembly space, thus leading them to believe that using the gymnasium as a dance hall or a graduation hall is quite appropriate and safe.

Because minimum occupant load is so subject to interpretation, the designer should meet with a code official early in the design process in order to determine what the code official's interpretations will be concerning minimum occupant loads. It would be a very difficult situation if a designer submitted a set of construction documents to a code official for plans review only to find that the code official's interpretations of the applicable minimum occupant load factors were so different from the designer's interpretations that the building, for all practical purposes, had to be redesigned. Minimum occupant load factors can greatly affect the design of a building.

NUMBER OF EXITS

Once a designer has determined the number of people for which he or she is designing an egress scheme, the designer must determine the minimum number of exits and means of egress that must be incorporated into the scheme. It is a fundamental rule of the four major codes that a building's occupants will have a choice of at least two different directions of travel when egressing a building or space because of a fire or other emergency (Figure 10-4). This helps ensure that if one exit or means of egress is blocked by an emergency condition, another exit or means of egress in a separate location will remain functional. As the population of a building or space increases, the num-

Figure 10-4 *Two directions of travel*

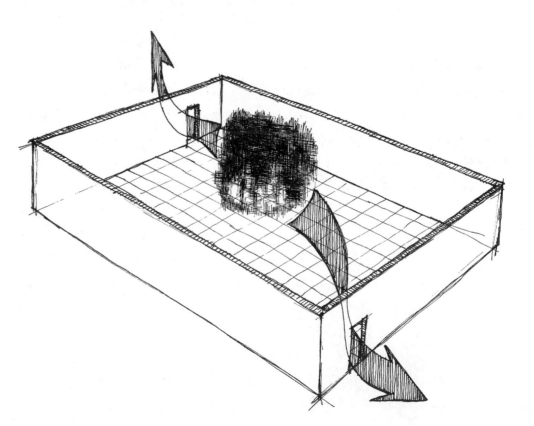

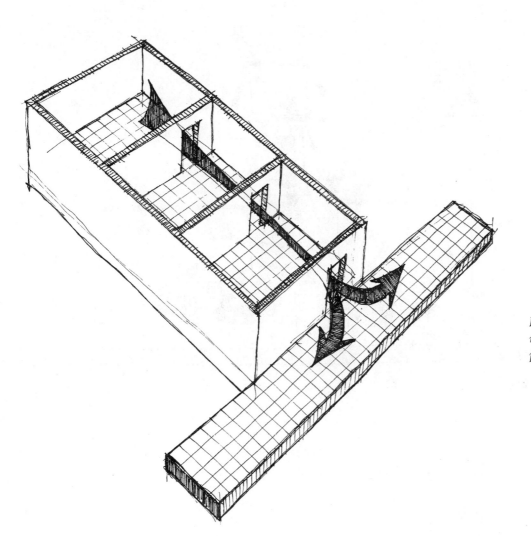

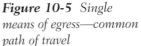

Figure 10-5 *Single means of egress—common path of travel*

ber of required exits or means of egress may increase. A large population may mandate three or even four separate routes out of a building or space.

There are exceptions in codes to the requirement for at least two different routes from a building or space in the event of an emergency. Many smaller spaces or tenant suites are required to have only one means of egress, as they are common paths to travel (Figure 10-5). Common paths of travel and dead-end spaces (Figure 10-6) are spaces with only a single direction of travel towards an exit, and they are allowable by codes as long as their lengths are not too great. Codes often permit a single means of egress for buildings which are considered safe because of their occupancy classification, their size, and the number of occupants they contain. One can also find single means of egress requirements in codes for mezzanines when the mezzanines meet certain strictly defined design parameters (Figure 10-7).

A good example of a code's allowing a single means of egress for a building based on that building's occupancy classification and safe design parameters can be found in the Standard Building Code:

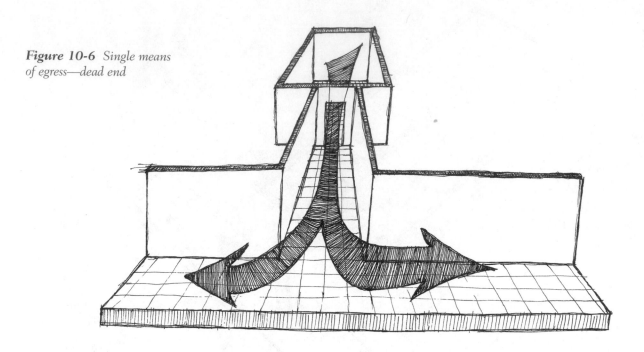

Figure 10-6 *Single means of egress—dead end*

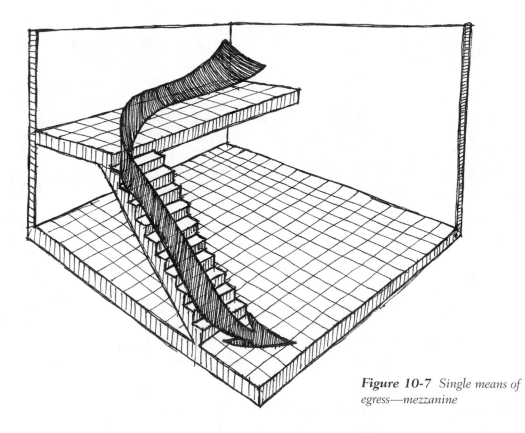

Figure 10-7 *Single means of egress—mezzanine*

A single exit is permitted in Group B occupancies when meeting the following conditions:

1.   Maximum two stories in height.

2.   Each floor area served by that exit does not exceed 3,500 sq. ft (325 m²).

3.   There are no more than 40 persons above the street floor as determined by Table 1003.1.

4.   The maximum distance of travel to the exit does not exceed 75 ft (23m). (Southern Building Code Congress International, Inc. 1996)

First, the Standard Building Code is permitting a single exit in this case because the building is of a low hazard occupancy classification—business. Second, the Standard Building Code is permitting a single exit, because the design parameters of the building do not pose a significant risk (Figure 10-8). The building is not tall; the building is not great in area; there are not many people using the building; and those people do not have to walk very far in order to egress the building. Whether or not this combination of occupancy classification and safe design parameters warrants the use of only a single means of egress is debatable, but the code officials who promulgate the Standard Building Code seem to feel that a single exit provides sufficient egress in this case.

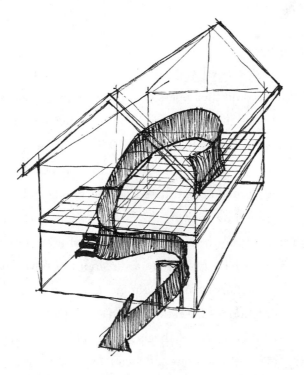

Figure 10-8 *Single means of egress—building*

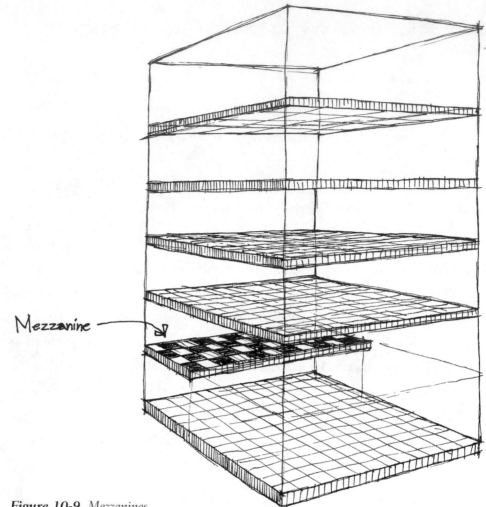

Mezzanine

Figure 10-9 *Mezzanines*

As discussed in Chapter 5, mezzanines are intermediate floors, which because of their size and their openness to the rooms or spaces in which they are located, are not counted as allowable stories of height when considering the maximum allowable height in stories of buildings (Figure 10-9). These mezzanines are often allowed by codes to have a single means of egress if they meet certain parameters as defined by codes. These parameters are based on the number of people occupying the mezzanine (as determined by applying the factors of minimum occupant load), as well as the travel distance from the most remote point of a mezzanine to a place where the mezzanine occupants have two different directions of travel towards an exit. In the case of a single set of stairs from a mezzanine, a point where the occupants would have two different directions of travel towards an exit would begin minimally at the bottom of the stairs and could conceivably begin at a point beyond the bottom of the stairs depending on the layout of partitions and locations of doors at the floor area to which the stairs lead.

WIDTH OF EGRESS

Egress Capacity

The number of people occupying a building or space as determined by minimum occupant load factors is not only necessary for determining the number of required means of egress for that building or space, but is also necessary for determining the ultimate width of those means of egress. This width of means of egress is referred to as egress capacity, and egress capacity is calculated for stairways, ramps, corridors, and doors if they are part of a means of egress. An egress capacity factor is multiplied by the number of occupants of a building or space in order to determine the width of the egress components serving that building or space. Egress capacity factors are divided into two major categories: level travel (ramps, corridors, and doors) and stair travel (Figure 10-10). Egress capacity factors for stairs are wider than level travel factors

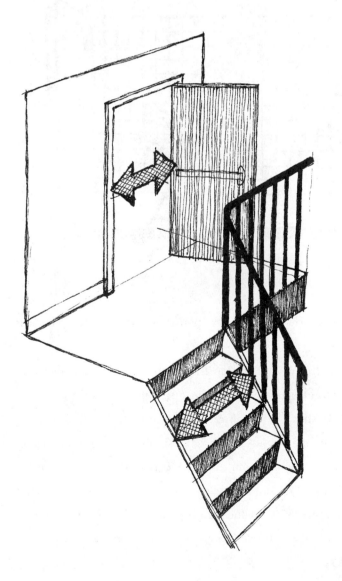

Figure 10-10 *Egress capacity factors*

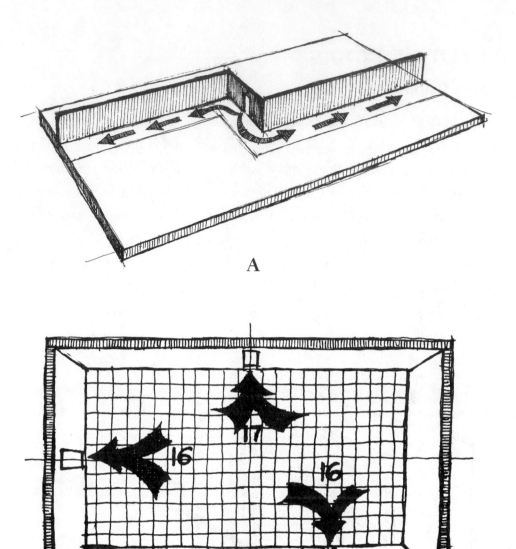

A

B

because people travel more slowly on stairways than they do when traveling through corridors and doors.

Codes are not written with the assumption that each exit or means of egress will need to accommodate the total egress load of the building or space they serve, but rather with the assumption that the minimum occupant load will be distributed amongst the different exits or means of egress. In designing for egress capacity, one would look at the area served by the different means of egress and divide the minimum occupant load by the number of different means of egress serving that area (Figures 10-11a and b). For example, if a one-story business occupancy had a total minimum occupant load of 49 people and had three exits, one would assume that 16 people each

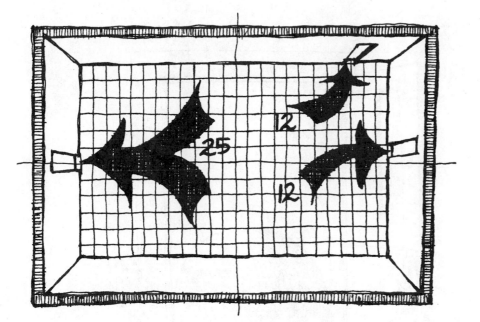
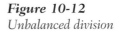

Figure 10-12
Unbalanced division

would exit through two of the exits and that 17 people would egress through the third exit. Of course, the proximity of the exits to one another may encourage the code official to require the egress capacity of each exit to be a little less balanced in certain instances (Figure 10-12).

Assembly occupancies usually have additional requirements for the distribution of the buildings' or spaces' occupants amongst the different means of egress. Most people who enter an assembly occupancy will try to exit through the main entrance of the building in the event of a fire unless that main entrance is clearly blocked by the fire. Codes, therefore, require that assembly occupancies provide a certain percentage of egress capacity at both the main entrance to the building and at all other peripheral exits. This ensures that the egress capacity will be sufficient at the exit that most of the building occupants are likely to use, as well as at all other exits in the event that the main exit is unusable. This additional assembly occupancy requirement for the distribution of egress capacity acknowledges that code officials are concerned with the number of occupants within assembly spaces and the general lack of familiarity of those occupants with those spaces.

Minimum Widths

The egress capacity factors referenced in codes are used for calculating the minimum widths of egress components necessary to accommodate the population of the building or space served. Codes also specify minimum widths for different egress com-

Figure 10-13 *32-inch clear*

ponents, regardless of the population served. Egress doors must be at least 32 inches in the clear, meaning that a 32-inch sphere could be rolled through the door opening when the door is opened perpendicular to the wall (Figure 10-13). Corridors, ramps, and stairs also have set minimum egress widths which can not be reduced. Minimum egress widths help guarantee that egress components are at least wide enough to remain functional for all, including individuals with disabilities. When designing egress components, one would use either the minimum egress widths, or the egress widths determined by applying egress capacity factors, whichever is greater.

MAXIMUM OCCUPANT CONTENT

The number of people permitted to occupy a building or space is not limited by the minimum occupant load factors, but rather by the amount of egress provided for that building or space. The actual number of people allowed to occupy a building or space is referred to as the maximum occupant content (depending on the code). If a designer determined from minimum occupant load factors that a particular room would have an occupant load of 100 people, then the designer would have to design an egress

Occupant Content

The maximum legal occupant content for this place of business is ___ persons. The minimum number of approved independent exits accessible to this occupancy is _____ .

Location: _____

_____

_____	_____
Building Official	**Fire Marshall**

It shall be unlawful to remove or deface this Notice.

Figure 10-14 *Maximum occupant content*

scheme for that room that would accommodate a minimum of 100 people. If the designer consequently designed the egress scheme for that same room to accommodate 400 people, the maximum occupant content for that room would be 400 people. Maximum occupant content can be calculated by dividing the actual width of egress components by the egress capacity factors. Maximum occupant content is also contingent, of course, on all other aspects of the egress design for that room meeting all applicable codes. Therefore, the egress design for the room could not violate any other egress requirements such as number, location, arrangement, and width of exits and exit access, and so on. Each code also specifies a maximum number of people per square foot allowed to occupy a room or space. Minimum occupant load dictates the minimum number of people that an egress scheme must accommodate, whereas maximum occupant content reflects the maximum number of people that can actually use a building or space. In assembly occupancies, the maximum occupant content must be posted in a conspicuous area (Figure 10-14).

ARRANGEMENT OF EXITS

The arrangement of exits and exit access is critical to ensuring safe means of egress from a building in the event of an emergency. Means of egress must be arranged so that the occupants of a building are within certain minimum travel distances of at least one exit. Means of egress must also be arranged to minimize the possibility that one emergency situation such as a fire can block more than one exit or exit access at the same time. Though all of the codes agree with these basic principles for arranging means of egress, they differ as to the actual specific requirements necessary to achieve these principles.

Travel Distance

Codes specify travel distances to exits for each building based on the building's occupancy classification and based on whether or not the building is sprinklered. Every building occupant must be within the maximum travel distance of at least one exit, no matter how remotely located that occupant is within the building (Figure 10-15). Each code varies in what it considers as an acceptable maximum travel distance. Maximum travel distance requirements help guarantee that no building occupant has to walk too far to reach an exit in the event of an emergency.

Figure 10-15 *Travel distance*

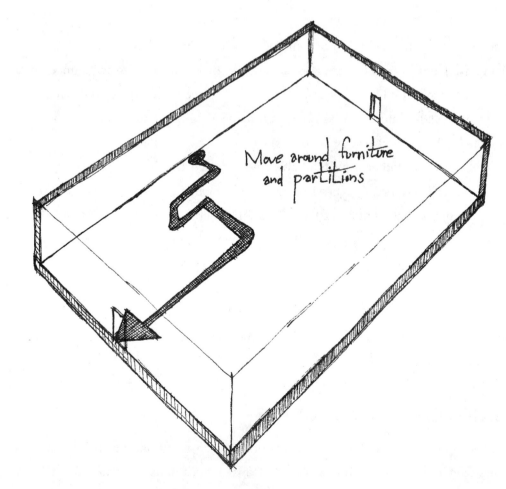

Separate Exits and Exit Access

In order for exits and exit access to provide for safe exiting, it is necessary to arrange them in a manner that provides for different paths of travel in separate directions, that the occupants of a building can always egress away from a fire or other emergency situation. Codes provide for multiple egress choices in two ways. One, codes specify a means of calculating a minimum distance between the required exits or exit access; and two, codes require that all separate exits and exit access be located such that their location minimizes the possibility that any two of them can be blocked by the same emergency condition.

The four major codes require that multiple building exits and multiple exit access serving rooms be located a distance apart equal to one-half of the diagonal of the building or area served by the exits or exit access (Figures 10-16a and b). This one-half diagonal separation is plotted as a straight line dimension between the entrances to the exits or exit access. Each of the codes allow the designer to trace the one-half diagonal dimension along the pathway of an exit access corridor if that exit access cor-

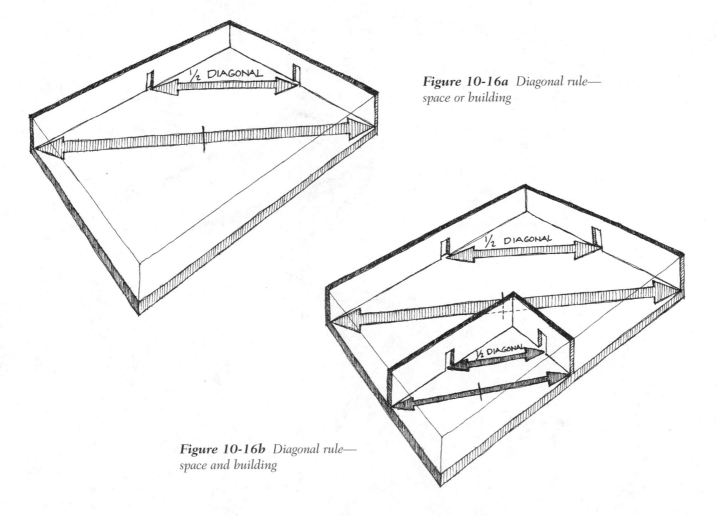

Figure 10-16a *Diagonal rule— space or building*

Figure 10-16b *Diagonal rule— space and building*

ridor is constructed in accordance with each individual code's exit access corridor requirements, including the requirements for a one-hour rated corridor with proper opening protectives (Figure 10-16c). Some codes allow the diagonal fraction dimension to be reduced in length if the building is fully sprinklered. Calculating the diagonal of a space or building served can be very subjective and should be done with the code official. Unusually shaped buildings may lead to many different interpretations as to where the diagonal is calculated (Figure 10-16d). This one-half the diagonal dimension rule is a means of assuring that all exits and exit access will be located a certain minimum distance apart from each other, thus granting the building occupants more egress choices. However, the more important rule (and often the more ignored rule) is perhaps the standard that all exits and means of egress shall be located to min-

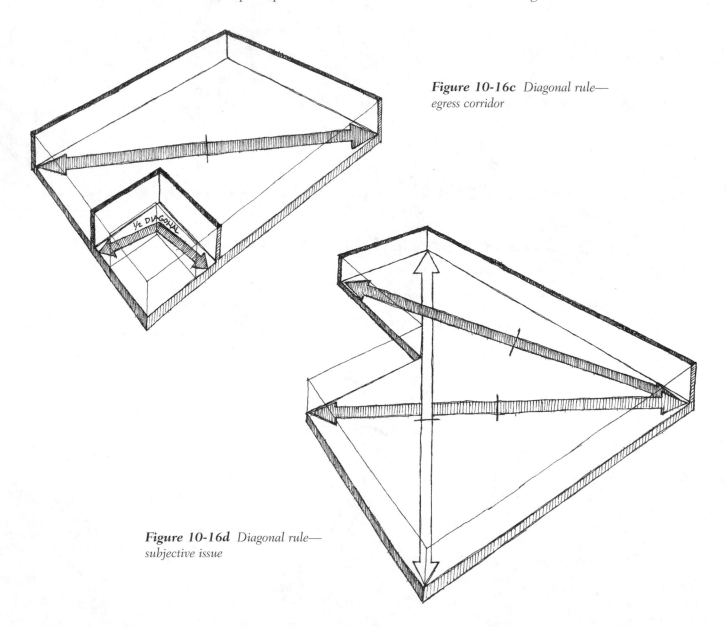

Figure 10-16c *Diagonal rule—egress corridor*

Figure 10-16d *Diagonal rule—subjective issue*

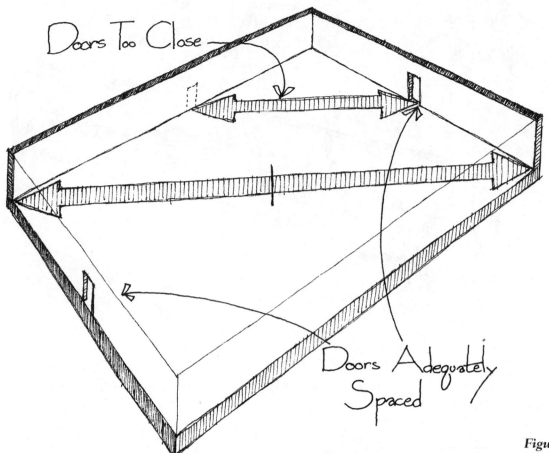

Figure 10-17 *Minimize blockage*

imize the possibility that any two will be blocked by the same fire or other emergency condition (Figure 10-17).

Dead-End Spaces

Whenever one enters a narrow space that has only one direction of travel towards an exit then one may have entered a dead-end space, commonly referred to as a dead-end corridor. Actually the term "dead-end corridor" is a misnomer, as a dead-end space may be formed by library shelves, by built-in casework, by partial height partitions, or by other elements, in addition to being formed by corridor walls (Figure 10-18). Codes specify maximum lengths for dead-end spaces, and some codes vary those lengths by occupancy classification, or by whether or not the building is fully sprinklered. The danger presented by a dead-end space is that, in the event of a fire, anyone egressing by this dead-end space may feel that the dead-end space leads to an exit. They may then travel to the end of the dead-end space only to find a locked door. Meanwhile, they may have lost valuable time, and they may also have become disoriented. This result-

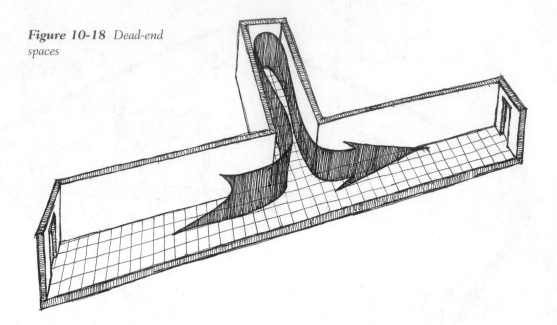

Figure 10-18 *Dead-end spaces*

ing loss of time and disorientation may prove fatal. The problems associated with dead-end spaces can become exacerbated when the dead-end spaces are full of smoke from a fire.

Common Paths of Travel

Common paths of travel are similar to dead-end spaces in that they are spaces with only one direction of travel towards an exit (Figure 10-19). When one enters a common path of travel, however, it is usually obvious which direction is the proper direction of travel towards an exit, whereas in a dead-end space, one may perceive that one is traveling towards an exit when in fact, one is traveling away from it. Common paths of travel are regulated by each of the codes as to maximum length, because the danger inherent to any space with only one direction of travel towards an exit. Not all of the four major codes include the term common path of travel. Just as with dead-end spaces, some codes vary the maximum distance of common paths of travel based on sprinkler protection and occupancy classification.

Accessible Means of Egress

When designing buildings for people with disabilities, one must design for access issues and egress issues. Access issues, or getting people with disabilities into buildings and to the services provided within buildings, are covered in Chapter 11. This section deals with egress issues, or getting people with disabilities out of buildings in the event

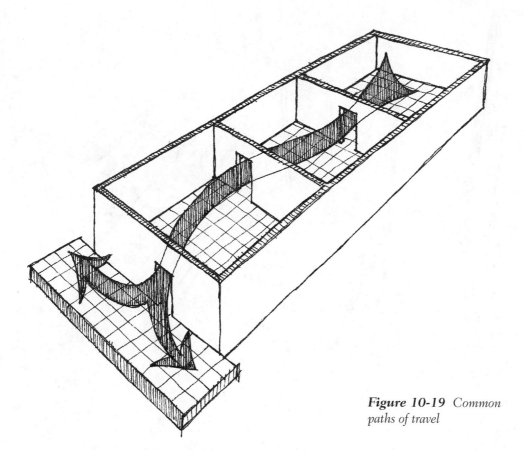

Figure 10-19 *Common paths of travel*

of an emergency. Providing some method for dealing with means of egress for people with disabilities is a relatively new concept for accessibility standards. Of course, there are now many different accessibility standards which deal with egress and keeping up with which standard and which requirements apply to any given building can be somewhat cumbersome for a designer.

As a general rule, when any exits in a building are not accessible to people with disabilities and the building is not protected throughout by a supervised automatic sprinkler system, then areas of rescue assistance (some codes refer to these "safe haven" areas as areas of refuge) must be provided at each inaccessible exit (Figure 10-20a-g). Each code, as well as the Americans with Disabilities Act (ADA), varies somewhat in what they require for accessible egress, as well as varies as to which buildings are required to have accessible means of egress. Areas of rescue assistance provide a place for people with disabilities to wait until fire personnel can help them evacuate from the building. An area of rescue assistance is a protected area with two-way audible and visible communication. The stairway adjacent to an area of rescue assistance must be wide enough for fire department personnel to assist individuals with disabilities in egressing from the areas of rescue assistance.

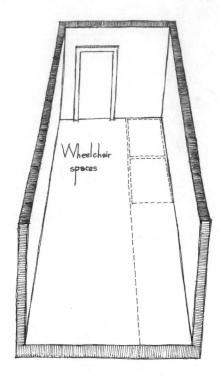

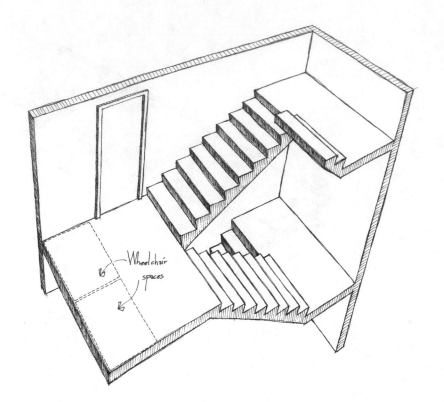

Figure 10-20a-g *Areas of rescue assistance*

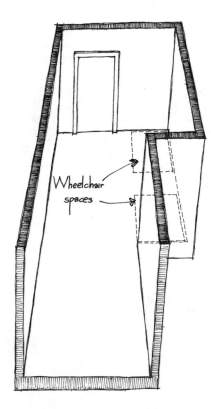

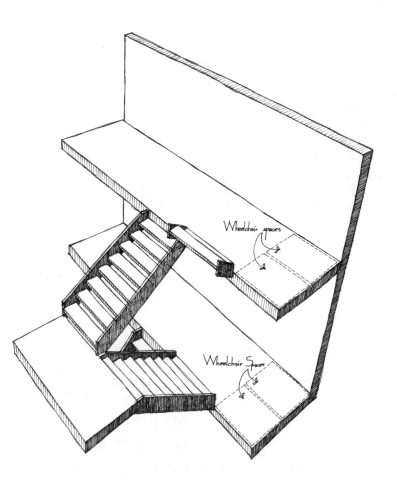

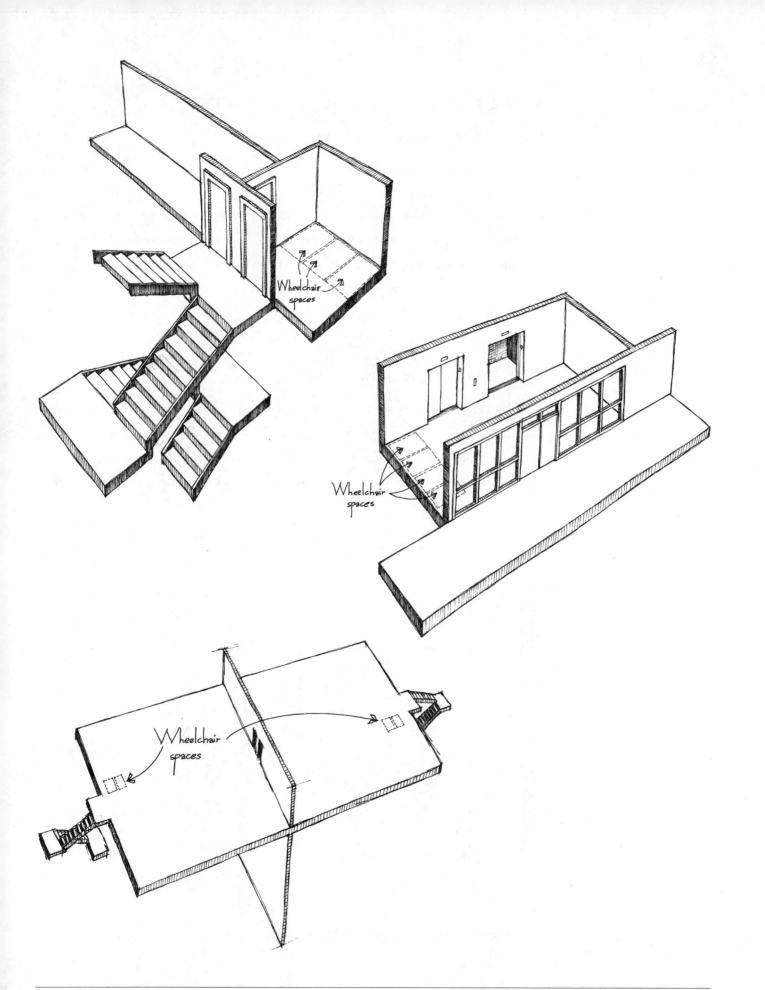

Wheelchair spaces

Wheelchair spaces

Wheelchair spaces

SPECIAL EXIT REQUIREMENTS

Boiler, Incinerator, Furnace Rooms

Some boiler, incinerator, and furnace rooms are required by codes to have two means of egress because of the hazardous nature of the fuel-fired equipment within these rooms. The egress requirements are usually based on the size of the rooms and the Btu input capacity of the equipment. Maximum travel distances may be stipulated by codes, as well as requirements governing the arrangement of the egress doors (Figure 10-21). Where oil fire equipment is used, codes may require the construction of dikes at entrances to the rooms to contain fuel spillage. Codes may also prohibit openings from certain occupancies into boiler, incinerator, or furnace rooms.

Exit Access Corridors

Exit access corridors are usually required by codes to be enclosed in one-hour fire rated construction. Their openings are usually required to be protected openings, employing rated doors and frames (Figure 10-22). Codes may vary these rating and protection requirements based on a building's or space's occupancy classification, or based

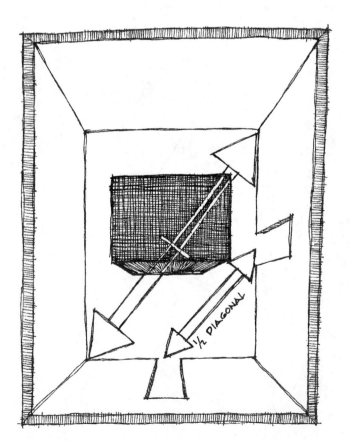

Figure 10-21 *Boiler rooms*

Figure 10-22 *Exit access corridors*

on whether or not the building is sprinklered. Codes usually disallow the use of exit access corridors as return air ways.

Emergency Egress Openings

Sleeping rooms on certain levels of buildings are required by codes to have emergency egress openings which must be capable of providing a certain minimum amount of clear opening. The clear opening must also maintain a specified minimum clear height and a specified minimum clear width. These dimensions are specified in order to ensure that a fire official with a breathing apparatus can gain entrance to the sleeping room in order to help egress the occupants from that room (Figure 10-23). Egress openings must be within a specified minimum distance from the finished floor of the sleeping rooms which they serve. Egress windows must also be operable without the use of special tools. An exterior door from a sleeping room may serve as the emergency egress opening for that sleeping room.

Smokeproof Enclosures

Code officials are concerned with the potential danger presented by high-rise buildings because of the difficulty in fighting fires in upper levels of multistory build-

Figure 10-23 *Emergency egress openings*

ings, and because of the difficulty in egressing building occupants whenever the egress involves stairways. In order to buy time for people egressing through stairways in tall buildings, codes require the stairways in these buildings to be smokeproof enclosures. Some smokeproof enclosures are stairways that are pressurized, so that they maintain a positive pressure in relation to the spaces leading to them, thus preventing the passage of smoke into the smokeproof enclosures (Figure 10-24). This pressurization is provided by mechanical ventilation. Other smokeproof enclosures rely on outside air to remove the products of combustion through natural ventilation. Smokeproof enclosures provide an egress pathway that will allow the occupants of a tall building the time necessary to egress at a natural pace.

STAIRWAYS

Stairway Protection

Exit stairways provide a safe passage for building occupants to egress through in the event of an emergency. They are therefore required to be protected from the rest of the building with some sort of fire-rated construction and opening protectives. There are some exceptions to providing protection for stairways used for egress, as in the cases of

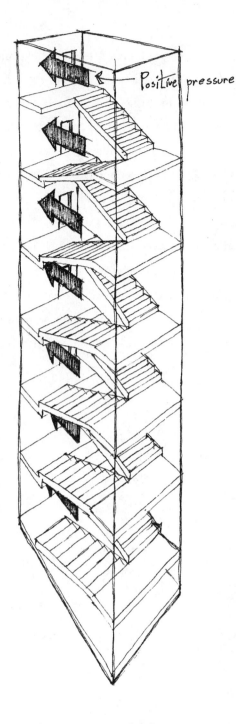

Positive pressure

Figure 10-24 *Smokeproof enclosures—mechanical ventiation*

certain open stairways from mezzanines, but as a general rule, exit stairways are protected, and their type of protection varies according to whether they are enclosed stairways or exterior exitway stairways.

Enclosed Stairways

Enclosed stairways are protected with rated construction separating them from the rest of the building. If a four-sided exit stairway were an interior stairway, completely surrounded by the rest of the building, then all four sides of that stairway would be built of fire-rated construction (Figure 10-25a). However, if only one side of an enclosed exit stairway were separating that stairway from the rest of the building, then only that separating side would need to be built of fire-rated construction, providing no other section of the applicable code required the other three sides to be rated (Figure 10-25b). The fire resistance ratings of walls separating enclosed exit stairways from other parts of buildings vary based on the number of stories the stairways serve and based on the occupancy classifications of the buildings.

Penetrations in enclosed exit stairways are only allowed to occur if they serve the purpose of the exit stairway, and they must maintain the integrity of the fire-resistant construction separating the stairway from the rest of the building. Doors into enclosed exit stairways are limited as to the amount of wired glass in a steel frame that they may contain, and must be rated one-and-a-half hours if they are installed in a two-hour fire-rated wall assembly, or must be rated one hour if they are installed in a one-hour fire-

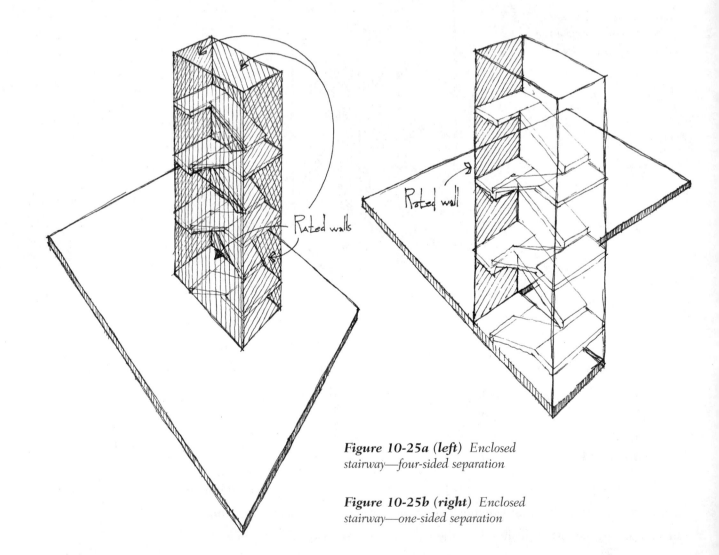

Figure 10-25a (left) *Enclosed stairway—four-sided separation*

Figure 10-25b (right) *Enclosed stairway—one-sided separation*

rated wall assembly. These doors are also required to be tested for temperature rise on the unexposed side (the stairway side) in order to assure that they will not radiate enough heat in the event of a fire to render the stairway useless for egress.

Exterior Exit Stairway

Codes go to great lengths to protect exterior exitway stairs from the threat of fire exposure (Figure 10-26). These stairs are required, with some exceptions, to be separated from the structure they serve with rated construction. Exterior exitway stairs must also be located a certain minimum distance from adjacent buildings. Openings within close proximity to exterior exitway stairs must be protected. Furthermore, codes specify the minimum widths of exterior balconies serving exterior exitway stairs when applic-

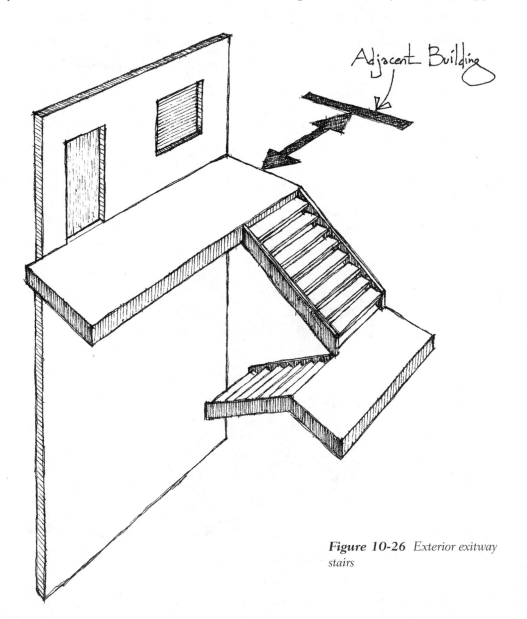

Adjacent Building

Figure 10-26 *Exterior exitway stairs*

able. Exterior exitway stairs may be restricted to buildings of certain heights and of certain occupancy classifications.

Stairway Construction

When interior and exterior stairways are used for exits, it is necessary to design them in such a manner that they provide building occupants a safe path of travel to the public way (Figure 10-27). Therefore, exit stairs have strict requirements governing their construction. They must be built to the requirements of the construction type of the building they serve, and they may even have to exceed the requirements of the construction type of the building they serve, because of the occupancy classification of the area which they serve. Whenever a closet is constructed underneath exit stairs, the closet must be separated from the exit stairs with rated construction. To keep those who egress through any enclosed exit stairway from becoming confused as to which level of the stairway is the level of exit discharge, all enclosed exit stairways must have some

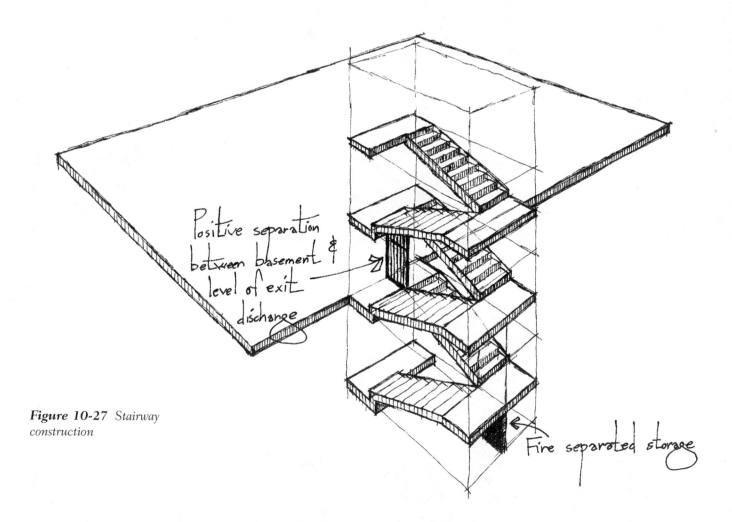

Positive separation between basement & level of exit discharge

Fire separated storage

Figure 10-27 *Stairway construction*

obvious means of separation at the level of exit discharge whenever these stairways continue beyond the level of exit discharge. The dimensions of the individual components of exit stairways are also regulated to ensure that they can be safely used.

Riser heights and tread depths are critical to how easily a stairway can be used, and as a consequence, codes regulate their dimensions (Figure 10-28). Though most codes and accessibility standards require a maximum riser height of seven inches and a minimum tread depth of eleven inches, there are still some codes which allow greater riser heights and lesser tread dimensions. Research has shown that stairs utilizing the "7/11" riser-tread limitations are safer than stairs which allow greater riser heights and lesser tread depths, and that the safest stairs utilize risers heights between 6.3 inches and 7.2 inches, and tread depths of at least 11.5 inches (Templer 1992).

The ratio of riser height to tread depth is dynamic, changing to reflect the gait of the "average" stair climber, as the riser height increases, the tread depth decreases. Many codes require that the sum of two risers plus the depth of one tread be equal to some range of numbers which supposedly reflect the proper average gait for designing stairways, though often the ranges employed by modern codes reflect archaic mea-

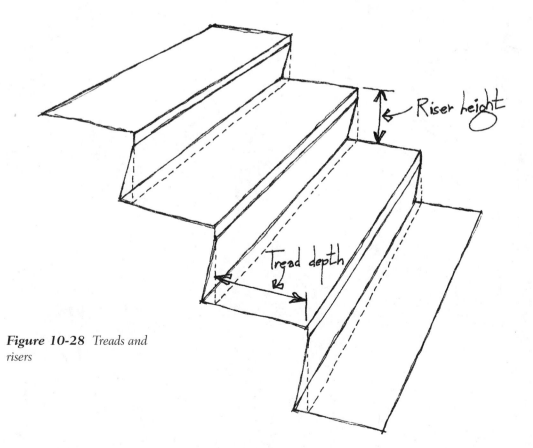

Figure 10-28 *Treads and risers*

surements of gait (Templer 1992). If the ratios of risers and treads do not reflect a comfortable gait for a stair climber, then the chance that the stair climber will fall due to a misstep is greatly increased.

Consistency of the riser heights and tread depths utilized in any single stair run is also essential to the design of safe stairs. Codes often specify the allowable variation in height between adjacent stair risers and between the tallest and the shortest risers in a flight of stairs. Most stair climbers quickly judge several treads and risers, and then proceed to ascend or descend the stairs with only an occasional glance at the treads and risers to recalculate their dimensions, so variations in treads and risers often lead to stairway accidents.

Codes require that landings occur at certain maximum height intervals to ensure that stair flights are not too long for safe ascent or descent (Figure 10-29). These intervals vary according to the occupancy classification served. Stairway landings must be at least as wide as the stairs they serve and at least as great in depth as the

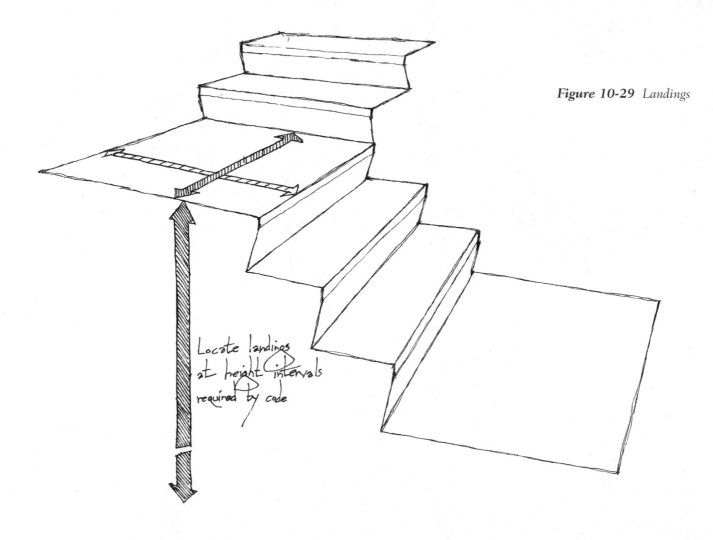

Figure 10-29 *Landings*

Locate landings at height intervals required by code

width of the stairs they serve. Often codes vary guardrail requirements at landings where the landings serve as intermediate landings for two flights of stairs reversing direction.

Handrails are used to stabilize oneself when ascending or descending stairs. Codes specify height ranges for handrails in order to ensure that they are installed at heights accessible to most individuals (Figure 10-30). The size and cross-sectional shape of handrails are also regulated to ensure that most handrail users can adequately grasp the handrails they use. One should be careful when specifying handrails, as many codes and accessibility standards disagree as to what shapes and sizes of handrails are adequate. Codes require additional intermediate handrails when stairs exceed certain widths so that virtually everyone using a set of stairs can reach a handrail. Along open edges of stairs, handrails are required to be continuous. At the tops and bottoms of

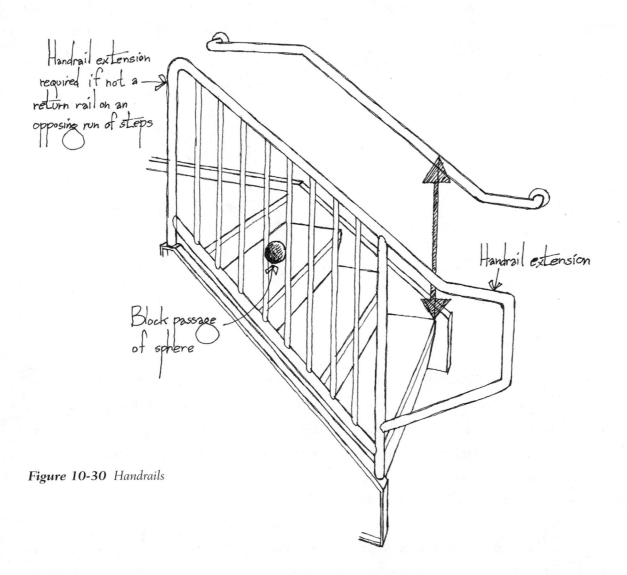

Figure 10-30 *Handrails*

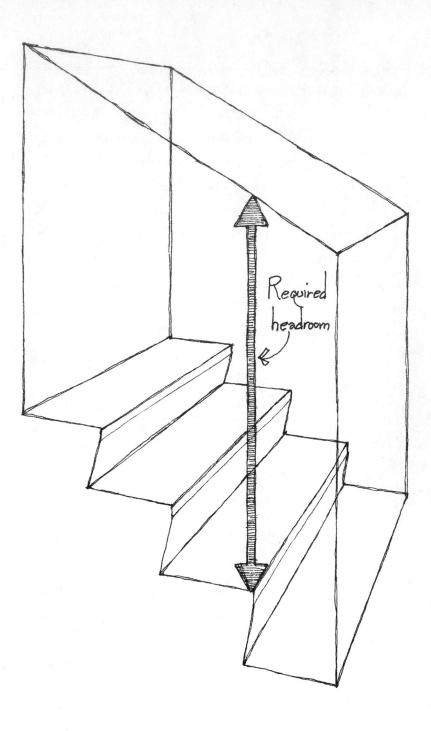

Figure 10-31 *Width and headroom*

handrail runs, they must terminate with a specified minimum length of run parallel to the landing, so that they can be used for support by individuals with disabilities when beginning an ascent or descent of a flight of stairs. Handrails along open sides of stairs may require some sort of ornamental enclosure that blocks the passage of a sphere of a certain prescribed dimension (the dimension varies according to the code being used, see guardrail discussion in this chapter).

Stairways must be wide enough and have sufficient enough headroom to accommodate the building occupants who use them for egress. Codes allow projections into stairway egress widths (except the minimum clear widths between handrails for stairs serving areas of rescue assistance) to accommodate handrails and supporting structure. These projections are limited by codes to certain maximum dimensions. Stairways must also maintain a headroom clearance of six feet, eight inches. Headroom clearance is measured as shown in Figure 10-31.

Special stair configurations such as winders, spiral stairways, circular stairways, and alternating tread stairways must conform to their unique individual dimensional requirements as specified in codes in order to ensure that they are safe as egress stairways. Codes also limit the situations in which some of these stairs can be used. See Figures 10-32a, 10-32b, 10-32c, and 10-32d for types of dimensional requirements of special stairs.

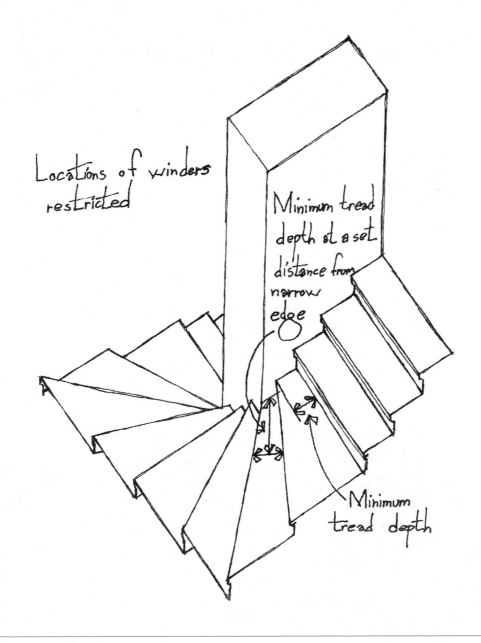

Figure 10-32a Special stairs—winders

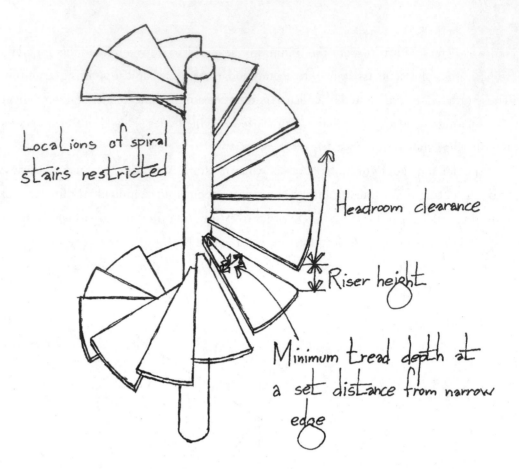

Figure 10-32b *Special stairs—spiral*

Locations of spiral stairs restricted

Headroom clearance

Riser height

Minimum tread depth at a set distance from narrow edge

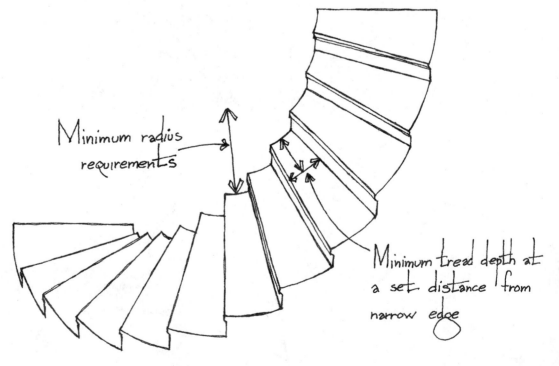

Figure 10-32c *Special stairs—circular*

Minimum radius requirements

Minimum tread depth at a set distance from narrow edge

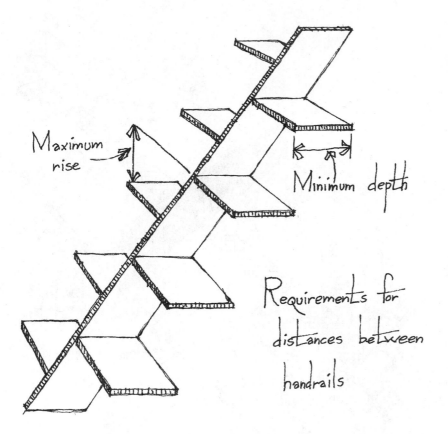

Maximum rise

Minimum depth

Requirements for distances between handrails

Figure 10-32d *Special stairs—alternating treads*

HORIZONTAL EXITS

Horizontal exits are comprised of fire-rated walls separating structures into two or more compartments, and fire-rated doors through these walls. In the event of a fire, the occupants within the fire area of a building can pass through the horizontal exit to gain refuge from the fire. The rated components of the horizontal exit would then serve to delay the fire from progressing to the non-fire side of the horizontal exit, thus buying time for the occupants of the building to egress in a more orderly fashion (Figure 10-33). Because they provide some protection from fire and therefore they allow a building's occupants more time to egress, horizontal exits permit designers some tradeoffs in designing egress schemes for buildings—increased travel distances to exits and decreased egress capacity of certain exits.

Horizontal exits allow designers to increase travel distances to exits by becoming intermediate exits. One can calculate the maximum required travel distance to the entrance to a horizontal exit, enabling a building to be potentially twice as large as the same building with no horizontal exit. One must still provide exits directly outside from each compartment adjacent to a horizontal exit; however, one only has to provide exit capacity from any compartment defined by horizontal exits for the occupant load of that

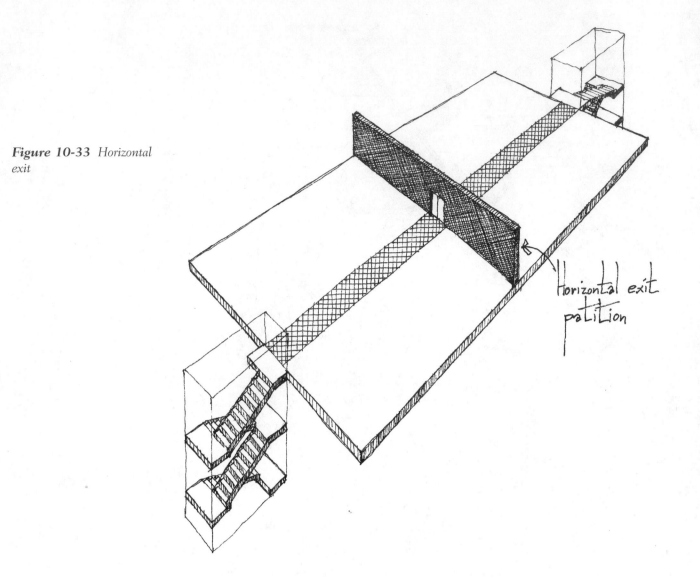

Figure 10-33 *Horizontal exit*

Horizontal exit patition

individual compartment. One does not have to provide exits within a single compartment for both the occupant load of that single compartment plus the occupant load of the compartments exiting into that single compartment through the horizontal exits. This allows designers to halve the capacity of external exits if they provide for the exiting of at least one-half of their building's occupants through horizontal exits. Horizontal exit sections in codes also require standing space in the compartments which the horizontal exit leads to, so that people egressing through the horizontal exit from a fire area can wait for their turn to egress from the non-fire area. The amount of square feet per person for standing space varies based on the occupancy classification served by the horizontal exit. Horizontal exits are often used as a means of maintaining existing exit arrangement requirements when a building addition blocks an existing required exit.

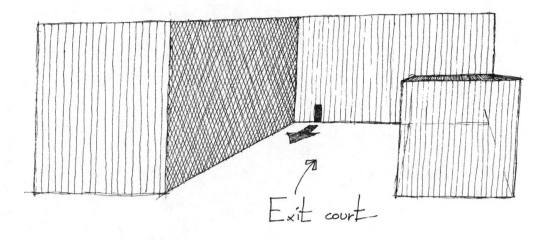

Figure 10-34 *Exit courts*

Exit court

EXIT DISCHARGE

Exit discharge is defined by codes as being between an exit and the public way. Though it is true that all exit discharges lead to a public way, it is not true that all exits lead to an exit discharge, as some exits lead directly to a public way. Examples of exit discharge are exit courts, exit lobbies, exit passageways, and exit vestibules. Each code treats the term "exit discharge" differently, and the particular code one is using at a given time may not include the above referenced spaces under the category of exit discharge. Most of these spaces act as a termination point for calculating required maximum travel distance, but one must still exit from each one of these spaces.

Exit Courts

Exit courts are outdoor spaces surrounded on three or more sides (Figure 10-34). Exit courts must lead to a public way. If exit courts are very narrow, windows opening onto them may be required to be provided with approved opening protectives.

Exit Passageways

Exit passageways are horizontal paths of travel used only for the purposes of exiting, and enclosed in construction like that used for enclosing exit stairways (Figure 10-35). Often, people confuse horizontal exits with exit passageways, thinking perhaps that since building occupants travel horizontally along exit passageways and that since exit passageways are exits, then exit passageways must be horizontal exits. Actually, horizontal exits are two-hour rated walls with protected openings that divide buildings into separate compartments, whereas exit passageways are exit corridors. Exit passageways are exits and one can calculate the maximum travel distance to the entrance of an exit passageway, but one must still exit from an exit passageway.

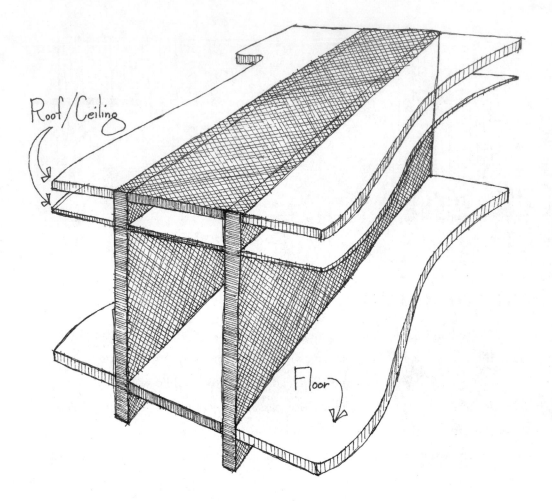

Figure 10-35 *Exit passageway*

An exit passageway must be constructed in accordance with the same requirements for constructing a vertical shaft. Its walls must go from floor to floor or from floor to roof deck, with no communication between the interstitial spaces formed by roof-ceiling construction and by floor-ceiling construction. The only openings allowed into exit passageways are the openings consistent with their use as an exit, such as egress doorways or penetrations for plumbing for sprinklering the passageway.

Exits through Lobbies

As a general rule, exits must lead directly to the outside of a building towards a public way. Codes do allow exits to empty into interior spaces in certain circumstances, however, based primarily on the protection of those spaces and on the capacity of the exits emptying into those spaces. A common means of exiting into an interior space is that of exiting through lobbies which meet the following restrictions (Figure 10-36):

1. No more than 50 percent of the number of exits and the capacity of exits is served by lobby exits;

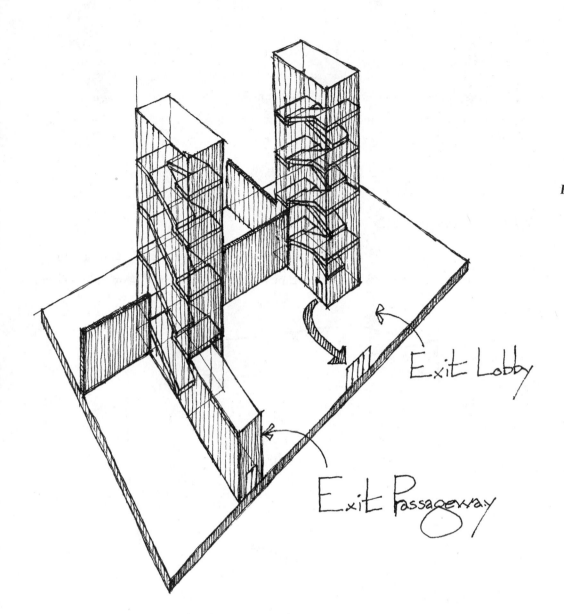

Figure 10-36 *Exit lobby*

Exit Lobby

Exit Passageway

2. The exits terminate in a lobby where the exit from the building is readily visible;

3. Any floor beneath the level of exit discharge is separated from the level of exit discharge with construction of a fire resistance rating equal to that of the stairway shaft terminating into the lobby;

4. The level of exit discharge is sprinklered; and

5. Any area on the level of exit discharge which is not sprinklered is separated from the level of exit discharge with construction of a fire resistance rating equal to that of the stairway shaft terminating into the lobby.

Each code must be consulted as to variations to the rules above for exit passageways.

Vestibules

Exit vestibules are spaces where a rated stairwell can terminate in a small foyer-like space which maintains separation from the rest of the level of exit discharge with labeled wired glass in steel frames (Figure 10-37). Codes specify the allowable widths and depths of exit vestibules. Exit vestibules must still provide an exit directly to a public way.

FIRE ESCAPES

Fire escapes are not the safest means of providing egress for occupants of a building, yet there are certain cases where fire escapes are the only means of providing egress.

Figure 10-37 *Exit vestibule*

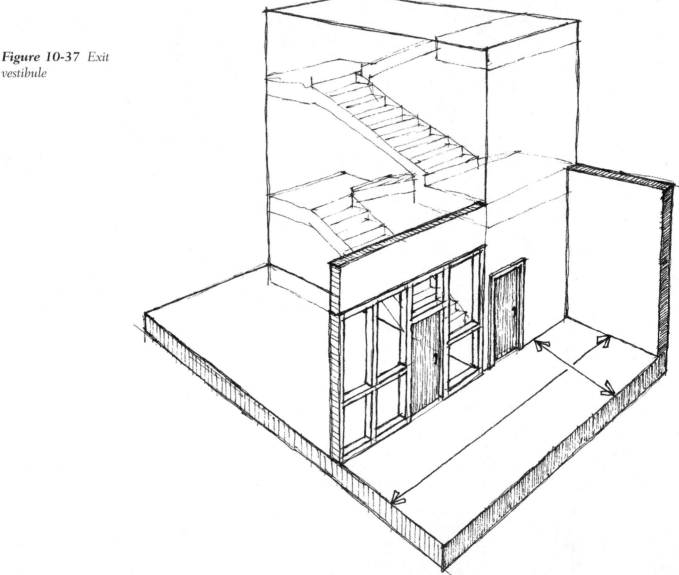

Fire escapes are usually employed in existing buildings where the physical constraints of the buildings prevent any other means of providing adequate egress, a situation which is much safer than a building with only one exit. Codes provide requirements for the design of fire escapes and detail how to properly construct fire escapes to minimize the dangers associated with their use (Figure 10-38).

Figure 10-38 *Fire escape*

DOORS

Egress chapters of codes have many requirements pertaining to doors (Figure 10-39). There are regulations governing the amount of force needed to open doors, the type of action required to open doors (i.e., whether the doors are side hinged or not), the minimum width of doors, the minimum number of doors, and the direction that doors swing, as well as many other door regulations. As a general rule, exit doors must swing in the direction of exit travel. There are exceptions to this rule based on the travel distance within an area to the egress door serving that area, and based on the occupant load served by that door. Egress doors that do not serve many people or which do not serve very large areas can usually swing into the area that they serve. A typical example of this situation would be a door opening into a private office. The number of doors serving a room or space is also dependent on the occupant load of that room or space.

Figure 10-39 Door

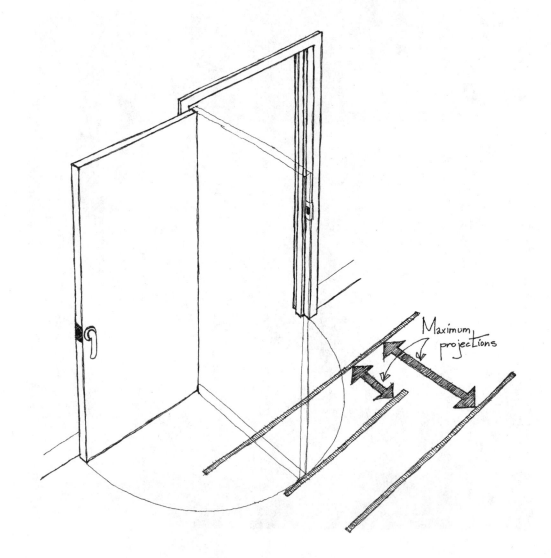

Doors are strictly regulated by codes as to how much of an egress pathway they can restrict. The rules vary based on whether a door is reducing the egress width of an exit access corridor as opposed to reducing the egress width of an exit stairway. In most cases, landings at doors must be at the same level as the space served by the door. With some exceptions, exit doors must not be lockable with locks requiring keys, tools, or special knowledge to operate them.

The force necessary to operate doors and door hardware are detailed in codes. Codes and accessibility standards often vary in their requirements for door operating forces. In the case of the Americans with Disabilities Act (ADA), a maximum force of five pounds is required to push and pull a door, yet the ADA exempts exterior doors and fire-rated doors from this requirement, as these doors must maintain their respective weather-separation and fire-separation integrity. However, if exterior doors or fire-rated doors can be installed to maintain a swinging force of five pounds or less and still serve their respective weather-separation and fire-separation functions it would be good to provide such doors, as they would be able to serve more people.

Special doors such as power-operated doors, revolving doors, and horizontal sliding doors have unique requirements in codes to ensure that they can be used in a safe manner. The requirements usually govern their acceptable locations and their operation in an egress situation or during a loss of power.

RAMPS

Although ramps permit many people to gain access to buildings, ramps can also prove to be dangerous if they are poorly designed. Sloped surfaces are difficult for many people to walk over, and the greater the slope, the more difficult it is to walk. Excessive cross-slopes (where the slope is perpendicular to the ramp's direction of travel) can prevent individuals who use wheelchairs from being able to use ramps. Proper ramp design also includes the placement of landings periodically so that those who use ramps can rest.

Codes require ramps to slope no more than one in 12 (8.33 percent), but many accessibility standards stipulate that ramps must maintain the least slope possible. Ramps with a slope steeper than one in 20 (Five percent) must be provided with handrails on both sides so that people can support themselves when using the ramps. Many ramps must have guardrails along their sides because of drop-offs along their sides. Landings must be provided at the tops and bottoms of ramps, where ramps change directions, and where doors open onto ramps (Figure 10-40). Ramps must have slip-resistant surfaces and must be designed to prevent water accumulation.

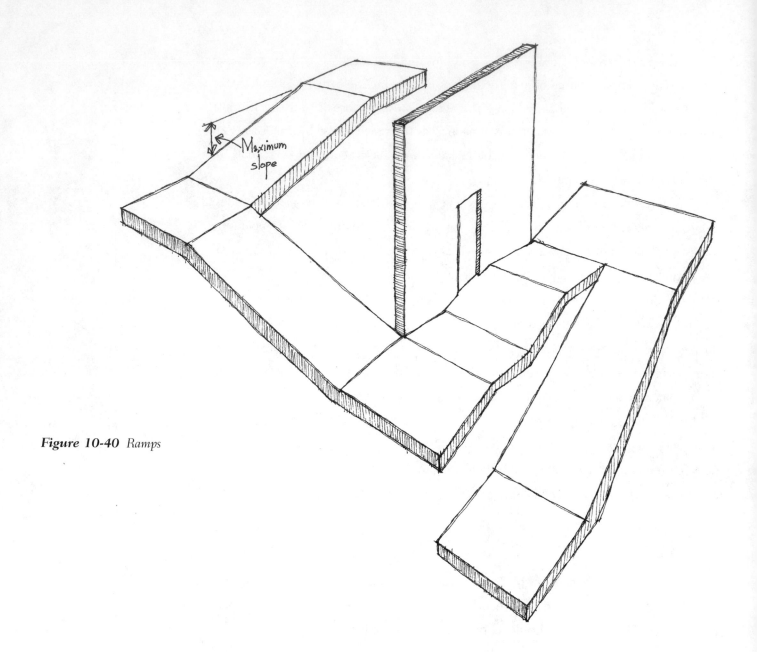

Maximum
slope

Figure 10-40 *Ramps*

GUARDRAILS

Guardrails are required wherever the distance from a walking surface to an adjacent lower surface is great enough that serious injuries could occur due to one's falling from the higher surface to the lower surface (Figure 10-41). Guardrails, along with their ornamental enclosures provide a barrier of sufficient strength, height, and closure to prevent one from passing from one side of the guardrail to the other. The required height of guardrails and their required locations are detailed in each of the four major codes.

Though all of the codes have similar guardrail requirements, they also have some differences, especially in their requirements for the ornamental enclosures that actual-

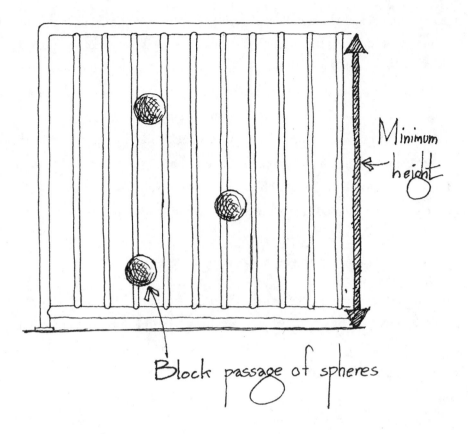

Minimum height

Block passage of spheres

Figure 10-41 *Guardrails*

ly resist the passage of an individual from one side of a guardrail to the other. There is much debate about what is required to resist the passage of children through guardrails. In his 1993 article entitled "The Elimination of Unsafe Guardrails—A Progress Report," Elliott O. Stephenson wrote that the following has been proven:

1. that almost every child six years in age and younger can pass completely through an opening six inches in width;

2. that approximately 95 percent of all children 18 months old can pass through an opening five and one-half inches in width;

3. that approximately one-half of all children 13 to 18 months in age can pass completely through an opening five inches in width; and

4. that virtually no child one year old or older can pass completely through an opening four inches in width (Stephenson, 1993).

It is obvious from this information that ornamental enclosures should block the passage of a sphere four inches in diameter to be truly effective. Actual research shows that ideally, guardrail ornamental enclosures should block the passage of a sphere three and one-half inches in diameter in order to be effective. Most of the four major codes call for ornamental enclosures which prohibit the passage of a sphere four inches in diameter in occupancies where children are likely to be, but some codes still use the archaic standard of blocking the passage of a sphere six inches or more in diameter.

Another concern with guardrail ornamental enclosure design is the prevention of a child's climbing over a guardrail. Young children have a propensity to climb and often they do not have the capacity to fully understand the potential danger posed by great heights. The use of horizontal bars as ornamental enclosures for guardrails is, though often aesthetically pleasing, a dangerous practice at best, as children often find these horizontal bars easy to climb. When children fall from climbing over guardrails, their falls often result in costly medical treatment, or perhaps even the loss of life.

IDENTIFYING MEANS OF EGRESS

Means of egress must be properly identified in order to ensure that the occupants of a building will know which way to travel when exiting a building during an emergency situation such as a building fire. Exits and exit access must remain illuminated, sometimes even when a loss of electrical power occurs; all exit doors, many exit access doors, and many routes leading to exit doors must be marked with signs (Figure 10-42); and some stairways must identify the floor level at each landing adjacent to a floor level.

Codes specify the required level of means of egress illumination based on the use

Figure 10-42 *Exit signs*

of the space. The locations of that illumination are also specified by codes. In buildings with certain occupant loads, emergency power is required for that egress illumination.

Signs must be provided to identify exits and identify exit access routes in locations specified by codes. These signs must meet certain dimensional and illumination requirements. Exit signs must remain illuminated even in the event of a loss of power, either through the use of an emergency power source or by self-luminance if self-luminous signs are approved by the code official. In some buildings, signs are required in stairways which identify the floor level as well as give directional information about roof access, and the exit discharge.

CHAPTER 11

Accessibility for Individuals with Disabilities and the Americans with Disabilities Act

This chapter discusses different accessibility codes, standards, and laws that regulate accessibility for individuals with disabilities. The discussion includes general information concerning state accessibility codes, the model codes, and the accessibility standards adopted by model codes, as well as specific information concerning the Americans with Disabilities Act (ADA). The ADA is treated in greater detail because it is a Civil Rights Act, and is the most comprehensive regulatory document governing accessibility for individuals with disabilities. The relationships of different accessibility codes, standards, and laws to one another will also be covered in this chapter.

Accessibility regulations for individuals with disabilities have grown and developed over the years beginning in 1960 with the efforts of the Easter Seal Society, the President's Committee for Employment of the Handicapped, and the American National Standards Institute (ANSI) in developing the ANSI A117.1 Standard. This was the first national standard for the design and construction of facilities accessible to individuals with disabilities. The initial ANSI A117.1 was approved by the ANSI committee in 1961, and was only six pages long, a far cry from the present CABO/ANSI A117.1, Accessible and Usable Buildings and Facilities. ANSI A117.1 was refined over the years with its first rewrite in 1980 as the result of an initiative of the Department of Housing and Urban Development. ANSI A117.1 became the basis of the Minimum Guidelines and Requirements for Accessible Design (MGRAD) developed by the Architectural and Transportation Barriers Compliance Board (ATBCB), also known as the "Access Board." The MGRAD was developed to help federal agencies develop consistent standards for the design of buildings accessible to individuals with disabilities. Two more rewrites of ANSI A117.1 occurred in 1986 and in 1992, and the present-day standard is a combined effort of ANSI and the Council of American Building Officials (CABO).

In 1968, the Architectural Barriers Act (ABA) became law, requiring all buildings that were designed, constructed, altered, and leased with federal financial assistance to be accessible to individuals with disabilities. The ABA initially adopted the provisions of ANSI A117.1 as its Standards for Accessible Design, but eventually adopted the Uniform Federal Accessibility Standards (UFAS) instead. The enforcement responsibilities of the ABA fall on the shoulders of the Access Board. The UFAS was developed by the Department of Defense, the General Services Administration, the Department of Housing and Urban Development, and the Postal Service in 1984. The UFAS have served as the dominant federal Standards for Accessible Design for years and were eventually the primary accessible design standards used for adherence to the Rehabilitation Act of 1973 (Rehab Act). The Rehab Act broke new ground by requiring not just buildings, but programs and activities receiving any form of federal financial assistance, to be accessible to individuals with disabilities.

Accessibility for individuals with disabilities eventually moved into the arena of civil rights protection. The Fair Housing Amendments Act of 1988 prohibited discrimination against individuals with disabilities in any activities relating to the sale or rental of dwellings, in the availability of residential real-estate transactions, or in the provision of services and facilities in connection therewith.

In 1990, Congress passed the Americans with Disabilities Act (ADA) which affords civil rights protection for individuals with disabilities by prohibiting discrimination against them in employment, public accommodations, state and local governments, and telecommunications. The ADA requires nongovernment entities to use the Americans with Disabilities Act Accessibility Guidelines (ADAAG) as their Standards for Accessible Design. The ADAAG was developed by the Access Board as guidelines for accessible design, but was adopted by Title III of the Americans with Disabilities Act as its Standards for Accessible Design, making it the official legal architectural accessible design standards for title III which regulates private entities. State and local government entities are allowed to choose between the use of the ADAAG and the UFAS as their Standards for Accessible Design. It is the intent of the federal government to eventually discontinue the use of the UFAS as recognized Standards for Accessible Design in favor of an expanded ADAAG.

This chapter attempts to establish the differences between the ADA and accessibility codes by discussing the ADA in great detail. Since other accessibility regulations behave more or less like building codes do, the administration chapter of this book provides a model for understanding these other regulations. The ADA behaves very differently from other accessibility standards and the detailed discussion of the ADA in this chapter should make those differences obvious.

WHICH RULES APPLY?

The short history above illustrates that just as with building codes, there are many different accessibility codes, standards, and laws (Figure 11-1). Federal accessibility regulations include the Architectural Barriers Act of 1968, the Rehabilitation Act of 1973, the Fair Housing Amendments Act of 1988, and the Americans with Disabilities Act of 1990. Individual states and even some municipalities have their own accessibility laws, and in some states the accessibility laws are relatively weak in comparison to such nationally recognized regulations as the ADA or the American National Standards Institute's "Accessible and Usable Buildings and Facilities" (CABO/ANSI A117.1). Other states have strong accessibility regulations which often exceed or conflict with the nationally recognized accessibility regulations. Whenever one is required to design for, build to, or inspect for the provisions of more than one of these accessibility regulations at the same time, the most stringent provisions of any two differing accessibility documents will control. And whenever any two applicable accessibility documents conflict, federal law supersedes state and local law, and state law supersedes local law.

The scoping provisions of accessibility codes, standards, and laws are frequently overlooked. The story of a local code official attempting to enforce the Americans with

Figure 11-1 *Typical accessibility standards*

Disabilities Act (ADA) or a designer attempting to design by the ADA and going straight to the Standards for Accessible Design without reading a word of the other regulatory language is a common one. This usually results in interpretations of the law which are either far too lenient or far too stringent. I often hear of code officials and designers applying the technical requirements of the Americans with Disabilities Act Accessibility Guidelines (ADAAG) or the Uniform Accessibility Standards (UFAS) incorrectly because of their not having read the scoping provisions of those documents. The scoping provisions of accessibility regulations identify the limits for complying with these codes, standards, and laws. Scoping provisions provide the "standards of care" expected for any given situation. I usually recommend that individuals not try to memorize construction regulations, but rather that they try to memorize where to look in these regulations for answers to their questions. However, if one wishes to commit any portion of accessibility regulations to memory, then one should first memorize the scoping provisions.

An understanding of the scoping provisions of accessibility regulations becomes even more critical when one considers that often but not always, one will have to meet the requirements of two or more of these regulatory documents. The ADA regulates programs and facilities within existing buildings, as well as alterations of existing facilities and new construction, but does not directly affect churches, because religious entities are exempt from this federal Civil Rights Act. On the other hand, state accessibility laws do not usually regulate existing facilities, but they do regulate alterations of existing facilities and new construction, including the alterations and new construction of churches. The scoping provisions of the ADA and a typical state accessibility law would inform a designer to use both regulatory documents when designing an office building, but to use only the state law when designing a church (Figure 11-2).

ADA DESCRIPTION

The Americans with Disabilities Act (ADA) of 1990 prohibits discrimination against individuals with disabilities in the areas of employment, public accommodations, state and local government services, and telecommunications. The ADA provides comprehensive civil rights protection in these areas for individuals with disabilities. The ADA is broader in scope than "traditional" accessibility codes and standards in that it not only addresses buildings and facilities, but also programs and services. The ADA is also broader in scope than most other accessibility codes and standards in that it addresses existing buildings and facilities, as well as alterations to buildings, facilities and new construction.

Though many of the ADA's provisions are not architectural in nature, this chapter discusses many of these nonarchitectural provisions because it is necessary to understand them in order to fully understand those provisions which are mainly architectural in nature. These nonarchitectural provisions are related mainly to ongoing requirements and the corrections of problems associated with these provisions often involve the talents of designers and builders. Many clients depend on their designers and builders to initially inform them of any duties these clients may have as a result of the ADA. Though this dependence on designers and builders may not be justified, should a private or public sector client become involved with a complaint against them under the ADA which involves an architectural barrier, that client will probably look in the future for design and construction services from designers and builders who are knowledgeable of the ADA. This chapter only discusses those provisions of title I (employment provisions) which relate to titles II and III. This chapter will not discuss the telecommunications provisions of title IV nor the miscellaneous provisions of title V.

Terms of Art

As with any regulatory document, the Americans with Disabilities Act employs many "terms of art" to implement the provisions within it. A thorough knowledge of these terms of art is necessary in order for one to become intimately familiar with the requirements of the ADA. Many of these terms of art are specific to certain sections of

Figure 11-2

ADA VERSUS ACCESSIBILITY CODES AND STANDARDS

Americans with Disabilities Act (ADA)

Accessbility Codes and Standards (as adopted by State and local governments)

Existing and Ongoing Provisions
    Programs and Activities
    Facilities

Existing Facilities are not covered by most codes

Alterations – Facilities

Alterations – Facilities

New Construction – Facilities

New Construction – Facilities

Exempt Entities *
    Religious Entities
    Private Clubs
    Housing
    Federal Government
    Other entities exempted from the Civil Rights
        Act of 1964

All Entities Covered **

* See discussion in this chapter for limitations to these exemptions
** Some accessibility codes do exempt certain entities

WHICH LAWS APPLY

(the ADA or the laws enacting State and local accessibility codes and standards)?

Existing Churches

Neither law applies—exempted entity under ADA and accessibility most codes do not cover existing facilities

Church Alterations or Newly Constructed Churches

Accessibility code applies—attempted entity under ADA but most codes have no exempt entities

Existing Office Buildings

ADA applies—ADA covers existing facilities, accessibility codes do not

Office Building Alterations or Newly Constructed Office Buildings

Both laws apply—offices are not exempt entities under the ADA and both the ADA and accessibility codes regulate alterations and new construction

The Issuance of Municipal Drivers Licenses

ADA applies—ADA covers programs, accessibility codes usually do not

the ADA, whereas others are more general in nature; that is, they may be relevant to more than one section of the ADA, or may be even relevant to all sections of the law.

There are many terms associated with the ADA, and several ADA terms sound similar to other ADA terms though there is often no relation between them. For example, the term "public entity" sounds similar to the term "public accommodation," often causing confusion, though these two terms are not related. The terms public entity and public accommodation are not even relevant to the same titles of the ADA. The same could be said for public accommodation and the term "reasonable accommodation." This chapter attempts to isolate terms of art and discuss them only when addressing the sections of the ADA in which they are used. Figure 11-3 lists many of the terms of art employed by the ADA with some references to corresponding areas of the law where they are used.

A couple of key general terms one should know when reading the Americans with Disabilities Act are the terms "act" and "part." Act refers to the Americans with Disabilities Act, and part refers to the individual parts or titles of that act. For example, part 35 is title II of the ADA and part 36 is title III of the ADA.

Figure 11-3

ADA TERMS OF ART

Title III (Private Entities) Existing and Ongoing Provisions (See also Appendix to Title III Regulations 36.406)

Readily Achievable Regulations 36.304 Removal of barriers

Places of Public Accommodation Regulations 36.104 Definitions

Commercial Facilities Regulations 36.104 Definitions

Recommended Barrier Removal Prioritization Regulations 36.304 Removal of barriers

Alternative Methods to Barrier Removal Regulations 36.305 Alternatives to barrier removal

Undue Burden for Auxiliary Aids and Services Regulations 36.309 Examinations and courses

Title II (Public Entities) - Existing and Ongoing Provisions

Program Access Regulations Subpart D Program Accessibility

Viewed in its Entirety Regulations 35.150 Existing facilities

Most Integrated Setting Possible Regulations 35.150 Existing facilities

Self-Evaluation Regulations 35.105 Self-evaluation

Transition Plan Regulations 35.150 Existing facilities

Undue Financial or Administrative Burden Regulations 35.150 Existing facilities

Alterations (See also Appendix to Title III Regulations 36.406)

Path of Travel Regulations 36.403 Path of travel; ADAAG 4.1.6 Accessible Buildings: Alterations

Primary Function Regulations 36.403 Path of travel; ADAAG 4.1.6 Accessible Buildings: Alterations

Maximum Extent Feasible Regulations 36.402 Alterations; ADAAG 4.1.6 Accessible Buildings: Alterations

Disproportionate Regulations 36.403 Path of travel; ADAAG 4.1.6 Accessible Buildings: Alterations

Technically Infeasible ADAAG 4.1.6 Accessible Buildings: Alterations

New Construction (See also Appendix to Title III Regulations 36.406)

Work Areas ADAAG 4.1.1 Minimum Requirements: Application (3)

Work Stations Title I

Common Use Areas ADAAG 3.5 Definitions

Public Use Areas ADAAG 3.5 Definitions

Structurally Impracticable Regulations 36.401 New construction; ADAAG 4.1.1 Minimum Requirements: Application (5)

General (See also Appendix to Title III Regulations 36.406)

Disability Regulations 36.104 Definitions

Readily Accessible to and Usable by Regulations 36.401 New construction

ADA Accessibility Guidelines (ADAAG) or "Standards for Accessible Design" (Standards)—Appendix A to the Regulations

Equivalent Facilitation ADAAG Appendix A2.2

Facility Regulations 36.104 Definitions

Structural Changes (Title II only) Regulations 35.150 Existing facilities

Administrative Methods (Title II only) Regulations 35.150 Existing facilities

Elevator Exemption (Title III only) Regulations 36.404 Alterations: Elevator exemption; Regulations 36.401 New construction; ADAAG 4.1.3 Accessible Buildings: New Construction (5)

Historical Significance Regulations 36.405 Alterations: Historic Preservation; Regulations 35.151 New construction and alterations; ADAAG 4.1.7 Accessible Buildings: Historic Preservation

Fundamental Alteration Regulations 36.309 Examinations and courses; Regulations 35.150 Existing facilities

Direct Threat Regulations 36.208 Direct threat

Enforcement Title III Regulations Subpart D - Enfocement; Title II Regulations Subpart F - Compliance procedures

Standards of Care

The Americans with Disabilities Act (ADA) provides for different "standards of care" based on the particular area that the law is regulating. This is not to be confused with an architect's "standard of care" for professional services. State and local government entities are held to a different standard of care under the ADA than are nongovernment entities. There are also different standards of care for each of the following: existing buildings and programs, alterations to existing buildings, and new construction. These different standards of care or levels of responsibility allow the ADA to assign the highest responsibility for accessibility to new construction where providing accessibility for people with disabilities is most affordable, while assigning a lower reponsibility to alterations in order to keep the costs of improving the accessibility of buildings and facilities from becoming disproportionate to the cost of the alterations. The lowest standard of care required by the ADA is assigned to existing private entity programs and facilities that house no state or local government programs. A completely different standard of care is applied to state or local government entities, a relatively high standard of care that affects programs as well as buildings.

Standards for Accessible Design

Not only are there different standards of care for the level of accessibility to provide based on whether a facility is existing, being altered, or newly constructed, but there are also different standards of care based on which set of design standards one employs when altering or constructing accessible facilities for individuals with disabilities. The Americans with Disabilities Act references the Americans with Disabilities Act Accessibility Guidelines (ADAAG) and the Uniform Federal Accessibility Standards (UFAS) as applicable standards for use when designing and constructing for accessibility. Private entities must use the ADAAG as their Standards for Accessible Design and public entities may choose between the ADAAG (without the elevator exemption) and the UFAS as Standards for Accessible Design. Many states are seeking certification of their accessibility standards as meeting or exceeding the ADAAG for regulating the design and construction of accessible facilities. This certification is available under title III of the ADA for private entity facilities. Subpart F, Certification of State Laws or Local Building Codes, of title III of the ADA addresses the rules and the process of this certification. The process is a lengthy one, but is helpful to facility owners, designers, and builders alike, because once a state law becomes certified as equivalent to the minimum requirements of the ADAAG for accessibility and usability of facilities, then one's meeting the requirements of that law will be viewed as providing an equivalent standard of care as that provided by the ADAAG. Portions of State and local laws can also be certified as equivalent to applicable portions of the ADAAG.

Relationship to Other Laws

Because it is a federal law, the Americans with Disabilities Act (ADA) supersedes any state or local laws unless the state and local Laws are more stringent than the ADA. Section 36.103 Relationship to other laws, of title III of the ADA, and section 35.103 Relationship to other laws, of title II of the ADA state,

> Other laws. *This part does not invalidate or limit the other remedies, rights, and procedures of any other Federal laws (including State common law) that provide greater or equal protection for the rights of individuals with disabilities or individuals associated with them.*

Whenever the ADA is more stringent than state or local laws, the ADA applies; whenever the ADA conflicts with state or local laws, the ADA applies; and whenever the ADA is less stringent than state or local laws, the state or local laws apply. Titles II and III of the ADA also clarify that the ADA should not be construed to apply a lesser standard of care than the standards applied under title V of the Rehabilitation Act of 1973. Section 36.103 of title III of the ADA adds that if a private entity receives federal financial assistance and is required to comply with the requirements of section 504 of the Rehabilitation Act of 1973, the ADA does not negate that requirement to comply with section 504.

CIVIL RIGHTS ACT

The Americans with Disabilities Act is a Civil Rights Act, not a construction code. The ramifications of being a civil rights act are very different from the ramifications of being a construction code. First, codes are enforced during the plans review process and the inspection process (see Chapter 2), whereas the ADA is enforced by our legal system. Second, when applying the provisions of the ADA, one must constantly consider whether or not the design and construction of a particular element or the implementation of a particular program would discriminate against individuals with disabilities. Though accessibility codes and the ADA both seek similar results as far as facilities are concerned, the ADA by nature of being a civil rights act often receives more attention from designers and builders, as the liability for violating the ADA can be great. Also, because the ADA addresses programs as well as construction, the ADA is much more comprehensive than the average accessibility portion of a code. The ADA requires a different mindset for designers and builders when applying its provisions from that used when applying the provisions of traditional accessibility codes.

The ADA is enforced by our legal system. Accessibility portions of codes are different from the ADA in that they are enforced by the plans review and inspection procedures of the state or local entity which adopts the particular code in question. Buildings and facilities are checked for compliance with any state or locally adopted accessibility codes by plans reviewers, and by inspectors who inspect construction in the field in order to determine that the construction adheres to the requirements of those accessibility codes. Should an element of a building which is required to be accessible by an accessibility code be ignored or missed by the designers, plans reviewers, builders, and inspectors involved in the project, chances are that the building element will not be corrected. There is usually no procedure for correcting that element unless the correction is made by those involved in the construction and inspection process. Under the ADA, however, an individual with a disability can file a complaint or a lawsuit over an inaccessible barrier when confronted with that barrier, no matter how long after the building has been occupied, if that barrier is within a building or facility covered by the ADA.

When dealing with construction projects that are covered by the ADA, owners, designers, and builders must consider whether or not the design and construction of any particular building element will create a barrier which is inaccessible to individuals with disabilities, and therefore will result in discrimination against individuals with disabilities. For example, the ADA would not require fire alarms in a conference room, but if a model code required fire alarms in certain conference rooms, the ADA would require those fire alarms to be accessible to individuals with disabilities. This means that those fire alarms would have to be accessible to individuals who cannot hear, as well as accessible to individuals who cannot see, so the fire alarms would have to be both audible and visible. The designer and builder must always consider the question, "If I provide this element for some people, how do I make it accessible to all people?" Of course, there are provisions in the ADA that help limit the degree of accessibility required in any given situation. These limitations will be discussed later in this chapter.

As already stated, the Americans with Disabilities Act (ADA) prohibits discrimination against individuals with disabilities in the areas of employment, public accommodations, state and local government services, and telecommunications. The ADA definition of a disability is a three-part definition, and can be found in title II of the law under section 35.104 Definitions, and in title III of the law under Section 36.104 Definitions, where it is stated that,

> Disability *means with respect to an individual, a physical or mental impairment that substantially limits one or more of the major life activities of such individual; a record of such impairment; or being regarded as having such an impairment.*

The term "physical or mental impairment" is broad in scope under the ADA and includes many impairments which are not affected by the design and construction of buildings and facilities, but which may be affected by the services provided within and without buildings and facilities. Sections 35.104 of title II and 36.104 of title III further state that:

> (1) *The phrase* physical or mental impairment *means—*
> (i) *Any physiological disorder or condition, cosmetic disfigurement, or anatomical loss affecting one or more of the following body systems: neurological; musculoskeletal; special sense organs; respiratory, including speech organs; cardiovascular; reproductive; digestive; genitourinary; hemic and lymphatic; skin; and endocrine;*
> (ii) *Any mental or psychological disorder such as mental retardation, organic brain syndrome, emotional or mental illness, and specific learning disabilities;*
> (iii) *The phrase physical or mental impairment includes, but is not limited to, such contagious and noncontagious diseases and conditions as orthopedic, visual, speech, and hearing impairments, cerebral palsy, epilepsy, muscular dystrophy, multiple sclerosis, cancer, heart disease, diabetes, mental retardation, emotional illness, specific learning disabilities, HIV disease (whether symptomatic or asymptomatic), tuberculosis, drug addiction, and alcoholism;*
> (iv) *The phrase* physical or mental impairment *does not include homosexuality or bisexuality.*

These sections state further that:

> (5) *The term* disability *does not include—*
> (i) *Transvestism, transsexualism, pedophilia, exhibitionism, voyeurism, gender identity disorders resulting from physical impairments, or other sexual behavior disorders;*
> (ii) *Compulsive gambling, kleptomania, or pyromania; or*
> (iii) *Psychoactive substance use disorders resulting from current illegal use of drugs.*

The ADA definition of disability centers around any physical or mental impairment that substantially limits one or more of the major life activities of an individual. "Major life activities" are defined as meaning "functions such as caring for one's self, performing manual tasks, walking, seeing, hearing, speaking, breathing, learning, and working." However, the ADA definition of disability also includes individuals having a record of an impairment and individuals regarded as having an impairment. This broad definition of disability grants certain civil rights to individuals with disabilities, as well as to individuals who are incorrectly perceived as having certain disabilities. Of course, these latter two parts of the definition of disability have no real effect on design and construction, but rather they affect employment situations, and are therefore more related to title I of the Americans with Disabilities Act than they are to titles II or III.

It is unlawful to discriminate against an individual who has a record of having had an impairment which substantially limits one or more major life functions. "Has a record of such impairment" is defined under the ADA definition of "disability" as meaning "has a history of, or has been misclassified as having, a mental or physical impairment that substantially limits one or more major life activities." For example, I once had a gentleman in one of my classes who told me he had been paralyzed for several years. In his case, it was not known why he had become paralyzed, nor why he had recovered fully from his paralysis. When I met him, he was able to walk without so much as a hint of the fact that he had once had to use a wheelchair for several years. If a potential employer familiar with this gentleman's history of having had a physical impairment used that history to deny him a job, that potential employer would be guilty of violating the Americans with Disabilities Act.

It is unlawful to discriminate against an individual who is regarded as having an impairment which substantially limits one or more major life activities. The ADA states that,

> *The phrase is* regarded as having an impairment *means—*
> *(i) Has a physical or mental impairment that does not substantially limit major life activities but that is treated by a private entity as constituting such a limitation;*
> *(ii) Has a physical or mental impairment that substantially limits major life activities only as a result of the attitudes of others towards such impairment; or*
> *(iii) Has none of the impairments defined in paragraph (1) of this definition but is treated by a private entity as having such an impairment.*

We have all heard of companies that wanted their employees to have a certain "look" in order to portray to the public an image of being "healthy." If such a company policy led to the denying of a job to an applicant because of a birthmark on that applicant's face, the policy could mean real trouble for that company, because it would be in violation of the Americans with Disabilities Act. Since it is illegal to deny employment or access to goods and services to an individual with a physical or mental impairment based solely on that impairment, it is certainly illegal to deny employment or access to goods and services to an individual incorrectly perceived as having a physical or mental impairment.

The three-part definition of "disability" established by the Americans with Disabilities Act helps set the stage for the ADA to provide for the mainstreaming of individuals with physical or mental impairments, as well as individuals mistakenly perceived as having physical or mental impairments. Though access to employment, goods, and services cannot be denied on the basis of disability, there are certain limitations to providing employment, goods, and services to people with disabilities. For example, one would not have to hire an individual with a disability if that individual were not the most qualified candidate for the job in question. Other limitations to providing employment, goods, and services to people with disabilities are discussed later in this chapter.

THE FIVE TITLES OF THE ADA

Title I of the Americans with Disabilities Act seeks to eliminate discrimination against individuals with disabilities by employment practices. The regulations of title I do not concern designers and builders unless they are employers, or unless employees with disabilities are discriminated against by the design and construction of inaccessible buildings and facilities. Title I is regulated mainly by the Equal Employment Opportunity Commission (EEOC). When seeking private sector advice on title I of the ADA, one should talk with an attorney who is familiar with employment law, and especially with the ADA.

Title II of the Americans with Disabilities Act seeks to eliminate discrimination against individuals with disabilities by public entities (state and local governments and agencies thereof). Title II regulates the services and, design, and construction practices of these public entities. Private (nongovernment) entities are not regulated by title II, except where public entity programs and services are provided by private entities or within private entity buildings and facilities. Title II does not regulate the federal government, but may regulate state and local governments when they administer certain federal programs and services.

Title III of the Americans with Disabilities Act seeks to eliminate discrimination against individuals with disabilities by private entities (nongovernment entities). Title III regulates private entity services, and private entity design and construction. A private entity building housing a public entity program may be subject to the requirements of both titles II and III of the ADA.

Title IV of the Americans with Disabilities Act seeks to eliminate discrimination against individuals with disabilities by telecommunications equipment and procedures.

Title V contains miscellaneous provisions that amplify many of the requirements of the other titles of the ADA.

EXEMPT ENTITIES

Private Clubs and Religious Institutions

In title III of the Americans with Disabilities Act (ADA), Section 36.102 Application states,

> (c) Exemptions and exclusions. *This part does not apply to any private club (except to the extent that the facilities of the private club are made available to customers or patrons of a place of public accommodation), or to any religious entity or public entity.*

A right coveted by many Americans is the right for one to congregate with whomever one pleases, as long as that congregation is not used to circumvent the requirements of certain laws such as the ADA. The ADA also seeks to preserve the separation of church and state that is an essential part of our democracy. Therefore, the ADA excludes private clubs and religious entities from its regulations; however, one cannot assume that all private clubs or religious entities are exempt from the provisions of the ADA.

Private Clubs

"Private clubs" are defined in title III of the Americans with Disabilities Act under Section 36.104 Definitions, as meaning "a private club or establishment exempted from coverage under title II of the Civil Rights Act of 1964 (42 U.S.C. 2000a(e))." The commentary section of title III which addresses the definition of private club lists several factors that courts have considered to determine whether or not a particular private club is exempt from the provisions of title II of the Civil Rights Act of 1964. The factors are

> the degree of member control of club operations, the selectivity of the membership selection process, whether substantial membership fees are charged, whether the entity is operated on a nonprofit basis, the extent to which the facilities are

open to the public, the degree of public funding, and whether the club was created specifically to avoid compliance with the Civil Rights Act.

The implication of this commentary is clear that these criteria will be used in determining which private clubs qualify as exempt entities under the ADA.

I have lived in cities where state law prohibited the sale of alcoholic beverages on Sundays except in private clubs. When entering public restaurants, I would often be asked if I were a member of the restaurant. A negative reply would lead to an offer of a one dollar membership or even a free membership to that restaurant. By making its patrons members, the restaurant would establish itself as a private club, and therefore would qualify to serve alcoholic beverages on Sundays. This "cheap membership" policy would keep many bars and restaurants in business on Sundays, but would not qualify those bars or restaurants for the private clubs exemption under the ADA. The criteria for establishing private club status under the ADA are much more stringent than the criteria used to determine whether state law will allow a bar or restaurant to serve alcoholic beverages on Sundays.

Private clubs which allow public accommodations to operate in their private club facilities must meet the requirements of title III of the ADA in all or part of their facilities. If I were to conduct a seminar open to the public and within the facilities of a private club, that seminar and certain areas of those facilities would have to be accessible to individuals with disabilities. This would be required by title III of the ADA, because I would be operating a place of public accommodation within that private club (places of public accommodation are discussed under the barrier removal section of this chapter). The responsible party for ensuring that the private club facilities were accessible to individuals with disabilities would either be my seminar business, the private club, or both parties as determined by my contract with the private club. If the private club wanted to remain exempt from the requirements of title III of the ADA, that club would need to avoid making its facilities available to public accommodations. However, if that private club desired to generate revenue from the rental of its facilities to nonexempt private or even public entities, it would be wise for that private club to make its facilities accessible to individuals with disabilities as no private entity nor any public entity could legally afford to lease those private club facilities.

Religious Entities

"Religious entities" are defined in title III of the Americans with Disabilities Act under Section 36.104 Definitions, as meaning "a religious organization, including a place of worship." This definition is very broad and not only applies to the worship facilities of religious organizations, but also applies to facilities operated by religious organizations which would normally be considered as places of public accommodation. The commentary within title III of the ADA which addresses the definition of religious entities states that one need not consider the nature of the service provided by the religious entity, but rather who is providing the service. Therefore, religious schools and hospitals are exempt entities under the ADA even though private schools and private hospitals would normally be considered to be public accommodations.

As with private clubs, religious entities cannot transfer their exempt status to public accommodations. If religious entities desired to generate income from making their facilities available to public and nonexempt private entities, the religious entities would be well served by making their facilities accessible to individuals with disabilities. Otherwise, private entities and public entities would be required to contract with other entities who operated accessible facilities. For example, a public concert held at a religious facility by a nonreligious entity would not receive the exempt status that is given to the religious entity that operated the facility.

It should also be noted that a religious entity may not transfer its exempt status to public entities covered under title II of the ADA, if that religious entity administers certain state or local government programs. Public entities are not allowed to contract with entities that discriminate against individuals with disabilities, whether those entities are exempt from the provisions of the ADA or not. For example, if a church were subsidized by a local government to serve meals to homeless people at a community kitchen within the church's facilities, those facilities would have to be accessible to individuals with disabilities. If the facilities were not accessible, the local government would be in violation of the ADA, because that local government entity would be discriminating against individuals with disabilities in the administration of one of its programs (public entity program accessibility is discussed under the title II section of this chapter). The desire to administer a community kitchen with state or local government funding might be the incentive for a religious entity to make their facilities accessible.

Housing

The Americans with Disabilities Act exempts certain housing from its requirements. One should consider the following questions when determining whether housing is exempt from the ADA:

1. Is the housing a place of lodging as defined in title III Section 36.104 Definitions under the definition of "places of public accommodation" (see places of public

accommodation in this chapter)? If the answer is yes, then places of lodging are regulated by title III of the ADA as places of public accommodation.

2. Are certain social services provided within the housing, as in certain homeless shelters and other facilities? If the answer is yes, then the facilities housing the social services are regulated by title III of the ADA as places of public accommodation.

3. How long is the length of stay of the residents of the housing? The length of stay may affect whether certain types of housing are treated as places of lodging. Often shelters such as homeless shelters and time-share condominiums are treated as places of lodging and are therefore regulated by title III of the ADA as places of public accommodation. Though dormitories are considered to be places of lodging under the ADA, one would not use time-related criteria to determine which dormitories were regulated, as all dormitories are places of lodging.

4. Is the housing provided by a state or local government program, such as low income housing? If the answer is yes, then program accessibility as regulated by title II of the ADA for public entities would mandate that the housing program be accessible to individuals with disabilities.

5. Is a place of public accommodation operated from the housing, such as a professional office located in a single family residence? If the answer is yes, then the professional office may be a place of public accommodation regulated by title III of the ADA (see the discussion of places of public accommodation located in private residences later in this chapter).

6. Are places of public accommodation provided adjacent to the private housing, such as a club house at an apartment complex? If the answer is yes, then places of public accommodation are regulated by title III of the ADA.

Accessibility for individuals with disabilities within multifamily housing is regulated by the Fair Housing Amendments Act. Places of lodging provided by private entities are regulated by title III of the ADA. Public housing provided by state and local governments is regulated by title II of the ADA. It is possible to have a housing situation where both the ADA and the Fair Housing Amendments Act apply, such as a hotel that allows long-term and short-term leases. The area of the building used for long-term leases would be subject to the requirements of the Fair Housing Amendments Act, whereas the area of the building used for short-term leases would be subject to the requirements of the Americans with Disabilities Act. However, if a housing facility allowed long-term and short-term stays and did not designate specific rooms for either long-term or short-term residency, the entire facility would have to meet the requirements of the Fair Housing Amendments Act and the ADA.

Federal Government

The federal government is covered by the Architectural Barriers Act (ABA) of 1968 and all federal facilities must meet the requirements of the Uniform Federal Accessibility Standard (UFAS). Because of the supposed accessibility provided within in federal facilities under the ABA, Congress exempted the federal government from the Americans with Disabilities Act. However, it has been my experience that many Federal departments and agencies have received mandates from their respective "heads" that they will maintain some sort of voluntary compliance with the ADA.

Others

Other entities exempted from the Americans with Disabilities Act are those "other" entities which are also exempted from the Civil Rights Act of 1964.

GENERAL PROHIBITION OF DISCRIMINATION
Title III—Private Entities

Title III of the Americans with Disabilities Act is titled, "Nondiscrimination on the Basis of Disability by Public Accommodations and in Commercial Facilities." Section 36.101 Purpose, states that its purpose

> is to implement title III of the Americans with Disabilities Act of 1990 (42 U.S.C. 12181), which prohibits discrimination on the basis of disability by public accommodations and requires places of public accommodation and commercial facilities to be designed, constructed, and altered in compliance with the accessibility standards established by this part.

Section 36.102 Application clarifies that title III applies to not only places of public accommodation and commercial facilities, but also to any private entity that offers examinations or courses related to applications, licensing, certification, or credentialing for secondary or post-secondary education, professional, or trade purposes.

Section 36.201 General, of title III "sets up" the general rule for prohibition of discrimination by stating,

> (a) Prohibition of discrimination. No individual shall be discriminated against on the basis of disability in the full and equal enjoyment of the goods, services, facilities, privileges, advantages, or accommodations of any place of public

accommodation by any private entity who owns, leases (or leases to), or operates a place of public accommodation.

Title III of the ADA prohibits discrimination against individuals with disabilities by private entities (nongovernment entities). This general prohibition of discrimination is followed by several sections in title III which further develop what is meant by a prohibition of discrimination.

Section 36.202 Activities, states that a public accommodation cannot deny individuals with disabilities from participating in or benefiting from the goods, services, facilities, privileges, advantages, or accommodations of a place of public accommodation; that a public accommodation cannot afford individuals with disabilities with the opportunity to participate in or benefit from a good, service, facility, privilege, advantage, or accommodation that is not equal to that afforded to other individuals; that a public accommodation cannot provide individuals with disabilities with a good, service, facility, privilege, advantage, or accommodation that is different or separate from that provided to other individuals, unless such action is necessary to provide the individuals with disabilities with a good, service, facility, privilege, advantage, or accommodation, or other opportunity that is as effective as that provided to others. These prohibitions of discrimination are afforded to individuals with disabilities or classes of individuals with disabilities. "Individuals with disabilities or classes of individuals with disabilities" refers to the clients or customers of the public accommodation that enter into contractual, licensing, or other arrangements. It should also be noted that public accommodations cannot discriminate as mentioned above either directly, or through contractual, licensing or other arrangements.

Section 36.203 Integrated settings, requires a public accommodation to afford its goods, services, facilities, privileges, advantages, and accommodations to individuals with disabilities in the most integrated settings appropriate to the needs of the individuals. These are to be provided so that individuals with disabilities will not have to participate in programs or activities that are separate or different. Section 36.203 further states, "Nothing in this part shall be construed to require an individual with a disability to accept an accommodation, aid, service, opportunity, or benefit available under this part that such individual chooses not to accept." This section also makes it clear that the section is not an authorization for the representative or guardian of an individual with a disability to decline essential needs for that individual with a disability such as food, water, medical treatment, or medical services.

Three more sections detail some of the rights granted by the ADA, some of which usually have little bearing on the design and construction of a facility. Section 36.204

Administrative methods, disallows discrimination against individuals with disabilities, either directly or contractually by public accommodations through the utilization
of standards or criteria, or methods of administration. Section 36.205 Association,
prohibits discrimination by a public accommodation against individuals or entities,
because of their relationship or association with an individual with a disability.
Section 36.206 Retaliation or coercion, clarifies that it is unlawful for a public
accommodation to discriminate against any individual who has opposed any act or
practice made unlawful by the ADA, who has made a charge or participated in any
proceedings as a result of the ADA, who has enjoyed any of the rights granted by the
ADA, or who has aided or encouraged any other individual in enjoying the rights
granted by the ADA.

Section 36.208 Direct threat, of title III of the ADA provides a limitation to
accessibility, when the provision of accessibility would in any case pose a direct threat
to the health or safety of others. Direct threat is not a limitation to the provision of
accessibility if in a particular instance, making a facility or program accessible would
pose a risk to the individual with a disability for whom the accessibility was provided. Section 36.208 states,

> (a) *This part does not require a public accommodation to permit an individual
> to participate in or benefit from the goods, services, facilities, privileges, advan-
> tages, and accommodations of that public accommodation when that individ-
> ual poses a direct threat to the health or safety of others.*
> (b) Direct threat *means a significant risk to the health and safety of others
> that cannot be eliminated by a modification of policies, practices, or proce-
> dures, or by the provision of auxiliary aids or services.*
> (c) *In determining whether an individual poses a direct threat to the health or
> safety of others, a public accommodation must make an individualized assess-
> ment, based on reasonable judgment that relies on current medical knowledge
> or on the best available objective evidence, to ascertain: the nature, duration,
> and severity of the risk; the probability that the potential injury will actually
> occur; and whether reasonable modifications of policies, practices, or proce-
> dures will mitigate the risk.*

Title III addresses several other issues involving the determination of limitations
regarding the prohibition of discrimination towards individuals with disabilities.
These three areas of concern do not involve the built environment and are primarily
employment issues. They are covered under section 36.209 Illegal use of drugs, section 36.210 Smoking, and 36.212 Insurance.

Title II—Public Entities

Title II of the Americans with Disabilities Act is titled, "Nondiscrimination on the Basis of Disability in State and Local Government Services." Section 35.101 Purpose, states that its purpose "is to effectuate subtitle A of title II of the Americans with Disabilities Act of 1990, (42 U.S.C. 12131), which prohibits discrimination on the basis of disability by public entities." Section 35.102 Application, clarifies that title II "applies to all services, programs, and activities provided or made available by public entities."

Section 35.130 General prohibition against discrimination, of title II establishes the general rule for prohibition of discrimination by stating, "(a) No qualified individual with a disability shall, on the basis of disability, be excluded from participation in or be denied the benefits of the services, programs, or activities of a public entity, or be subjected to discrimination by any public entity." Title II of the ADA prohibits discrimination against individuals with disabilities by public entities (state and local government entities and agencies thereof). Section 35.130 further details what is meant by a general prohibition against discrimination by public entities.

In providing aids, benefits, or services, either directly or through contractual, licensing, or other arrangements, public entities may not on the basis of disability, deny qualified individuals with disabilities the opportunity to participate in or benefit from their aids, benefits, or services; public entities may not on the basis of disability afford individuals with disabilities with the opportunity to participate in or benefit from aids, benefits, or services that are not equal to that afforded to other individuals; public entities may not on the basis of disability provide individuals with aids, benefits, or services that are not as effective in affording equal opportunities to obtain the same results, to gain the same benefits or to reach the same levels of achievement as that provided to others; public entities may not on the basis of disability provide separate aids, benefits, or services to qualified individuals with disabilities than is provided to others unless such action is necessary to provide qualified individuals with aids, benefits, or services that are as effective as those provided to others; public entities may not on the basis of disability aid or perpetuate discrimination against qualified individuals with disabilities by providing significant assistance to agencies, organizations, or persons that discriminate on the basis of disability in providing aids, benefits, or services to beneficiaries of the public entities' programs; public entities may not on the basis of disability deny qualified individuals with disabilities the opportunity to participate as members of planning advisory boards; and public entities may not on the basis of disability otherwise limit qualified individuals with disabilities in the enjoyment of any rights, privileges, advantages, or opportunities enjoyed by others receiving their aids, benefits, or services.

Public entities cannot deny qualified individuals with disabilities the right to participate in services, programs, or activities that are not separate, even if separate services, programs, or activities are provided for individuals with disabilities. Public entities cannot utilize criteria or methods of administration, either directly or through contractual or other arrangements that discriminate against qualified individuals with disabilities that defeat or impair the accomplishments of any programs with respect to individuals with disabilities, and that perpetuate the discrimination against qualified individuals with disabilities by other public entities if all of the public entities are subject to common administrative control. Sites and locations of public entity facilities must be selected so that the facilities and the programs offered in the facilities will be accessible to qualified individuals with disabilities. When selecting procurement contractors, public entities may not use criteria that discriminate against qualified individuals with disabilities.

Licensing and certification programs of public entities cannot discriminate against qualified individuals with disabilities. Public entities cannot establish requirements for the programs or activities of licensees or certified entities that discriminate against qualified individuals with disabilities. Section 35.130 adds, "The programs or activities of entities that are licensed or certified by a public entity are not, themselves, covered by this part." That is not to say that the programs or activities of entities that are licensed or certified by a public entity are not covered by other provisions of title II of the ADA, or even covered by title III of the ADA.

In order to ensure accessibility to individuals with disabilities, public entities must make reasonable modifications in policies, practices, and procedures, unless it can be demonstrated that such modifications would fundamentally alter the nature of the service, program, or activity.

Public entities may not use eligibility criteria that selectively disallow individuals with disabilities "from fully and equally enjoying any service, program, or activity, unless such criteria can be shown to be necessary for the provision of the service, program, or activity being offered."

Public entities must administer services, programs, or activities "in the most integrated setting appropriate to the needs of qualified individuals with disabilities."

Individuals with disabilities may refuse any accommodation, aid, service opportunity, or benefit provided under title II of the ADA, but any representative or guardian of an individual with a disability is not authorized by title II to decline food, water, medical treatment, or medical services for that individual.

Public entities may not place surcharges on individuals with disabilities in order to pay for the accommodations necessary to provide accessibility for those individuals with disabilities.

Section 35.130 of title II of the ADA ends with the proviso that public entities cannot discriminate against individuals who have associations or relationships with individuals with disabilities.

EXISTING AND ONGOING PROVISIONS

Unlike most accessibility codes, the Americans with Disabilities Act (ADA) regulates existing facilities and existing programs as well as employment issues. Both the ADA and accessibility codes regulate new construction and alterations, but the ADA prohibits discrimination against individuals with disabilities in existing facilities and programs as well. Existing facilities are buildings and facilities with no planned improvements, and therefore the ADA's provisions regulating existing facilities are retroactive in nature.

When considering the ramifications of the ADA towards existing programs and facilities, it is helpful to identify three areas of concern in order to separate the different standards of care required for each situation—title I employment provisions, title II program accessibility, and title III private entity barrier removal. Title III requires private entities to remove barriers to individuals with disabilities which are readily achievable to remove within places of public accommodation. Public entities are required by title II to make all programs and services accessible to individuals with disabilities. Employment provisions are covered by title I of the ADA and relate to both private and public entities. Employee provisions require employers to make reasonable accommodations in order for employees with disabilities to be able to perform the functions of their jobs. It should be noted that the Title I employment provisions do not apply to certain small entities, but titles II and III apply to all nonexempt entities regardless of size.

The provisions of the ADA which regulate these three areas are ongoing provisions. In other words, they must meet these provisions continually. Any new or altered facility and any new program must maintain forever the applicable standards of care applied to existing programs and facilities. Also, employers must never discriminate against an employee with a disability.

How do ADA existing provisions relate to designers and builders? Since many of these existing and ongoing provisions affect programs and employment, the solutions required to improve accessibility are not always architectural in nature, nor do they always require any design or construction. However, programs and employment opportunities offered by designers and builders must comply with the ADA. Also, barrier removal in places of public accommodation and program accessibility for public entities may require architectural modifications in many cases. Architectural modifications may even be necessary in order to make an area accessible where an employee with a disability works, so it is not uncommon for designers to be employed to help private entities and public entities identify inaccessible features of their facilities, as well as help remedy certain situations.

The ADA requires accessible features of facilities and equipment to be maintained in accessible condition. Being a Civil Rights Act, the ADA covers the "ongoing" aspects of accessibility. It is not enough to provide accessibility for individuals with disabilities, but one must also maintain that accessibility, so that facilities and equipment do not become inaccessible over time. This is significant as the neglect of accessible features may ultimately lead to public accommodation's being accused of discriminating against individuals with disabilities.

Section 35.133 of title II and Section 36.211 of title III Maintenance of accessible features, states,

> (a) A public accommodation shall maintain in operable working condition those features of facilities and equipment that are required to be readily accessible to and usable by persons with disabilities by the Act or this part.
>
> (b) This section does not prohibit isolated or temporary interruptions in service or access due to maintenance or repairs.

Title III—Private Entities

Key Terms

In order to fully understand the Americans with Disabilities Act's prohibition of discrimination for private entities, one must become acquainted with some key terms of art. The terms necessary for understanding this prohibition of discrimination are commercial facility, place of public accommodation, and public accommodation.

COMMERCIAL FACILITIES

Commercial facilities are defined in title III of the ADA under Section 36.104 Definitions, which states,

Commercial facilities *means facilities—*
(1) Whose operations will affect commerce;

(2) That are intended for nonresidential use by a private entity; and

(3) That are not—

(i) Facilities that are covered or expressly exempted from coverage under the Fair Housing Act of 1968, as amended (42 U.S.C. 3601-3631);

(ii) Aircraft; or

(iii) Railroad locomotives, railroad freight cars, railroad cabooses, commuter or intercity passenger rail cars (including coaches, dining cars, sleeping cars, lounge cars, and food service cars), any other railroad cars described in section 242 of the Act or covered under title II of the Act, or railroad rights-of-way. For purposes of this definition, "rail" and "railroad" have the meaning given the term "railroad" in section 202(e) of the Federal Railroad Safety act of 1970 (45 U.S.C. 431[e]).

When a facility meets any of the section 36.104 criteria for defining a commercial facility, then the entire facility is a commercial facility. Portions of commercial facilities may or may not be places of public accommodation as defined below. Places of public accommodation are located within a commercial facility. What does commerce mean? Section 36.104 states,

Commerce *means travel, trade, traffic, commerce, transportation, or communication—*

(1) Among the several states;

(2) Between any foreign country or any territory or possession and any State; or

(3) Between points in the same State but through another State or foreign country.

This is obviously a broad definition and reflects the intent of Congress for the ADA to be far-reaching in scope.

PUBLIC ACCOMMODATIONS AND PLACES OF PUBLIC ACCOMMODATION

Places of public accommodation encompass those areas of a private entity facility where the public has access to goods and services intended for public use. Places of public accommodation are the areas where one shops, dines, rests, is entertained, is educated, seeks employment, and so on. One who owns, operates, leases, or leases to a place of public accommodation is a public accommodation. Public accommodations are ultimately responsible for seeing that their places of public accommodation meet the requirements of the ADA. When I provide my seminars in hotels, I am a public accommodation because I operate my seminars which are places of public accommodation. Any hotel which leases a seminar space to me is also a public accommodation, because they are leasing a place of public accommodation to me. We could both be responsible, depending on our tenant/landlord agreement, for ensuring that the place of public accommodation meets the requirements of the ADA.

Section 36.104 Definitions of title III of the ADA states,

Place of public accommodation *means a facility, operated by a private entity, whose operations affect commerce and fall within at least one of the following categories—*

(1) An inn, hotel, or motel or other place of lodging except for an establishment located within a building that contains not more than five rooms for rent or hire and that is actually occupied by the proprietor of the establishment as a residence of the proprietor;

(2) A restaurant, bar, or other establishment that serving food or drink;

(3) A motion picture house, theater, or concert hall, stadium, or other place of exhibition or entertainment;

(4) An auditorium, convention center, lecture hall, or other place of public gathering;

(5) A bakery, grocery store, clothing store, hardware store, shopping center, or other sales or rental establishment;

(6) A laundromat, dry cleaner, bank, barber shop, beauty shop, travel service, shoe repair service, funeral parlor, office of an accountant, lawyer, pharmacy, insurance office, professional office of a health car provider, a hospital, or other service establishment;

(7) A terminal, depot, or other station used to supply public transportation;

(8) A museum, library, gallery, or other place of public display or collection;

(9) A park, zoo, amusement park, or other place of recreation;

(10) A nursery, elementary, secondary, undergraduate, or postgraduate private school or other place of education;

(11) A day care center, senior citizen center, homeless shelter, food bank, adoption agency, or other social service center establishment; and

(12) A gymnasium, bowling alley, golf course, or other place of exercise or recreation.

Places of lodging as defined under item (1) of the list above include time-share condominimums. The burden of proof as to whether a time-share condomimium is a place of lodging may actually depend on the average length of stay of the different owners or renters. That critical length of stay should be verified with the Department of Justice until precedence can be established in a courtroom.

Private residences are usually not covered by title III of the ADA, but when a place of public accommodation is located within a private residence, title III of the ADA does apply. An example of a place of public accommodation in a private residence might be an office of a professional, such as a psychologist or small restaurant within a private residence. Section 36.207 Places of Public Accommodation Located in Private Residences, states,

> *(a) When a place of public accommodation is located in a private residence, the portion of the residence used exclusively as a residence is not covered by this part, but that portion used exclusively in the operation of the place of public accommodation or that portion used both for the place of public accommodation and for residential purposes is covered by this part.*
>
> *(b) The portion of the residence covered under paragraph (a) of this section extends to those elements used to enter the place of public accommodation, including the homeowner's front sidewalk, if any, the door or entryway, and hallways; and those portions of the residence, interior or exterior, available to or used by customers or clients, including restrooms.*

Existing Facilities—Readily Achievable Barrier Removal

Existing facilities of private entities are regulated by title III of the Americans with Disabilities Act, and are required to remove architectural barriers from places of public accommodation which deny access for individuals with disabilities to the goods and services provided within the facilities. If any of these architectural barriers cannot be removed without great effort or expense, modifications can be made to programs and services through alternative methods in order to accommodate individuals with disabilities. If either the removal of a particular structural barrier or modifications to programs and services to eliminate that barrier would involve great effort or expense, then no actions would be required to remove that particular barrier. The ADA would see the removal of that barrier as being in excess of the "readily achievable" standard of care for existing private entity facilities. This barrier removal should have occurred as of January 26, 1992.

Existing private entity barrier removal is required by title III, section 36.304 Removal of barriers which states, "(a) *General.* A public accommodation shall remove architectural barriers in existing facilities, including communication barriers that are structural in nature, where such removal is readily achievable, i.e., easily accomplishable without much difficulty or expense." This general rule is loaded with ADA jargon which may require some explanation. It is important for one to remember when trying to understand the full implications of this general rule, that the ADA requires the lowest standard of care for existing private entity facilities and programs.

Existing private entity facilities consist of all private entity facilities whether or not any such facility is scheduled to be renovated, expanded, or demolished. Facilities that are renovated or expanded were existing facilities before their renovation or expansion, and are existing facilities during and after their renovation and expansion, and are therefore subject to the ADA provisions for existing facilities. Of course, they are also subject to the ADA requirements for alterations. As soon as a newly constructed private entity facility is completed, it becomes an existing facility, which results in its being subject to the ADA provisions for existing facilities.

Private entities must anticipate that different individuals with different disabilities will occupy the places of public accommodation within their existing private entity facilities. These private entities must remove the accessibility barriers which are readily achievable to remove from the places of public accommodation. Areas of existing private entity facilities which are not places of public accommodation are held to a different standard of care than are the places of public accommodation. In the areas of a facility that are not places of public accommodation, one would remove the barriers that prevented an employee with a disability from performing the functions of his or her job, upon hiring that employee. These reasonable accommodations for an employee with a disability are required by title I of the ADA and are discussed later in this chapter.

So existing private entities are first held to an "architectural" standard of care, and then to an "alternative methods" or program access standard of care within places of public accommodation. Public entities (state and local government entities), on the other hand, may choose from the onset between program adjustments and architectural solutions for maintaining accessibility, but they are held to a higher standard of care as to total accessibility. Existing public entity programs are covered later in this chapter.

Architectural Barriers

The term "architectural barriers" is defined within the commentary on section 36.304 of title III of the ADA. The commentary states, "The requirement to remove architectural barriers includes the removal of physical barriers of any kind." Obviously, the removal of attitudinal and administrative barriers do not require architectural or "structural" modifications. Attitudinal and administrative barriers are covered under the title III prohibition of discrimination provisions already discussed.

Readily Achievable

When providing architectural barrier removal for existing private entity facilities, the standard of care required by the ADA is defined by the term, "readily achievable".

Section 36.104 Definitions, of title III explains that, *"Readily achievable* means easily accomplishable and able to be carried out without much difficulty or expense." The readily achievable standard will rarely provide the ultimate level of accessibility up to and within any facility; nevertheless, because of the considerable expense often found in removing barriers to accessibility from existing facilities, the readily achievable standard is viewed as a fair standard of care. Higher standards of care are applied to alterations and new construction, as accessibility is more affordable to provide when "starting from scratch."

The following is a list of factors from section 36.104 of title III which are used to consider whether or not an action is readily achievable:

(1) The nature and the cost of the action needed under this part;
(2) The overall financial resources of the site or sites involved in the action; the number of persons employed at the site; the effect on expenses and resources; legitimate safety requirements that are necessary for safe operation, including crime prevention measures; or the impact otherwise of the action upon the operation of the site;
(3) The geographic separateness, and the administrative or fiscal relationship of the site or sites in question to any parent corporation or entity;
(4) If applicable, the overall financial resources of any parent corporation or entity; the overall size of the parent corporation or entity with respect to the number of its employees; the number, type, and location of its facilities; and
(5) If applicable, the type of operation or operations of any parent corporation or entity, including the composition, structure, and functions of the workforce of the parent corporation or entity.

What would be necessary to meet the readily achievable standard for a restaurant that was an individual franchise of a large restaurant corporation with hundreds of franchises, is not the same as what would be necessary to meet the readily achievable standard for a small single location "mom and pop" restaurant. The intent of the readily achievable standard is not to burden the rich more heavily than the poor, but rather the intent is to provide as much accessibility in existing private entity facilities as is considered fair, while not financially exhausting the resources of smaller businesses. It would not help individuals with disabilities at all for the ADA to put out of business those small companies that might eventually employ, provide services to, or receive services from individuals with disabilities.

Some existing private entity facilities have no places of public accommodation, and therefore have no areas where the readily achievable barrier removal standard is applied. Often, factories and other industrial facilities have no or few places of public accommodation. Be aware that within these facilities, offices used for seeking employment, areas open for public tours, and dining areas open to the public, as well as any other similar areas are considered places of public accommodation.

There are some private entities where it may not be readily achievable in a given year to provide any barrier removal in places of public accommodation. One must understand that it would be a rare circumstance for a private entity not to be able to remove any barriers to accessibility in a readily achievable fashion. Furthermore, one must understand that readily achievable barrier removal within existing private entity facilities is an ongoing standard, and though it may not be financially possible for a private entity to provide readily achievable barrier removal in a given year, the readily achievable standard will be applied every year, and it is not likely that a private entity will never have the financial wherewithal to remove any to accessibility in a readily achievable fashion. In fact, a more likely scenario would be that of a private entity having the financial resources to remove some barriers to accessibility in a readily achievable fashion one year, while other barriers to accessibility would be removed in a readily achievable fashion in later years. Some barriers to accessibility may never be readily achievable to remove.

BARRIER REMOVAL

When trying to determine which barriers are readily achievable for a private entity to remove, one may use as a guide, the list found in title III under Section 36.304 Removal of barriers:

(b) Examples. *Examples of steps to remove barriers include, but are not limited to, the following actions—*

1. *Installing ramps;*
2. *Making curb cuts in sidewalks and entrances;*
3. *Repositioning shelves;*
4. *Rearranging tables, chairs, vending machines, display racks and other furniture;*
5. *Repositioning telephones;*
6. *Adding raised markings on elevator control buttons;*
7. *Installing flashing alarm lights;*
8. *Widening doors;*
9. *Installing offset hinges to widen doorways;*
10. *Eliminating a turnstile or providing an alternative accessible path;*
11. *Installing accessible door hardware;*
12. *Installing grab bars in toilet stalls;*
13. *Rearranging toilet partitions to increase maneuvering space;*

14. *Insulating laboratory pipes under sinks to prevent burns;*

15. *Installing a raised toilet seat;*

16. *Installing a full length bathroom mirror;*

17. *Repositioning the paper towel dispenser in a bathroom;*

18. *Creating designated accessible parking spaces;*

19. *Installing an accessible paper cup dispenser at an existing inaccessible water fountain;*

20. *Removing high pile low density carpeting, or*

21. *Installing vehicle hand controls.*

This list is not exhaustive as there are many other options for readily achievable barrier removal which one could apply. Title III of the ADA calls for the consideration of additional barrier removal options which apply to seating in assembly areas, examinations and courses, transportation provided by public accommodations, check-out aisles, and certain other areas where strict adherence with the Standards for Accessible Design would not be readily achievable.

When considering which barriers are readily achievable to remove in existing assembly seating areas, one should consider the many different aspects of seating enjoyed by the patrons of assembly areas. Section 36.308 Seating in assembly areas, requires that a reasonable number of wheelchair seating spaces be provided, as well as a reasonable number of seats with removable aisle-side arm rests. The wheelchair seating spaces are required to be located to ensure that they:

[A] *Are dispersed throughout the seating area;*

[B] *Provide lines of sight and choice of admission prices comparable to those for members of the general public;*

[C] *Adjoin an accessible route that also serves as a means of egress in case of emergency; and*

[D] *Permit individuals who use wheelchairs to sit with family members or other companions.*

Section 36.308 adds that if the removal of any assembly area seats to create wheelchair seating areas is not readily achievable, then portable chairs should be provided adjacent to wheelchair seating areas, if readily achievable, for family members or companions of individuals with disabilities to use.

Title III of the ADA addresses examinations and courses in Section 36.309 Examinations and courses. Section 36.309 stipulates that examinations and courses which are related to applications, licensing, certification, or credentialing for secondary or post-secondary education, professional, or trade purposes will be accessible to individuals with disabilities that have impaired sensory, manual, or speaking skills.

Modifications must be made to examinations and courses or to the locations where examinations and courses are offered in order to achieve accessibility for individuals with disabilities.

It is possible that in many situations accessibility for examinations and courses can only be achieved through the provision of auxiliary aids. Auxiliary aids and services for examinations include taped examinations, interpreters, of other effective methods of making orally delivered materials available to individuals with hearing impairments, Brailled or large print examinations and answer sheets or qualified readers for individuals with visual impairments or learning disabilities, transcribers for individuals with manual impairments, as well as other similar aids and services. Auxiliary aids and services for courses include taped texts, interpreters, or other effective methods of making orally delivered materials available to individuals with hearing impairments, Brailled or large print texts or qualified readers for individuals with visual impairments or learning disabilities, classroom equipment adapted for use by individuals with manual impairments, as well as other similar aids and services.

Those public accommodations which provide public transportation but which are not primarily engaged in the business of transporting people, must remove transportation barriers in existing vehicles and rail passenger cars when the removal of those barriers is readily achievable as stated in Section 36.310 Transportation provided by public accommodations. Examples of the types of transportation vehicles covered by section 36.310 are shuttle services operated between transportation terminals and places of public accommodation, customer shuttle bus services operated by private companies and shopping centers, hotel shuttles, student transportation systems, and transportation provided within recreational facilities such as stadiums, zoos, amusement parks, and ski resorts. Section 36.310 does not require public accommodations to remove barriers in any of these existing vehicles and rail passenger cars "that can only be removed through the retrofitting of vehicles or rail passenger cars by the installation of a hydraulic or other lift."

Section 36.302 Modifications in policies, practices, or procedures requires stores with check-out aisles to keep open during store hours an adequate number of accessible check-out aisles. This is to ensure that an equivalent level of convenient service is provided for individuals with disabilities. An example of modifying policies, practices, and procedures given in section 36.302, suggests that if an express check-out aisle is the only accessible check-out aisle in a particular existing store, then that store should make that express check-out aisle available at all times to all persons requiring an accessible check-out aisle.

PRIORITIZATION

When the costs of removing barriers exceed what is readily achievable for a given year, the public accommodation must decide which barriers should be removed first, based on what is readily achievable and on which barriers would take precedence for removal over other barriers. Title III of the ADA provides a suggested list of priorities in Section 36.304 Removal of barriers:

> (c) Priorities. *A public accommodation is urged to take measures to comply with the barrier removal requirements of this section in accordance with the following order of priorities.*
> *(1) First, a public accommodation should take measures to provide access to a place of public accommodation from public sidewalks, parking, or public transportation. These measures include for example, installing an entrance ramp, widening entrances, and providing accessible parking spaces (Figure 11-4).*
> *(2) Second, a public accommodation should take measures to provide access to those areas of a place of public accommodation where goods and services are made available to the public. These measures include, for example, adjusting the layout of display racks, rearranging tables, providing Brailled and raised character signage, widening doors, providing visual alarms, and installing ramps (Figure 11-5).*
> *(3) Third, a public accommodation should take measures to provide access to restroom facilities. These measures include, for example, removal of obstructing furniture or vending machines, widening of doors, installation of ramps, providing accessible signage, widening of toilet stalls, and installation of grab bars (Figure 11-6).*
> *(4) Fourth, a public accommodation should take any other measures necessary to provide access to the goods, services, facilities, privileges, advantages, or accommodations of a place of public accommodation (Figure 11-7).*

The rationale behind this priority list is fairly obvious. First, it serves no real purpose for the facility to be accessible if individuals with disabilities cannot gain entrance to the facility. Second, access to the goods and services within the facility are the central reason to gain entrance to that facility. Third, accessible toilet rooms grant more time for people with disabilities to enjoy the goods and services offered within the facility. And fourth, the ADA's central theme is the prohibition of discrimination against individuals with disabilities, and therefore all other goods and services, such as drinking fountains and telephones, should be made accessible. Though the above analysis of the barrier removal priority system attempts to establish logic for the priorities listed, the analysis is somewhat geared towards those with disabilities affecting mobility. It is important to note that there are many different types of disabilities, and a building that

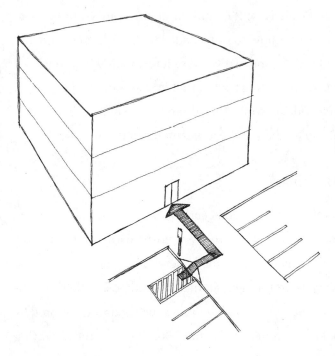

Figure 11-4 Entrance issues

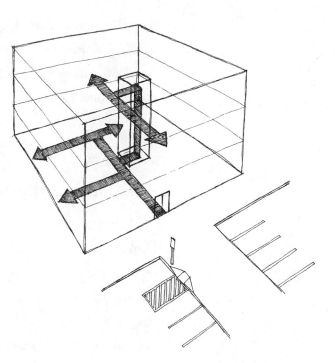

Figure 11-5 Interior issues

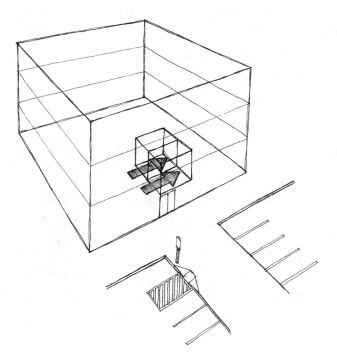

Figure 11-6 Restroom issues

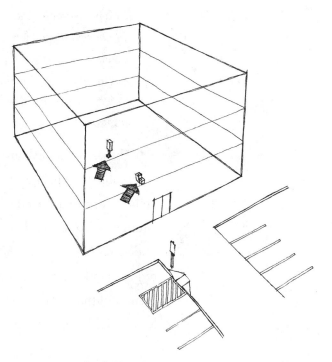

Figure 11-7 Other issues

is totally inaccessible to certain individuals with certain disabilities, may not be inaccessible, or may be only partially inaccessible to other individuals with other disabilities. With this in mind, one should not assume that because individuals who use wheelchairs cannot gain entrance to a certain existing facility, that it would not be possible to make the facility accessible to individuals with other disabilities, such as individuals who use crutches or individuals who are hard of hearing amongst others.

Alternatives to Barrier Removal

When it is not readily achievable for a public accommodation to remove barriers from a place of public accommodation, title III of the Americans with Disabilities Act requires the public accommodation to make its "its goods, services, facilities, privileges, advantages, or accommodations available through alternative methods, if those methods are readily achievable." These nonarchitectural alternative methods are required by Section 36.305 Alternatives to barrier removal. Section 36.305 lists the following actions as examples typifying alternatives to barrier removal:

(1) Providing curb service or home delivery;
(2) Retrieving merchandise from inaccessible shelves or racks;
(3) Relocating activities to accessible locations;
(c) Multiscreen cinemas. *If it is not readily achievable to remove barriers to provide access by persons with mobility impairments to all of the theaters of a multiscreen cinema, the cinema shall establish a film rotation schedule that provides reasonable access for individuals who use wheelchairs to all films. Reasonable notice shall be provided to the public as to the location and time of accessible showings.*

This is not an exhaustive list of alternative methods. If it is not presently readily achievable for a public accommodation to provide accessibility for individuals with disabilities within a place of public accommodation by removing barriers or by providing alternative methods, then the public accommodation will have no present obligation under the ADA, as the readily achievable standard is a limitation, as well as a minimum requirement. Remember also that the readily achievable standard is an ongoing requirement and that which may not be readily achievable to do in the present may be readily achievable to do in the future.

Landlord and Tenant Responsibilities

Section 36.201 General, of title III of the Americans with Disabilities Act clarifies that responsibility for accessibility within places of public accommodation is determined by the legal agreements between landlords and tenants. Section 36.201 states:

> (b) Landlord and tenant responsibilities. *Both the landlord who owns the building that houses a place of public accommodation and the tenant who owns or operates the place of public accommodation are public accommodations subject to the requirements of this part. As between the parties, allocation of responsibility for complying with the obligations of this part may be determined by lease or other contract.*

In all actuality most, if not all landlord/tenant agreements in place at the inception of the ADA had no language regarding the ADA whatsoever. This is probably not as true today. When entering into a lease agreement either as a tenant or as a landlord, one should have an attorney familiar with the ADA review the agreement before one signs it.

Limitations to Barrier Removal

SAFETY

Safety requirements may be imposed by a public accommodation if they are legitimate safety requirements and are not merely a means for avoiding compliance with the ADA. Section 36.301 of title III clarifies that safety requirements must be based on actual risk. Safety requirements cannot be based on mere speculation, stereotypes, or generalizations about individuals with disabilities.

UNDUE BURDEN FOR AUXILIARY AIDS AND SERVICES

Section 36.303 Auxiliary aids and services, of title III of the Americans with Disabilities Act states,

> (F) Alternatives. *If provision of a particular auxiliary aid or service by a public accommodation would result in a fundamental alteration in the nature of the goods, services, facilities, privileges, advantages, or accommodations being offered or in an undue burden, i.e., significant difficulty or expense, the public accommodation shall provide an alternative auxiliary aid or service, if one exists, that would not result in an alteration or such burden but would nevertheless ensure that, to the maximum extent possible, individuals with disabilities receive the goods, services, facilities, privileges, advantages, or accommodations offered by the public accommodation.*

Examinations and courses are also granted the undue burden limitation concerning auxiliary aids and services under section 36.309 Examinations and Courses.

The definition of "undue burden" is defined in Section 36.104 Definitions, of title III as,

> significant difficulty or expense. In determining whether an action would result in an undue burden, factors to be considered include—
> (1) The nature and the cost of the action needed under this part;
> (2) The overall financial resources of the site or sites involved in the action; the number of persons employed at the site; the effect on expenses and resources; legitimate safety requirements that are necessary for safe operation, including crime prevention measures; or the impact otherwise of the action upon the operation of the site;
> (3) The geographic separateness, and the administrative or fiscal relationship of the site or sites in question to any parent corporation or entity;
> (4) If applicable, the overall financial resources of any parent corporation or entity; the overall size of the parent corporation or entity with respect to the number of its employees; the number, type, and location of its facilities; and
> (5) If applicable, the type of operation or operations of any parent corporation or entity, including the composition, structure, and functions of the workforce of the parent corporation or entity.

Often, a private entity may wish to cite undue burden as a reason for not complying with a particular provision of title III of the ADA. The undue burden limitation is made available to private entities only for auxiliary aids and services, however, as it may be impossible to provide some auxiliary aids and services on short notice. Section 36.303 Auxiliary Aids and Services lists the following examples of auxiliary aids and services:

> (1) Qualified interpreters, notetakers, computer-aided transcription services, written materials, telephone handset amplifiers, assistive listening devices, assistive listening systems, telephones compatible with hearing aids, closed captioning, telecommunications devices for deaf persons (TDD's), videotext displays, or other effective methods of making aurally delivered materials available to individuals with hearing impairments;
> (2) Qualified readers, taped texts, audio recordings, Brailled materials, large print materials, or other effective methods of making visually delivered materials available to individuals with visual impairments;
> (3) Acquisition or modification of equipment or devices; and
> (4) Other similar services and actions.

If on the first day of one of my seminars, I had an individual register at the door and request a sign language interpreter because the seminar registrant was deaf, there is a good chance that it would be impossible for me to arrange for a sign language interpreter at the last minute. Most cities do not have many qualified sign language interpreters, and it is likely that they would all be committed to other functions weeks before. If I could not find a qualified sign language interpreter, I would have to claim undue burden, and try to make other arrangements for the individual who was deaf. If, on the other hand, that last-minute registrant was hard of hearing and he or she requested an assistive listening device, chances are I could probably arrange for the provision of an assistive listening device that day.

EXAMINATIONS AND COURSES

Section 36.309 Examinations and Courses of title III of the ADA allows limitations to accessibility for examinations and courses in addition to the "undue burden" limitation discussed above. If a private entity can show that a particular adjustment to an examination, in order to make it accessible to an individual with a disability, would fundamentally alter the measurement of the skills or knowledge the examination is intended to test, the private entity would not have to make that alteration. Similarly, if a private entity can show that a particular adjustment to a course, in order to make it accessible to an individual with a disability, would fundamentally alter the course, the private entity would not have to make that alteration.

Expanding on the example given above for undue burden, if on the first day of one of my seminars, an attendee who is deaf requested a sign language interpreter, I would try to locate one. I would not, however, start my seminar late because of an inability to locate a qualified sign language interpreter. The participants in my seminars expect a course taught at a specific time as advertised in my brochures. They may have set up meetings and travel arrangements according to the published schedule. To change the schedule dramatically would be a fundamental alteration of the service provided.

RELATIONSHIP TO ALTERATIONS

In title III of the Americans with Disabilities Act, section 36.304 Removal of barriers establishes limitations for readily achievable barrier removal in places of public accommodation based on alteration provisions. Barrier removal efforts are required to meet the requirements for alterations under title III of the ADA as long as those barrier removal efforts do not exceed the readily achievable standard. However, barrier removal in existing places of public accommodation need not ever exceed the requirements for alterations under title III of the ADA. The alterations path of travel requirements discussed later in this chapter are not triggered by ADA-mandated readily achievable barrier removal within places of public accommodation.

RELAXING STANDARDS

When compliance with the ADA alterations provisions cannot be attained in a readily achievable fashion, other readily achievable measures for barrier removal can be employed which may provide less accessibility than called for in those alteration requirements, as provided in section 36.304 Removal of barriers. Examples of such an "easing" of the alterations requirement given in section 36.304 are "providing a ramp with a steeper slope or widening a doorway to a narrower width than that mandated by the alterations requirements." Any variation from the alterations requirements can only be made if it is not readily achievable to meet the alterations requirements, and if such variation does not create a health or safety risk to anyone.

PORTABLE RAMPS

Section 36.304 Removal of barriers of title III allows the use of a portable ramp if the use of a permanent ramp is not readily achievable. When using a portable ramp one should consider the safety of the individuals who will use that ramp. Features of a portable ramp which affect safety include the ramp surface treatment, the railings, the anchoring of the ramp, and the strength of the materials used to construct and support the ramp.

SELLING OR SERVING SPACE

Section 36.304 Removal of barriers of title III provides a limitation to barrier removal to those public accommodations who sell merchandise. Section 36.304 states, "(F) Selling or serving space. The rearrangement of temporary or movable structures, such as furniture, equipment, and display racks is not readily achievable to the extent that it results in a significant loss of selling or serving space." It is not the purpose of the ADA to cause public accommodations to go out of business, but it is its purpose to make the goods and services of public accommodations accessible to individuals with disabilities. A store manager, for example, can train employees to assist individuals with disabilities, including reaching for merchandise when warranted.

PERSONAL DEVICES AND SERVICES

Title III of the ADA does not require public accommodations to provide personal devices and services to its customers, clients, or participants with disabilities. Section 36.306 Personal devices and services gives as examples of personal devices wheelchairs and individually prescribed devices such as eyeglasses or hearing aids. Examples of personal services listed under section 36.306 are assistance in eating, toileting, or dressing.

ACCESSIBLE OR SPECIAL GOODS

Section 36.307 Accessible or Special Goods of title III of the ADA states that a public accommodation is not required to stock accessible goods for sale, if those goods are not a regular part of the public accommodation's inventory. However, if the public accommodation, as a normal course of operation, orders goods for its customers, and if the public accommodation can receive accessible goods from the suppliers the public accommodation customarily does business with, then the public accommodation would be required to order accessible goods on request by individuals with disabilities. Section 36.307 lists examples of accessible goods as being Brailled versions of books, books on audio cassette, closed-captioned video tapes, special sizes or lines of clothing, and special foods to meet particular dietary needs.

Public Entities

Program Access

Existing programs of state and local government (public) entities are regulated by title II of the Americans with Disabilities Act, and are required to be accessible to individuals with disabilities. Barriers to accessibility in public entity programs may be architectural in nature, or may be more administrative or attitudinal in nature, however, public entities may choose whether to provide access for individuals with disabilities to programs by modifying policies and practices, or by making architectural modifications. This choice of program solutions or architectural solutions is different from what is required for private entities under title III of the ADA. As previously discussed, title III requires existing private entities to remove architectural barriers in a readily achievable fashion from places of public accommodation, and then utilize readily achievable alternative methods to remove those barriers if it is not readily achievable to remove the barriers architecturally. The barriers can remain if there are no readily achievable solutions available, either through architectural modifications or through alternative method solutions. Though public entities may choose to maintain accessibility through program adjustments or architectural modifications, there is no readily achievable limitation available for public entities; they must make all of their programs accessible to individuals with disabilities with few exceptions. The terms "readily achievable" and "barrier removal" do not exist in title II of the ADA. They have no bearing on public entities unless a facility contains both public entities (covered by title II) and private entities (covered by title III), in which case the facility may have to meet the requirements of both titles II and III of the ADA. Public entities should have achieved full program access as expeditiously as possible after January 26, 1992, but no later than January 26, 1995.

Existing public entity program adjustment is mandated by title II of the Americans with Disabilities Act section 35.149 which states that except as otherwise provided in section 35.150,

> *no qualified individual with a disability shall, because a public entity's facilities are inaccessible to or unusable by individuals with disabilities, be excluded from participation in, or be denied the benefits of the services, programs, or activities of a public entity, or be subjected to discrimination by any public entity.*

Section 35.150 Existing facilities, states further,

> *(a) General. A public entity shall operate each service, program, or activity so that the service, program, or activity, when viewed in its entirety, is readily accessible to and usable by individuals with disabilities.*

The phrase "when viewed in its entirety" is a key phrase which accents the philosophy that title II requires public entity programs to be completely accessible though they may achieve that accessibility at one location when similar programs are offered at other locations. The title II "undue burden" standard of care limiting the accessibility of State and local government programs is a much higher standard of care than the title III "readily achievable" standard of care for existing private entity places of public accommodation (undue financial or administrative burden is discussed later in this chapter). Though a private entity may have to modify more facilities than would a public entity operating similar type facilities, in most cases the public entity ultimately has to provide a higher level of accessibility for individuals with disabilities.

Public entities are not required by section 35.150 "to make structural changes in existing facilities where other methods are effective in achieving compliance" under program access, nor are public entities required to make each of their facilities accessible to individuals with disabilities. Different methods available to public entities for compliance with the program access standard of care are listed in section 35.150. A public entity may achieve program access by:

> *redesign of equipment, reassignment of services to accessible buildings, assignment of aides to beneficiaries, home visits, delivery of services at alternate accessible sites, alteration of existing facilities and construction of new facilities, use of accessible rolling stock or other conveyances, or any other methods that result in making its services, programs, or activities readily accessible to and usable by individuals with disabilities.*

Those areas of existing public entity facilities where the public does not venture are held to a different standard of care than are the more public areas of facilities. In the areas of a facility which are employee-only areas, one would provide reasonable accomodations so that an employee with a disability could perform the functions of his or her job, upon the hiring of that employee. These reasonable accommodations for an employee with a disability are required by title I of the ADA and are discussed later in this chapter.

Limitations

HISTORIC PROPERTIES AND HISTORIC PRESERVATION PROGRAMS

Section 35.150 Existing facilities of title II of the Americans with Disabilities Act states that the act does not "require a public entity to take any action that would threaten or destroy the historic significance of an historic property." Any particular modification for accessibility that would destroy or threaten the historical significance of an historic property would not have to be implemented, but those programs which are implemented in historic properties must be maintained in an accessible manner. Historic preservation programs must give precedence to methods that provide physical access to individuals with disabilities. If the inaccessible second floor of an historic house can not be made accessible without impeding the historical significance of the house, for example, a video tape of that second floor can be provided on the first floor for viewing by individuals with disabilities. If the second floor of that historic house happens to be the location for a public entity health clinic, the health services provided by that clinic must be made available at an accessible location for individuals with disabilities.

FUNDAMENTAL ALTERATION IN THE NATURE OF A SERVICE, PROGRAM, OR ACTIVITY

If a public entity can prove that by taking a particular action to make a service, program, or activity accessible, it would result in a fundamental alteration to the nature of the service provided, that public entity will not be obligated to take that particular action. The limitation of accessibility of "fundamental alteration to the nature of the service, program or activity provided is discussed in title II of the ADA under section 35.150 Existing facilities. The determination that the provision of accessibility for a service, program, or activity offered by a public entity would fundamentally alter the nature of the service, program, or activity provided must be made by the head of the public entity or his or her designee. This determination must be made after considering the resources available for the funding and the operation of the service, program, or activity provided. The determination must be submitted in writing with the reasons cited for reaching that determination.

UNDUE FINANCIAL OR ADMINISTRATIVE BURDEN

If a public entity can prove that by taking a particular action to make a particular service, program, or activity accessible, it would result in an undue financial or administrative burden, that public entity will not be required to take that particular action. As with claiming "a fundamental alteration to the nature of the service, program, or activity" provided, a public entity claiming "undue financial or administrative burden" would need to submit written reasons for making that claim by the head of the public entity or by his or her designee. The claiming of "undue financial or administrative burden" should be made with great care, as there are not that many situations involving the provision of program accessibility which would cause an undue financial or administrative burden to a public entity.

Self-Evaluation, Notice, and Designated Employees

Title II of the Americans with Disabilities Act requires public entities to have performed a self-evaluation of their then-current services, policies, and practices, and the effects thereof by January 26, 1993. If any of the services, policies, and practices did not meet the requirements of title II of the ADA, the public entity should have corrected them. This self-evaluation process is called for in title II under section 35.105 Self-evaluation. Public entities are required to have permitted individuals with disabilities and groups representing individuals with disabilities to participate in the self-evaluation process. If a public entity employs 50 or more people, it is required to have maintained records of the self-evaluation for three years following its completion, and to make those records available for public inspection. Those records were to include:

(1) A list of the interested persons consulted;
(2) A description of areas examined and any problems identified; and
(3) A description of any modifications made.

Section 35.106 Notice, of title II of the ADA adds "A public entity shall make available to applicants, participants, beneficiaries, and other interested persons information regarding the provisions of this part and its applicability to the services, programs, or activities of the public entity." The information must be made available in such manner as determined by the head of the public entity, that will inform individuals with disabilities of the protection against discrimination assured them by the ADA. If a public entity employs 50 or more persons, then title II, section 35.107 Designation of responsible employee and adoption of grievance procedures, requires the public entity to designate an employee to coordinate its efforts to comply with and carry out the responsibilities mandated by the ADA. The designated employee must also carry out any responsibilities involving communicated complaints that the public entity is discriminating against individuals with disabilities as determined by the ADA. The public entity must make available the designated employee's name, office address, and office telephone number. If more than one employee is designated to coordinate a public entity's ADA responsibilities, then all of their names, office addresses and telephone numbers must be made available. Public entities that employ 50 or more persons must also adopt and publish grievance procedures providing for prompt and equitable resolution of ADA-related complaints.

Transition Plan

If a public entity employing 50 or more people made any structural changes to achieve program access, those structural changes are required by title II of the Americans with Disabilities Act to have been detailed in a transition plan. Section 35.150 Existing facilities requires the transitional plan to have been published within six months of January 26, 1992, and requires that the transitional plan have included the steps necessary to complete the called for structural changes. The plan should include identification of the physical obstacles limiting the accessibility of the public entity's programs or activities; a detailed description of the methods that were to be used to make the facilities accessible; the schedule for taking the steps necessary to make the facilities accessible; and indicate the public entity official who was responsible for the plan. If a public entity had responsibility or authority over streets, roads, or walkways, that public entity is required to have included in its transitional plan, a schedule for providing curb ramps or other sloped areas where pedestrian walks crossed curbs, especially when walkways served any entities covered by the ADA.

Surveying for Barriers

Readily Achievable and Program Access

When private entities engage in readily achievable barrier removal procedures, and when public entities perform self-evaluations, they often require the assistance of architects in locating inaccessible structural elements and determining what is necessary to make those elements accessible. Architects can provide valuable expertise as to what blocks accessibility to individuals with disabilities, as well as to what can be done to correct such blockage. The process for investigating what aspects of the built environment deny access to individuals with disabilities is much the same for title III barrier removal as it is for title II program access. The ultimate solutions to rectifying such inaccessible features will vary greatly depending on whether one is a title III entity or a title II entity however, as each entity is subject to two very different standards of care.

Reports

The survey reports of inaccessible features provided by architects for private and public entities should be informative while not committing the architect to any liability that should not be borne by the architect. For example, an architect should never make the legal determination for a title III client as to which barriers are readily achievable to remove, for that architect cannot make that determination without an intimate understanding of the client's financial resources. However, the architect has a responsibility to the client to inform him or her what readily achievable actually means, and to provide enough survey information for the client to make an intelligent assessment of which barriers must be removed. A high-quality accessibility survey report should discuss issues from the Americans with Disabilities Act relevant to the report, such as "readily achievable" in a title III report and "program access" in a title II report. The report should give locations of inaccessible elements, the reasons the elements are inaccessible, and the remedies required to make the elements accessible. One may choose to prioritize which elements should be corrected first. For private entities such prioritization should reflect the priorities suggested in title III for readily achievable barrier removal, where the highest priority is the provision of accessibility to and through the entrance to a facility, the second highest priority is the provision of accessibility to the goods and services provided within the interior of the facility, the third highest priority is accessible restrooms, and all other accessible elements are of the lowest priority. Some reports include ratings of each inaccessible element as to the magnitude of the lack of accessibility, that is whether the problems associated with the element present a hazard, block access, are a major inconvenience, or are a minor inconvenience. Clients may pay for extra features in reports like listing several solutions for each inaccessible element, providing photographs of the inaccessible elements, or providing cost information for correcting inaccessible elements. Architects may also be asked to provide construction documents and construction administration services for correcting inaccessible elements.

Title I—Employment Provisions

Both public entities and private entities are required by title I of the Americans with Disabilities Act (ADA) to provide reasonable accommodations for employees with disabilities in order for the employees to be able to perform the functions of their employment. Reasonable accommodations, such as the lowering of shelves or the provision of telecommunications devices for the deaf (TDDs), would be provided upon hiring individuals with disabilities and not in anticipation that particular individuals with particular disabilities would eventually be hired. Title I employment provisions apply to all public and private entities regardless of where these entities are housed, in existing facilities, in altered facilities, or in new construction.

Potential employers cannot use the costs associated with reasonable accommodations as justification for refusing employment to qualified individuals with disabilities. The ADA does not require an employer to hire an individual with a disability if that individual is not the most qualified candidate for the job. Title I advice should come from attorneys and not from architects, as employment provisions are not specifically an architectural matter. Discrimination against employees with disabilities can be caused by architectural barriers, however, and thus may trigger some involvement by architects in the solutions to correcting those barriers. Title I is under the purview of the Equal Employment Opportunity Commission (EEOC).

NEW CONSTRUCTION

Readily Accessible to and Usable by

The Americans with Disabilities Act's new construction requirements for public entity facilities under title II and for private entity facilities under title III are essentially the same if the public entity chooses to meet the Americans with Disabilities Act Accessibility Guidelines (ADAAG). The ADA applies its highest standard of care for facilities to new construction—readily accessible to and usable by individuals with disabilities. It is most affordable to make a facility accessible to individuals with disabilities when the facility is first constructed; therefore, the ADA requires the greatest standard of care for accessible design in new construction. Section 35.151 New construction and alterations of title II of the ADA provides a general design and construction rule for public entity facilities:

> (a) Design and construction. *Each facility or part of a facility constructed by, on behalf of, or for the use of a public entity shall be designed and constructed in such manner that the facility is readily accessible to and usable by individuals with disabilities, if the construction was commenced after January 26, 1992.*

Private entity facilities are required to meet new construction standards by title III, section 36.101 Purpose, which "requires places of public accommodation and commercial facilities to be designed, constructed, and altered in compliance with the accessibility standards established by this part." Section 36.102 of title III references "Subpart D, New Construction and Alterations" as the section for establishing criteria for the design and construction of places of public accommodation and commercial facilities. Private entity facilities which must comply with the title III provisions for new construction are those facilities designed and constructed for first occupancy after January 26, 1993. Title III section 36.401 New construction, defines "first occupancy after January 26, 1993" as meaning that the last certified complete application for a permit or a permit extension for a facility was after January 26, 1996 and the first certificate of occupancy for the facility was issued after January 26, 1993. Of course, all new construction must now meet the ADA new construction standards, but these dates remain significant for determining the standard of care that facilities constructed in the past were required to meet when a compliant is filed.

Standards for Accessible Design

New construction must be designed and constructed in accordance with certain standards for accessible design. Section 35.151 New construction and alterations, of title II of the Americans with Disabilities Act allows public entities to choose between the Uniform Federal Accessibility Standards (UFAS) and the Americans with Disabilities Act Accessibility Guidelines (ADAAG) as the standards for accessible design for new construction and alterations. A public entity can use the UFAS for one facility and the ADAAG for another facility, however the public entity cannot select different provisions from each standard for the same facility, choosing the provisions from each that are most favorable to that public entity. If a public entity selects the ADAAG for any of its facilities, the elevator exemption at sections 4.1.3(5) and 4.1.6(1)(j) of the ADAAG may not be used by the public entity. Title III of the ADA requires private entity facilities to use the Standard for Accessible Design attached as Appendix A to part 36 (title III) of the ADA. These standards for accessible design are the Americans with Disabilities Act Accessibility Guidelines (ADAAG), and are required by section 36.406 Standards for new construction and alterations.

ADAAG Limitations

There are some important limitations available for those entities using the ADAAG as the standards for accessible design for new construction. The federal government intends for the ADAAG to eventually become the only Standards for Accessible Design for public entities under title II of the ADA, as it is already for private entities under title III of the ADA. Presently, public entities can choose between the use of the ADAAG or of the UFAS as the Standards for Accessible Design. Because the federal government intends for an updated ADAAG to eventually become the Standards for Accessible Design for new construction of public entity facilities, and because the federal government requires the ADAAG as the Standards for Accessible Design for new construction of private entity facilities, the limitations and standards of care discussed in this section will be those of the ADAAG.

When new construction is required to meet the ADAAG, the entire facility must meet the requirements of the ADAAG unless a specific exemption is granted. For example, a building with twenty public and employee toilet rooms will be required to have 20 accessible toilet rooms, not a single set of accessible toilet rooms with directional signs placed within the facility so that they can be located. The ADA attempts to "mainstream" our environment for individuals with disabilities. The new construction exemptions or limitations granted to those public entities that choose to design by the ADAAG and to all private entities are "work areas" and "structural impracticability." An additional exemption related to elevators is available to private entities as well.

Work Areas

In order to fully understand the "work area" and "work station" limitations, one must become familiar with what is required by the Americans with Disabilities Act for

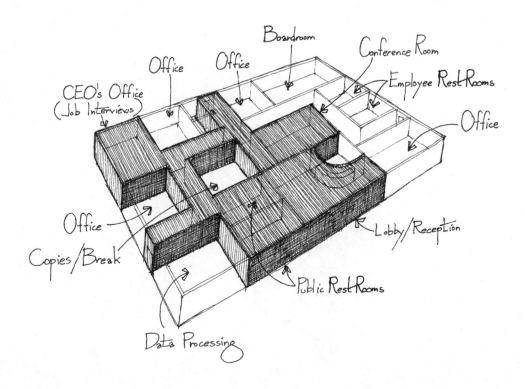

Figure 11-8 *Public use*

"public use areas" and for "common use areas." "Public use" areas are the areas of a facility where the public can be found. They are essentially the same areas as the places of public accommodation within private entities (Figure 11-8). The Americans with Disabilities Act Accessibility Guidelines (ADAAG) requires all public use areas to be designed in full compliance with the ADAAG.

Section 3.5 Definitions, of the ADAAG defines "common use" as "those interior and exterior rooms, spaces, or elements that are made available for the use of a restricted group of people (For example, occupants of a homeless shelter, the occupants of an office building, or the guests of such occupants)." Common use areas occur in "employee only" or "member only" areas and are treated by the ADAAG like public use areas (Figure 11-9). They must also be designed in full compliance with the ADAAG.

"Work areas" are discussed in the ADAAG in section 4.1.1 Application, which states that

> Areas that are used only by employees as work areas shall be designed and constructed so that individuals with disabilities can approach, enter, and exit the areas. These guidelines do not require that any areas used only as work areas be constructed to permit maneuvering within the work area or be constructed or equipped (i.e., with racks or shelves) to be accessible.

Work areas are not made accessible for individuals with disabilities until those individuals are employed in a capacity that will require them to use the work areas (Figure 11-10). In this case, reasonable accommodations will be made to ensure that the indi-

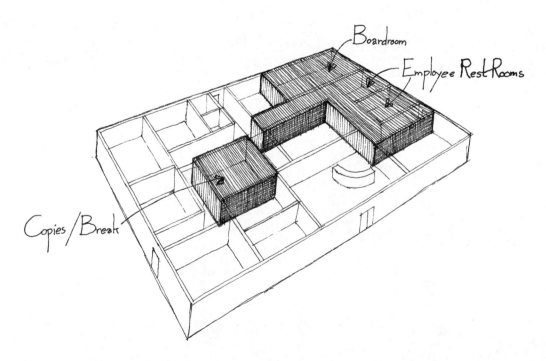

Figure 11-9 *Common use*

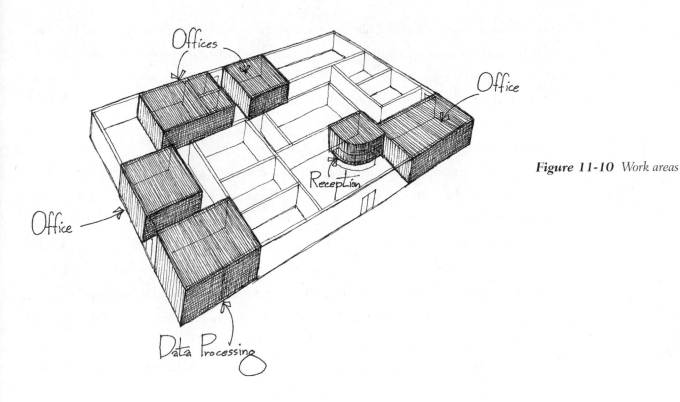

Figure 11-10 Work areas

viduals with disabilities can perform the functions of their job as required by title I of the ADA. Until an individual with a disability has been hired to work in a particular work area, that work area must be designed to meet three requirements; the work area must be located on an accessible route, must allow individuals with disabilities to enter it, and must allow individuals with disabilities to exit it. There is no requirement for

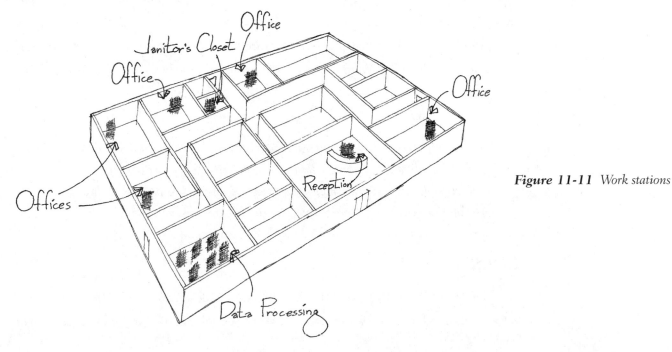

Figure 11-11 Work stations

work areas to provide a clear turning space for individuals who use wheelchairs, but that turning space may be required in the future as a reasonable accommodation for an employee who uses a wheelchair. When reviewing a building design or alteration, it is always helpful to identify those portions of the facility that are work areas, in order to contrast the level of accessibility required for those areas versus public use and common use areas.

"Work stations" are the actual locations where individual employees perform the functions of their work (Figure 11-11). Work stations need only be made accessible when an individual with a disability is hired to work at that work station. Work stations may be located in work areas, common use areas, or public use areas. A work station might be an individual desk in an office (work area), which has three desks (work stations). A work station might be a reception counter in a lobby (public use area). In the case of a reception counter in a lobby, public use area requirements would require the portions of that counter, which are used to serve the public, to be made accessible, while the receptionist's area (work station) would only need to be made accessible if the receptionist was an individual with a disability.

Structurally Impracticable

The Americans with Disabilities Act Accessibility Guidelines (ADAAG) state in section 4.1.1(5)(a) that, "Full compliance will be considered structurally impracticable only in those rare circumstances when the unique characteristics of terrain prevent the incorporation of accessibility features." If it is structurally impracticable to make a particular element of a facility accessible to individuals with disabilities, title III of the ADA would not require that particular feature to be accessible. All other elements of the facility would still have to be accessible however, unless any of them qualified for some other new construction limitation. Section 36.401 New construction, of title III gives this example:

> If providing accessibility in conformance with this section to individuals with certain disabilities (e.g., those who use wheelchairs) would be structurally impracticable, accessibility shall nonetheless be ensured to persons with other types of disabilities (e.g., those who use crutches or who have sight, hearing, or mental impairments) in accordance with this section.

Elevators

The Americans with Disabilities Act (ADA) provides private entity facilities an elevator limitation for new construction in title III, section 36.401 New construction. The

Americans with Disabilities Act Accessibility Guidelines (ADAAG) also provides an elevator exemption for new construction under section 4.1.3 (5). The elevator exemption is not available to public entities as stated in section 35.151 New construction and alterations of title II of the ADA.

In new construction of private entity facilities, elevators are not required in facilities two stories or less in height, nor are elevators required in facilities of any height if none of the stories are 3,000 or more square feet in area. Exceptions to this limitation are shopping centers or shopping malls, and professional offices of health care providers, all of which must have elevators if they are multistory facilities. Multistory facilities containing terminals, depots, or other stations used for specified public transportation must also have elevators, and must also provide an accessible route from an accessible entrance to any area housing passenger services, including boarding and debarking, loading and unloading, baggage claim, dining facilities, and other common areas open to the public.

Section 36.401 of title III defines "professional office of a health care provider" as meaning,

> a location where a person or entity regulated by a State to provide professional services related to the physical or mental health of an individual makes such services available to the public. The facility housing the "professional office of a health care provider" only includes floor levels housing at least one health care provider, or any floor designed or intended for use by at least one health care provider.

"Shopping center or shopping mall" is defined by section 36.401 as meaning,

> (A) A building housing five or more rental establishments; or (B) A series of buildings on a common site, either under common ownership or common control or developed either as one project or as a series of related projects, housing five or more sales or rental establishments.

Section 36.401 clarifies that for the purposes of the section, places of public accommodation defined under the definition of places of public accommodation as,

> a bakery, grocery store, clothing store, hardware store, shopping center, or other sales or rental establishment,

are considered sales or rental establishments. Finally, section 36.401 adds that,

> The facility housing a "shopping center or shopping mall" only includes floor levels housing at least one sales or rental establishment, or any floor level designed or intended for use by at least one sales or rental establishment.

The private entity facilities elevator limitation does not negate the fact that the facilities utilizing the elevator exemption must meet all other accessibility requirements.

ALTERATIONS TO EXISTING FACILITIES
Standards for Accessible Design

As in new construction, alterations to existing facilities are required to be designed and constructed in accordance with certain Standards for Accessible Design. Section 35.151 New construction and alterations of title II of the Americans with Disabilities Act allows public entities to choose between the Uniform Federal Accessibility Standards (UFAS) and the Americans with Disabilities Act Accessibility Guidelines (ADAAG) as the Standards for Accessible Design for new construction and alterations. For alterations, a public entity can use the UFAS for one facility and the ADAAG for another facility, however the public entity cannot select different provisions from each standard for the same building. If a public entity selects the ADAAG for any of its facilities, the elevator exemption under sections 4.1.3(5) and 4.1.6(1)(j) of the ADAAG may not be used by the public entity. Title III of the ADA requires private entity facilities to use the Standards for Accessible Design attached as Appendix A to part 36 (title III) of the ADA when altering existing facilities. These Standards for Accessible Design are the Americans with Disabilities Act Accessibility Guidelines (ADAAG), and are required by section 36.406 Standards for new construction and alterations.

As mentioned under new construction, this chapter does not discuss the standards of care or the limitations of the UFAS in any great detail, as the federal government intends for the ADAAG to eventually become the only designated ADA Standards for Accessible Design. The alterations section of this chapter is therefore written with the assumption that the requirements for altering public entity facilities under title II are the same as the "alterations: path of travel" requirements for altering private entity facilities under title III. These path of travel requirements are in both title III and the ADAAG, so any public entity which choses the ADAAG as its Standards for Accessible Design will indeed be subject to the "alterations: path of travel requirements."

Though this chapter will not discuss the provisions of the UFAS per se, it is important to know that many of the UFAS alteration requirements hinge on the concept of "substantial alteration." If the total costs of renovations to a facility within a twelve-month period meet or exceed 50 percent of the full and fair cash value of the facility, then the facility must undergo a substantial accessibility upgrade. There are many other provisions within the UFAS concerning accessibility within altered facilities as well as discussion of how to apply the substantial alteration provisions, and only a thorough review of that document will acquaint one with these rules.

Private Entity Facilities and ADAAG Compliant Public Entity Facilities

The standards of care applied by the Americans with Disabilities Act to alterations are different than the high standard of care (readily accessible to and usable by) applied to new construction, and the low standard of care (readily achievable barrier removal) applied to existing title III facilities. Title III of the ADA holds private entity facilities to two standards of care when those facilities are altered. One, the altered areas of a private entity facility must be readily accessible to and usable by individuals with disabilities; and two, funds may have to be spent to provide accessibility along the path of travel to and from the altered areas based a percentage of the total alteration costs. Title II simply requires altered public entity facilities to be readily accessible to and usable by individuals with disabilities. However, when public entities elect to use the Americans with Disabilities Act Accessibility Guidelines (ADAAG) as their Standards for Accessible Design, the Department of Justice applies the title III private entity alteration requirements as precedence for determining the standard of care for public entity facilities when they are altered. This is true only if the public entity elects to use the ADAAG as the Standards for Accessible Design for alterations instead of the Uniform Federal Accessibility Standards (UFAS), as the ADAAG also requires path of travel improvements for alterations. Since this chapter of this book does not discuss the standards of care or the limitations found in the UFAS, for the purposes of this section, the phrase "altered facility(ies)" means altered public entity facilities covered under title II of the ADA which elect to use the ADAAG as their alterations Standards for Accessible Design, and all altered private entity facilities covered under title III of the ADA.

Section 35.151 New construction and alterations of title II of the ADA states,

(b) Alteration. *Each facility or part of a facility altered by, on behalf of, or for the use of a public entity in a manner that affects or could affect the usability of the facility or part of the facility shall, to the maximum extent feasible, be altered in such a manner that the altered portion of the facility is readily accessible to and usable by individuals with disabilities, if the alteration was commenced after January 26, 1992.*

This general rule is all is all that section 35.151 has to say about alterations except for some discussion of applicable Standards for Accessible Design and some limitations to this rule. The general alterations rule for title III of the ADA is similar and states under section 36.402 Alterations,

> (a) General. (1) Any alteration to a place of public accommodation or a commercial facility, after January 26, 1992, shall be made so as to ensure that, to the maximum extent feasible, the altered portions of the facility are readily accessible to and usable by individuals with disabilities, including individuals who use wheelchairs.

Title III further refines the general requirements for alterations to private entity facilities in section 36.403 Alterations: Path of travel, which adds,

> (a) General. An alteration that affects or could affect the usability of a facility that contains a primary function shall be made so as to ensure that, to the maximum extent feasible, the path of travel to the altered area and the restrooms, telephones, and drinking fountains serving the altered area, are readily accessible to and usable by individuals with disabilities, including individuals who use wheelchairs, unless the cost and scope of such alterations is disproportionate to the cost of the overall alteration.

To best understand this "alterations: path of travel" rule, one has to become familiar with several key terms and concepts: alterations, usability, primary function, maximum extent feasible, path of travel, and disproportionate.

Alterations are defined in title III of the ADA, section 36.402 Alterations, which states,

> (b) Alteration. For the purpose of this part, an alteration is a change to a place of public accommodation or a commercial facility that affects or could affect the usability of the building or facility or any part thereof.
> (1) Alterations include, but are not limited to, remodeling, renovation, rehabilitation, reconstruction, historic restoration, changes or rearrangement in structural parts or elements, and changes or rearrangement in the plan configuration of walls and full-height partitions. Normal maintenance, reroofing, painting or wallpapering, asbestos removal, or changes to mechanical and electrical systems are not alterations unless they affect the usability of the building or facility.

The ADAAG states further under section 4.1.5 that additions to existing buildings or facilities are to be regarded as alterations, so additions to buildings are treated as both new construction and as alterations by title III and by the ADAAG. Therefore, altered facilities must meet the requirements of both new construction and alterations.

Section 36.402 of title III continues,

*(2) If existing elements, spaces, or common areas are altered, then each such
altered element, space, or area shall comply with the applicable provisions of
Appendix A to this part.*

As already stated, alterations to existing facilities must comply with the "alterations:
path of travel" rule, but all altered elements must also comply with new construction
requirements. This is analogous to a renovation of a major portion of an existing building and how a code official would treat that renovation. The code official would certainly require that renovation to meet all of the applicable current codes and standards,
but the code official may also require other areas of the building to be upgraded
because of the size of the initial planned renovation. Similarly, the ADA requires the
alterations of all altered facilities to meet the ADAAG, but also requires improvements
to be made to the path of travel area leading to the altered areas when alterations affect
the usability of primary function areas.

Only alterations that affect primary function areas trigger the "alterations: path of
travel" rule. The definition of primary function is given in section 36.403 Alterations:
Path of travel, of title III, which reads,

(b) Primary function. *A "primary function" is a major activity for which the
facility is intended. Areas that contain a primary function include, but are not
limited to, the customer services lobby of a bank, the meeting rooms in a conference center, as well as offices and other work areas in which the activities of the
public accommodation or other private entity using the facility are carried out.
Mechanical rooms, boiler rooms, supply storage rooms, employee lounges or lock-
er rooms, janitorial closets, entrances, corridors, and restrooms are not areas containing a primary function.*

My own definition of a primary function area is that it is, in most cases, the same
as a typical building code definition for "net area" (see Figure 5-11, page 120). Primary
function areas are the areas where employees' work stations are located, as well as the
areas where the public goes to receive the goods and services offered in a facility. An
exception to equating primary function areas with net areas would be that of a roadside
service station, where one could argue that one of the principal services provided are
the restrooms, and that therefore the restrooms would be primary function areas.
Restrooms would not be considered by building codes to be net area, even in roadside
service stations, nor are they generally considered to be primary function areas.

Altered facilities where the alterations occurred exclusively in corridors and
mechanical rooms would not be subjected to the "alterations: path of travel" rule, as

corridors and mechanical rooms are not primary function areas. Altered facilities where the alterations included offices and dining areas would be subjected to the "alterations: path of travel" rule, as offices and dining areas are primary function areas.

Only alterations that affect the usability of primary function areas trigger the "alterations: path of travel" rule. Section 36.403 Alterations: Path of travel, of title III states,

> (c) Alterations to an area containing a primary function. (1) Alterations that affect the usability of or access to an area containing a primary function include, but are not limited to-
> (i) Remodeling merchandise display areas or employee work areas in a department store;
> (ii) Replacing an inaccessible floor surface in the customer service or employee work areas of a bank;
> (iii) Redesigning the assembly line area of a factory; or
> (iv) Installing a computer center in an accounting firm.
> (2) For the purposes of this section, alterations to windows, hardware, controls, electrical outlets, and signage shall not be deemed to be alterations that affect the usability of or access to an area containing a primary function.

Remember also that the previously discussed definition of "alterations" in section 36.402 states, "Normal maintenance, reroofing, painting or wallpapering, asbestos removal, or changes to mechanical and electrical systems are not alterations unless they affect the usability of the building or facility." The alterations definition states that these items do not affect the usability of a primary function area and therefore do not affect accessibility.

If an entity planned to replace the wallpaper throughout a facility, the facility would become an altered facility but would not be subjected to the "alterations: path of travel" rule, as wallpaper removal and replacement does not affect the usability of a space by individuals with disabilities. If on the other hand, an entity planned to replace the carpet throughout a facility or planned to relocate partitions within a facility, the facility would become an altered facility and would be subjected to the "alterations: path of travel" rule. This is because the piling and thickness of carpet and the location of partitions do affect the usability of a space by individuals with disabilities.

So when private entities and ADAAG-compliant public entities alter elements of primary function areas that affect usability, the entities are required to improve the path of travel to and from the altered areas to the maximum extent feasible, and in a manner that is not disproportionate to the costs of the total alterations. The definition of "path of travel" can be found in section 36.403 Alterations: Path of travel, of title III which states, *(e)* Path of travel. *(1) A "path of travel" includes a continuous, unobstructed way of pedestrian passage by means of which the altered area may be approached, entered, and exited, and which connects the altered area with an exterior approach (including sidewalks, streets, and parking areas), an entrance to the facility, and other parts of the facility.*

(2) An accessible path of travel may consist of walks and sidewalks, curb ramps and other interior or exterior pedestrian ramps; clear floor paths through lobbies, corridors, rooms, and other improved areas; parking access aisles; elevators and lifts; or a combination of these elements.

(3) For the purpose of this part, the term "path of travel" also includes the restrooms, telephones, and drinking fountains serving the altered area.

It is important not to miss the fact that toilet rooms, telephones, and drinking fountains serving the altered area are considered as part of the path of travel to and from that altered area.

The "alterations: path of travel" rule requires that modifications to the path of travel be made to the maximum extent feasible, and in a manner that is not disproportionate to the total costs of the renovation. Section 36.402 Alterations, of title III of the ADA explains,

(c) To the maximum extent feasible. *The phrase "to the maximum extent feasible," as used in this section, applies to the occasional case where the nature of an existing facility makes it virtually impossible to comply fully with applicable accessibility standards through a planned alteration. In these circumstances, the alteration shall provide the maximum physical accessibility feasible. Any altered features of the facility that can be made accessible shall be made accessible. If providing accessibility in conformance with this section to individuals with certain disabilities (e.g., those who use wheelchairs) would not be feasible, the facility shall be made accessible to persons with other types of disabilities (e.g., those who use crutches, those who have impaired vision or hearing, or those who have other impairments).*

Disproportionality is defined by section 36.403 as follows:

(F) Disproportionality. *(1) Alterations made to provide an accessible path of travel to the altered area will be deemed disproportionate to the overall alteration when the cost exceeds 20% of the cost of the alteration to the primary function area.*

(2) Costs that may be counted as expenditures required to provide an accessible path of travel may include:

(i) Costs associated with providing an accessible entrance and an accessible route to the altered area, for example, the cost of widening doorways or installing ramps;

(ii) Costs associated with making restrooms accessible, such as installing grab bars, enlarging toilet stalls, insulating pipes, or installing accessible faucet controls;

(iii) Costs associated with providing accessible telephones, such as relocating the telephone to an accessible height, installing amplification devices, or installing a telecommunications device for deaf persons (TDD);

(iv) Costs associated with relocating an inaccessible drinking fountain.

When altering elements of a primary function area that affect the usability of that primary function area for individuals with disabilities, the path of travel to and from that altered area (including restrooms, telephones, and drinking fountains serving that altered area) must be made accessible to the maximum extent feasible, but at a cost not exceeding 20 percent of the total cost of the alteration to the primary function area. If a one hundred thousand dollar alteration occurred which affected the usability of a primary function area of a facility, 20 percent of that budget alteration would be 20 thousand dollars. The entity responsible for the altered facility would be required to budget as much as 20 thousand dollars improving the path of travel to the altered primary function area, including improving the accessibility of restrooms, telephones, and drinking fountains serving that altered area. If the only improvement that could be made to improve the accessibility of the path of travel to and from the altered primary function area involved a single element that would cost more than 20 thousand dollars to make accessible, such as the addition of an elevator, no expenditures improving that path of travel would be required by the ADA (Figure 11-12), as the 20 percent limitation is a maximum limitation. However, if the only improvements that could be made to improve the accessibility of the path of travel to and from the altered primary function area involved many different elements that would cost a total of 12 thousand dollars to make accessible, such as improvements to an existing elevator and costs associated with making restrooms and a front entrance accessible, the ADA would require 12 thousand dollars to be budgeted towards improving that path of travel (Figure 11-13). If the improvements necessary to make the path of travel to and from the altered primary function area involved many different elements that would cost more than 20 thousand dollars total to make accessible, a budget allotting 20 thousand dollars to improve that path of travel (20 percent maximum) would be required by the ADA (Figure 11-14).

In the last case mentioned above, the entity responsible for the altered facility would have to prioritize which elements along the path of travel to the altered area, were necessary to make accessible since the 20 percent limitation would not pay for the cost associated with making that entire path of travel accessible to individuals with dis-

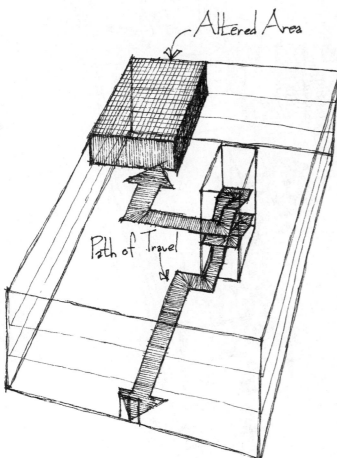

Altered Area

Path of Travel

Figure 11-12 Accessible— no elevator

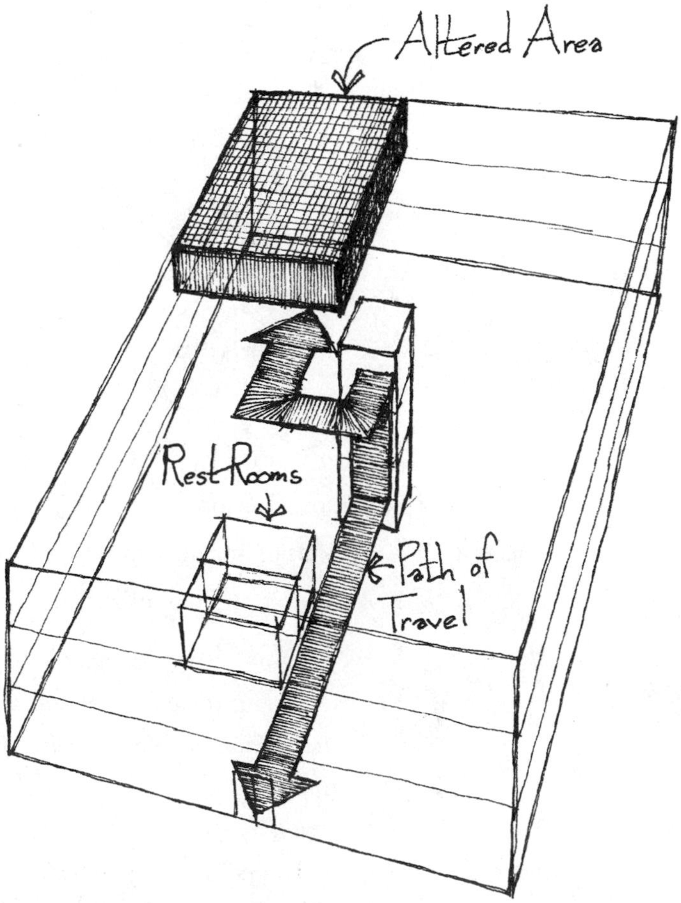

Altered Area

Rest Rooms

Path of Travel

Figure 11-13 Almost accessible

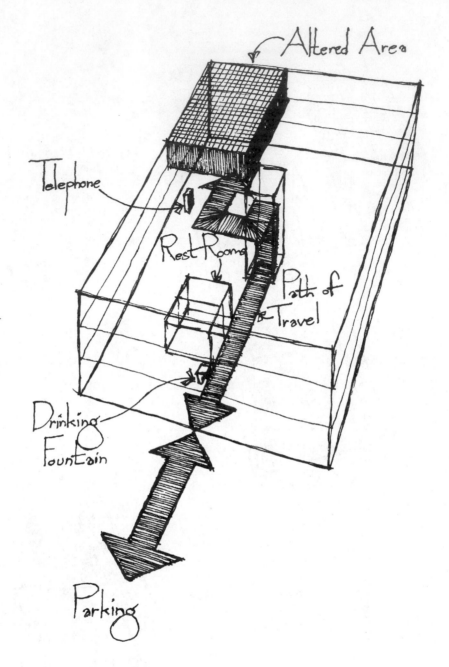

Altered Area

Telephone

Rest Rooms

Path of Travel

Drinking Fountain

Parking

Figure 11-14 *Many inaccessible elements*

abilities. Section 36.403 Alterations: Path of travel, of title III of the ADA provides a list of priorities for determining which elements along the path of travel to an altered primary function area must be made accessible. Section 36.403 states,

(g) Duty to provide accessible features in the event of disproportionality.
(1) *When the cost of alterations necessary to make the path of travel to the altered area fully accessible is disproportionate to the cost of the overall alteration, the path of travel shall be made accessible without incurring disproportionate costs.*
(2) *In choosing which accessible elements to provide, priority should be given to those elements that will provide the greatest access, in the following order:*

(i) An accessible entrance;

(ii) An accessible route to the altered area;

(iii) At least one accessible restroom for each sex or a single unisex restroom;

(iv) Accessible telephones;

(v) Accessible drinking fountains; and

(vi) When possible, additional accessible elements such as parking, storage and alarms.

This list of priorities is different from the suggested list of priorities for readily achievable barrier removal in title III regulating existing private entity facilities.

Should an entity responsible for an altered facility try to circumvent the "alterations: path of travel" rule by scheduling several different small renovations affecting the usability of a primary function area so that 20 percent of the total cost of any of the renovations would not support the cost of making a particular item accessible, title III of the ADA has an additional requirement. Section 36.403 Alterations: Path of travel, of title III states,

> *(h) Series of smaller alterations. (1) The obligation to provide an accessible path of travel may not be evaded by providing a series of small alterations to the area served by a single path of travel if those alterations could have been performed as a single undertaking.*
>
> *(2) (i) If an area containing a primary function has been altered without providing an accessible path of travel to that area, and subsequent alterations to that area, or a different area on the same path of travel, are undertaken within three years of the original alteration, the total cost of alterations to the primary function areas on that path of travel during the preceding three year period shall be considered in determining whether the cost of making that path of travel accessible is disproportionate.*
>
> *(ii) Only the alterations undertaken after January 26, 1992, shall be considered in determining if the cost of providing an accessible path of travel is disproportionate to the overall cost of the alterations.*

If three different alterations were made affecting the usability of a primary function area, each costing 100 thousand dollars, and the only improvement that could be made to the accessibility of the path of travel to and from the altered primary function area involved a single element that would cost more than 20 thousand dollars but less than 45 thousand dollars to make accessible, such as the addition of an elevator, the entity responsible for the altered facility would be required to make that single element accessible, as the cost of improving the path of travel would be less than 20 percent of the total cost of the three renovations. This would, of course, be contingent on those three renovations all having occurred within a three-year time period, and the first renovation having occurred after January 26, 1992.

Limitations

Landlord/Tenant

Whenever a tenant alters the usability of primary function areas within a tenant space only, that alteration will not "trigger" the path of travel concerns for the landlord of that facility. This is discussed in title III of the Americans with Disabilities Act under section 36.403 Alterations: Path of travel. Of course, the tenant would be obligated to meet the requirements of the "alterations: path of travel" rule within the tenant space.

Technically Infeasible

The Americans with Disabilities Act Accessibility Guidelines (ADAAG) provide for a "technically infeasible" limitation which states that if compliance with the alterations requirements is technically infeasible, then the alteration shall provide accessibility to the maximum extent feasible. Section 4.1.6 (1)(j) states, "Any elements or features of the building or facility that are being altered and can be made accessible shall be made accessible within the scope of the alteration." Technically infeasible is defined by ADAAG section 4.1.6 as meaning,

> with respect to an alteration of a building or a facility, that it has little likelihood of being accomplished because existing structural conditions would require removing or altering a load-bearing member which is an essential part of the structural frame; or because other physical or site constraints prohibit modification or addition of elements, spaces, or features which are in full and strict compliance with the minimum requirements for new construction and which are necessary to provide accessibility.

The technically infeasible limitation is often related to the existing structure of a facility that is being altered, in that it usually would be technically infeasible to relocate structural elements in order to accommodate the accessible design of a particular element.

Elevators

Private entity facilities are granted an elevator exemption under title III of the Americans with Disabilities Act, section 36.404 Alterations: Elevator exemption, and under the Americans with Disabilities Act Accessibility Guidelines (ADAAG), section

4.1.6 (k). Once again, title II does not grant public entities an elevator exemption, even for alterations of existing facilities. The elevator exemption granted private entity facilities for alterations of existing facilities, is identical to the elevator exemption granted by the ADA for new construction of private entity facilities. See the "new construction" section of this chapter for discussion of the elevator limitation.

Historic Facilities

Title III of the Americans with Disabilities Act (ADA) covers the alterations of historic private entity facilities under section 36.405 Alterations: Historic preservation, whereas title II of the ADA covers the alterations of historic public entity facilities under section 35.151 (d) Alterations: Historic properties. What these two sections have to say is essentially the same. Entities are not required to make any particular element of a historic facility accessible to individuals with disabilities if such a provision would threaten or destroy the historic significance of the facility. However, alternative methods of access must be provided if possible, to make the facility or the programs and services offered within the facility accessible. Many people mistakenly assume that if they operate their business or programs from an historic facility, they are not obligated to meet the requirements of the ADA. This is not true, as the historic facilities limitation under the ADA is applied to one architectural feature at a time. If the alteration of a particular feature of a facility would threaten or destroy the historical significance of the facility, that feature may not have to be altered under the ADA. Most historic structures are held to the existing facilities provisions of the ADA. Public entities under title II will be held to a higher standard of care (program access) than will be private entities under title III (readily achievable barrier removal).

The Americans with Disabilities Act Accessibility Guidelines (ADAAG) covers the alterations of historic facilities under section 4.1.7 Accessible Buildings: Historic Preservation. The ADAAG is more explicit in stipulating which elements must be made accessible and how they are to be made accessible in historic facilities. Of course, private entities will have to meet the requirements of both title III and the ADAAG. Public entities which opt to use the ADAAG as their standards for accessible design, will have to meet the requirements of title II, as well as the ADAAG. There is an affirmative duty for historical property owners to have their accessibility plans accepted by a State Historic Preservation officer.

Medical Care Facilities

Medical care facilities are required by the Americans with Disabilities Act Accessibility Guidelines (ADAAG section six), to provide a certain percentage of accessible patient bedrooms and toilets based on the type of medical care facility, whether they are general purpose hospitals, hospitals and rehabilitation facilities that specialize in treating conditions that affect mobility, or long-term care facilities. ADAAG section 6.1 (4) Alterations to patient bedrooms, allows medical care facilities that are undergoing alterations to "phase" in the number of accessible bedrooms based on a percentage of the number of bedrooms being altered. For example, ten percent of general purpose hospital bedrooms are required to be accessible, so if a 30-bedroom patient wing of a 100-bed general hospital were being altered, the ADAAG would require three of the patient bedrooms in the altered area to be accessible even if the existing hospital had no accessible patient bedrooms.

Accessible Transient Lodging

Accessible transient lodging is addressed in section nine of the Americans with Disabilities Act Accessibility Guidelines (ADAAG). Section nine defines accessible transient lodging as hotels, motels, inns, boarding houses, dormitories, resorts, and other similar places of lodging. Time-share condominiums are considered by the Department of Justice to be accessible transient lodging if their turnover is frequent enough. The accessible transient lodging section of the ADAAG establishes the criteria for accessible sleeping rooms and suites, as well as for other rooms and suites not required to be accessible. It is extremely important to note that section 9.4 of the ADAAG requires all sleeping rooms and suites, other than the accessible sleeping rooms and suites, to have doors within them that provide a 32-inch clear opening (Figure 10-13). This includes bathroom doors and walk-in closet doors. It does not matter that the bathrooms in these suites are not accessible. The rationale behind this requirement is that individuals with disabilities may need a sleeping room at a transient lodging facility after all the accessible rooms are rented, and that an inaccessible room is better than no room as long as an individual with a disability can access it and can access the bathroom and closet. Section 9.4 does not require any latch-side clearance, accessible hardware, sloped thresholds, maneuvering space, or any other accessible features—just the 32-inch clearance. Presently, the Department of Justice is very serious about enforcing this requirement.

Egress and Areas of Rescue Assistance

New construction is required by the Americans with Disabilities Act Accessibility Guidelines (ADAAG) to provide areas of rescue assistance adjacent to every inaccessible exit located in facilities that are not equipped with a supervised automatic sprinkler system. The ADAAG also requires accessible routes in new construction to serve as means of egress for emergencies or to connect to an accessible area of rescue assistance. ADAAG section 4.1.6(g) exempts alterations from having to meet these egress and area of rescue assistance requirements. Areas of rescue assistance are illustrated in figure 19-7.

ENFORCEMENT

One of the principle differences between the Americans with Disabilities Act (ADA) and accessibility codes is how the ADA is enforced. Rather than relying on plans reviewers and inspectors, the ADA uses our legal system to enforce its requirements. One can file a complaint or file a lawsuit when one feels that an entity has not met their ADA obligations. It is not completely accurate to say that the ADA does not involve plans reviewers or inspectors, as complaints may be filed after one has reviewed a set of construction documents and determined that a project is not going to be constructed in accordance with the ADA, and as the Department of Justice (DOJ) relies on inspectors to investigate facilities (planned or built) for compliance with the ADA. Also, the DOJ encourages state and local building inspectors to check facilities for compliance with the ADA.

If an individual feels he or she has been discriminated against because of his or her disability, that individual can file a lawsuit against the alleged discriminatory entity under the ADA. The language of the ADA encourages the use of alternate means of dispute resolution as opposed to filing a lawsuit, but does not mandate it. Alternate means of dispute resolution includes settlement negotiations, conciliation, facilitation, mediation, fact-finding, minitrials, and arbitration. The Attorney General can investigate potential ADA violations whenever he or she feels a violation exists, or if requested to do so by other complainants. If the Attorney General finds violations of the ADA, he or she can commence a civil action in any appropriate United States district court. The Attorney General can also commence civil action based on the belief that an entity is violating the ADA; an investigation is not required. Should a defendant be found guilty of noncompliance with the ADA, that defendant can be assessed the plaintiff's court costs, as well as be required to remedy the discriminatory policy or barrier. Under Title

TITLE III—PRIVATE ENTITIES ENFORCEMENT

Figures 11-15a and b
Enforcement diagram

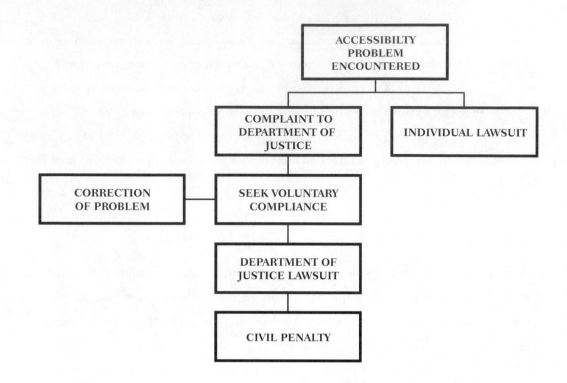

TITLE II—PUBLIC ENTITIES ENFORCEMENT

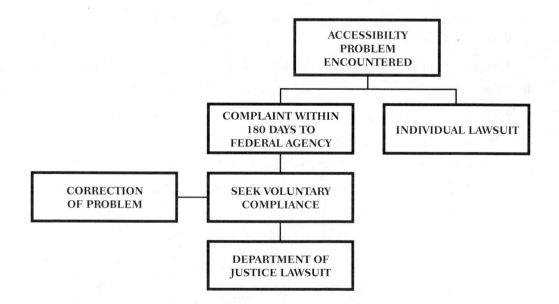

III, the defendant can also be assessed 50 thousand dollars for the first violation and 100 thousand dollars for each subsequent violation. Title three of the ADA in section 36.504(b) states that, "a determination in a single action, by judgment or settlement, that the covered entity has engaged in more then one discriminatory act shall be counted as a single violation."

Enforcement of the ADA is covered in title III under Subpart E, Enforcement, and is covered in title II under Subpart F - Compliance Procedures (Figure 11-15a and b). The requirements for both titles are substantially similar except that title II complaints can be made to one of eight departments of the federal government depending on the nature of the complaint. The eight departments are the Department of Agriculture, the Department of Education, the Department of Health and Human Services, the Department of Housing and Urban Development, the Department of Interior, the Department of Justice, the Department of Labor, or the Department of Transportation. Complaints against public entities must be made within 180 days of the alleged infraction.

STATE AND LOCAL ACCESSIBILITY CODES AND STANDARDS

Scoping Provisions

The scoping provisions of state and local accessibility codes and standards are very different from the scoping provisions of the Americans with Disabilities Act (ADA) of 1990. State accessibility codes typically address more occupancies than does the ADA. Because the ADA is a federal Civil Rights Act, it does not regulate such entities as religious entities, private clubs, and private residences, for example. However, the ADA provides broad civil rights protection and does regulate existing facilities, as well as alterations to facilities, and new construction. On the other hand, state accessibility codes address almost every type of occupancy (depending on the state), but they usually address only alterations to facilities and new construction, not existing facilities.

Inspectors in the Field

One of the most significant differences that can be found between the Americans with Disabilities Act (ADA) and State and local accessibility codes and standards is in the area of enforcement. The ADA is enforced primarily through a legal complaint process, whereas state and local accessibility codes and standards are usually enforced by inspectors at the design and construction phases of a facility. This means that one will receive immediate "feedback" from state and local inspectors as to how to best make a facility accessible to individuals with disabilities. Unfortunately, it may also mean that a local inspector who is not familiar with the ADA may try to enforce some local provision that would be in violation of the ADA. The best solution to this problem is for the state or local government entity to seek certification of equivalency for their accessibility design standard, as discussed under the section of this chapter entitled "Standards for Accessible Design." Then meeting the state or local design standard would be viewed as having met the title III requirements of the ADA, depending on how much of the standard was submitted and how much of the standard was certified.

Model Codes

The three major building codes all contain scoping provisions for accessible design, as well as references to the CABO/ANSI A117.1, Accessible and Usable Buildings and Facilities. Though there are jurisdictions that enforce the provisions of the model codes concerning accessibility for individuals with disabilities, there are many states where a state accessibility standard overrides the provisions of the building codes. As of the writing of this book, the three major building code organizations are meeting with federal task force members to generate a consensus-based code that parallels the federally required standards for accessible design. This process should help designers and code enforcers by eventually leading to the establishment of one nationally recognized accessibility standard.

Interior Environment

Chapter 12 discusses the many health-related concerns associated with interior environments. Typical concerns addressed are the provision of adequate lighting and ventilation for building spaces, the provision of surfaces in toilet rooms, and shower rooms and rodent-proofing.

The three major building codes each contain requirements regulating the interior environments of buildings. Though these three codes have similar chapter formatting, they each place different requirements for interior environments in different chapters. Interior environment requirements are in building codes in order to provide for some measure of health safety for the occupants of buildings. These health safety-related requirements help ensure that buildings are provided with adequate lighting and that buildings are properly ventilated. Health safety-related requirements for sanitary surfaces and for rodent-proofing help maintain interior environments free of infection and disease. Sound transmission control requirements help maintain safe noise levels within buildings by regulating the construction of building assemblies, such as wall assemblies, floor-ceiling assemblies, and roof-ceiling assemblies. Other codes, such as plumbing and mechanical codes, complement building codes in the provision of buildings and structures which promote health safety.

LIGHT

Building codes contain regulations which require adequate light for the utilization of building spaces. Lighting is necessary for the many functions which buildings house, as well as for the egressing of occupants from buildings or building areas when emergencies occur. Windows and translucent wall systems are sources for natural light, and may

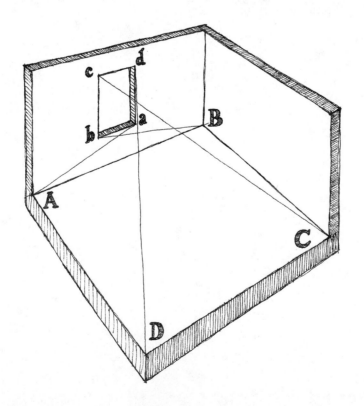

Figure 12-1 *Window areas*

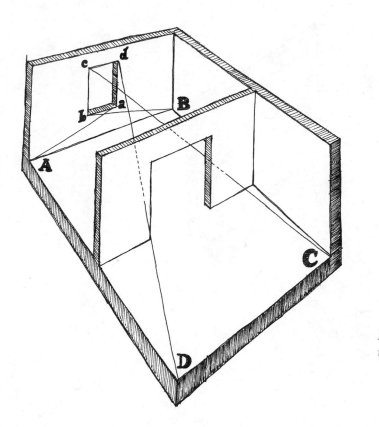

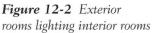

Figure 12-2 *Exterior rooms lighting interior rooms*

be used for lighting building interiors if their dimensional properties provide adequate light. Building codes require certain amounts of window area, based on the area of rooms served by the windows (Figure 12-1). When interior rooms are located adjacent to rooms with exterior windows or translucent window systems, the interior rooms may use the natural lighting of the exterior rooms to satisfy the natural lighting requirements for the interior rooms, if two conditions are met (Figure 12-2). First, the opening between any interior room and an exterior room must be adequately sized, as prescribed by each code, to permit the passage of sufficient light from the exterior room to the interior room. Second, the windows or translucent wall systems in the exterior room must be sized in order to provide for the adequate percentage of natural light, as prescribed by each code, based on the floor area of both the exterior room and the interior room. Building codes allow the use of artificial lights to enhance limited natural lighting, or as a substitute for natural lighting if adequate light levels are maintained by the artificial lighting.

VENTILATION

Ventilation of interior spaces is regulated by building codes so that the air quality within buildings will remain safe for the occupants of such buildings. Interior spaces of buildings may be ventilated naturally by operable windows, vents, or louvers, or by

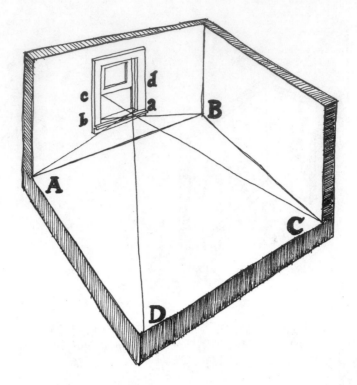

Figure 12-3 Ventilation opening

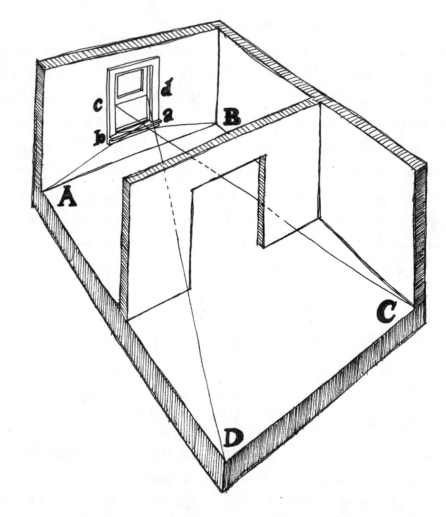

Figure 12-4 Rooms sharing ventilation

mechanical means. Mechanical ventilation is allowed as a substitute for natural ventilation when the design and construction of the mechanical ventilation system is deemed by each code to provide equivalent ventilation to its natural ventilation requirements.

When operable windows are used to provide natural ventilation, they are regulated as to the amount of clear opening area they must contain as a minimum. They must allow a certain percentage of clear opening area based on the floor area of the room or rooms which they serve (Figure 12-3). This percentage of required clear opening area varies from code to code. When interior rooms occur without any exterior wall openings, such interior rooms must share the natural ventilation provided by adjacent rooms with exterior wall openings. In order for an interior room to be able to utilize the exterior wall openings of an adjacent room to satisfy natural ventilation requirements, the opening between the interior room and the exterior room must meet two requirements (Figure 12-4). First, the opening between the interior room and the exterior room must be adequately sized, as prescribed by each code, to permit adequate air movement from the exterior room to the interior room. Second, the openings in the exterior room must be sized in order to provide the adequate percentage of natural ventilation, as prescribed by each code, based on the floor area of both the exterior room and the interior room.

In order to ensure that an adequate supply of fresh air is available for providing natural ventilation, building codes may require ventilation openings to open onto yards, public spaces, or onto courts which meet certain dimensional requirements, depending on the code. If a court is inadequately constructed, arranged, or sized, it can complicate matters by serving as a source for a contaminated air supply rather than as a source for a fresh air supply. Therefore, certain building codes address the dimensions, shapes, construction, and amount of enclosure of courts when courts are used for ventilation air supply.

ROOM DIMENSIONS

It is entirely possible that the physical dimensional requirements in building codes pertaining to rooms and spaces are for the purpose of maintaining spaces which are usable by the occupants who buy and lease buildings. This would be more of a quality-of-life concern than a health safety concern, yet one can easily imagine that minimum dimensional requirements for rooms and spaces would also promote better dilution and circulation of interior air, and hence would promote health safety (Figure 12-5). Building codes specify minimum square footage areas for certain rooms, and also specify minimum widths and minimum ceiling heights for certain rooms (Figure 12-6). The most stringent dimensional requirements are applied to habitable spaces. Habitable spaces are spaces in structures for living, sleeping, eating, or cooking, and do not include support spaces like bathrooms, halls, storage spaces, and so on. Other rooms, such as kitchens (though kitchens are rooms for cooking and are therefore habitable spaces),

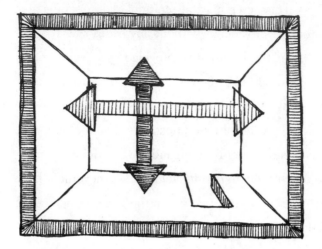

Figure 12-5 *Room dimensions*

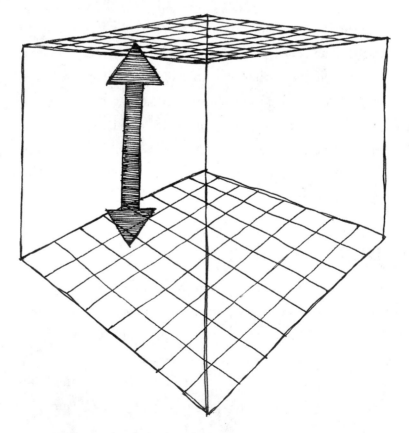

Figure 12-6 *Ceiling heights*

bathrooms, corridors, storage rooms, etc., may have lower ceiling heights (Figure 12-7). Building codes allow adjustments to minimum ceiling heights when projections into the minimum ceiling heights occur, such as beams or furred-down ceilings (Figure 12-8). Codes also specify how to calculate minimum ceiling heights in rooms with sloped ceilings where portions of the ceilings are located at a height lower than the minimum required ceiling height (Figure 12-9).

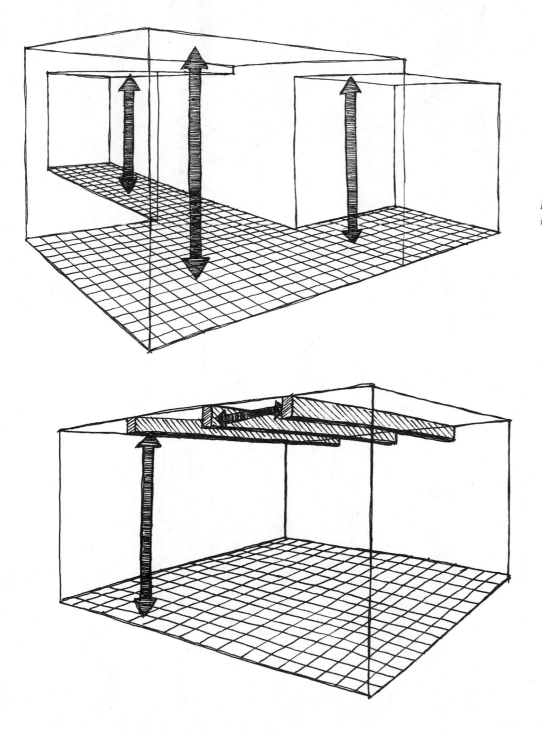

Figure 12-7 *Lower ceiling heights*

Figure 12-8 *Projecting beams*

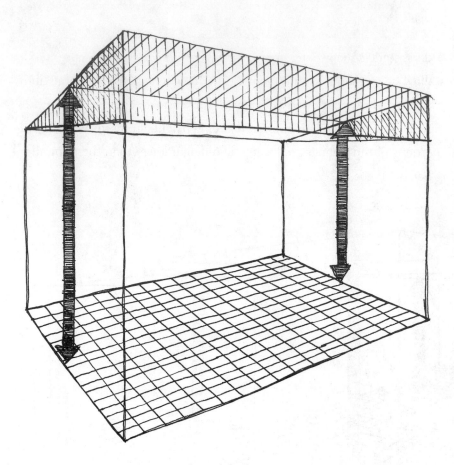

Figure 12-9 *Sloped ceilings*

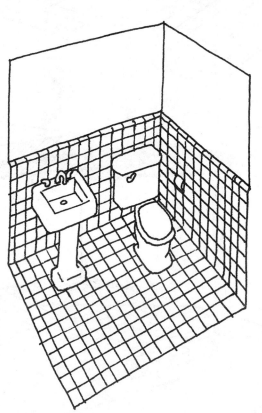

Figure 12-10 *Sanitary surfaces*

SANITATION

Building codes contain requirements for the installation of hard, impervious surfaces in areas where wall and floor surfaces will be exposed to the types of uses that augment unsanitary conditions. These requirements vary from code to code and usually address wall and floor surfaces in toilet and shower rooms (Figure 12-10). In order to maintain sanitary conditions, floors and portions of walls in these rooms are required to have smooth, hard, and nonabsorbent surfaces. Sanitation requirements may also require the joints between plumbing fixtures and water resistant wall surfaces to be waterproofed, so that water cannot gain entry to these joints. Building codes may also require the separation of a toilet room from food preparation areas with a tight-fitting door. This helps provide some minimal separation between the contaminated toilet room air and the air in the kitchen where food is prepared.

RODENT-PROOFING

Rodents potentially introduce filth and disease into buildings; therefore, rodent-proofing is required by building codes in spaces containing feed, foodstuff, or food. The spaces which mandate rodent-proofing are those used for storing, preparing, processing, serving, or selling the food items. Building codes require the protection of openings (e.g., crawl-space openings, etc.) from the potential entry of rodents (Figure 12-11). Furthermore, codes require the protection of certain building elements, such as wood-

Figure 12-11 *Crawl space opening protection*

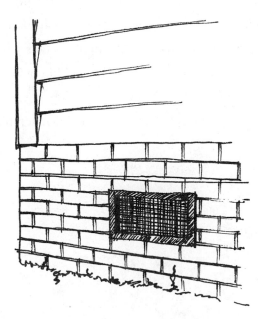

Figure 12-12 *Wooden door with sheet metal rodent protection*

en doors, from the potential gnawing by rodents in order to gain entry (Figure 12-12). Other code provisions deter rodents from climbing pipes and other appurtenances in order to gain entry.

SOUND TRANSMISSION CONTROL

Loud noise levels can be injurious to one's hearing, so some building codes contain requirements regulating sound transmission control. The sources of sound transmission regulated by codes may be structural systems which transmit noises as they move, or may be the daily activities occurring within buildings like concerts, talking, machinery operation, or other such sources. Certain fire resistance directories also assign sound transmission ratings to walls, floor-ceiling assemblies, and roof-ceiling assemblies.

Energy Conservation

Chapter 13 discusses the types of provisions covered by the Model Energy Code (MEC) promulgated by the Council of American Building Officials (CABO). As many of the requirements of the MEC are very technical in nature, one would need to consult other resources to fully understand how to apply them.

As our world population continues to increase, energy conservation becomes increasingly more a timely concern because of the increasing demand placed on our energy resources which are already taxed. Most states have in place either a state-promulgated energy code or some sort of legislation adopting some nationally recognized energy conservation standard for construction. Probably the most recognized national standard for energy efficient design is the Model Energy Code (MEC) (Figure 13-1) formerly published by the Council of American Building Officials (CABO) and now administered by the International Code Council (ICC). This chapter is based on the MEC and only attempts to discuss the types of requirements contained within that code; this chapter does not involve a discussion of how to use the MEC, as that discussion would be more appropriate for a commentary on the MEC.

The intent of the Model Energy Code (MEC) is established under the administration chapter of the code where it is stated, "The provisions of this code shall regulate the design of building envelopes for adequate thermal resistance and low air leakage and the design and selection of mechanical, electrical, service water-heating and illumination systems and equipment which will enable effective use of energy in new

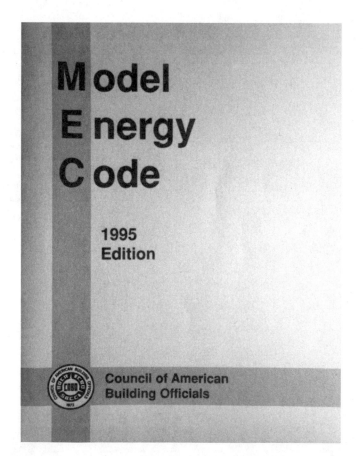

Figure 13-1 Model Energy Code

building construction (International Code Council, 1995)." The MEC requires residential buildings (in this case, detached single-family residences, detached duplex residences, and any other residential buildings less than four stories in height) to comply with the provisions of one of three methods of energy-efficient design: Design by Systems Analysis and Design of Buildings Utilizing Renewable Energy Sources, Design by Component Performance Approach, or Design by Acceptable Practice. All other buildings, including other residential occupancies, must meet different nationally recognized standards for energy efficient design as referenced by the MEC. The provisions of the MEC pertain to new construction and additions. With few exceptions, existing construction is exempt from the MEC's provisions.

Insulation is required to be properly labeled and marked with pertinent information about its performance (e.g., required minimum thickness for blown or sprayed insulation or *R*-values for other insulation). The installation of insulation must be done in a manner where the code official can verify the pertinent information. Any maintenance required for insulation must be included in its label. The MEC requires *U*-values to be determined for windows, doors, and skylights, and this information must be included in the labeling of these construction products. The code official may require plans and specifications to be submitted for the purpose of proving compliance with the MEC.

General design conditions are specified by the Model Energy Code (MEC) so that all energy efficiency design methods are based on the same assumptions. These standards for design establish hot weather and cold weather design temperatures and criteria for mechanical ventilation. One may have to use several referenced standards to establish the design criteria called for in the MEC.

METHODS

The Design by Systems Analysis and Design of Buildings Utilizing Renewable Energy Sources method involves a comparison between the building one is designing and a hypothetical building with essentially the same energy design parameters (e.g., energy sources, floor area, area of thermal envelope, exterior design conditions, occupancy, climate data, and usage operational schedule). One would compare the energy consumption of the two, based on an energy analysis of the designed building and an energy analysis of the hypothetical building if the hypothetical building were designed in accordance with Method two, Design by Component Performance Approach. If the energy usage of the designed building were shown not to exceed the energy usage of the hypothetical building, the designed building would meet code. This explanation is somewhat oversimplified as the Model Energy Code specifies many other parameters that must be met when choosing this design method. The MEC outlines procedures that must be followed when applying this method, and outlines the documentation required for presenting the analysis.

Method two, Design by Component Performance Approach, is a method for calculating the energy usage of a building by performing heat loss and heat gain calculations. This method is intended for all heated and cooled residential buildings. The design parameters for performing the calculations are specified for this method in the Model Energy Code (MEC). There are also other design parameters within the MEC for buildings designed under this method.

The third method, Design by Acceptable Practice, is similar to Method two in that it requires some heat loss and heat gain calculations. However, this method does not require one to calculate as many values for building elements from scratch. Method three applies to residences that are five thousand square feet or less in area and are three stories or less in height. The Model Energy Code (MEC) specifies other design parameters for buildings designed under this method.

The Model Energy Code (MEC) refers all buildings not covered by the methods discussed above to certain sections of the Standard RS-22 Codification of ASHRAE/IES 90.1-1989, Energy Efficient Design of New Buildings Except Low-Rise Residential Building <CW> 1993. The sections of RS-22 considered applicable by the MEC are specifically referenced. The MEC also specifies some options as to which RS-22 sections may be used by the designer applying the requirements of the standard.

Exterior Wall Coverings

Chapter 14 discusses exterior wall coverings and what sorts of code requirements are used to ensure that exterior wall coverings are durable and provide weather protection. The bulk of the requirements discussed in Chapter 14 pertain to exterior veneers. The three building codes are inconsistent as to what they require for exterior wall coverings, so many of the requirements discussed in this chapter may reflect the requirements of only one or two of the major building codes. One should consult their code carefully when attempting to determine just what is required.

Exterior wall coverings provide weather protection for buildings. Exterior wall coverings are not structural in nature, but rather, are applied to structural systems (Figure 14-1). In order for exterior wall coverings to perform their intended functions, they must obviously be applied in a manner that resists the passage of rain, snow, and wind. Building codes require exterior wall coverings to be constructed of durable materials, and to be constructed in a manner that affords enough structural integrity for exterior wall coverings to remain in place. Building codes also address the fire resistance of exterior wall coverings, so that the likelihood of fire moving from one building to another is reduced.

Building codes do not regulate the appearance of exterior wall coverings though zoning ordinances may regulate such aesthetic issues. Energy codes regulate the heat loss and heat gain characteristics of exterior wall coverings (see Chapter 13). Within building codes, the properties of exterior wall coverings (materials, durability, weather resistance, structural integrity, and fire resistance) are often regulated in many different chapters. For example, a brick veneer wall may be required to be a fire-resistant assembly in one chapter of a building code because of the wall's proximity to a property line, while the bricks in that wall will be required to meet a referenced standard for material design in another chapter of the code. Yet another building code chapter will require that same brick veneer wall to be constructed in a manner which resists the passage of rain and which ensures that the wall will have sufficient structural stability to remain in place. Ultimately, one has to look at several different chapters of a building code, as

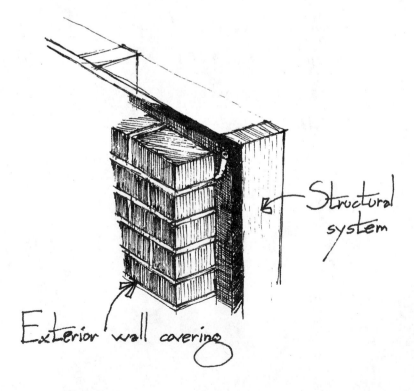

Figure 14-1 *Exterior wall coverings are applied to structural systems*

Figure 14-2a, b and c
Typical veneers, a. Brick veneer, b. Exterior insulated finish system (EIFS), c. Horizontal lapped siding

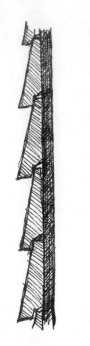

Figure 14-3 *Self flashing veneer*

well as look at other regulatory documents in order to ascertain just what is required of any particular exterior wall covering.

VENEERED WALLS

A veneered wall consists of a wall with a veneer facing attached to it. The veneer facing is not structural and cannot be assumed to add to the strength of the wall. Veneers are selected for their appearance, ease of maintenance, durability, weather resistance, and insulation characteristics. Typical veneers are brick, tile, concrete, masonry units, metal, porcelain coated metal panels, glass, wood, and vinyl (Figure 14-2a, b, and c).

Building codes require exterior veneered walls to provide weather protection for buildings. The veneered walls are required to be properly flashed in order to provide such weather protection, unless the veneer material is self-flashing (Figure 14-3). Codes require veneered walls to use sealant where the use of flashing is not practical. Depending on the type of veneer used, building codes detail many requirements for the proper design and installation of veneered wall systems.

Masonry Veneer

Masonry veneer utilizes individual masonry units which are attached to one another with mortar joints, and which create a wall capable of providing weather protection.

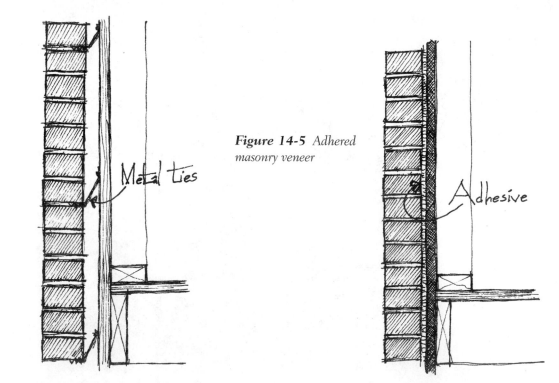

Figure 14-4 *Masonry veneer*

Metal ties

Figure 14-5 *Adhered masonry veneer*

Adhesive

It is an old cliché to question whether the mortar joints serve the purpose of holding the individual masonry units together or of holding them apart. In other words, the mortar joints are the "weak link" structurally in a masonry-veneered wall, as their compressive strength is less than that of the individual masonry units and they have very little tensile strength. There are two principal types of masonry-veneered wall systems—anchored masonry veneer and adhered masonry veneer. Anchored masonry veneer consists of individual masonry units mortared together and secured to a backing with mechanical fasteners which are approved by the code official (Figure 14-4). Adhered masonry veneer consists of individual masonry units, mortared together, and secured and supported to a backing through the use of approved adhesive bonding materials (Figure 14-5).

Anchored Masonry Veneer

Anchored masonry veneer wall coverings are regulated by building codes as to the types of materials and the dimensions of those materials which can be used as veneers and used as anchoring elements. Codes also govern the means by which anchored masonry veneers are supported structurally, both vertically and horizontally (laterally). The code requirements for structural support vary based on the type of masonry veneer used.

Building codes require anchored masonry veneers to meet the standards for materials referenced in the masonry construction chapters of the codes. Each type of masonry veneer material must be of a certain minimum thickness in order to be considered acceptable for use as an exterior wall covering. The quality and dimensional requirements for these materials are necessary for assuring that anchored masonry veneers are durable and structurally capable of remaining in place.

In order to remain in place, anchored masonry veneers must be able to resist vertical and lateral loads. Vertical loads are imposed by the weight of the individual masonry units themselves (Figure 14-6). Horizontal loads consist of loads imposed by nature, such as wind loading (Figure 14-7). Resistance to vertical and horizontal loads are addressed in building codes by requirements for supporting anchored masonry veneers both vertically and laterally.

Anchored masonry veneers must be supported vertically on footings and foundations which are noncombustible, except that certain wood foundation systems are allowed for support by each code. When considering the strength of walls, anchored masonry veneers cannot be assumed to add to the strength of the walls. Because of the potential for the veneer portions of walls to expand and contract at a different rate than

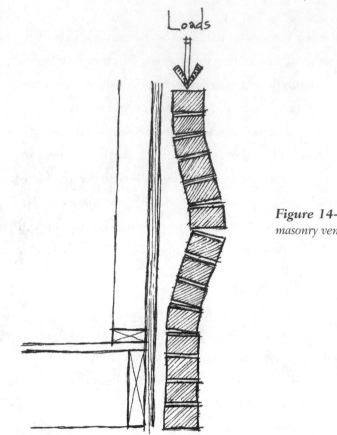

Loads

Figure 14-6 *Vertical loads on masonry veneer*

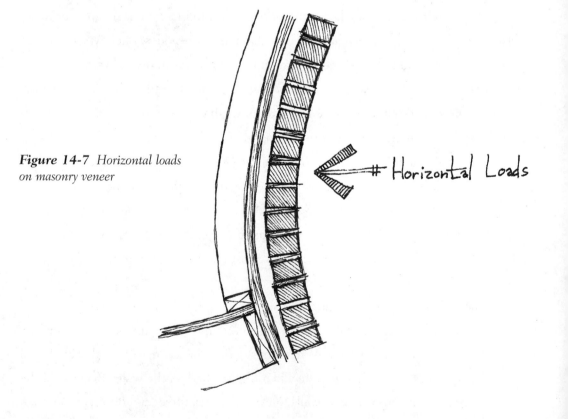

Figure 14-7 *Horizontal loads on masonry veneer*

Horizontal Loads

the structural portion of walls, the design and construction of anchored masonry veneers must account for differential movement. Building codes help account for this differential movement by requiring air spaces of certain dimensions between anchored masonry veneers and their backings.

Horizontal support is provided for anchored masonry veneers by attaching the veneers to backings with different types of fasteners. A wall which acts as a backing for an anchored masonry veneer must be able to support the loads imposed by the anchored masonry veneer, as well as any other loads the wall is intended to support. Building codes specify the types of fasteners (ties) acceptable for attaching anchored masonry veneers to different backings. Codes also specify the spacing limitations of those ties, and the depth, where applicable, to which certain types of ties must be anchored in a backing. These code requirements ensure that anchored masonry veneers will have a sufficient number of attachments to backings to prevent the veneers from buckling, and that the ties will be attached firmly enough to continue to provide support for the veneers. Whenever a backing for an anchored masonry veneer consists of sheathing applied to a wall system, building codes require that the sheathing be of a certain minimum thickness, so that it is rigid enough to support the veneer.

Adhered Masonry Veneer

Like anchored masonry veneer wall coverings, adhered masonry veneer wall coverings are regulated by building codes as to the types and dimensions of materials used as veneers, and as to what types and thicknesses of bonding materials are acceptable. Codes also govern the shearing stress of the bond. The code requirements for structural adhesion vary based on the type of backing and the type of masonry veneer used.

Metal Veneers

Metal veneers are required by building codes to be of a certain minimum thickness so that they are strong enough to be considered a durable finish. They must be attached to supports with corrosion resistant fasteners. Corrosion may occur due to oxidation from exposure or due to galvanic action. Galvanic action is a process which occurs when two dissimilar metals are placed in contact with one another; one of the metals will eventually corrode and begin coating the other metal. Depending on the two metals adjacent to one another, this corrosion process can occur relatively quickly (i.e., quickly enough for it to be considered improper to use the two metals in contact with one another for building construction), or can take so long to occur that it causes no concern to the code official. Metal veneer fasteners must be spaced in such a manner that they provide proper attachment for the metal veneers to the supports.

Supports for exterior metal veneers and fasteners are required by codes to be able to resist certain minimum wind loads. When exterior metal veneers are attached to metal supports, the supports must be protected from water penetration by painting, galvanizing, or some other equivalent method. When exterior metal veneers are attached to wood supports, the wood must be pressure-treated or must be protected by some other acceptable method.

Whenever metal veneer joints or ends are exposed to weather, codes require some effort to protect them from moisture penetration. The protection may be provided by painting, by the use of sealants, or by some other reliable means. If metal veneers are not attached to grounded metal supports, the veneers must be properly grounded. Each code references different requirements for grounding metal veneers.

Glass Veneers

Glass veneers are called thin structural glass veneers and concern code officials because the breakage of such veneers can be dangerous to pedestrians below. Glass

Figure 14-8 *Glass above walking surfaces*

located above walking surfaces is of particular concern, as falling glass is extremely dangerous (Figure 14-8). Building codes regulate the thickness of thin structural glass veneers, as well as the allowable size of individual glass panels.

The attachment of thin structural glass veneers is critical because of the need to keep the glazing in place, and because the expansion and contraction of thin structural glass veneers due to temperature changes can cause breakage if the glazing is in contact with materials that do not expand or contract at the same rate. Codes regulate the fastening of thin structural glass veneers, and require expansion joints where the glazing must be afforded uninhibited movement.

Wood Veneers

Wood veneers include board siding (vertical and horizontal), panel siding (e.g., plywood siding, particleboard siding, and hardboard siding), wood shingles, and shakes (Figure 14-9). Building codes regulate the thickness of different wood sidings in order to guarantee enough rigidity for them to remain in place and to provide weather protection. Supports for wood veneers have certain spacing requirements so that the supports provide adequate structural stiffness. Codes regulate the depth of penetration of fasteners for wood veneers. The manner in which wood veneers are installed may oblige one to take certain measures to provide for proper fire protection. For example, if wood veneers are applied to furring, the interstitial spaces created by the furring may necessitate the installation of fire blocking or draftstopping.

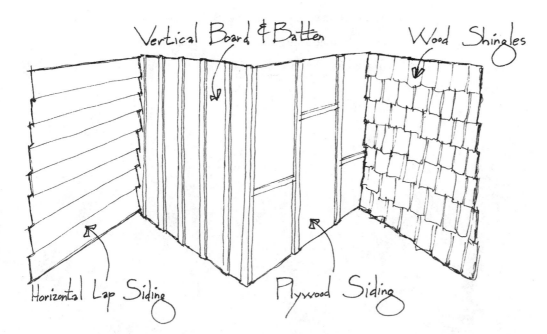

Figure 14-9 *Wood shingles and shakes*

Asbestos Shingles

Some building codes contain exterior wall covering requirements for asbestos shingles. Typical requirements include the types of sheathing allowed as backing for asbestos shingles, and the types of fasteners used to attach the sheathing and the shingles. Asbestos shingles are also required by codes to be manufactered of a specific minimum thickness.

Vinyl Siding

Depending on the code being referenced, vinyl siding may have to meet the requirements of that code or of some other referenced standard. Requirements may deal with such issues as the ability of vinyl siding to resist different wind loads, the backing required for vinyl siding, and the type and spacing of fasteners required to attach vinyl siding to its backing. Restrictions of the use of vinyl siding may be mandated by codes based on the type of construction of the building.

COMBUSTIBLE MATERIALS ON THE EXTERIOR SIDE OF EXTERIOR WALLS

Whenever combustible materials occur on the exterior side of exterior walls, building codes regulate the type of materials used as well as the proper installation of those materials. The materials must meet applicable referenced tests and standards to ensure that they are safe to use in each specific application. Codes also require combustible exterior finish materials to be completely backed with exterior walls, and may restrict the location of the combustible materials. In the case of balconies and bay windows, codes place restrictions on what they are constructed of based on the type of construction of the building.

Roofs and Roof Structures

Chapter 15 discusses building code requirements for roof structures and roof coverings, as well as building code requirements for parapet walls. Requirements for parapet walls which relate to fire-resistant construction are discussed in Chapter 7 of this book. The parapet wall requirements covered in this chapter are concerned with water protection for the parapet wall and the drainage of roofs through parapet walls.

Roofs provide weather protection for buildings. A roof consists of some sort of structural system which either supports a roof deck or which is an integral part of the roof deck (e.g., a concrete slab), and the roof covering. Roof structures are comprised of penthouses, tanks, cooling towers, cupolas, domes, and other structures located on the roofs of buildings (Figure 15-1). Building codes regulate roofs and roof structures to ensure that they are structurally sound and that they provide proper weather protection.

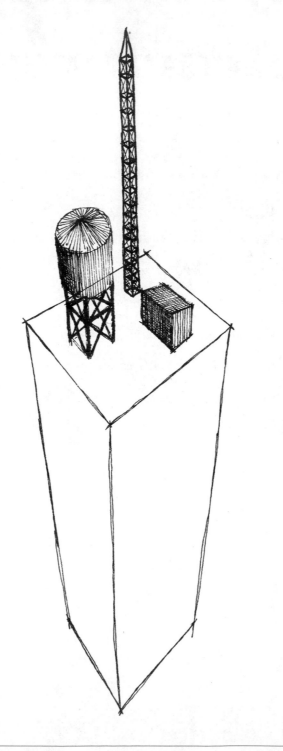

Figure 15-1 *Roof structures*

Roof structures are further regulated as to their type of construction and materials, their support, and in the case of tanks, their provisions for drainage. One must look at several chapters of a building code to learn all of the requirements pertaining to roofs and roof structures.

PARAPET WALLS

Building codes require parapet walls to be designed and constructed in a manner that will prevent rain water from entering the wall at its top and at its junction with the roof covering (Figure 15-2). Codes require proper drainage of water from roof areas behind parapet walls. The tops of parapet walls must be covered with weatherproof noncombustible copings which are as wide as the walls are thick. Flashing must be used to prevent water from entering parapet walls at the coping joints and at the intersections of the parapet walls and the roof planes. If interior drainage of roof areas behind parapet walls is not provided, then those roof areas must drain through parapet walls by means of scuppers. Codes specify material, sizing, and location requirements for scuppers, both for normal roof drainage and for overflow drainage if no other means of overflow drainage has been provided.

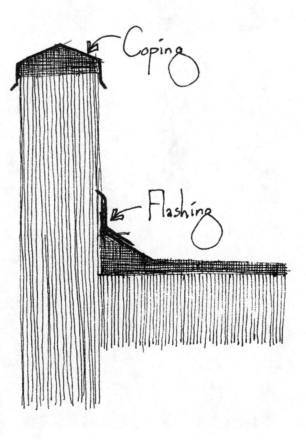

Figure 15-2 *Parapet wall*

ROOF COVERINGS

Building codes must address many different types of roof coverings. Roof coverings may consist of asphalt shingles, mineral fiber shingles, slate shingles, concrete or clay tile roofs, wood shingles or shakes, built-up roofs, slate or mineral surfaced roll roofing, metal roofs, synthetic sheet membrane roofs, etc. (Figure 15-3). Codes must also address many characteristics of roof coverings, including their installation, their fire resistance, their resistance to wind, and their ability to provide weather protection.

Figure 15-3 *Roof coverings*

Roof coverings are required by codes to provide weather protection at the roof. The manner by which each type of roof covering provides weather protection varies based on the particular roof covering in question. Some roof coverings are designed to employ the forces of gravity and route water off of a roof as quickly as possible. Other roof coverings provide a waterproof separation between ponding water and the building spaces below, and then utilize drains and scuppers to eventually remove the water from the roof. The slopes of roofs vary based on the method of weather protection and the properties of the roofing materials used.

Flashing

In order for a roof covering to provide complete weather protection, flashing must be used where the roof slope changes direction (e.g., gables, hips, and valleys) (Figure 15-4), at junctions of roofs and vertical planes (such as where roofs abut walls) (Figure 15-5), and where elements penetrate roofs (e.g., curbs and supports for equipment, skylights, chimneys, plumbing vents, and other mechanical vents) (Figure 15-6). Building codes require flashing to be of certain specific materials based on the location of the flashing and on the type of roof covering employing the flashing. Depending on the type of flashing used and the location of the flashing, codes may specify the required thickness of the flashing, the weight of the flashing, the width of the flashing, or any other property of the flashing necessary to ensure that the flashing is durable and contributes to the weather protection integrity of the roof covering. It is important that flashing be

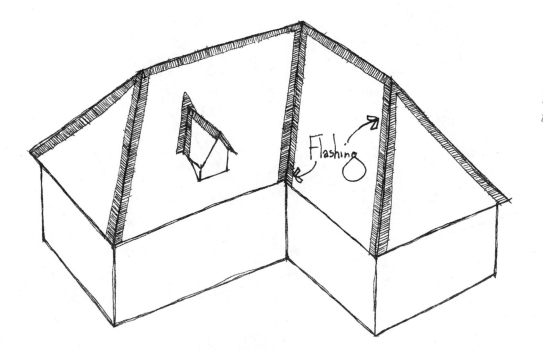

Figure 15-4 *Flashing—gables, hips, valleys*

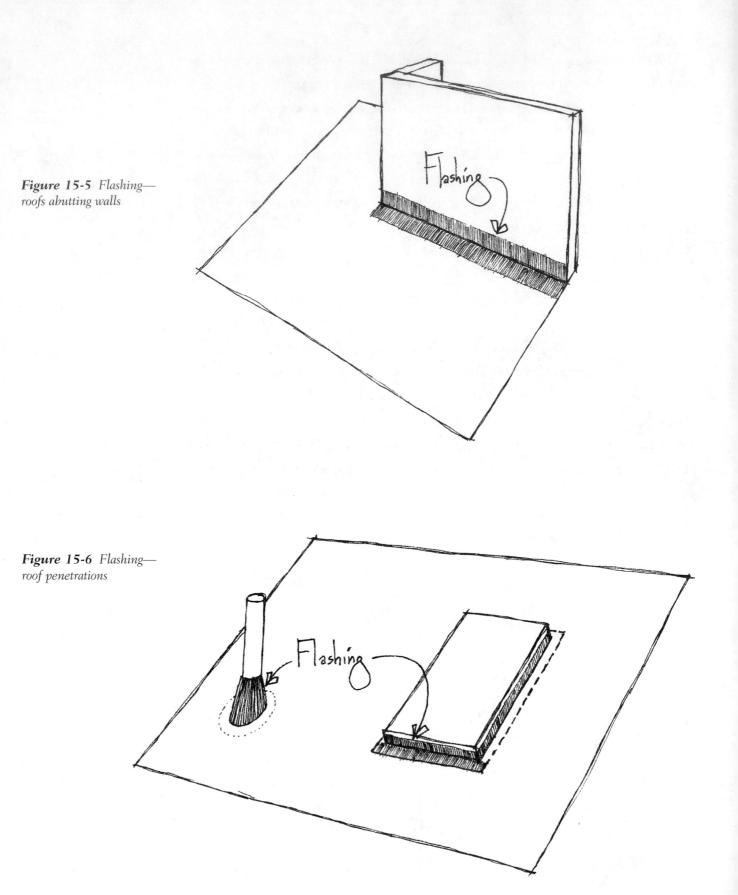

Figure 15-5 Flashing—
roofs abutting walls

Figure 15-6 Flashing—
roof penetrations

made of a material that is chemically and electrically compatible with the materials adjacent to it, so that the flashing will not corrode or cause other materials to corrode.

Fasteners

Building codes regulate the types of fasteners used for roof coverings, as well as their installation. Fasteners are used for attaching roofing underlayment to a roof deck, for attaching a roof finish to a roof deck, and for attaching flashing when flashing is required. Fastening may be accomplished mechanically, by adhesives, or by both depending on the circumstances. Fasteners must be made of materials that will not corrode nor cause adjacent materials to corrode. Building codes regulate the types of fasteners used for roof coverings, as well as the dimensions and spacing of those fasteners.

Roof coverings are required by building codes to resist wind loads. The structural components of roof assemblies (i.e., roof decks, rafters, etc.) are regulated for wind resistance by the structural chapters of building codes. Roof coverings must also resist wind, however, as they must remain effective as weatherproofing agents. Different types of roof coverings must meet different requirements for wind resistance. For example, certain shingles may be required to have self-seal strips or may be required to be interlocking. Fastener schedules may also change based on the location and application of the roof shingles.

Fire-Resistance Classification

Roof coverings are classified for fire resistance by building codes in accordance with a referenced standard. They are classified as Class A, Class B, or Class C roof coverings. Class A roof coverings include masonry, concrete, slate, tile (Figure 15-7), and any other roof covering listed as a Class A roof covering; Class B roof coverings include corrugated steel sheets, galvanized steel sheets, galvanized steel shingles (Figure 15-8), and any other roof covering listed as a Class B roof covering; and Class C roof coverings include fiberglass asphalt shingles (Figure 15-9) and any other roof covering listed as a Class C roof covering. Building codes dictate where roof coverings of each classification are permitted for use. There are roof coverings which are not classified for fire resistance that are allowed by codes to be used in certain limited situations, such as for carports and farm buildings amongst others.

Types

Building codes contain many different requirements for the different types of roof coverings available. Roof coverings are required to be installed in accordance with

Figure 15-7 *Typical Class A roof covering*

Figure 15-8 *Typical Class B roof covering*

Figure 15-9 *Typical Class C roof covering*

building code requirements, as well as with the listings provided by the manufacturers of the roof coverings. Requirements for roof coverings addressed by building codes include the types and installation of underlayments, the types and spacing of fasteners, the exposures of shingles, the specifications for flashing, and many other requirements. Figure 15-10 lists several different types of roof coverings and typical building code requirements for each type.

Reroofing a structure may consist of replacing the roof or recovering the roof. Replacing a roof consists of removing an existing roof, making repairs to the roof decking and structure as needed, and then installing a new roof covering, including underlayment. Recovering a roof consists of preparing the old roof to receive a new roof covering, and then installing a new roof covering over that existing roof. One must realize that some codes and certain mortgage lenders allow no more than two roof coverings on a structure.

Some building codes require replacement of roofs rather than recovering of roofs when conditions do not warrant the installation of a new roof over an existing roof. The reasons for not recovering an existing roof are fairly obvious. If the condition of an existing roof structure or roof covering will not structurally support a new roof covering, or will cause the installation of a new roof covering to be ineffective, then one must replace the existing roof structure or covering rather than recover it. When an existing

Figure 15-10

TYPE OF ROOF COVERING	TYPICAL CODE REQUIREMENTS
Asphalt Shingles	Type of underlayment
	Location and fastening of underlayment
	Overlapping of underlayment
	Special locations of asphalt shingles
	Types of fasteners
Mineral Fiber Shingles	Type of underlayment
	Location and fastening of underlayment
Slate Shingles	Minimum slope
	Type of underlayment
	Maximum exposure
Concrete and Clay Tile Roof	Thickness of tile
	Test requirements for tile
	Identification of tile
	Installation of tile
	Condition of substrate
	Type of underlayment
	Standards for membrane
	Types of fasteners
	Flashing requirements
	Adhesive/sealant requirements
	Mortar requirements
	Eave closure requirements
	Lumber requirements
Wood Shingles and Shakes	Locations permitted
	Minimum grades of shingles and shakes
	Types of allowable shingles and shakes
	Type of underlayment
	Identification of shingles and shakes
	Exposure of shingles and shakes
	Types of fasteners
	Standards and identification of fire retardant treated shingles and shakes

TYPE OF ROOF COVERING	TYPICAL CODE REQUIREMENTS
Built-Up Roofs	Deck requirements and preparation
	Cant strip requirements
	Base ply fastening requirements
	Fastening requirements for additional plies
	Types of fasteners
	Surface treatment requirements
	Material requirements
	Aggregate requirements
Slate- or Mineral-Surfaced Roll Roofing	Weight of roofing
	Exposure of sheets
	Type of fasteners
Metal Roofs	Minimum weight of different metal roofs
	Types of fasteners
	Minimum slopes
	Seam and joint requirements
	Thickness of shingles, if applicable
Synthetic Sheet Membrane Roofs	Requirements for structural system
	Requirements for nailers
	Thickness of flashing
	Preparation of substrate
	Ballast requirements, if applicable
Liquid Applied Coatings	Coating material requirements
	Minimum coating thickness
	Surface preparation
	Application requirements
	Minimum slope

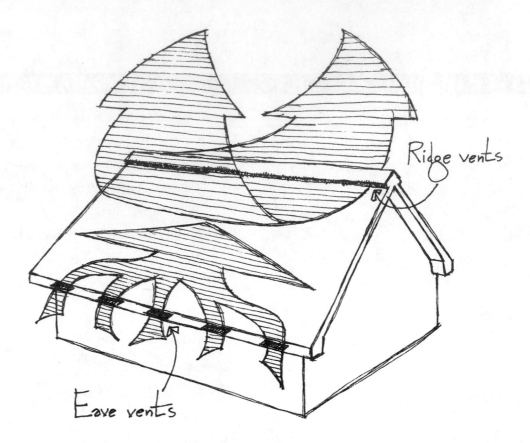

Figure 15-11 Attic ventilation

Ridge vents

Eave vents

Figure 15-12 Attic access

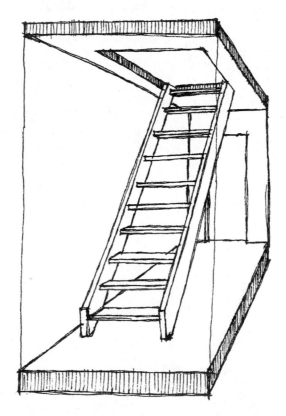

roof has too many roof coverings, one must replace the roof coverings rather than recover it. Certain types of roofs, such as tile roofs, are not allowed to be covered with another roof. Each code varies as to what is required of flashing when recovering an existing roof.

ATTICS

The attic spaces formed by roofs and ceilings must be adequately ventilated in order to remove moisture buildup that can cause damage to the structure. Building codes specify the amount of attic ventilation openings one must provide based on the area of the attic (Figure 15-11). These openings must be protected against the potential intrusion of rodents and birds. Codes allow a reduction in the amount of ventilation opening required if certain measures are taken to enhance the flow of ventilating air through the attic space. It should be noted that the amount of ventilation required by codes is often inadequate to properly ventilate attic spaces in some humid areas of the country.

Attic spaces must be provided with an access opening (Figure 15-12). Codes prescribe the minimum dimensions of attic access openings. If equipment is installed in attic spaces, such as mechanical systems, codes require attic access openings to be large enough to remove the largest piece of equipment.

Structural Loads, Tests, and Inspections

Chapter 16 discusses the types of structural loads that buildings and structures are exposed to and what types of issues codes are concerned with when designing buildings and structures that must resist those loads. This chapter does not discuss the structural engineering of facilities to resist loads, as that discussion would be beyond the purview of this book. However, this chapter does attempt to familiarize designers with the types of issues confronted by structural engineers when they design the structural systems for different facilities.

Structural chapters of building codes regulate design and construction for structural design. That is, they regulate what must be done so that buildings and structures will remain standing by resisting the forces imposed on them. Any structure is exposed to many different types of loads. The weight of the structure itself imposes dead loads on the structure; and additional live loads are imposed on the structure as a function of how the structure is used (by the introduction of occupants, furnishings, vehicles, machinery, etc.). Nature imposes loads on structures in the form of rain, snow, earthquakes, and wind. Building codes use structural chapters to describe the types of loads imposed on structures, as well as to prescribe the types of considerations that must be taken into account by designers when determining how to apply those loads to their designs. Structural design is affected by the shape of a structure, the height of a structure, whether a structure is enclosed or open, whether or not a structure is raised and open underneath, and by many other attributes of a structure's physical design (Figure 16-1). The duration of any load on a structure will also affect its design, as structural

Figure 16-1 *Shape of structure*

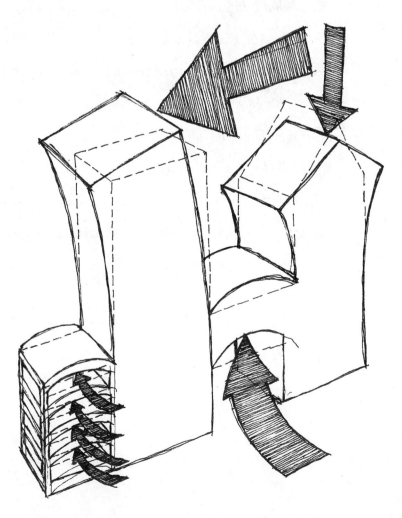

loads that are longer in duration will subject a structure to more stress than will equivalent structural loads that are not as long in duration. Code officials must determine that any structure erected in their jurisdiction is properly designed and constructed in accordance with all locally adopted codes and standards.

WRITING STRUCTURAL REGULATIONS

Structural chapters of building codes represent some of the most debated material within codes. Alterations to the text of structural chapters often affect several different building materials, creating a situation where one type of material is difficult to use in a given circumstance, whereas another type of material lends itself quite well to the same circumstance. Therefore, changing the provisions of structural chapters may raise the ire of one group of material manufacturers, while placating another. The end result is a great deal of debating at code change hearings whenever substantial modifications to structural chapters are proposed.

There are other reasons for frequent debate when modifications are proposed to structural chapters of building codes, amongst which is the difference in philosophy that many code officials have regarding structural design. Some code officials believe that good structural design should be so all-encompassing as to protect building occupants from virtually any foreseeable load, no matter how great; this group might wish for buildings that would not fail in even the most severe of hurricanes. Other code officials believe that good structural design should balance "adequate" structural load conditions with economy of construction. This latter group may feel that no one can design for immense hurricanes and that structural designs based on ultimate criteria may be so costly that individuals will find ways to circumvent codes rather than to meet them.

CONSTRUCTION DOCUMENTS

The chapters of building codes dealing with the structural design of buildings are some of the most technical chapters of the codes. They are often too technical for a code official to understand. As a result, many code officials often rely on structural engineering staff or consultants when reviewing plans and specifications for adherence to the structural provisions of building codes. Though many code officials feel that it is their duty to check all of the calculations of structural engineers, it is generally considered acceptable for a code official to check the loads, shape factors, and any other relevant input factors of a structural design in order to maintain that the designer used the proper loads and factors referenced by the code, while assuming that the engineer is professionally capable of performing all the necessary calculations. Of course, a code official may have good reasons for checking the calculations of some designers more carefully, but the code official should rely on the consulting of a qualified individual when checking structural calculations if that code official is not competent to check the calculations him or herself. Similarly, many architects in a given situation may need to check the input loads and factors of a structural engineer, but should an architect feel that he or she should check certain structural calculations, that architect should rely on the advice of a qualified consultant unless the architect is qualified by training.

TYPES OF LOADS

Dead Loads

Dead load is defined by building codes as being the weight of all of the components of a building, structural and nonstructural, including walls and partitions, floors, roofs, ceilings, beams, girders, trusses, columns, stairways, and fixed service equipment (Figure 16-2). Fixed service equipment includes plumbing stacks and risers, electrical

Figure 16-2 Dead loads

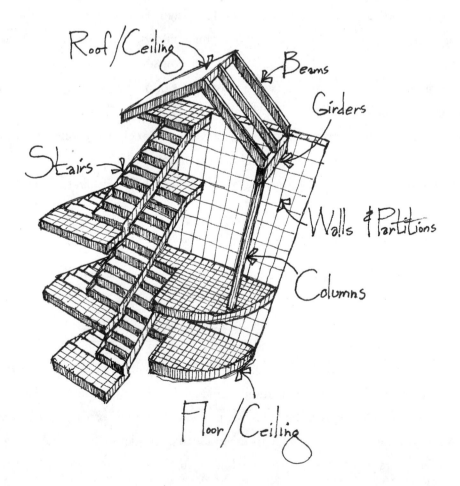

feeders, heating, ventilation, air conditioning, and fire protection systems. When designing for the dead load of a structure, one must use the actual weight of the different building components. If the actual weight of a particular component is not known, then one must determine the weight of the component by some means acceptable to the code official (perhaps by the use of a referenced standard).

As already mentioned, the weight of partitions must be included when determining dead loads. It is not always known, however where partitions will be located in a structure. For example, in many multi-tenant buildings (e.g., shopping centers and multi-tenant office buildings), tenant separation partitions and other partitions are not installed or even located until a tenant has signed a lease and a tenant space design has been approved. To compensate for this lack of knowledge as to the actual location of potential dead loads, building codes require some load factor to be added to the known dead loads for the purpose of calculating structural systems.

Live Loads

Live loads are loads that are produced as a result of the use and occupancy of structures (Figure 16-3). They do not include crane loads, dead loads, earthquake loads, snow loads, or wind loads. Live loads are generated by the occupants of a structure, as well as by furnishings, supplies, special equipment, and so on. Live loads are applied to all structural elements, including floors, walls, roofs, beams, girders, trusses, and columns. A sleeping room in a residence would be subjected to a different live load than would be the lobby of an office building. Similarly, the area of a library where the stacks are located would be subjected to a greater live load than would be the reading area of the library. Variation in the occupancy and use of spaces changes the intensity of the live loads imposed on the spaces. Building codes require live loads to be calculated as the greatest loads that are likely to be produced by the occupancy and use of the structure in question.

Building codes also require that live load calculations reflect the weight of special concentrated live loads. These concentrated live loads are created within a structure by the introduction of heavy items, such as machinery, vehicles, or the like. The weight imposed by concentrated live loads or by heavy uniform live loads may actually affect the design of many different structural assemblies if more than one assembly are acting in concert with one another.

Machinery and equipment, and certain occupancy situations may cause impact loads on a structure. The movement imposed by impact loads is quite different than the loads imposed by stationary occupants and equipment. For example, sports fans at a

Figure *16-3* *Live loads*

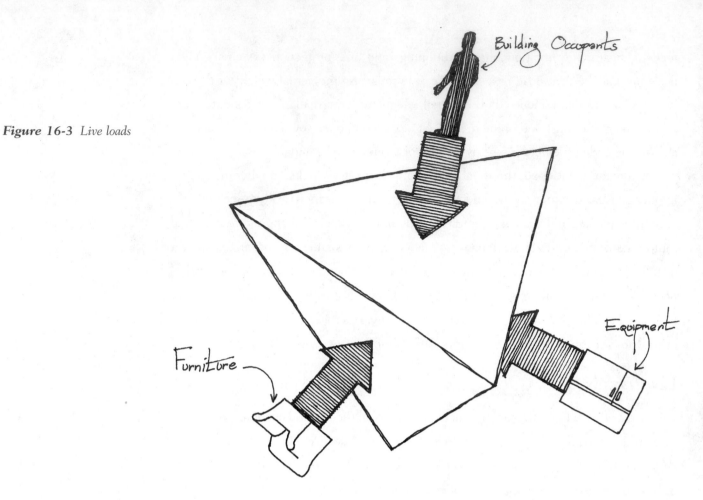

stadium jumping in unison can exert a harmonic load which must be accounted for in structural design. Building codes require structural designers to consider all applicable impact loads in their design and analysis of a structure.

Snow Loads

Snow imposes loads on structures which can be quite heavy and which can remain in place for an extensive amount of time depending on the climate. Building codes compensate for the variations in amount of snowfall through the use of figures which delineate the amount of snowfall to be considered for structural design, based on where the structure is to be located geographically. One must be cautious when applying snow loads from a referenced figure however, as there may be some local variation in the actual amounts of snowfall, because of the altitude of the locality in question, or because of some other geographic constraint. One may be required to use greater snow loads locally than would otherwise be required by a code figure which adjusts factors based on the snowfall activity in certain geographical regions. The structural design is required by codes to reflect the actual snow load conditions.

The slopes of roofs affect the structural design of buildings and structures for snow loads (Figure 16-4). A flat roof would be subjected to a higher snow load than a sloped roof, as the snow remains on a flat roof longer. Obviously, a steeply sloped roof would normally be subjected to less snow load than would be a roof with a low slope.

The shapes of roofs can also affect the structural design of buildings and structures for snow loads (Figure 16-5). Sawtooth roofs, barrel vault roofs, and any roofs where the slopes change or where the juncture of two roofs can trap snow may lead to unbalanced snow loads. Unbalanced snow loads may also be created by projections from roofs, such as penthouses or mechanical equipment (Figure 16-6). Unbalanced loads may create a situation where certain areas of a roof are subjected to higher snow loads than the roof would normally be subjected to if the snow were not trapped. In the event of an unbalanced snow load, building codes require the structural designer to consider the effects of the unbalanced load when determining a structural design.

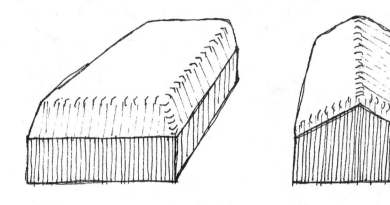

Figure 16-4 Snow loads—roof slopes

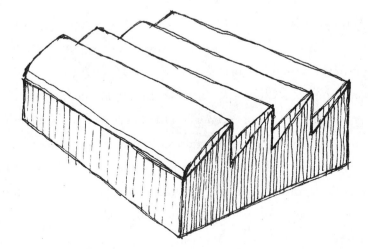

Figure 16-5 Snow loads—roof shapes

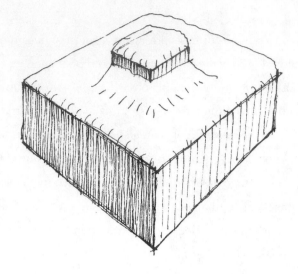

Figure 16-6 Snow loads—
unbalanced loads

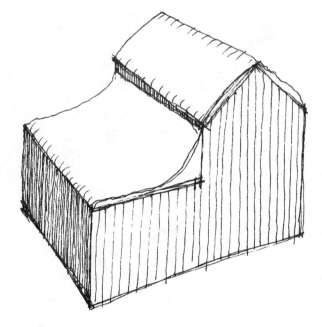

Figure 16-7 Snow
loads—roof locations

The locations of roofs affect the structural design of buildings and structures for snow loads, as the location of a roof relative to other roofs has a direct relation as to how much snow accumulates on the roof (Figure 16-7). A roof that abuts a wall which supports a higher roof will receive the snow drifts from the higher roof. Snow can drift from higher roofs to lower roofs even when the lower roof is not directly adjacent to the wall supporting the higher roof. Wind-driven snow may emanate from a high roof and travel some horizontal distance before landing on a lower roof. Whenever a lower roof receives snow drifts from two separate roofs simultaneously, the structural designer must consider the weight of the heavier drift when determining structural loads for the lower roof.

Wind Loads

Wind loads subject buildings and other structures to a great amount of structural loading. Building codes require structures to be designed to resist the forces imposed by wind loads. Building codes reference figures which establish design wind speeds by geographical region in order to compensate for the fact that different regions historically have different wind speeds. One must note, however, that the wind speeds shown in these building code figures are often altered by state or local government entities. Adjusting design wind speeds by locale keeps structures from being over regulated when they are located in areas with relatively low wind speeds, while ensuring that structures in areas with high wind speeds are adequately regulated.

There are many aspects of any structure's design which affect how it reacts to high winds. The shape of a structure may help the structure resist wind forces or may hin-

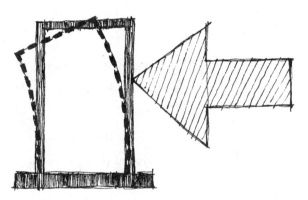

Figure 16-8 *Wind loads—roof shapes*

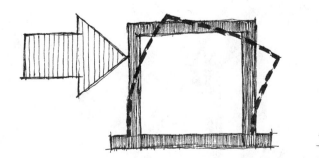
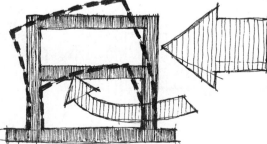

Figure 16-9 *Wind loads—open vs. enclosed structure*

Figure 16-10 *Wind loads—eaves*

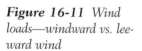

der the structure's efforts to resist wind forces (Figure 16-8). If a structure is an open structure, it will behave differently when high winds occur than will an enclosed structure (Figure 16-9). Structures raised up from grade by piles, for example, will be subjected to uplift forces that may literally pull the structure out of the ground, if the structure is not designed to resist such forces. Eaves on buildings may also be subjected to uplift forces (Figure 16-10).

The effect of forces exerted by wind pressures can often be subtle to those who are unaware of the ramifications of such forces. On August 24, 1992, hurricane Andrew swept across South Florida leaving mass destruction in its wake. Many of the buildings that were destroyed by this devastating hurricane were not constructed in accordance with local building codes, and their destruction could be traced to certain flaws in their structural design. For example, there were several large buildings with tilt-up concrete panel walls and structural tee roof systems which collapsed completely. Investigation of these structures showed that they were designed as enclosed structures, the design of which is different from the design that would be used for open structures, as enclosed structures and open structures behave very differently under wind loading. These buildings were indeed enclosed structures, but the flaw in their design was that the exterior overhead door assemblies were not designed to resist the wind pressures referenced by local codes. The overhead doors therefore collapsed prematurely, the result of which was the enclosed structures became open structures. High winds then rushed into the unobstructed door openings, lifting structural tees off of their supporting walls, and then blowing the walls down. An error in the structural designs of the overhead doors ultimately led to the collapse of the buildings.

Figure 16-11 *Wind loads—windward vs. leeward wind*

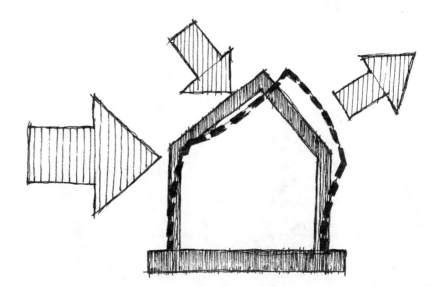

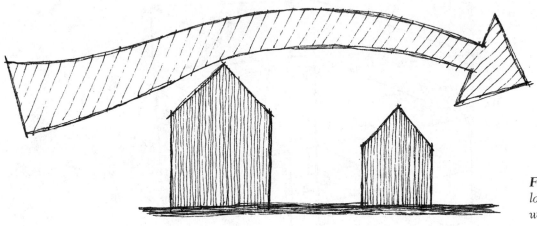

Figure 16-12 Wind loads—Building blocking wind

Much of what is covered in structural chapters in building codes concerning wind loads has to do with the shape of structures and the closure of structures. Just as wind forces act differently on an enclosed structure than they do on an open structure, wind forces also act differently on structures of different shapes. A vertical wall resists wind loads differently from a sloped wall. A sloped roof surface facing a strong wind (windward) behaves differently than a sloped roof surface on the opposite side of a building from the wind source (leeward) (Figure 16-11). Structures may also vary in their resistance to wind loads because of their proximity to other buildings blocking the wind, but building codes do not allow for decreases in structural design wind loads based on other structures (Figure 16-12). Obviously, the other structures may be removed eventually, negating their ability to perform as a wind block.

Earthquake Loads

Earthquakes create many different types of load conditions, including loads which can literally shake a building apart (Figure 16-13). As with wind loads and snow loads, building codes use figures to assign various earthquake design loads to different geographical areas. The earthquake motions which affect the structural system of a building are influenced by the location of the building relative to a fault. Buildings located in higher risk areas must be designed with more earthquake-resistant features than would buildings located in lower risk areas.

Soil profiles also influence the structural system of a building when a building is subjected to earthquake motions. Some soil conditions support buildings better during earthquakes than do other soil conditions. As a result, building codes require the structural analysis of a building for earthquake-resistant design to include consideration for the type of soil supporting the building.

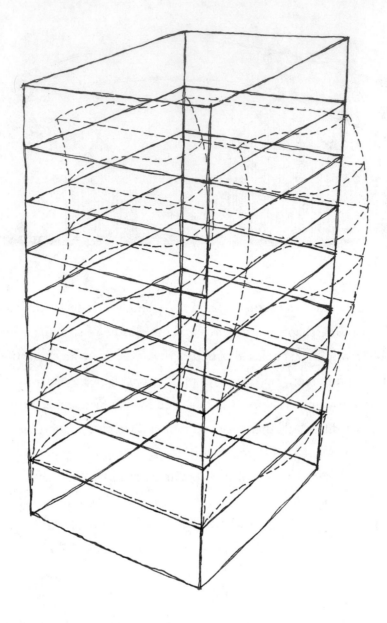

Figure 16-13 *Earthquake loads—building shape*

Building codes use other criteria for determining the ultimate earthquake-resistant design for any building required to resist earthquakes. How a building is used is important, because of the number of occupants within the building or because of the nature of the services provided within the building. The shape and height of a building are important when analyzing the building for earthquake-resistant design, as they affect how the building will perform when subjected to earthquake motions.

Special Loads

Structures are often subjected to special loads based on the unique use characteristics of each structure. These special loads are structural loads which do not fit into the classifications of dead loads, live loads, or weather-related loads. Two examples of the types of special loads addressed by codes and standards are the loads imposed on basement walls and the loads imposed on handrails and guardrails.

Basement walls are structurally loaded by pressure from soil and ground water adjacent to them. They must resist lateral pressure that is created by the soil retained, and they must resist hydrostatic pressure caused from the water retained in that soil. Building codes require basement walls to be designed with consideration given for these pressures. Of course, basement walls may also be subjected to dead loads and live loads from the structure above.

Guardrails are subjected to loading from building occupants, as well as from vehicular traffic. Building codes require handrails, guardrails, and parking guardrails to be designed for horizontal loads which vary according to the use of the rail in question. Parking guardrails must be designed to resist the horizontal load imposed by automobiles, whereas guardrails at balconies, stairs, and ramps must be able to resist the horizontal load imposed by pedestrians. Pedestrian guardrails and handrails must be designed for specific bearing strengths also, so that they can support the weight imposed on them by the occupants using them.

DEFLECTIONS

The loading of structural assemblies causes them to deflect. Structural codes and standards allow for certain maximum deflections in structural members, recognizing that if a structural member's deflection is too great, it will ultimately fail. Building codes also specify maximum deflection limitations based on the finish materials applied to structural members. For example, floor-ceiling assemblies which encompass a gypsum board ceiling are allowed by codes to have a greater deflection than are floor-ceiling assemblies encompassing a plaster ceiling. Gypsum board can flex more than plaster without cracking, and therefore gypsum board can be designed for a greater deflection than plaster.

It is important to understand that the allowable building code deflections for structural assemblies are often too great for achieving a quality design. Remember that codes often present minimum standards, and do not necessarily present the best means for designing and building any particular element. To illustrate this point, consider that when codes specify maximum deflections for floor joists, codes are concerned with the structural capabilities of the floor joists and whether or not the ceiling finish will crack or fail. However, if one uses the minimum numbers and sizes of floor joists allowed by codes in a house design, the house will almost certainly have some rooms in which the floors have so much bounce, one will literally cause objects (such as picture frames, china, etc.) to bounce off of furniture by simply walking through these rooms. The sorts of design decisions that lead to the stiffening of floors for the convenience of the owners are the sorts of design decisions not generally considered to be within the purview of codes and standards. Codes and standards are concerned with a floor's ability to remain structurally sound and to provide an adequate structural support for ceiling finishes if indeed the floor supports a ceiling finish. Codes and standards provide minimum structural guidelines, and the designer must know when to exceed those guidelines.

TESTING AND INSPECTIONS

Building codes allow for the testing and inspection of structural materials, products, design, and construction. Some tests or inspections may be performed many times as part of an ongoing process to ensure compliance. For example, high-strength bolts are required by codes to be checked periodically to ensure that they are properly installed and tightened. Other tests or inspections may occur only once in response to a particular concern that a code official may have, or because of some indication that a structural situation is not reliable. The failure of a concrete core sample may lead to a major load test of a structure in order to determine whether the structure can actually withstand the loads it will be required to support.

Foundations and Retaining Walls

Chapter 17 discusses many aspects of foundation design, beginning with excavations, then continuing with discussion of soils, followed by discussion of footings and foundations. Other requirements for foundations are discussed including required openings in foundation walls, along with waterproofing and dampproofing of foundations. The chapter closes with discussion of piles and their design and installation, as well as many other requirements necessary for the safe design and construction of pile foundations.

Foundations and footings provide bases upon which buildings and structures are built. Foundations must be designed and constructed to respond to the nature of the soils, rock, and water wherever they are located. Soils analysis must be performed to determine the qualities of the subgrade before the construction process can even begin. Once all tests and analyses of a site have taken place, excavation can occur. Building codes have much to say about executing the excavation process so that construction workers are protected from the potential collapse of earthen walls. Once excavation is complete, footings are poured and foundation systems are constructed. Foundation walls are then waterproofed or dampproofed according to the hydrolic properties of the site regarding water. Piles may be installed as part of the foundation system, because of the excessive design loads of a particular structure, or because of some inadequacies found in the uppermost soils of the site. Building codes regulate all of these aspects of foundation design and construction.

EXCAVATIONS

Any excavations made for the purpose of providing foundation systems affect the soil adjacent to the excavations and may affect other foundations adjacent to the excavated areas. Unsupported or poorly supported earth adjacent to excavated areas can collapse, causing injury or even death to construction workers. Improperly designed or con-

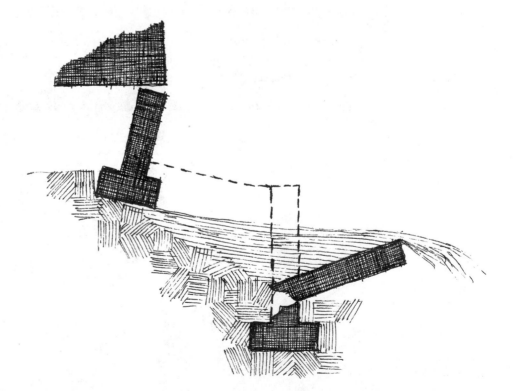

Figure 17-1 *Earth flowing from foundation into excavation*

structed retaining walls may fail, releasing previously retained earth, and consequently leading to human injury or death, or to the structural failure of other nearby foundation systems. The flow of earth into an excavated area may rob an adjacent foundation of the very support on which it stands if that flow is not prevented (Figure 17-1). Whenever any site excavations are made, building codes require measures to be taken to ensure that the earth and foundation systems adjacent to the excavations do not collapse. Codes also assign responsibility for the provision of adequate structural support of foundation systems adjacent to excavated areas when the excavated areas are adjacent to deeded property lines. In some cases, the responsibility for shoring up existing foundations adjacent to newly excavated areas falls on the shoulders of the owners of the existing foundations. In other cases, the responsibility for such shoring-up is that of the parties responsible for the excavations.

FOOTINGS AND FOUNDATIONS

Soils

Foundations transmit the loads of a structure to the earth below, be it soils or rock. The foundation bases which are in contact with the earth are called footings. It is absolutely imperative that the earth below footings and foundations provide adequate bearing for the foundation structure as well as the superstructure to remain stable

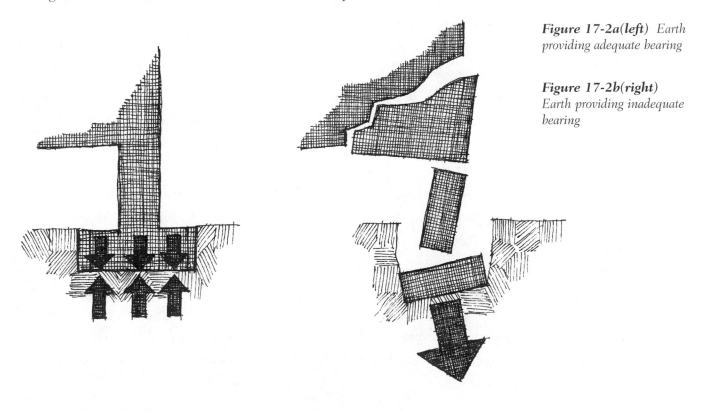

Figure 17-2a(left) Earth providing adequate bearing

Figure 17-2b(right) Earth providing inadequate bearing

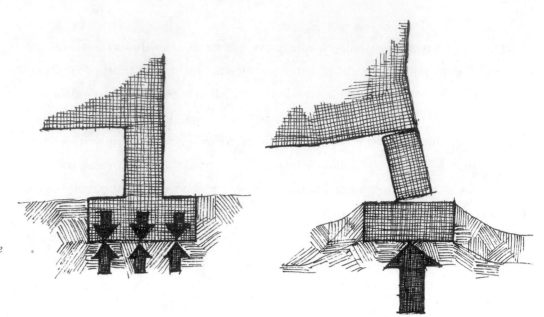

Figure 17-3a(left) Stable soils

Figure 17-3b(right) Heaving soils

(Figures 17-2a and b). Much of what codes have to say about the bases beneath footings and foundations has to do with what is necessary for ensuring that such bases remain stable. Certain soils have a propensity to erode because of their make-up, while other more stable soils may erode due to water runoff. Soils with high clay content may heave when exposed to water, causing foundations to move (Figures 17-3a and b).

Building codes require footings to be located on firm soils, either undisturbed soils of proper bearing capacity or properly compacted fill. Soils used for supporting structures must be free of vegetation, roots, and any other foreign materials, so that they remain consistent and do not experience any settling such as might be caused by soils shifting into voids left by decaying vegetation. Backfill must also be free of vegetation and any foreign materials. Where water may cause soils which support structures to erode, consideration must be given to such potential runoff problems during the design and construction of the structures, so that the erosion is stopped. Finished grade must slope away from foundations in order to keep water from affecting the performance of the foundations (Figure 17-4). Footings are required to bear on earth below the frost penetration depth (Figure 17-5), because the constant freezing and thawing of soils above frost penetration depths causes footings to move. In the coldest climates, footings may be required to bear on the permafrost, as the most stable soils in those areas are the soils that never thaw. Codes require footings to be located at a minimum depth of twelve inches (which in many areas is deeper than minimum frost penetration depths) as an added precaution against the disturbance of the subgrade due to freeze/thaw action or some other disturbance. Codes use map figures to establish minimum frost penetration design depths for different regions.

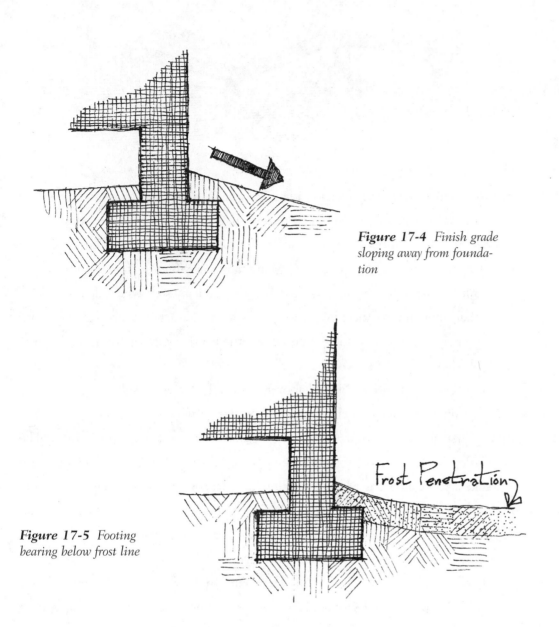

Figure 17-4 *Finish grade sloping away from foundation*

Figure 17-5 *Footing bearing below frost line*

Footings transmit to the earth those loads imposed on foundations by the structure above; therefore, the soils beneath footings must be able to carry the loads transmitted by the footings. Should the soil on a construction site not be able to adequately bear the loads imposed by the footings at the site, the foundation system for the structure in question will fail. The failure of the foundation system may translate into a sinking foundation system or differential settlement over the structure supported by the foundation system (Figure 17-6). The ultimate result could be a structure where it is difficult to open and shut doors and where floors are sloped, or even a structure where total structural collapse occurs, perhaps a life threatening situation.

In order to ensure that any soil is capable of supporting the loads imposed on it by a structure, the code official may require a soils investigation to be performed. A soils

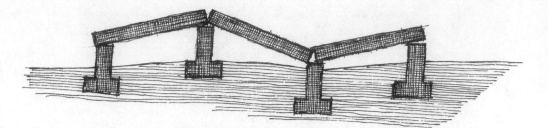

Figure 17-6 *Differential settlement*

investigation may include soils tests, and buildings codes contain sections which establish some of the requirements for such testing. It is not unheard of for a designer to require soils testing on his or her own in order to ascertain whether or not a site can adequately support a planned structure. Many tables and figures in codes presume a certain minimum soil-bearing pressure for their use, and any soils which do not provide at least that minimum soil bearing pressure may be inadequate for structural support. Thus, one may require test results to determine the bearing capacity of the soil at particular job sites.

Soils investigation also involves determining whether soils are subjected to shifting or moving, differential settlement, high groundwater, or whether they are expansive in nature. When shifting or moving soils are present, building codes require footings to be taken to depths where stable soils exist. One must design footings and foundations for the weakest soil conditions whenever a site contains soils of varying bearing capacity and differential settlement is consequently likely to occur. High water tables may subject basements to flooding, and therefore the designer must consider measures such as waterproofing when designing for areas with high water tables.

Expansive soils are soils which expand when in contact with water. Because of their propensity to expand when saturated, they move footings and foundations with each expansion and contraction. This lack of stability generally renders them inadequate for supporting structures, unless the structures can withstand the movement. Expansive soils can be removed so that other more stable soils can be placed where the expansive soils were located. One can even support a structure on expansive soils if the swell pressure of the soils is less than the confining pressure created by the weight of the structure, or by the weight of the structure plus the weight of the added stable soils.

One means of avoiding problems with expansive soils is to dig through the expansive soils until one reaches soils more suitable for the support of footings. Should one choose this tact, one must ensure that any foundation walls that traverse through expansive soils are strong enough laterally to resist the forces imposed on them by the swelling of the expansive soils (Figure 17-7). One must also design the footings penetrating the expansive soils so that they are not subject to uplift forces incurred from the

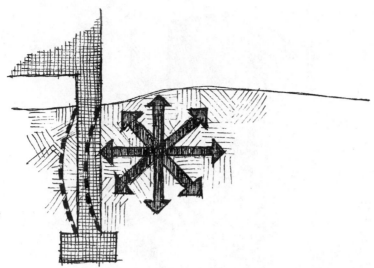

Figure 17-7 *Lateral rigidity through expansive soils*

expansive soils' swelling. As expansive soils heave, they can literally lift structures out of the ground if one does not design for uplift forces.

Another means of combating expansive soils is to neutralize their adverse affects. The process of neutralizing their adverse affects is called stabilization. By stabilizing expansive soils, one eliminates their tendency to change in volume, the elimination of which creates soil conditions which may be suitable for bearing footings and foundations. Stabilization may be achieved by dewatering the expansive soils or by saturating the expansive soils so that they remain constant in volume. One may also stabilize expansive soils by the use of chemicals.

Footing Requirements

Footings are the bases of foundations or column walls used to distribute the load over the subgrade (Olin, 1995). Footings push at the earth as a result of the loads they are carrying and the earth reacts by pushing back at the footing. As we all know, every action creates an opposite and equal reaction. If the earth does not push back adequately (soils with weak bearing pressures) or if the earth pushes back too much (as with expansive soils), footings may sink or lift resulting in foundation failure. The sizes of footings are dictated by the bearing pressures of the soils supporting them. If a column footing exerts a force of ten thousand pounds onto soils with a bearing pressure of 2500 pounds per square foot, then the footing will need to be at least four square feet in area (10,000 pounds divided by 2500 pounds per square foot equals four square feet) in order to keep from sinking into the soils (Figure 17-8). Codes require footing designs to be based on the actual bearing capacities of the soils providing support.

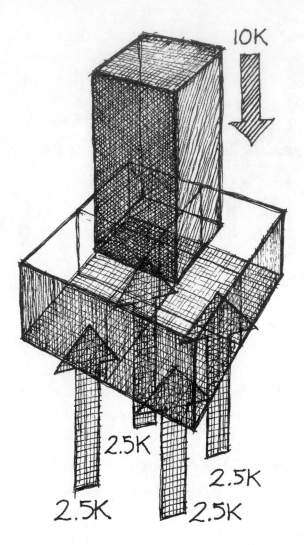

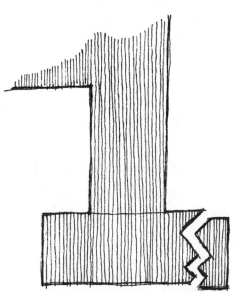

10K

2.5K

2.5K

2.5K

2.5K

Figure 17-8 *Footing size*

Figure 17-9 *Strength of footing*

The strength of the footing material is important as no footing will perform acceptably if it breaks up, because of its inability to resist the forces imposed on it by the structure and the earth pushing at one another (Figure 17-9). Building codes require concrete footings to obtain a certain minimum strength after 28 days of curing. The design of footings in certain locales may require the employment of seismic design methods such as seismic ties.

Foundation Walls

A foundation wall carries the loads imposed by the structure above and transfers those loads to the earth via a footing. In order to ensure sufficient support, codes usually require foundation walls to be at least as thick as the walls they are supporting. In some instances, codes may allow foundation walls to have a lesser thickness than the walls they are supporting if the foundation walls are corbeled as specified in the codes in order to receive the thicker walls above (Figure 17-10). Obviously, footings must be able to resist decay and termites as they are in constant contact with the earth. This does not necessarily preclude footings from being constructed of wood; some codes allow timber footings and wood foundation systems to be used if the wood is properly protected. Timber footings may be allowed if they are permanently below water or if they are properly treated with an approved preservative treatment. Wood foundation

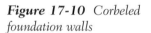

Figure 17-10 Corbeled foundation walls

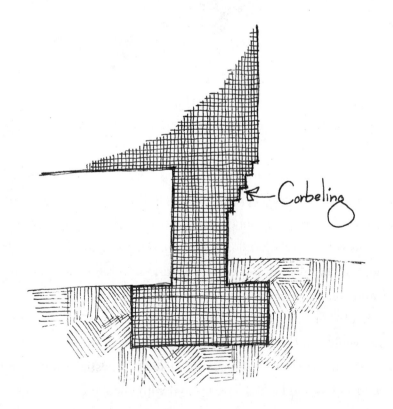

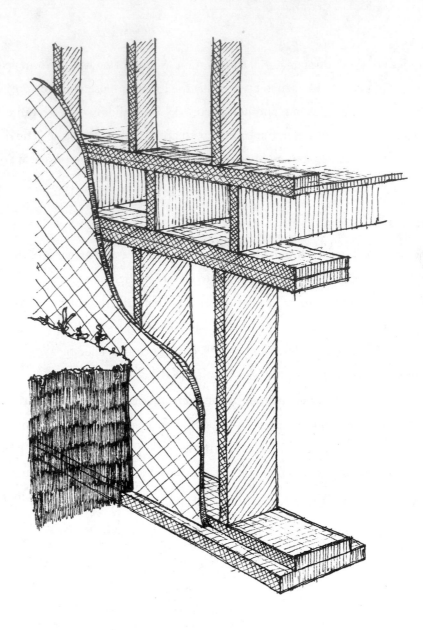

Figure 17-11 *Wood foundation systems*

systems may be allowed if they comply with approved technical standards referenced by codes (Figure 17-11).

In addition to supporting the loads from the structures above them, foundation walls must also resist the loads applied laterally to them by wind loading or by retained earth. Building codes require foundation walls to be properly braced or of adequate thickness to resist buckling when loads are imposed on them (Figure 17-12).

Imagine standing adjacent to a wooden yardstick with the stick standing on its end, one end bearing on the floor and the other end three feet above the floor supported by the tip of one of your fingers. If you were to push lightly on the end of the yardstick, the yardstick would bend slightly in the direction of one or the other of its printed sides (Figure 17-13). The harder you pushed, the more the yardstick would bend, and eventually the yardstick would break if you pushed with enough force (Figure 17-14). The

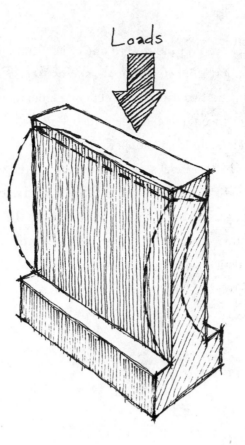

Figure 17-12 *Bracing of foundation walls*

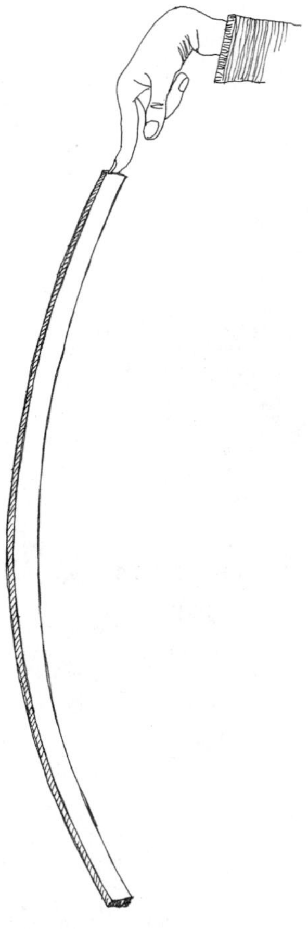

Figure 17-13
Pushing on yard stick

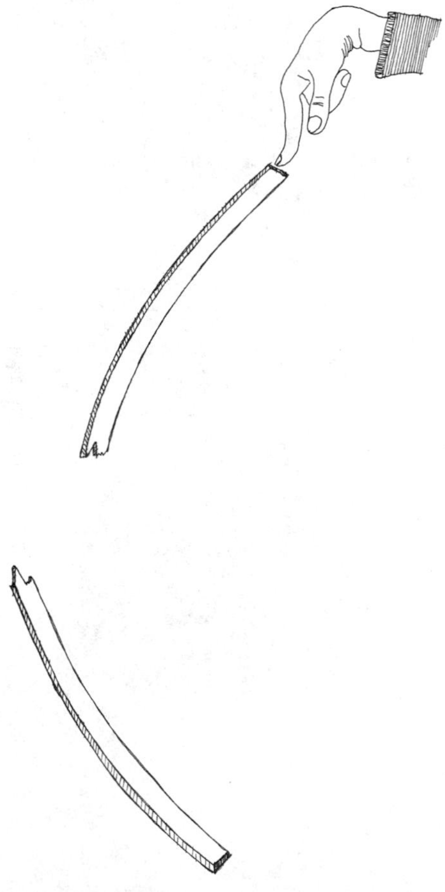

Figure 17-14
Breaking yard stick

yardstick would bend toward one of its printed sides, because the least amount of lateral support is inherent in its least cross-sectional dimension. The yardstick would not bend in the two opposite directions perpendicular to its printed sides, because those directions would require the yardstick to resist a cross-sectional dimension which provides adequate lateral support. This is the principle at play when thickening a wall to provide better lateral support—the thicker the wall, the more difficult it is to bend.

Now imagine you were to place a left hand finger adjacent to one of the printed sides of the yardstick and 18 inches above the floor at the midpoint of the yardstick, while supporting the top of the yardstick with a right-hand finger. A push at the end of the yardstick would not bend the yardstick if the push moved the yardstick in the direction of the left-hand finger provided that the left-hand finger were held rigidly at the

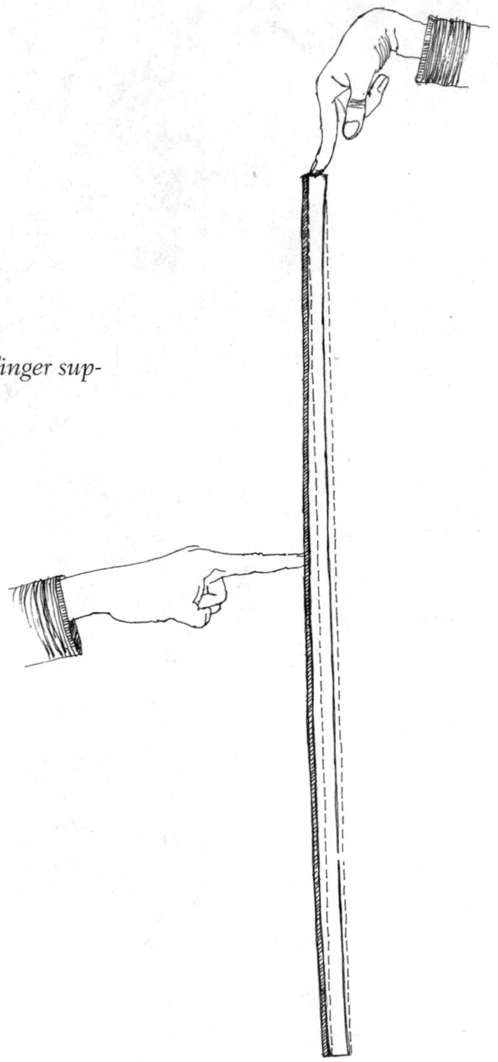

Figure 17-15 *Finger supporting yard stick*

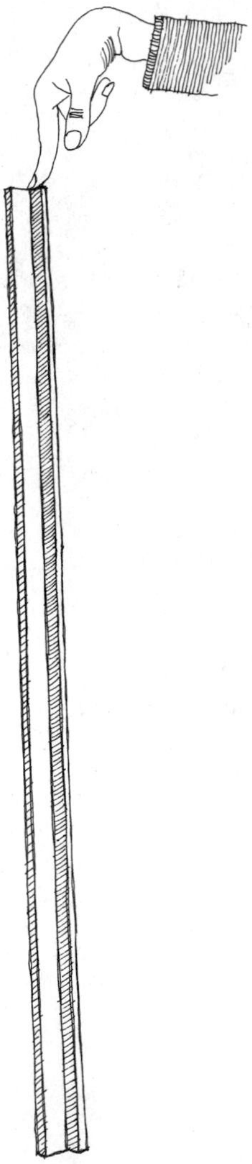

Figure 17-16 *Yard stick T column*

yardstick's midpoint (Figure 17-15). This is due to the fact that the left-hand finger is providing lateral support at the midpoint of the yardstick, which compensates for the lack of lateral support provided by the yardstick's thickness perpendicular to the bending direction. This type of lateral support is akin to the bracing of a wall with perpendicular or angular beams. The left-hand finger effectively divides the span of the yardstick into two shorter 18-inch spans which can withstand a greater load without bending than can the single three-foot span.

If you were then to take a second yardstick standing on end, and glue it to the first yardstick so that its printed sides were perpendicular to the printed sides of the first yardstick, you would find that it would be very difficult or even impossible to push down on the tops of the two yardsticks with a finger and cause them to bend or fail (Figure 17-16). Of course, if you loaded the tops of the two yardsticks with heavy enough weights, they would eventually fail, but they could withstand a much greater load acting together as a single unit than they could acting individually. The strongest cross-sectional dimensions of one yardstick would resist bending to your left or right, and the strongest cross-sectional dimensions of the other yardstick would resist bending to your front or back. This situation is analogous to providing lateral support for a wall by changing the direction of the wall, by providing pilasters or columns within the wall, or by intersecting the wall with other perpendicular planes such as floor-ceiling assemblies, roof-ceiling assemblies, or other walls (Figure 17-17a, b, c, d, and e).

Building codes require foundation walls to be provided with ample lateral support so that they will not collapse from loading, should the loading be weather-related loads, loads from retained earth, dead loads, live loads, or special loads from the structure above. Retaining walls are foundation walls and may have lateral support provided by the

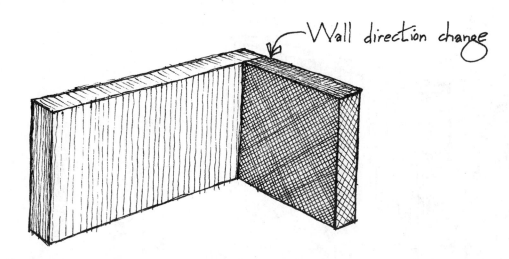

Figure 17-17a *Lateral support for walls—changing direction*

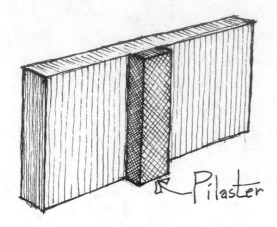

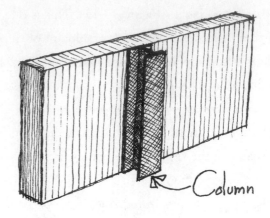

Figure 17-17b *Lateral support for walls—pilasters*

Figure 17-17c *Lateral support for walls—columns*

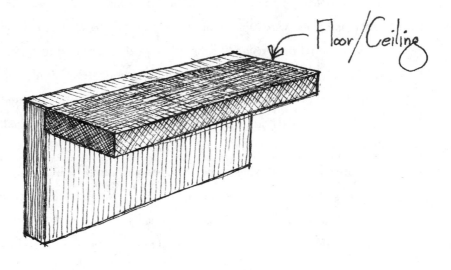

Figure 17-17d *Lateral support for walls—intersecting floor-ceiling*

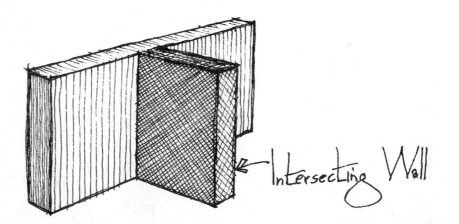

Figure 17-17e *Lateral support for walls—intersecting walls*

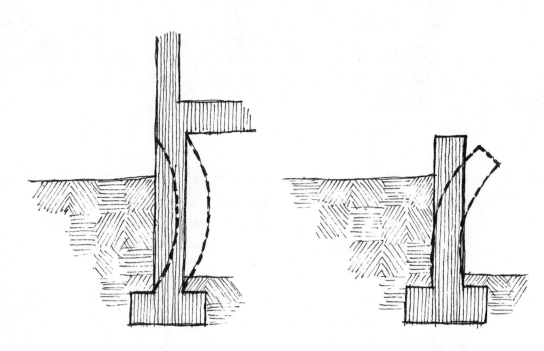

intersection of a floor-ceiling plane (Figure 17-18a), or may not have any lateral support provided as in the case of a terrace wall which retains earth on one side only (a cantilevered retaining wall) (Figure 17-18b). In order to withstand lateral pressures, unsupported cantilevered retaining walls require more thickness than do equal height retaining walls constructed of similar materials and which are supported by intersecting horizontal planes.

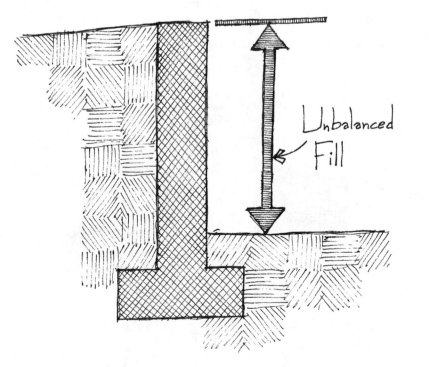

Figure 17-19
Unbalanced fill

Unbalanced Fill

The amounts of loads imposed on retaining walls by retained earth are a function of the height of unbalanced fill. Unbalanced fill simply means the height of retained earth on one side of a wall that is not balanced on the other side of the wall with more earth. Therefore, if a retaining wall were five feet high from bottom of footing to top of wall, and only three feet of the wall could be seen above grade on one side, while none of the wall could be seen on the other side because of the retained earth's being level with the top of the wall, one would say the wall had an unbalanced fill of three feet (Figure 17-19). Though the wall is five feet high, the bottom two feet of the wall have earth on both sides and are therefore experiencing no lateral pressures from retained earth. However, the top three feet of the wall are experiencing lateral forces from soil pressure and ground water pressure for a height of three feet with no counterbalancing effect on the other side. Therefore, this wall must be designed of materials with adequate strength, and thickness or bracing to resist such lateral pressures. Building codes compensate for the height of unbalanced fill when stipulating requirements for the thickness and bracing of foundation walls.

Openings

Foundation walls that enclose crawl spaces below buildings without basements are required by codes to have two types of openings. They must have openings which allow for the proper ventilation of crawl spaces (Figure 17-20). They must also have openings which permit human access to the crawl space for providing maintenance and for servicing equipment, as well as which permit the installation or removal of any equipment (i.e., a furnace, etc.) within the crawl space (Figure 17-21).

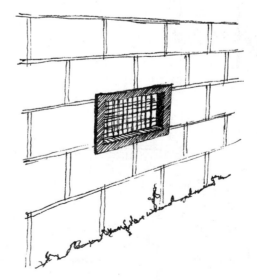

Figure 17-20 *Crawl space ventilation*

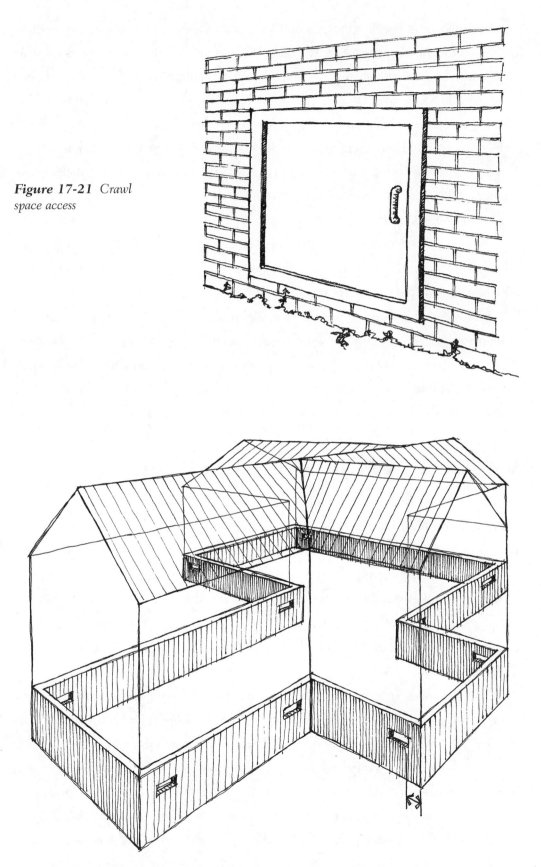

Figure 17-21 *Crawl space access*

Figure 17-22 *Crawl space ventilation locations*

Building codes specify the sizes and locations of ventilation openings so that the proper ventilation of crawl spaces will almost be certain. Ventilation openings must be arranged in a manner that promotes good cross-ventilation. For each crawl space, one must provide a certain minimum area of ventilation opening as a function of area of crawl space. The installation of an approved vapor barrier within a crawl space will reduce the required minimum area of ventilation opening for that crawl space. Vapor barriers reduce the amount of moisture in a crawl space, thus minimizing the negative effect that moisture can have on a poorly ventilated crawl space. The ventilation openings must be dispersed throughout the crawl space and must be located within a certain distance of each corner of the structure (Figure 17-22). Ventilation openings must contain corrosion resistant wire mesh that provides for sufficient passage of ventilating air while denying the passage of rodents.

Access openings must be provided to crawl spaces to allow for the maintenance of equipment and the structure. Building codes specify minimum dimensions for these access openings, and stipulate that the openings must be large enough to allow the passage of the largest piece of equipment located in the crawl space. Access openings must be covered with a door or some other panel or device that can be easily removed.

WATERPROOFING AND DAMPPROOFING

Whenever walls and floors of buildings are located below finished ground level, they must be protected from ground water or moisture. If hydrostatic pressures exist, the walls and floors must be waterproofed as specified in each of the building codes. Even without the existence of any hydrostatic pressures the walls and floors would need to be dampproofed as specified in each of the building codes. Any backfill applied to walls below grade must be placed in a manner that will not damage any waterproofing, dampproofing, or the foundation wall, so that the walls maintain their ability to retain water or resist moisture.

Building codes specify typical types of materials allowed for waterproofing and dampproofing, as well as the requirements for the overlapping and the sealing of the joints of such materials. In addition, specifications for coverage are given, codes stating where the topmost edge of the waterproofing or dampproofing must be located and where the bottommost edge of the waterproofing or dampproofing must be located. In the case of dampproofing, codes require drainage to be provided which will carry ground water away from the foundations. This drainage consists of gravel or crushed stone laid in a covered trench, drain tiles, or drain pipes (Figure 17-23). Drain tiles and

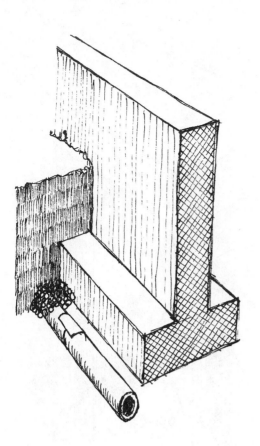

Figure 17-23 *Foundation drainage*

drain pipes are perforated at the top to allow the passage of water. All drain tiles and pipes, and all drain trenches must be covered with some approved membrane that will allow the passage of water, while filtering out any dirt or debris that can clog the drainage system. The drainage system must slope in a manner that will channel water away from the foundations as specified by codes.

PILES

Piles are used in construction where the soils below a structure cannot support it if a slab or spread footing foundation is used. Piles transmit the loads of structures through such soils and down to suitable points of bearing. There are two types of piles: friction piles (Figure 17-24), and point- or end-bearing piles (Figure 17-25). Friction-bearing piles are tapered towards their deepest end and rely on the friction between their sloped surface and the soils around them to create enough resistance to support the structure above. Point-bearing piles bear directly on some subsurface material such as rock, which provides a sound enough base to support the structure above. Obviously, friction-bearing piles rely on soils which can provide the resistance necessary to support the piles, whereas point-bearing piles do not necessarily rely on the qualities of the soils around them.

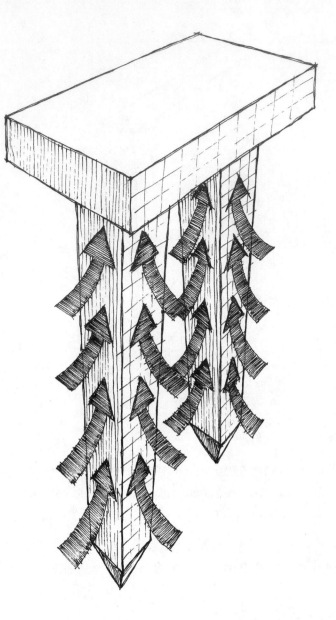

Figure 17-24 *Friction-bearing piles*

Before piles are designed and installed, building codes require thorough investigations and reports of the subsurface areas where the piles will be located. One must know how adequate the bearing conditions will be, and at what depths and locations one can find such adequate bearing conditions. Unless information is available on the subsurface conditions of any site where piles are to be located, one must perform the test and analysis oneself. Codes specify what types of information are needed before designing and installing piles. A typical investigation and report would include recommended pile types and installed capacities, driving criteria, installation and field inspection procedures, pile load test requirements, durability of pile materials, and designation of bearing stratum or strata. This list is not necessarily exhaustive. One can use special types of piles which are not referenced in the building codes if one can prove the adequacy of such piles, and if the local code official will approve the use of such piles.

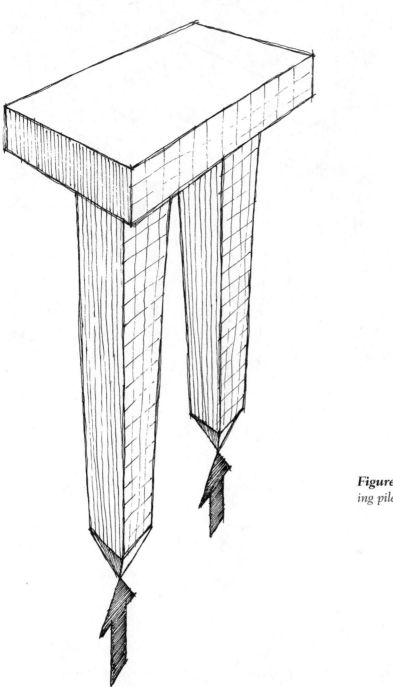

Figure 17-25 End-bearing piles

It is possible for a particular building site to have soils with properties that may adversely affect certain piles. The soils may contain too much water or chemical components which prove to be corrosive. Building codes require the design and installation of piles to address and compensate for soils problems when a site's soils can cause damage to the piles.

Just as with columns and walls, piles must have sufficient lateral support to keep from buckling when loaded (Figure 17-26). Piles located in soils which are not fluid are considered by codes to have sufficient lateral support from the soils around them.

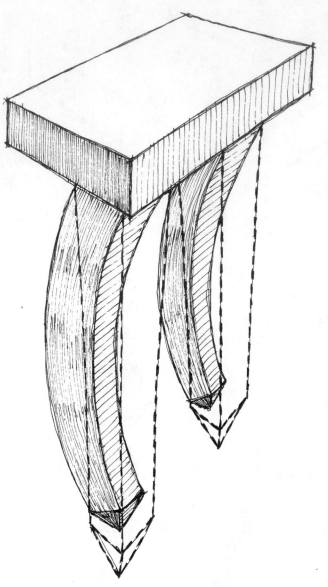

Figure 17-26 *Piles—lateral support*

However, if piles are located in water, air, or soils which do not provide sufficient lateral support, codes require the piles to be designed so that they act as columns and provide their own lateral support. In seismic areas, consideration must be given for the design of piles that will resist the bending imposed by an earthquake when the piles are located in soils that are conducive to such forces.

Furthermore, piles must have lateral stability—another property they have in common with columns and walls. If one were to arrange four popsickle sticks to form the shape of a square, and then connect them at their ends with rivets so that they could rotate freely around their connections, one could reconfigure the arrangement of popsickle sticks to form the shape of any number of parallelograms (Figure 17-27). This is the way that structural systems behave when subjected to loading, such as wood frame

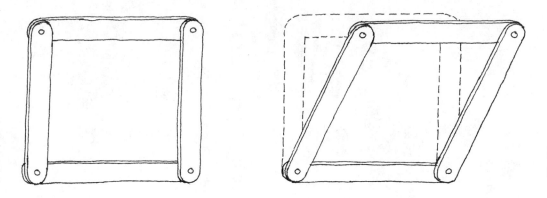

Figure 17-27 *Sticks— parallelogram*

walls or several piles in succession. Their members rotate around their connections, causing the structures to change shape and fail. One must provide lateral stability to keep the different structural members from rotating around their connections. One means of providing lateral stability would be through the use of triangulation. If one were to take three popsickle sticks and connect them at their ends with rivets to form a triangle, one could not reconfigure the shape of the triangle as the popsickle sticks would be arranged in a manner that would not permit them to move in any direction (Figure 17-28). This triangular arrangement provides for lateral stability, and is the basis for the provision of lateral stability for many different types of structural systems. Wood frame walls use triangulation to provide for lateral stability by bracing corners with straps, inlet bracing, or solid sheets of plywood or other approved wood products. The solid sheets act as triangular bracing as they provide structural support in both the horizontal direction and the vertical direction; in the case of these solid sheets, the triangles just happen to be filled solid. Another means of providing lateral stability would be to make a structural member's connections or anchoring at the foundation so rigid and strong that no rotation could occur when loads were imposed on the structural system. This latter method would relate more to pile construction.

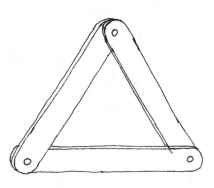

Figure 17-28 *Sticks— triangle*

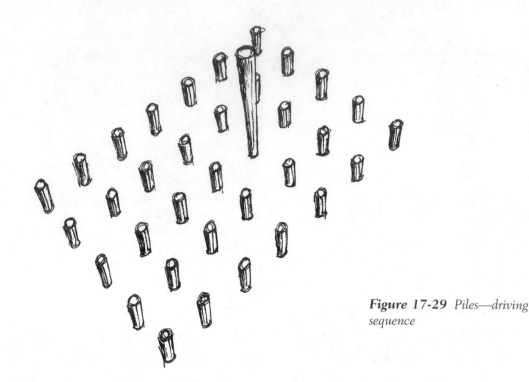

Figure 17-29 *Piles—driving sequence*

Building codes regulate many of the properties of piles. Codes regulate the minimum spacing of piles while the structural design will determine the maximum spacing of piles. The splicing of piles is regulated by codes in order to ensure that spliced piles do not lose their structural integrity due to splicing. Piles are regulated as to how much they must be embedded in pile caps. Pile caps are regulated as to how much they must extend beyond piles. Pile caps cannot be considered to provide any structural bearing on the earth below them, but rather all bearing must be considered to come from the piles themselves. In certain seismic zones, pile caps may be required to be connected to the piles with reinforcement and all pile caps may be required to be tied together.

Building codes require certain administrative procedures of the code official when pile foundations are used. A Pile Location Plan must be filed with the code official before the installation of piles. This plan must show the location and identification of each pile, the identification of which is consistent with the detailed records of each pile. The piles must be identified as meeting a specified grade by the manufacturer, and the identification must be maintained throughout installation, or the piles will be required to be tested to determine their grade at the job site. The code official must approve of a qualified inspector to be present on the site when piles are installed or tests are performed.

The actual installation of piles is also regulated by building codes. Piles must be of such dimensions and strength that permits their being driven without damage to their structural integrity. If existing piles are reused, information must be submitted to the building official which proves the piles to be sound and to meet all the requirements of the code. These piles must be redriven or tested to prove their bearing capacity. Any piles which heave when adjacent piles are driven must be redriven to their required penetration and load capacity. They must be tested as well to ascertain they meet such penetration and capacity. Accepted methods of analysis must be used to estimate the settlement of piles or pile groups. This settlement cannot hinder the structural integrity of the structure. Piles may be driven by vibratory drivers if proper load tests are carried out and upon approval by the code official.

When piles are installed, they may damage other piles or they may change the structural properties of the soils around them. The driving of friction piles further compacts the soils around them, and if they are driven in the wrong sequence, it may be difficult to place the last piles as the soils may be too compact to permit their installation (Figure 17-29). Building codes require piles to be installed in a manner and sequence that does not adversely affect the piles being installed or the piles that have already been installed.

Building codes require the use of approved formulas, load tests, or methods of analysis to determine the allowable axial and lateral loads on piles. There are many types of loads and many site characteristics which affect pile loading, and which mandate the investigation, in order to determine that piles are not overloaded. Codes require one to prove the piles' ability to provide proper bearing capacity, to withstand lateral loads, and to resist uplift.

Piles are made of many different materials and designs. Building codes have specific things to say about different types of piles. Figure 17-30 illustrates the types of concerns addressed by building codes for different types of piles.

Figure 17-30

BUILDING CODE CONCERNS FOR DIFFERENT PILES

Timber Piles
Referenced standards for piles
Referenced standards for preservative treatment
Allowable stresses
End-bearing pile resistance

Structural Steel Piles
Referenced standards
Allowable stresses
Minimum dimensions
Seismic design

Concrete-Filled Steel Pipe and Tube Piles
Referenced standards
Allowable stresses
Minimum dimensions
Reinforcement requirements
Placement of concrete

(continued)

Figure 17-30 (continued)

BUILDING CODE CONCERNS FOR DIFFERENT PILES

Cast-in-Place Concrete Piles

Strength and characteristics of
  concrete

Reinforcement requirements

Placement of concrete

Seismic design

Drilled or augered uncased piles
  concerns

    Allowable stresses

    Pile dimensions

    Installation

    Reinforcement requirements

Driven uncased piles concerns

    Allowable stresses

    Pile dimensions

    Installation

    Reinforcement requirements

Enlarged base piles concerns

    Aggregate requirements

    Allowable stresses

    Installation

    Pile-bearing capacity

    Concrete cover

Steel-cased piles concerns

    Material requirements

    Allowable stresses

    Installation

    Reinforcement requirements

    Seismic design

Precast Concrete Piles

Design and manufacture

Installation

Reinforced piles concerns

    Reinforcement design

    Material requirements

    Allowable stress

    Concrete cover

    Installation

Prestressed piles concerns

    Prestress design

    Concrete strength

    Allowable stress

    Installation

    Concrete cover

    Seismic design

Composite Piles

Design

Limitation of load

Splice requirements

Caisson Piles

Pile construction

Design and dimensions

Material requirements

Structural core requirements

Allowable stresses

Installation

Seismic design

Building Materials

Chapter 18 discusses common building code requirements that pertain to different types of building materials. Though each building code devotes entire chapters to each type of building material, the different materials are all included together in a single chapter of this book. The materials discussed in this chapter are concrete, light metal alloys, steel, masonry, wood, glass and glazing, gypsum board and plaster, and plastic. The discussion covering many of these materials is dominated by references to the same nationally recognized standards referenced by building codes for these materials. Often codes defer legislation of a particular concern to other standards.

Building codes regulate design for fire, structural, and health safety, but often overlooked are the requirements in codes for building materials and construction. The building materials chapters of codes look at buildings from their most basic components to determine how to properly piece together these components in a manner that ultimately provides building occupants with fire, structural, and health safety. If walls or roof structures are not properly constructed, their failure due to the forces of nature may negate their ability to achieve larger goals. For example, the water damage from a poorly constructed roof detail might eventually destroy a wall which provides structural support or fire separation. There are many methods for properly using the building materials discussed in this chapter other than those presented by codes. One may need to substantiate such methods to the code official with engineering calculations or tests by individuals who are qualified to present such proof. However, building codes do present the most common and acceptable methods of using building materials. These methods can be understood by most of the general public, however as codes become more complex, many sections of codes are becoming more difficult to understand by the layperson.

CONCRETE

Concrete is one of the most versatile materials used in construction. It is by far the most common foundation material, and is used for many superstructures as well. Molds called formwork shape the concrete when it is poured so that the concrete assumes the same form called for in its design (Figure 18-1). After placement, concrete cures to maximum strengths over a period of time, usually 28 days. Concrete is made of many materials including cements, aggregates, water, metal reinforcement, and admixtures. Cements, water, and aggregates make up the basic concrete mix. Metal reinforcement adds tensile strength to concrete, which is already very strong in compression. Admixtures serve several different purposes, such as creating concrete mixes which can cure in extreme heat or extreme cold. Many code officials are leery of admixtures, fearing that they weaken the concrete mix, so when using them, one should be prepared to show proper documentation illustrating that an admixture will achieve its desired results while not reducing the strength of the concrete mix below its required strength.

Design

Concrete must conform to the provisions of building codes and to the provisions of the American Concrete Institute's standard entitled Building Code Requirements for

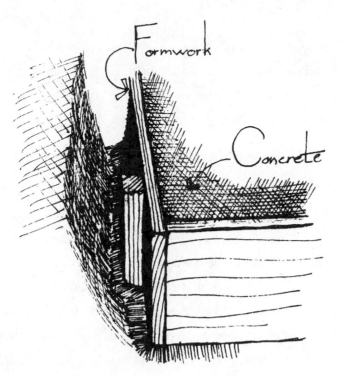

Figure 18-1 Formwork

Reinforced Concrete (ACI 318) as referenced by each code. Building codes require concrete to meet many special design requirements in areas where seismic activity is a concern. Codes require the materials in concrete to meet referenced standards for quality and consistency, and where applicable, to meet specific dimensional requirements. A code official may ask for some of the constituent materials of concrete to be tested for quality. Such testing would be performed by a recognized testing laboratory in accordance with standards referenced by the code.

Building codes require slabs on grade to be of certain minimum thicknesses. The thickness of a slab will usually be dictated by the slab's use (Figure 18-2). Vapor barri-

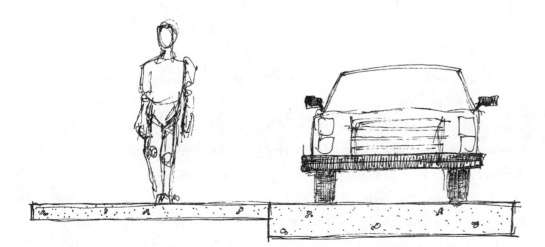

Figure 18-2 *Thickness of slab*

ers are required under slabs located below enclosed and heated spaces to prevent the migration of moisture from the soils through the slabs. Many codes specify the locations of control joints, which are placed to control the locations of cracking in the slab due to contraction during curing.

Durability and Quality

There are many durability requirements for concrete in building codes. Concrete may be exposed to extreme freeze/thaw conditions or to elements which promote corrosion such as salts in sea water. Codes require concrete mixes to be designed to compensate for these adverse conditions so that the concrete will retain its strength.

The quality of concrete is regulated by building codes to ensure that the concrete on a job performs as it is designed to perform. Concrete mixes vary for many reasons, not the least of which is for preparing a mix that will accommodate the method used to place the concrete. The process of pumping concrete requires a more fluid mix than does the process of placing concrete by wheelbarrow. Concrete mixes may be varied to obtain high strength early or to resist the effects of cold weather. Codes require concrete to achieve certain minimum strengths over specified periods of time, and require testing of that concrete to ensure that it obtains required strengths at certain specified intervals. Core samples of curing concrete are drilled at specified intervals and are tested with extreme loads until they fail. If one of the concrete test cylinders were to fail prematurely during testing, much more elaborate and expensive load tests would have to be performed. The testing of concrete is performed by independent testing agencies. All materials for concrete must be stored on job sites in a manner that will not allow the deterioration of the materials or the introduction of foreign matter into the materials.

Placement

Care must be taken in mixing and placing concrete in order to avoid contamination of the concrete or to avoid the separation of its constituents. Building codes require mixing equipment to be clean so that contamination will not occur. The mixing must be vigorous enough to mix all of materials in the concrete, but not so vigorous as to cause the materials to separate. Concrete must be placed as close to its final location as possible to decrease the chance that separation of materials occurs due to excessive dropping, rehandling, or flowing. The locations where concrete is placed are required to be free of water unless the code official approves otherwise. Curing of concrete must occur under controlled temperature conditions, or else a type of concrete must be used which can tolerate high or low temperature extremes.

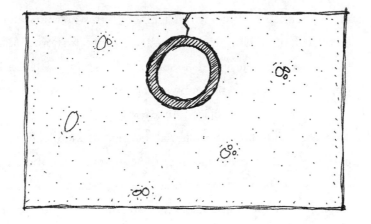

Figure 18-3 *Pipes in con-crete*

Concrete formwork is required by codes to be constructed tight and in a manner that will not permit the leakage of the concrete. This formwork must accommodate the design dimensions and other parameters for the foundations and structures. Formwork is required to be structurally capable of resisting the loads imposed on it by the place-

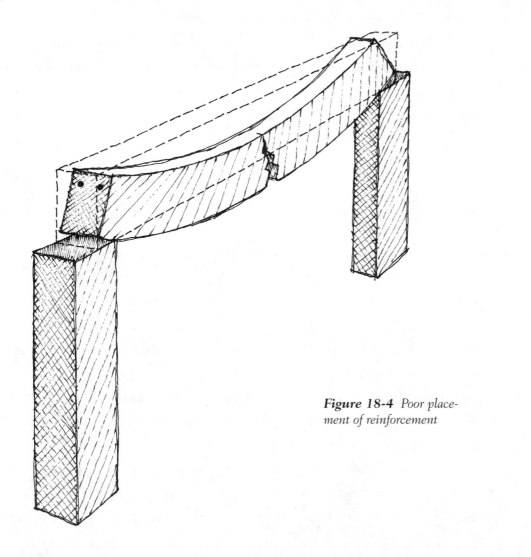

Figure 18-4 *Poor place-ment of reinforcement*

ment of concrete. Bracing or shoring of formwork must not be removed until the concrete structure, along with any other bracing or shoring still in place, can support the loads they were designed to support. The removal of formwork cannot damage the structure formed by the formwork or damage any structure already in place.

The introduction of conduits and pipes into concrete can present two problems. One, the conduit or pipe material may not be chemically compatible with the concrete, and may lead to deterioration of the concrete. Two, the area occupied by the conduits or pipes, or the location of the conduits or pipes may weaken the concrete structure (Figure 18-3). Building codes require the sizes and locations of conduits and pipes embedded in concrete to be approved by the engineer so that the structural integrity of the concrete will not be impeded. Codes also specify some limitations for the embedding of conduits and pipes in concrete. Furthermore, codes require that conduit and pipes placed in concrete consist of materials not harmful to the concrete.

Metal reinforcement gives concrete its tensile strength and must be applied properly in order to serve its purpose. Reinforcement must be clean and placed in the locations called for in the design of the structure. Poor placement of reinforcement may lead to its being located in an area of the structure where it will not perform adequately as a tension member (Figure 18-4). Reinforcing is required to have adequate concrete cover, as it must work in conjunction with the concrete; inadequate concrete cover may cause the concrete to separate from the reinforcement, and as a result the reinforcement and concrete may act as separate entities.

MASONRY

Masonry construction is often confused with masonry veneer construction. Masonry construction consists of masonry units forming walls and providing their own structural support. On the other hand, a masonry veneer wall is constructed of masonry units and relies on the wall to which it is attached for structural support. Masonry veneer may be attached to a wall of wood frame construction, steel stud construction, masonry construction, or some other method of construction (see Chapter 14).

Masonry construction consists of individual masonry units held together by mortar and placed on some type of support or foundation. The masonry units may be made of clay, concrete, glass, stone, or some other building material, and may be solid, hollow, or may have their cells filled with grout. Some masonry walls are composed of a single wythe while other masonry walls are composed of two or more wythes. A wythe is a single plane of masonry units, one unit in thickness (Figure 18-5). When a masonry wall

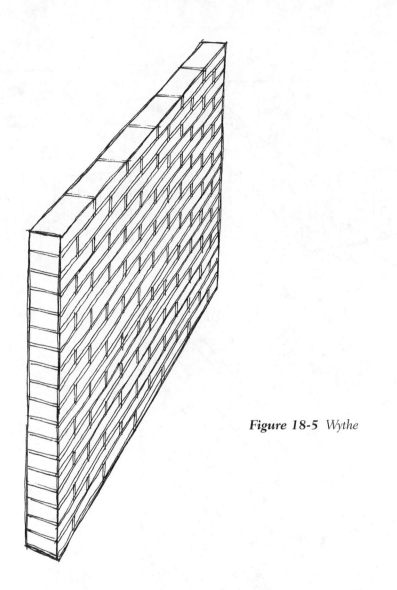

Figure 18-5 *Wythe*

has more than one wythe, the wythes may be directly adjacent to each other, or they may be spaced apart with either an air space or reinforcing and grout between them. Multiple wythes are tied together in some manner so that they act as a common structural entity. Depending on the type of masonry construction used, each wall has different strength characteristics.

Walls of solid masonry construction are composed of masonry units which are solid or nearly solid. Many solid masonry units may have holes in them, but the cumulative area of the holes are small enough to avoid the classification of hollow masonry units (Figure 18-6a and b). Hollow masonry units are used to build walls of hollow masonry construction. Solid and hollow masonry construction walls may consist of one or more wythes, with walls of multiple wythes acting together as a single wall through the use of metal ties or masonry headers which span both wythes (Figure 18-7).

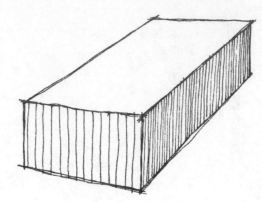

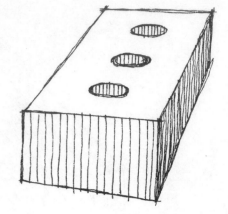

Figure 18-6a (left) *Solid masonry units*

Figure 18-6b (right) *Solid masonry units with holes*

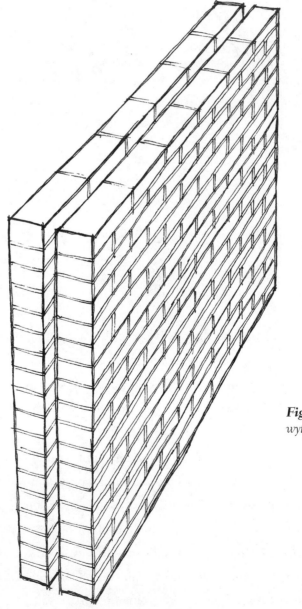

Figure 18-7 *Two or more wythes*

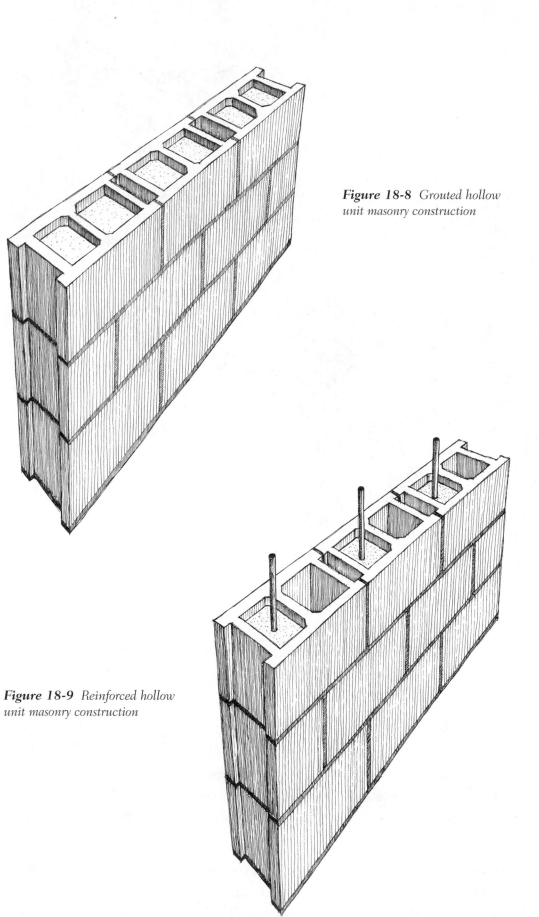

Figure 18-8 Grouted hollow unit masonry construction

Figure 18-9 Reinforced hollow unit masonry construction

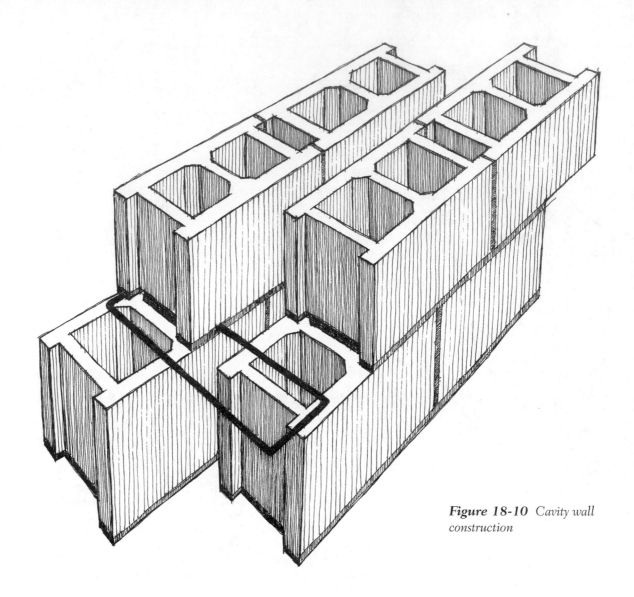

Figure 18-10 *Cavity wall construction*

By filling occasional vertical cells of a hollow masonry wall from bottom to top with grout, one creates grouted hollow unit masonry construction (Figure 18-8). This filling of certain vertical cells with grout strengthens the wall in a manner that will resist more lateral force. One can strengthen the wall even further by converting it to reinforced hollow unit masonry construction with the addition of reinforcing (Figure 18-9). The reinforcing would be added horizontally in the mortar joints at certain specified intervals and vertically within the cells which are completely filled with grout.

When a masonry wall is composed of two or more wythes, and there is an air space or cavity between each wythe, the wall is referred to as cavity wall construction (Figure 18-10). Filling that cavity solid with grout strengthens the wall and converts it to grouted multiple-wythe masonry construction. When reinforcing is added to that wall of multiple wythes with fully grouted cavities, the wall becomes even stronger and is referred to as reinforced grouted multiple-wythe masonry construction (Figure 18-11).

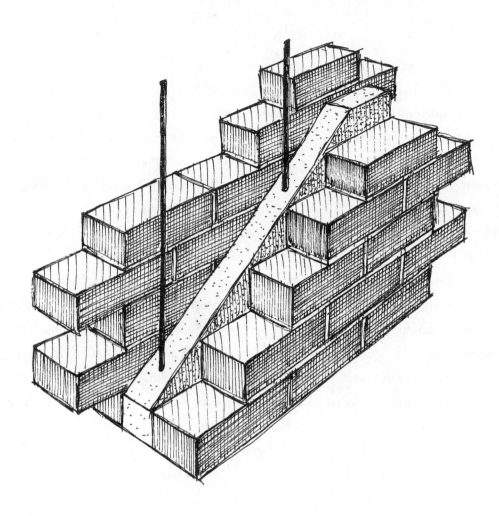

Figure 18-11 *Reinforced grouted multiple-wythe masonry construction*

Structural Considerations

Building codes require sufficient documentation to show that walls of masonry construction are properly designed and constructed. The documentation required varies based on the method chosen for designing masonry construction. If the height of the structure is not too great and the structure is located on a site with low seismic risk and low wind loads, one can use empirical design and rely on the specifications for masonry construction contained in the applicable building code, or in a standard referenced by that code. Empirical design implies relying greatly on one's observation and past experiences. If the height of the structure is too great or the site seismic risk and wind load conditions are too great, one will have to rely on acceptable engineering design for the masonry construction. Depending on the design method used, engineered or empirical, the documentation submitted to the code official will vary.

Building codes specify acceptable standards for the design of masonry construction, as well as for the different components of masonry construction. These referenced standards ensure that the materials used are adequate for their intended use. Any reuse of masonry units would require some proof that they are acceptable for reuse. There are standards for concrete masonry units, clay or shale masonry units, stone masonry units, ceramic tile, glass block, various types of mortars and grouts, surface-bonding mortar, metal reinforcement, adhesives, and so on. In order for any type of masonry construction to be successful, all of its constituents must be of proper quality and manufacture.

Masonry construction must begin with a firm base. This is true of any structural system, but with masonry construction, this truth is even more evident as inadequate support will cause the bond between individual masonry units to crack or even fail (Figure 18-12). Therefore with few exceptions, codes do not allow masonry to be supported by wood.

Building codes specify means for maintaining the lateral support of masonry walls (see discussion of lateral support in chapter seventeen under foundation walls). As discussed in Chapter 17, there are many ways to provide lateral support (e.g., shear walls, columns, pilasters, floor-ceiling assemblies, roof-ceiling assemblies, etc.). Thickening a masonry wall also increases its lateral support, as does adding grout and reinforcement to the wall. Building codes require proper anchorage between a masonry wall and any structural element used to support that wall laterally.

Masonry construction may also be used to provide lateral stability for a building (see discussion of lateral stability in Chapter 17 under piles). The rigidity of a masonry

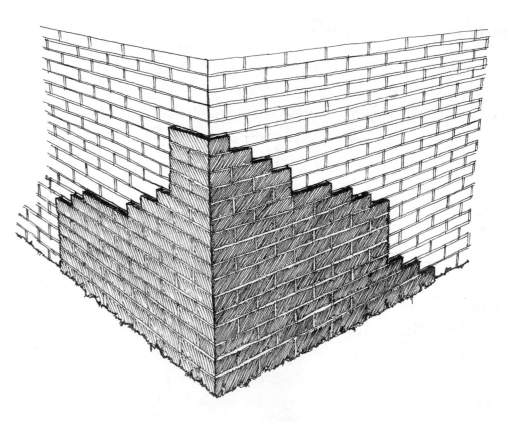

Figure 18-12 *Cracking masonry*

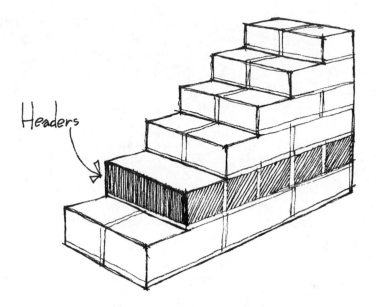

Headers

Figure 18-13
Overlapping header courses

wall lends itself well to resisting the rotation of connections responsible for a lack of good lateral stability in many other structural systems such as wood framing. When masonry walls are used for lateral stability, they must meet the dimensional requirements specified in codes for such use.

Another structural concern of code officials regarding masonry construction is the amount of compressive stress applied to masonry units when fully loaded. Too much load will cause the units to fail. Therefore, building codes require the compressive stresses resulting from all applicable loads to be analyzed and accounted for when designing for masonry construction. The allowable compressive stress for any masonry construction element is not only a function of its individual units, but also a function of the type of mortar between the units. Different types of masonry units and different types of mortars have different compressive strengths.

Bonding is the term used to describe the interconnecting of multiple wythes in a wall so that they act structurally as a single unit. Proper bonding may be achieved by metal ties or joint reinforcement (see Figure 18-10), or may be achieved by turning certain masonry units to form header courses which overlap different wythes (Figure 18-13). Depending on the type of bonding used, building codes specify how often these bonding elements must occur. The frequency of their occurrence is expressed in terms of area of wall or percentage of wall, as well as maximum vertical and horizontal dimensions between elements.

Bonding is also achieved by individual masonry units in a single wythe when they overlap each other in successive courses (running bond) (Figure 18-14a). Stack bond walls, where the units in one course are stacked directly over the units in the course below, are not as structurally sound as common bond walls because of the lack of bond-

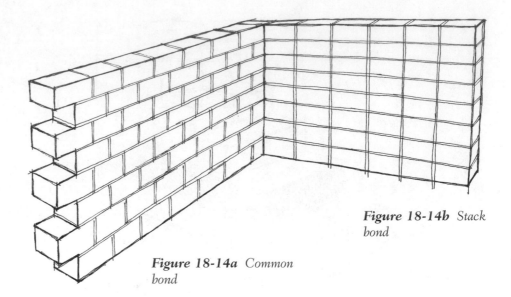

Figure 18-14b *Stack bond*

Figure 18-14a *Common bond*

ing between units horizontally and vertically (Figure 18-14b). Stack bond walls require extra reinforcing in order to provide some sort of horizontal bond.

Construction

Building codes regulate the proper methods of constructing with masonry. There are requirements in codes for the proper installation of mortar. These requirements specify where mortar must be placed and how thick its coverage must be. There are requirements for the provision of weep holes at the base of the exterior-most wythes of multiple wythe walls. This ensures that the water which gains access to the interior areas of the wall will be provided with a means to escape. It is important to remember that masonry and grout are porous and allow some water to enter a wall's interior. Wall ties are regulated as to the length to which they project into mortar joints and as to how much they are embedded in the mortar. Masonry must be properly braced during construction and any loads applied to masonry during construction must not exceed the loads that the masonry and the bracing are capable of carrying. Codes specify criteria for the proper corbeling of masonry should one want to thicken a masonry wall. Corbeling is the process of projecting successive courses of masonry at small increments until a desired thickness of wall is maintained (Figure 18-15). When individual corbels or a series of corbels project too far, they may fail.

The placement of grout is also a construction method regulated by building codes. If grout is dropped from too high a height, the individual constituents that make up the grout (e.g., portland cement, aggregates, etc.) may separate, resulting in an inadequate structural mix. Codes, therefore, require grout to be placed as masonry walls are constructed. The grout is placed in "lifts" of specified heights, and must be placed

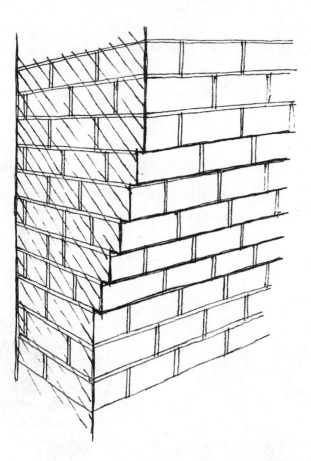

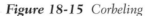

Figure 18-15 *Corbeling*

before a wall becomes so high that the vertical distance the grout must drop is excessive.

Weather affects masonry construction, as precipitation and temperature can alter the properties of mortar and grout. Too much water dilutes mortar and grout to the point where they are ineffective. Freezing weather prevents mortar and grout from curing properly, as heat is an important part of the chemical process which gives them their strength. Excessively hot weather can cause mortar and grout to give off too much moisture so that they do not properly cure or bond. Bonding between mortar and masonry units is affected by the moisture that is absorbed by the masonry unit from the mortar. Proper bonding actually pulls mortar closer and into masonry units.

Building codes require weather protection to be provided at the top of unfinished masonry work to deny the entrance of water, snow, or ice. Unprotected masonry work must not occur on wet days. When ambient temperatures drop below certain levels, codes require the temperature of the elements of masonry construction to be maintained at specified acceptable levels. What is required for cold-weather masonry construction varies based on the ambient temperatures. Wind breaks may be required if masonry construction is subjected to winds of certain speeds, as such winds can excessively cool the different elements of construction. When ambient temperatures are excessively hot, codes require quick placement of masonry units before too much water evaporates from the mortar. As an extra precaution against rapid evaporation, codes regulate how far mortar beds can extend before masonry units are laid on top of them.

Glass Block

Just as with masonry construction of concrete or clay brick units, masonry construction of glass block units is also regulated by building codes (Figure 18-16). Code requirements serve to minimize a wall's bending so that the mortar joints will not crack resulting in the wall's structural failure. Codes require glass blocks to be of a certain

Figure 18-16 *Glass block*

minimum thickness and to be located in panels of certain maximum dimensions. The panels must meet criteria for maximum allowable length, maximum allowable height, and maximum allowable area. The types of mortar used for glass block panels are regulated by codes, as are the dimensions of the mortar joints. Reinforcement is required in certain glass block mortar beds to add additional support to the panels. Additional anchorage is required for exterior glass block panels when they must resist wind loads and earthquake loads.

Masonry Chimneys and Fireplaces

When factory-built chimneys, fireplaces, and barbecues are installed, building codes require them to be installed in accordance with their listings. These products are carefully designed and thoroughly tested and are very safe to use as long as they are built by a reputable manufacturer. When one wants to build a masonry chimney, fireplace, or barbecue however, one must meet the requirements laid out in building codes for such appurtenances. The code requirements for these appurtenances regulate their fire safe construction and their ability to draw or exhaust the products of combustion.

Masonry chimneys must be supported by noncombustible construction (Figure 18-17). Building codes specify the total amount of corbeling allowed for masonry chimneys, in addition to the maximum dimensions of each individual corbel at each masonry course. Codes also specify the allowable types and thickness of masonry to be used for masonry chimneys. When chimneys pass through floors and ceilings, they must be separated from the building structure with noncombustible fireblocking. Building codes specify the distances that must be maintained between different combustible construction elements and chimneys. Chimneys may be required by some codes to have cleanouts so that the products of combustion can be removed.

Masonry chimneys are required to be lined with approved fireclay liners or listed liners of some other type. The joints of these liners must be smooth, as rough joints can catch creosote and the creosote may eventually ignite, resulting in a flue fire. Another concern of code officials regarding fireclay flue liners is the potential for a spark from the deteriorated joint of one flue liner to ignite the creosote leaking from another flue liner in the same chimney flue space. Clay flue liners in the same flue space are therefore required by codes to have their joints staggered and no more than two clay flue liners can be located in the same flue space. Codes specify where flue liners must begin in relation to the fireplace intake and where they must terminate in relation to the top of the chimney. Flue liners must have an air space between them

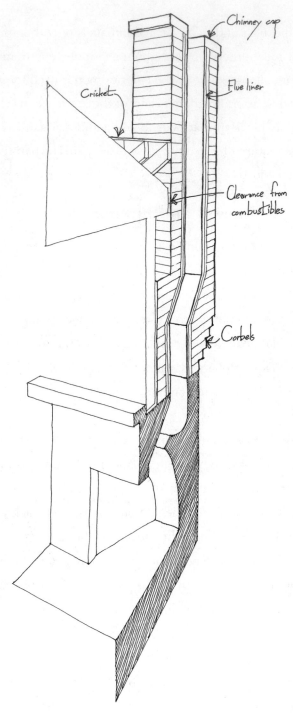

Figure 18-17 *Masonry chimney*

Chimney cap

Flue liner

Cricket

Clearance from combustibles

Corbels

and the masonry chimney as specified in each code to allow for differential expansion and contraction.

As with chimneys, codes regulate the allowable types and thickness' of masonry to be used for constructing masonry fireplaces (Figure 18-18). Typical dimensions of masonry fireplaces specified by codes include the thickness of backs, sides, and linings of fireplaces, the minimum depth of fireboxes, the minimum depth and width of

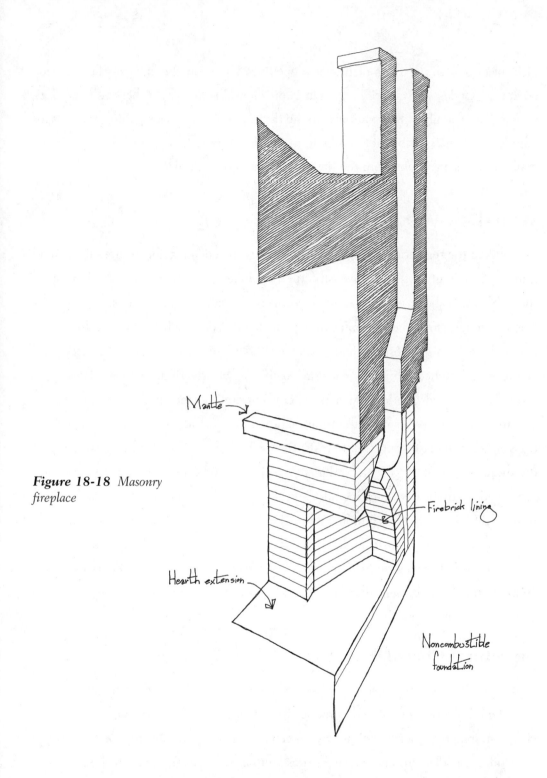

Figure 18-18 *Masonry fireplace*

Mantle

Firebrick lining

Hearth extension

Noncombustible foundation

throats, the minimum height of throats above fireplace openings, the cross-sectional areas of the openings above fireplaces, and the cross-sectional areas of flues.

Because of the heat and embers which pass through fire place openings, codes regulate the placement of combustible materials in the vicinity of fireplace openings. Noncombustible hearth extensions are required on the floors in front of fireplace openings. Codes specify the minimum distances that these hearth extensions must extend in front of and to the sides of fireplace openings based on the sizes of the fireplace openings. Codes also specify the minimum allowable distances between fireplace openings and combustible materials around the openings, such as paneling, mantles, or mantle supports. Combustible building materials around all sides of fire places must maintain the separations from the fire places that codes stipulate.

WOOD

The bulk of the regulations in building codes for wood construction address light wood framing which utilizes repetitive structural members and which does not support "heavy" loads. Whenever wood framing consists of heavy timber systems, or whenever wood framing carries heavy uniform or point loads, codes refer designers to several nationally recognized design standards, as well as require their designs to meet good engineering practice. Uniform loads are loads that are distributed over a large area, whereas point loads are loads which are concentrated in one small area. Light wood framing uses relatively small structural members (e.g., studs, joists, rafters, and light trusses), spaced closely together to resist the loads imposed on a structure. Because of the frequent repetition of structural members, light wood framing can resist many uniform loads without having to include large structural members such as columns and beams. By following the requirements in building codes for light wood framing, one does not need to have any training in structural engineering in order to build a structure. However, if one's structural situation includes heavy loads, or incorporates beams and columns in its design, then one should consult a designer who is competent to address such situations.

Structural Considerations

When designing wood structural systems, one can avail oneself of many excellent design guides for different wood products, such as heavy timber members, structural glued laminated timber, metal plate connected wood trusses, plywood beams, and so on. Building codes reference many of these publications, as it is part of their purview to establish criteria for proper design quality of these engineered systems. Even though one may not be trying to design a complicated structure, many of these systems may be used along with light wood framing, because of their outstanding structural capabilities and economy.

Codes also regulate the quality of materials like dimensional lumber, which are not part of engineered systems. Dimensional lumber is made up of the common wood members used for light wood framing: studs, joists, and rafters, particleboard, plywood, etc. Dimensional lumber is visually graded by inspectors who look at the grain of the lumber and who check for types and locations of imperfections, such as knots. The grade assigned to each piece of lumber ultimately denotes that piece of lumber as having specific structural capabilities. If two pieces of lumber with different grades are of the same size, the piece of lumber with the better grade will be capable of carrying more load.

Another aspect of dimensional lumber which affects its load carrying capacity is the moisture content of the lumber. Lumber which is kiln-dried (15 percent or less moisture content) can withstand more loading than lumber which is surfaced-dried (19 percent or less moisture content). When designing for dimensional lumber, one should become familiar with what type of lumber is readily available in local lumber yards. Building codes specify which grades of lumber are acceptable for use in any given structural application.

Lumber in contact with moisture must be protected against decay. Lumber in contact with the ground or in close proximity with the ground must be protected from termites. The level of hazard posed by decay and termite infestation varies based on the geographical location of the structure. Building codes require the use of pressure-treated lumber or lumber which is naturally resistant to decay or termites when applying the lumber to building locations that would warrant such protection. Pressure-treated lumber is used more often because of its affordability. A common mistake often made when using a species of wood which can be naturally resistant to decay and termites, is that of using sap wood instead of heartwood. Only the heart wood of most naturally resistant species is considered to actually resist decay and termites. Often, a deck is built of the sap wood of a naturally resistant species, only to rot away in five years because heartwood, which is more costly, was not used. Some species of wood are naturally resistant regardless of whether sap wood or heartwood are used.

The process of designing for dimensional lumber is a simple one. For example, if one were trying to size joists for a structure, one would first determine the grades of lumber most available in one's area and then attempt to use those grades as much as possible for economy's sake. Next, using approved span tables (Figure 18-19), one would select the sizes of lumber that would both meet the joists' span requirements, and that could be spaced at uniform dimensions which worked with other building products. It would not make sense to choose some large joists that could be spaced at 24 inches on center if the subflooring one were going to apply to those joists could only span 16 inches. The structural criteria which affect the number of pieces of dimen-

Figure 18-19 Span Tables for Joists and Rafters *and* Design Values for Joists and Rafters *provides a simplified system for determining allowable joist and rafter spans for common load conditions. Design values are included for the most common North American softwoods and hardwoods. Courtesy of the American Forest and Paper Association (AF&PA), Washington, DC*

sional lumber to use for uniform framing are the lengths of the members (spans), the center to center distance of the members (spacings), and the cross-sectional area of the members (sizes). It is important to remember that there are many other criteria to employ when selecting dimensional lumber other than those criteria considered important by building codes. A case in point would be the fact that often a uniformly framed floor might be structurally sound in the eyes of the code, but allow too much bounce in any building owner's opinion.

Once one has determined the sizes of dimensional lumber to be used for framing a structure, one must then determine the types, sizes, and numbers of fasteners to use for connecting the framing. Building codes list types, sizes, and numbers of fasteners for virtually any connection that one would encounter when framing with dimensional lumber. One can also consult applicable industry standards when determining the fasteners to use for engineered systems. There are other requirements for fasteners in codes which govern the composition of fasteners. For example, when applying fasteners to treated lumber, one needs to employ fasteners which are resistant to corrosion because of the chemicals used in treating lumber.

Floor Framing

Building codes detail acceptable means for light wood framing of structures, beginning with floors and continuing with walls and roofs. When foundation systems are comprised of concrete or masonry, wood structures resting on those foundations must

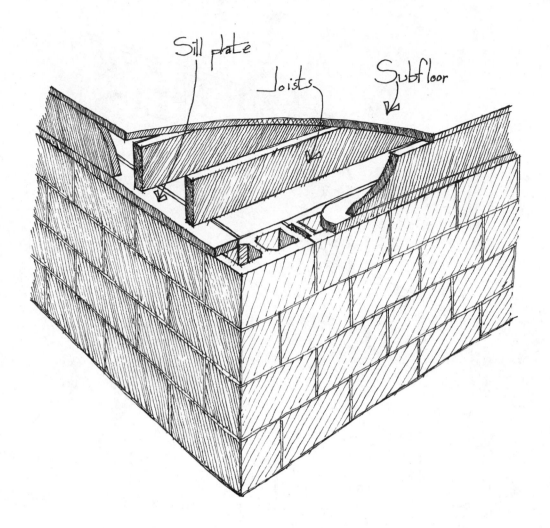

Sill plate

Joists

Subfloor

Figure 18-20 *Floor framing*

begin with a sill plate. Sill plates are regulated by codes as to their acceptable size, the spacing and anchorage of the bolts which fasten them to foundations, and the protection necessary for them to resist decay because of their contact with concrete or masonry. Sill plates on foundation walls in conjunction with beams and girders provide the support for floor framing. Codes regulate the acceptable means for splicing beams and girders, as well as the amount of bearing which must be provided for supporting beams and girders.

Floor joists support the subfloors and finished floors of structures and floor joists must be sized so that they can withstand the loads imposed on them (Figure 18-20). Building codes specify the different means by which floor joists can be supported, in addition to the minimum amount of bearing required based on what material their supports are made of. In order to keep joists in place and to keep them from twisting, blocking is required at their ends and in many cases blocking or bridging is required at certain intervals along their span. When one notches joists for support purposes or notches and cuts holes in joists for utilities access, one must do so in accordance with code

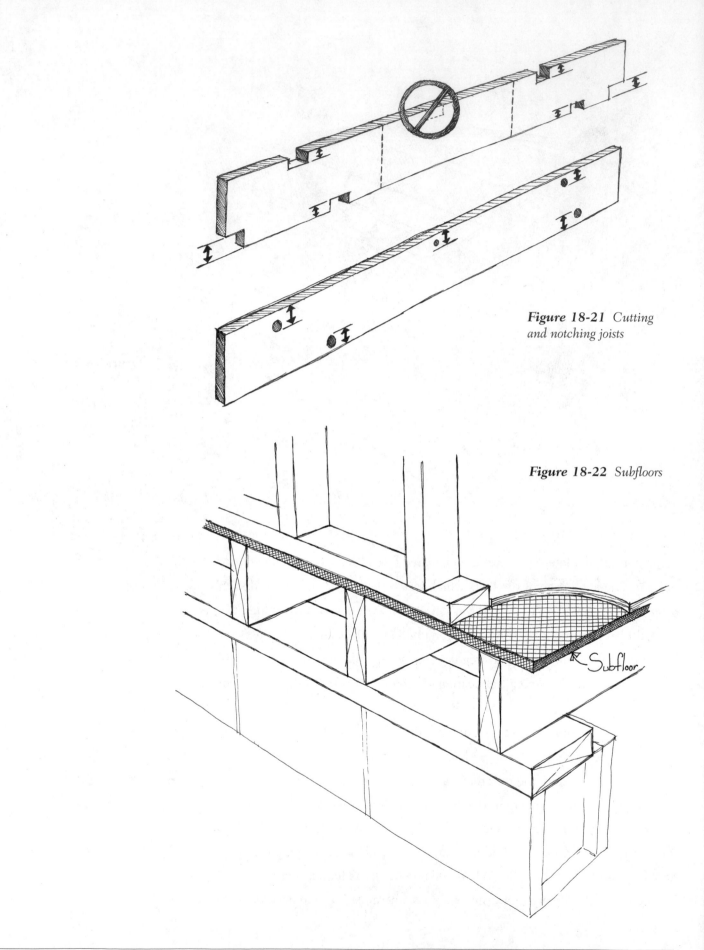

Figure 18-21 *Cutting and notching joists*

Figure 18-22 *Subfloors*

Subfloor

requirements for such cutting and notching (Figure 18-21). Furthermore, codes require bearing partitions supported by joists to be located directly above or near other supports based on whether the joists are running perpendicular to the bearing wall or are running parallel with the bearing wall. If a floor has an opening located in it (i.e., fireplace, stairway, or vent opening, etc.), code requirements specify how to treat the framing of that opening.

Subfloors are supported by joists and form the base for walls, finished floors, and stairs. Subfloors may consist of wood planks or of plywood or particleboard sheets (Figure 18-22). Codes regulate the types of products allowed for use as subfloors, and specify the support conditions for those subfloors, depending on the product used. Based on the thickness and types of subfloors and the spacing of the joists supporting them, some subfloor sheets may require clips to be installed at their junctions with other sheets in order to provide enough support to span joists without too much deflection.

Vertical Framing

Vertical framing refers to the framing of exterior walls and interior partitions, and code requirements pertaining to vertical framing regulate primarily the sizes and spacings of structural members, the connections of structural members, the bracing of walls and partitions, the sheathing of exterior walls, and the framing requirements for openings in walls and partitions. There are also requirements dealing with the cutting and notching of studs for plumbing and electrical service. Vertical framing sits on the subfloor, and ultimately supports the roofs, ceilings, and upper floors of a structure.

Building codes specify the grade and sizes of studs to be used for framing walls and partitions. The more cross-sectional area a stud has, the more load it can carry. The closer the spacing of studs in a wall, the more load the wall can carry. Often, it is prudent to space studs more closely together than codes will allow in order to better accommodate the finish materials attached to the studs. Studs are attached to a bottom plate at their base and terminate at their highest ends with two top plates (Figure 18-23). If joists or trusses bear on the doubled top plates, they must bear at or near studs or building codes will require extra strengthening of the top plates. Doubled top plates serve as bearing elements for joists, rafters, and trusses. They also provide a means to better connect intersecting walls to one another. Codes require top plates to provide for overlapping at wall corners and intersections (Figure 18-24a and b). Excessive notching, cutting, or boring of holes in studs and top plates can hinder their structural integrity, but because plumbing and electrical service must penetrate studs and top plates, codes include requirements regulating the proper means for penetrat-

Figure 18-23 *Wall framing*

ing wall framing elements. Some penetrations may warrant the use of metal straps to reinforce studs and top plates.

It is important to brace exterior stud walls to provide for lateral stability (see discussion of lateral stability under "piles" in Chapter 17). Lateral stability is provided by bracing the corners of a wood frame structure with structural sheathing, such as plywood, or by some other means acceptable to the code official (Figure 18-25). The rigidity provided by corner bracing keeps the structural members from rotating around their connections, thus preventing the structure from collapsing. Lateral stability must be accounted for whether the structural system is a post-and-beam or a uniform framing system.

Openings in walls and partitions for doors, windows, and vents must be framed properly so that any loads applied to the top of a wall with openings do not cause the lumber at the top of the opening to sag. This sagging usually results in doors and windows that will not open or shut correctly. Too much sagging could even lead to struc-

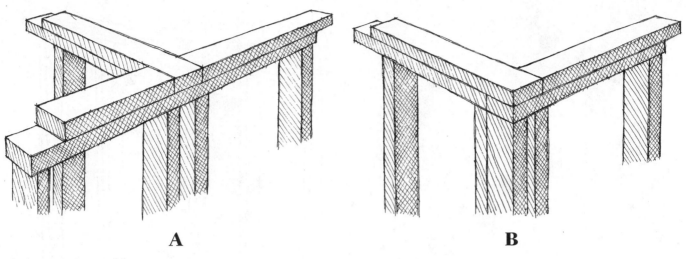

Figure 18-24a and b
Top plates overlapping

Figure 18-25 Corner bracing

Figure 18-26 *Headers*

tural failure. To prevent the tops of openings from deflecting too much, headers are placed at the tops of openings in walls and partitions (Figure 18-26). In wood frame construction, headers are usually made of doubled-up dimensional lumber, each member two inches in nominal thickness, and of a depth necessary to resist excessive deflection. Building codes prescribe the sizes that headers must be according to loads applied at the tops of the walls in question and based on the widths of the openings. Codes prescribe how to support those headers as well.

Roof and Ceiling Framing

Ceiling joists, roof rafters, and trusses rest on the top plates of walls and support ceilings and roofs, respectively. As with floor joists, building codes require ceiling joists and roof rafters to be sized according to their spans, spacings, and the loads they carry. Trusses are engineered and must be accompanied by the seal of a professional licensed to design trusses.

The forces resulting from loading roof rafters are different than the forces resulting from loading floor or ceiling joists. Joists push downward on their supports, whereas

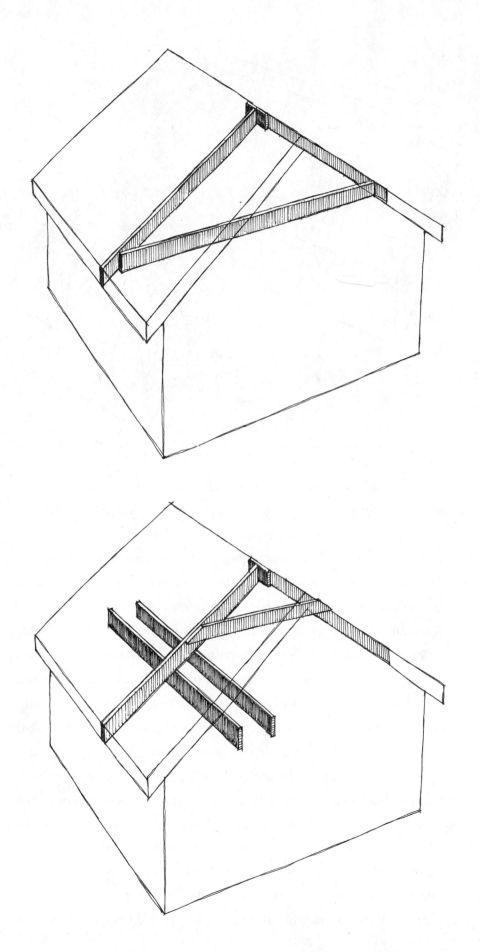

Figure 18-27 *Rafters and joists in parallel*

Figure 18-28 *Rafters and joists perpendicular*

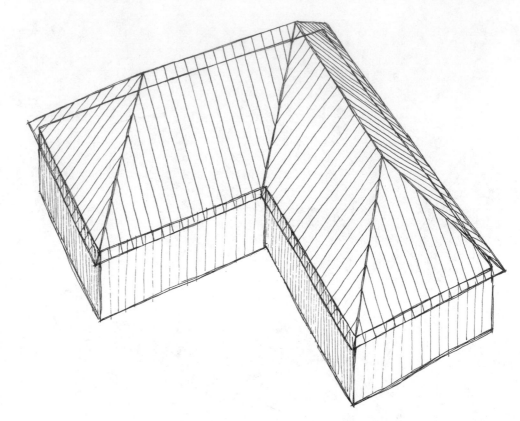

Figure 18-29 *Valleys and hips*

rafters push downward and outward. Therefore, building codes require rafters to be connected to ceiling joists when they run parallel to one another so that they act as a unit to prevent the exterior bearing walls from being pushed outward (Figure 18-27). If the ceiling joists run perpendicular to the rafters, one must use some other means as specified in codes for keeping the rafters from spreading the bearing walls (Figure 18-28). It is important for rafters to have solid bearing at roof ridges, hips, and valleys. Codes require rafters to terminate directly across from other rafters at these locations (Figure 18-29). This way, the push of one rafter will be countered by the push of another rafter. Trusses act more like floor joists and transmit loads directly downward.

Roof sheathing is supported by rafters and forms the base for roof coverings. Like subfloors, roof sheathing may consist of wood planks, or of plywood or particleboard sheets (Figure 18-30). Roof sheathing is also similar to subfloors in that codes regulate the types of products allowed for use as sheathing, and specify the support conditions for sheathing, depending on the product used. Based on the thickness and types of sheathing and the spacing of the support rafters, some sheet sheathing may have to have clips installed at the junction of one sheet with another sheet in order to provide enough support to span the supporting rafters without deflecting too much.

Often a design relies on structural diaphragms to provide resistance to shear. Diaphragms are panels made of sheet products (plywood or particleboard) attached to

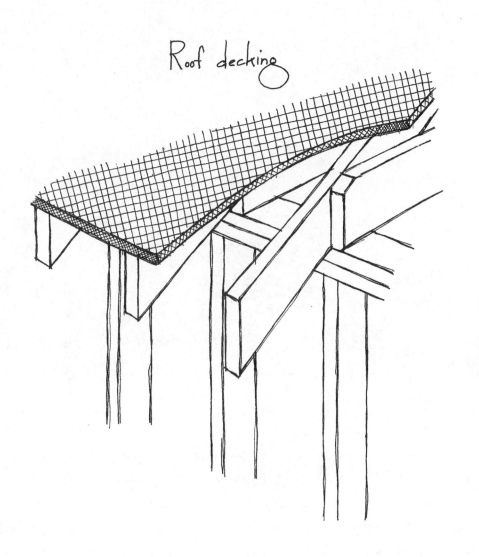

Roof decking

Figure 18-30 *Roof deck-ing (sheathing)*

each side of wood frames, and fastened in accordance with nailing schedules located in codes. These structural panels use all of the components, skin, frame, and fasteners to resist shear quite effectively over the entire panel. Diaphragms can be used in horizontal and vertical applications. One can also set up a conventional framing element (e.g., a floor-ceiling system or wall system) to act as a diaphragm if one chooses to by meeting all the requirements in codes for such a diaphragm.

Fire Protection

There are many ways to prevent the spread of fire when building with wood frame construction. One can slow the spread of fire from vertical interstitial spaces to horizontal interstitial spaces or vice-versa by using fireblocking. Vertical interstitial spaces are the spaces within walls and between the wall surfaces. Horizontal interstitial spaces are the spaces between ceilings and the floors above or the roofs above. One can slow the spread of fire by controlling drafts in attic spaces, floor-ceiling or roof-ceiling

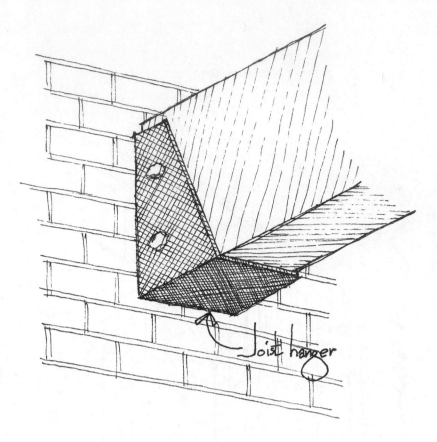

Figure 18-31 *Beam hanger*

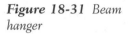

spaces, and cove spaces through the use of draftstopping. Fireblocking and draftstopping are discussed in Chapter 7 of this book. One can also slow the spread of fire through the use of fire-rated assemblies. Care must be taken to not introduce any building products into fire-rated assemblies that were not part of the fire resistance test, as the introduction of these products may negate the assemblies' ratings. When wood structural members enter masonry walls, codes provide one with ways to detail the connection, such as hangers or fire cuts so that the structure on the fire side of the wall will not pull the wall down (Figure 18-31).

METALS

The metals used in construction for structural purposes are aluminum and steel. These metals are noncombustible and are relatively light in comparison with concrete. In fire-resistant assemblies, metals must be protected with some other material, such as gypsum board, as the heat from fire causes aluminum and steel to deform. Often the cost of the gypsum board where several layers are required for fire resistance, creates a situation where concrete becomes more economically competitive than steel construction, as concrete withstands fire well.

Most of the requirements in building codes for aluminum and steel construction are references to nationally recognized standards. There are also required engineering factors in codes for designing structural steel systems. The referenced standards cited include standards for cold-formed steel construction, open web joist construction, structural steel cables, welding, and high-strength bolts. Like all construction methods, those employing aluminum and steel must meet all other requirements of building codes, including the applicable structural provisions cited in structural chapters of codes.

GLASS AND GLAZING

Glass and glazing, though desirable for the views they afford, are potential hazards because of the injuries that can incur from contact with broken glass. Impact injuries related to glass occur when one accidentally kicks reaches through, or walks through glass. Injuries from falling glass occur when sloped glazing or glazing above building occupants breaks and falls. Wind loads can blow glass out of its frame, such as in a glass door, and result in injury or even death. Glazing must be supported properly and must be designed so that it does not break from wind or snow loading. Building codes regulate all of these type situations by requiring glazing to meet different requirements which are applicable to each situation. Certain types of glass are required by codes to be permanently identified as to their type, so that code officials can verify that the proper type of glass has been used for a given application.

Impact loads are loads imposed on glazing by building occupants. Hazardous locations are locations where any glazing would be highly susceptible to impact loading. Glazing in hazardous locations must be of a type prescribed by codes for those locations. Codes require special types of glazing for hazardous locations, such as tempered glass. Tempered glass is manufactured so that when it breaks, it breaks into small, relatively harmless pieces. Glazing considered to be in hazardous locations includes certain glazing in doors, adjacent to doors, in enclosures for areas such as showers and tubs, in walls adjacent to walking surfaces, all glazing in railings, and certain glazing in fences enclosing swimming pools (Figure 18-32a–f).

Glazing in vertical applications and sloped glazing may be subject to wind loads, snow loads, or dead loads. Building codes require such glazing to be designed to resist these loads. One must use the structural loading provisions from codes to determine what loads apply to vertical and sloped glazing (see Chapter 16).

Glazing must be properly supported so that breakage to the glazing does not occur. Supports for glazing must hold the glazing firmly in place, and must also limit the

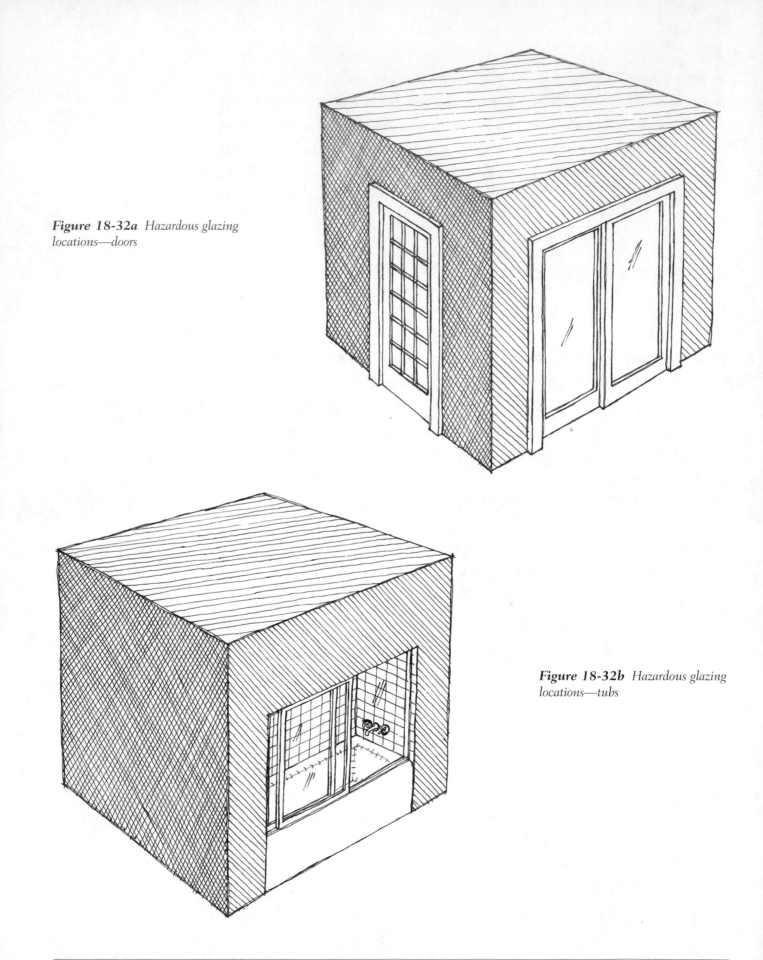

Figure 18-32a Hazardous glazing
locations—doors

Figure 18-32b Hazardous glazing
locations—tubs

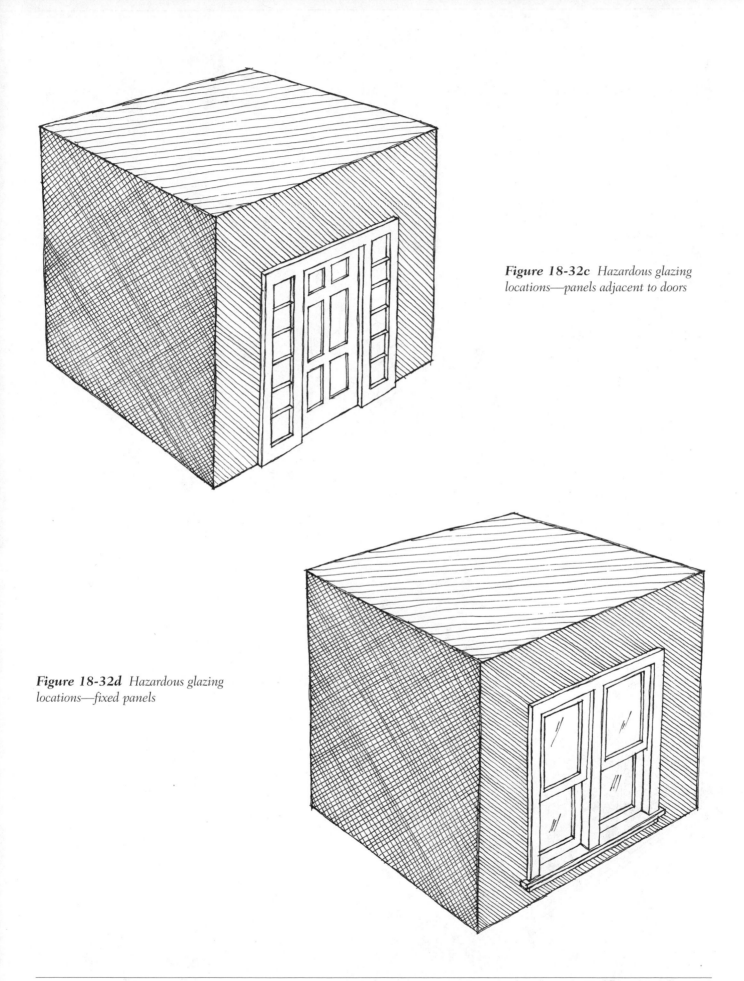

Figure 18-32c *Hazardous glazing locations—panels adjacent to doors*

Figure 18-32d *Hazardous glazing locations—fixed panels*

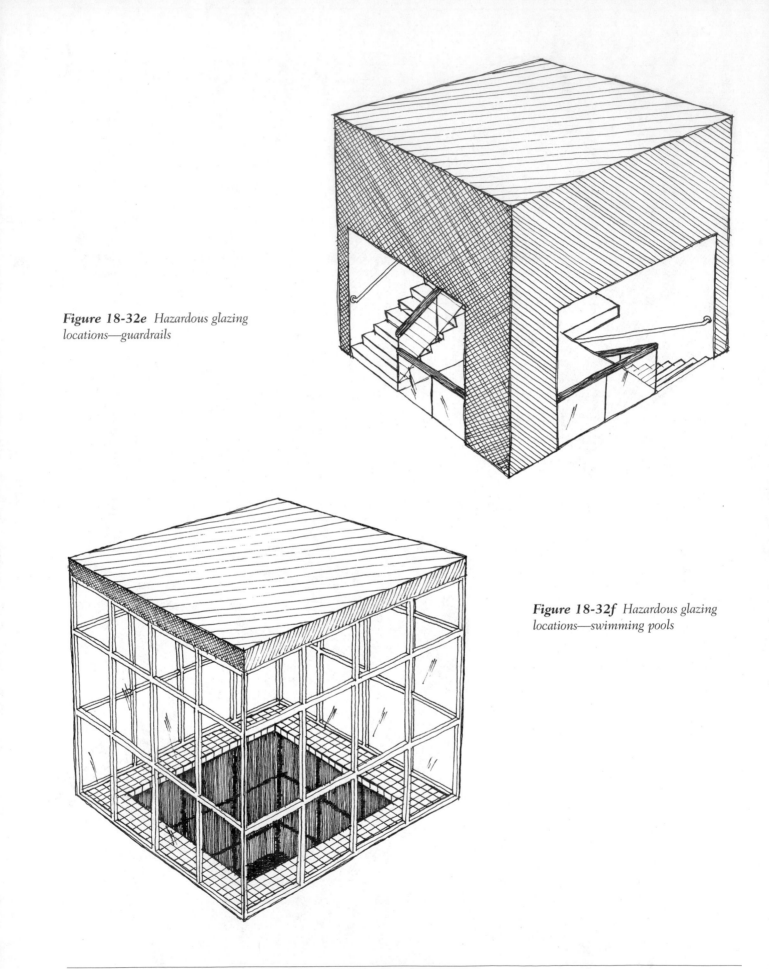

Figure 18-32e Hazardous glazing
locations—guardrails

Figure 18-32f Hazardous glazing
locations—swimming pools

deflection of the glazing. Codes address glazing supports, and describe in depth what is required in situations where glazing is supported against outward loads by silicone sealant/adhesive bonds to structural members. This is to ensure that these bonds offer equivalent support to that offered by mechanical supports.

GYPSUM BOARD AND PLASTER

Gypsum board is probably the most common interior construction finish and is a very versatile material which can afford a great deal of fire resistance, depending on the thickness and type of gypsum board. Gypsum board is usually attached to framing members or furring strips (Figure 18-33). When exposed to heat, gypsum board gives off moisture that was retained at its manufacturing. This release of moisture helps gypsum board provide fire resistance. Gypsum board can also be used to construct vertical structural diaphragms (see the discussion on wood in this chapter). In any given application, the thickness of gypsum board used is based on the actual application. A curved wall may necessitate the use of several thin layers of gypsum board, while fire resistance requirements may call for the use of a particular type and thickness of gypsum board.

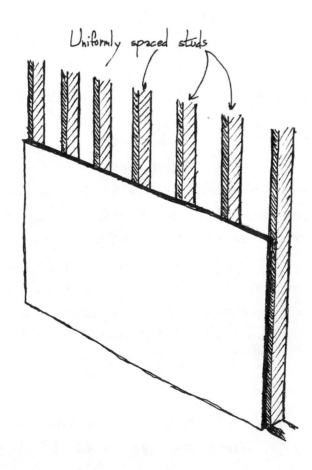

Figure **18-33** *Support of gypsum board*

Figure 18-34 *Application of plaster—wood lath*

Metal and wood studs, joists, rafters, trusses, and furring strips provide the support for gypsum board. Building codes specify the allowable heights and spacings of supports for gypsum board, as well as the types and spacings of fasteners used to attach gypsum board to supports. Codes also refer to many standards which govern the composition and the qualities of the materials used when installing gypsum board. Such materials include the different types of gypsum boards, joint reinforcing tapes and adhesives, and so on.

There are two types of plaster—portland cement plaster and gypsum plaster. Gypsum plaster is used in interior applications. Portland cement plaster may be used in both interior and exterior applications. Plaster is applied to a rough surface (e.g., lath, masonry, parging, or scored concrete) which is either structural in nature or supported by the building structure (Figure 18-34). As with gypsum board, building codes require the materials associated with the installation of plaster to meet all applicable referenced standards for composition and quality. Codes and standards govern the many aspects of plaster application including the types of lath used to support plaster, the types of fasteners used to attach lath to its supports, and the spacings of those fasteners.

PLASTIC

One of the principal concerns about plastics in construction is the potential deadly smoke emitted from plastics in the event of a fire. Smoke inhalation is responsible for more fire deaths than any other factor, and many plastics are capable of emitting dense, extremely toxic smoke. There are two primary uses of plastic which are addressed by building codes—foam plastic insulation and light-transmitting plastics. One should note that plastic is now being used for decking applications. Foam plastics are regulated by codes for fire-safe design and installation. Light-transmitting plastics are regulated for fire safety and structural safety.

Foam Plastic Insulation

Because of the concern with the smoke generated from plastics and their contribution to fire growth, foam plastic insulation in buildings is required to meet the requirements of ASTM E 84, Test for Surface Burning Characteristics of Building Materials for Class B finishes (see discussion on wall finishes in Chapter 8 of this book). Foam plastic insulation in buildings cannot have a flamespread rating in excess of 75, nor a smoke developed rating in excess of 450 when tested in accordance with ASTM E 84. Foam plastic insulation must be labeled to show its flamespread rating and smoke-developed rating.

Other measures are taken by building codes to protect building occupants from the fire and smoke hazards associated with foam plastic insulation. Thermal barriers are required in many construction assemblies to separate the insulation from interior spaces of buildings. The thermal barrier consists of ½-inch gypsum board or some equivalent material. In exterior walls, one may use foam plastic insulation in nonrated walls and in rated walls when they are a certain distance from property lines. As walls become closer to property lines and require ratings, codes allow foam plastic insulation only in walls where the insulation is part of the listed fire rated assembly. Code officials can call for tests as specified in building codes to prove that foam plastic insulation in a wall assembly meets the provisions of the codes.

Light-Transmitting Plastics

Light-transmitting plastics must meet the interior finish requirements discussed in chapter eight of this book. The principal applicable requirement is adherence to the requirements of ASTM E 84, Test for Surface Burning Characteristics of Building Materials. There are also building code requirements for the sizes of light-transmitting plastic panels allowed in walls, as well as requirements for the percentage of unprotected openings in a wall that can consist of light-transmitting plastics. Light-transmitting plastic panels used in exterior walls and roofs must meet many code requirements dealing with their allowable area, locations, detailing, minimum slope, and separation.

When used as light-diffusing systems in electrical fixtures, light-transmitting plastics must meet interior finish requirements. Building codes allow the use of light-transmitting plastics in interior signs if the plastics are of a certain specified maximum size, and if their edges are encased in metal.

Elevators and Conveying Systems

C hapter 19 discusses the requirements of building codes concerning elevators and escalators. These requirements are mostly fire protection requirements which affect life safety. Because their design affects life safety, the NFPA 101, Life Safety Code also addresses elevators and escalators. Much of the discussion in this chapter relates to the discussion in Chapter 7 about the design and construction of vertical shafts.

Elevators, escalators, and other conveying systems are similar in that they traverse multiple floor levels, potentially creating an opportunity for smoke, fire, and unburned gases to move from one floor to another, thus creating a hazard to the building occupants. Therefore, building codes have many requirements regulating the design of such conveying systems. Vertical openings between floors are either restricted or controlled by the use of vertical shafts. Elevators and escalators are regulated by codes as to how they relate to the means of egress schemes within buildings. Though the bulk of building code requirements for elevators pertain to life safety and fire protection, one may find other requirements for elevators within building codes. Some Codes may require certain buildings to have at least one elevator car in a building of a size that would accommodate an ambulance stretcher. Buildings with standby power may be required to meet additional requirements for elevator activation when standby power is initiated. Some codes detail the administrative procedures for the permitting, inspection, and testing of elevators.

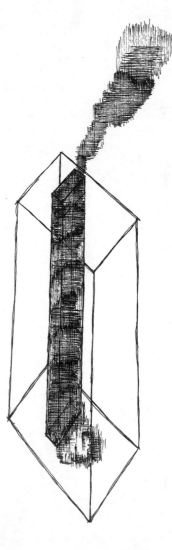

Figure 19-1 *Hoistways can act like chimneys*

ELEVATORS

Elevator Enclosures and their Construction

In order to keep smoke, fire, and unburned gases from entering elevator hoistways (vertical shafts) and consequently from spreading throughout buildings, elevator hoistways are required by building codes to be protected. This protection is provided by constructing the hoistways of fire-rated construction while protecting the openings in accordance with nationally recognized standards. These hoistways must be designed and constructed in accordance with the provisions of each code for vertical shafts, and are also required by codes to meet the enclosure provisions of the American National Standards Institute and the American Society of Mechanical Engineers (ANSI/ASME) A17.1, Standard Safety Code for Elevators, Dumbwaiters, Escalators and Moving Walks. If not protected, hoistways tend to act as chimneys, pulling smoke, fire, and unburned gases throughout buildings (see shaft discussion in Chapter 7) (Figure 19-1). By preventing these products of combustion from enter-

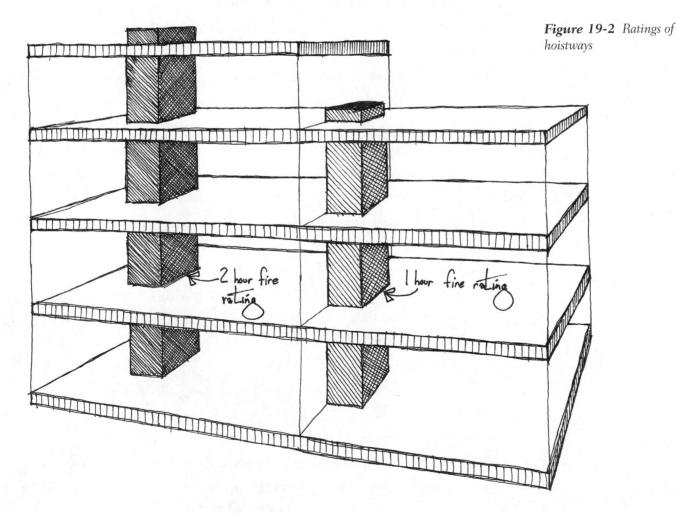

Figure 19-2 *Ratings of hoistways*

ing into elevator hoistways, the chances of their spreading to non-fire areas are greatly reduced.

Elevator hoistways must be constructed of fire-rated walls, and may be required to have fire-rated floor-ceiling assemblies, and roof-ceiling assemblies depending on the hoistway design. The amount of rating that elevator hoistway enclosures receive is based on the height of the elevator hoistway, as well as the occupancy classification of the structure (Figure 19-2). The walls and partitions that define elevator hoistways must be designed in accordance with the rules for vertical shafts. Consequently, these walls and partitions must continue from floor to floor and from floor to roof, and cannot terminate against the ceiling portion of an equivalently fire rated floor-ceiling or roof-ceiling assembly. The top of an elevator hoistway must terminate above a roof. Should an elevator hoistway terminate below a buildings' roof-ceiling assembly, then the top of the hoistway must carry the same fire resistance rating as do the hoistway walls. The bottoms of hoistways must terminate in pits at the ground level that have non-combustible floors. If the bottom of a hoistway terminates at a pit located above ground level, then the bottom floor-ceiling assembly of the hoistway must carry the same fire resistance rating as do the hoistway walls. Doors into elevator hoistways must be rated in accordance with shaft opening protection requirements.

Though codes attempt to prevent their passage into elevator hoistways, there is still a possibility that elevator hoistways will become polluted from smoke, fire, and unburned gases. Because of this, codes require more than one elevator hoistway within many buildings in the event that one of the hoistways becomes polluted. Building occupants are not usually allowed to use elevators in the event of a fire emergency (indeed many elevators will automatically return to the main floor level in the event of a fire emergency), however egress may be provided through elevators under the supervision of fire officials after they have arrived at the scene. Pressurized elevators may serve as egress for individuals with disabilities or for others. Codes allow elevators in buildings with three elevator cars or fewer to be located in a single hoistway (Figure 19-3). Codes require any building with at least four elevator cars to have at least two separate elevator hoistways (Figure 19-4). Codes also allow no more than four elevator cars to be located in a single hoistway (Figure 19-5).

In buildings where elevators serve three or more floors, the elevator hoistways are required to vent to the exterior of the buildings. This ventilation relieves hot gases and smoke which can accumulate at the top of elevator hoistways. If no relief is provided, such smoke and hot gases may build up to the point where they travel into other parts of buildings, causing a threat to life. Building codes specify the amount of ventilation

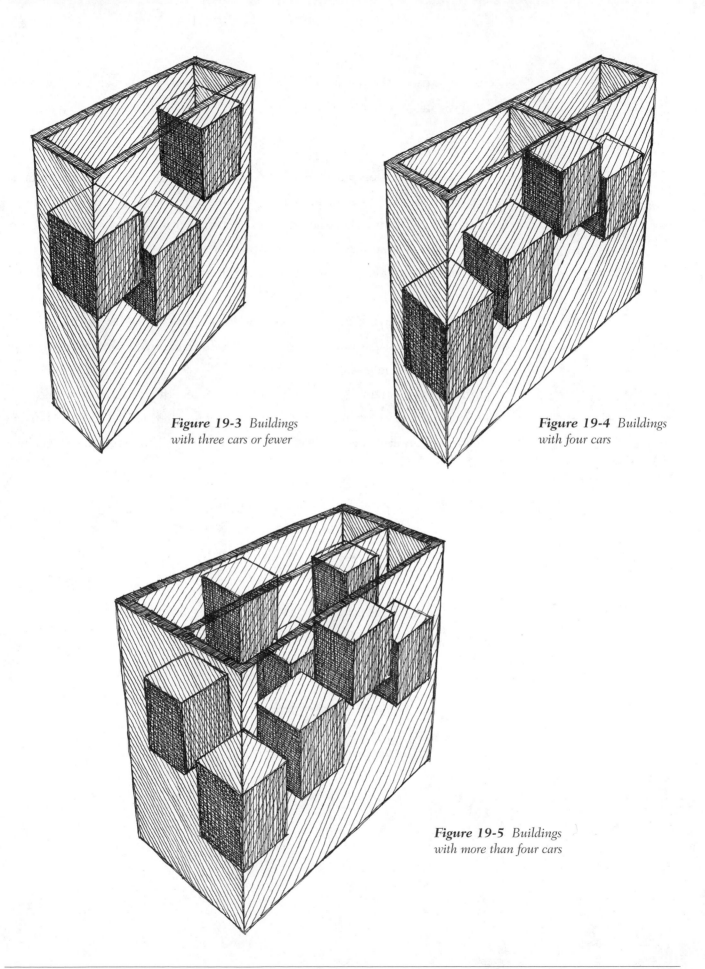

Figure 19-3 Buildings
with three cars or fewer

Figure 19-4 Buildings
with four cars

Figure 19-5 Buildings
with more than four cars

necessary for each hoistway, as well as how that ventilation must be achieved, and when one can use means other than ventilation to protect the hoistway.

Egress

An elevator's location can affect a building's egress design. Because of the potential for elevator hoistways to allow the passage of smoke from one level of a building to another, building codes construct rules to protect egress pathways from elevators. Codes require signs warning building occupants to use stairs in the event of an emergency. Elevators are not permitted to be located within a vertical shaft which is also used for a stairway. Moreover, one must be able to travel from one set of stairs to another without passing directly in front of elevator doors (Figure 19-6). By isolating elevator hoistways from egress pathways, codes maintain safe egress routes for the occupants of buildings to use in the event of a fire emergency.

Just as it is important to consider how elevators affect the egressing of people located in areas removed from the elevators, it is also important to consider the building occupants within elevators and elevator lobbies, and how to egress them. Building

Figure 19-6 No egress in front of elevators

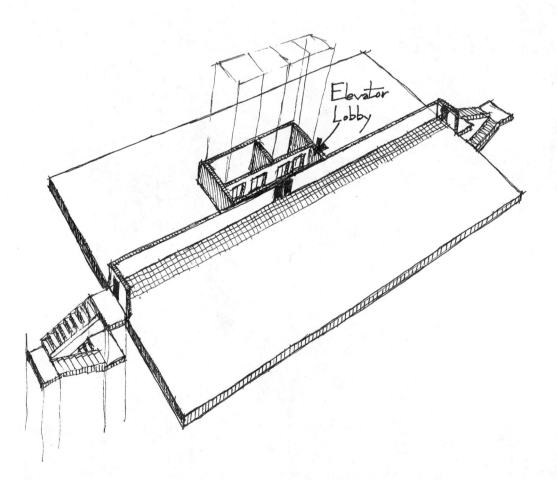

codes require egress to be provided from elevators and elevator lobbies. Elevator lobbies may be formed by retractable partitions that move into place upon the detection of smoke or fire within a building.

Accessibility

Means of egress for individuals with disabilities is one of the features of modern accessibility standards. For example, the Americans with Disabilities Act (ADA)

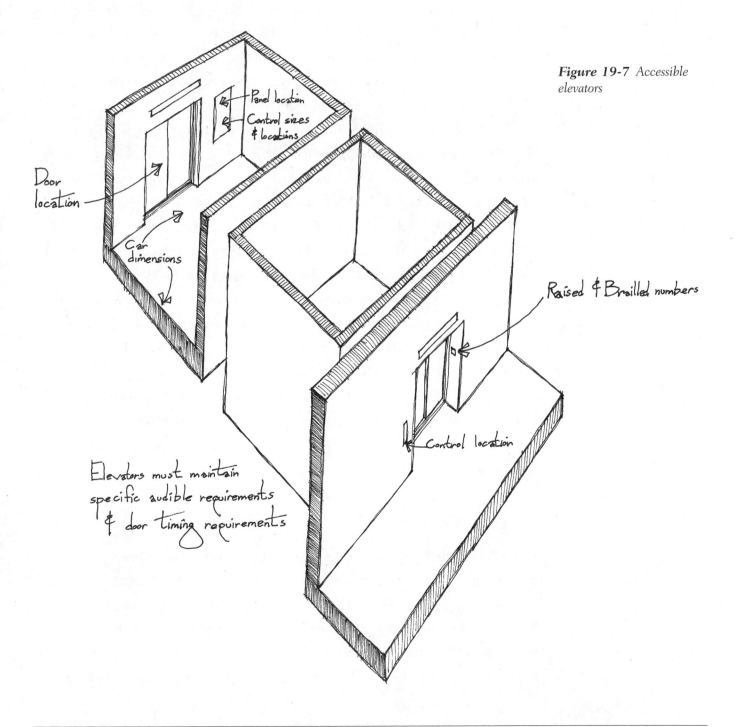

Figure 19-7 Accessible elevators

Panel location

Control sizes & locations

Door location

Car dimensions

Raised & Brailled numbers

Control location

Elevators must maintain specific audible requirements & door timing requirements

requires areas of rescue assistance at exits which are inaccessible to individuals with disabilities, and that are located in buildings which are not provided with supervised automatic sprinkler systems. Areas of rescue assistance are required in new construction only. These areas of rescue assistance are waiting spaces for individuals with disabilities with two-way communication between the areas of rescue assistance and the fire control areas of buildings. They provide individuals with disabilities with a protected place to wait for fire personnel who can help them egress a building in the event of an emergency. Many accessibility standards other than the ADA require areas of rescue assistance though they may call them something else, such as areas of refuge. The ADA and these other accessibility standards allow elevator lobbies to be used as areas of rescue assistance if the elevators are pressurized as prescribed by codes in order to prevent smoke and hot gases from entering the elevator hoistways.

There are many other requirements in codes and standards for making elevators accessible to individuals with disabilities (Figure 19-7). Elevator cars must be of certain minimum dimensions so that individuals who use wheelchairs can utilize them. All call buttons and car control buttons must be of certain dimensions and must be located at specific heights above the floor. Brailled and raised lettering must be located on both elevator jambs to identify floor levels and must be located within elevator cars to identify car control buttons. There are requirements for elevator cars to audibly signal when they are going up, when they are going down, and when they pass a floor level. Timing requirements ensure that elevator doors remain open long enough for individuals with disabilities to enter and exit elevator cars. The emergency phones in elevators must provide both visible and audible communication, so that individuals who cannot hear or speak are able to communicate in the event of an emergency. To know what must be done to make elevators accessible to individuals with disabilities, one must consult all applicable accessibility standards. Other measures than the ones above may be required.

ESCALATORS

Escalators, by their very nature, are located at openings between floors. Such openings potentially allow the passage of smoke and gases form fire to move from floor to floor (see Chapter 7) (Figure 19-8). Because of this risk, building codes require escalators to be located in areas which are already permitted by codes to be open to different floors. Building codes will also allow the use of escalators in other areas if certain protective measures are taken including providing the building with automatic

Figure 19-8 Escalators

sprinkler protection. Escalators are not permitted by building codes to be used for means of egress, as their designs are not compatible with the design standards considered to be acceptable for egress stairway design.

Plumbing and Mechanical

Chapter 20 takes a brief look at what types of requirements are found in codes pertaining to the design and construction of plumbing, and mechanical systems. This chapter does not attempt to discuss the code requirements of these systems in detail, but rather to illustrate what codes address concerning these building services. The codes discussed in this chapter are the International Plumbing Code and the International Mechanical Code promulgated by the International Code Council.

There are many codes by many different organizations which address the design and construction of plumbing, and mechanical systems, but the most dominant of these codes in the United States will soon be the International Plumbing Code and the International Mechanical Code. Though plumbing and mechanical systems are often designed by engineers with expertise in these areas, architects must be familiar with the codes for these systems, as there is some overlapping of design responsibility when designing for these systems. For example, a particular requirement in a mechanical code may necessitate the construction of fire-rated assemblies, or an architect may need to design rest rooms based on plumbing loads generated from a plumbing code.

PLUMBING

Building codes refer to nationally recognized plumbing codes for requirements pertaining to plumbing systems. Though many of the model code organizations publish a plumbing code, it is clear that eventually the most nationally recognized plumbing code will be the International Plumbing Code (IPC) as published by all three building code organizations acting jointly as the International Code Council, Inc. (ICC) (Figure 20-1). The requirements in the IPC are very similar to those found in other plumbing codes; therefore, this section is based on the provisions of the IPC only. The discussion in this section is very general, and attempts only to familiarize one with the sorts of things covered by plumbing codes. There are other requirements in plumbing codes which are not discussed in this chapter.

Plumbing systems start with water sources, wells or municipal supplies, and carry water to plumbing fixtures. Plumbing fixtures rely on water to dispense, wash, or flush and provide for the passage of the water and waste into drains. Drains carry the waste water to sewers, septic tanks, or some other means of waste disposal. Drain systems are supplied with vents to relieve the pressure in drains, halt the siphoning of the drainage system, and vent harmful gases to the outdoors. Individual fixtures are outfitted with traps that also keep odors and harmful gases from entering buildings. Plumbing codes provide the requirements necessary to construct safe and sanitary plumbing systems.

Administration and General Regulations

Just as with any code, plumbing codes begin with administrative provisions and definitions which establish the rules necessary for the enforcement of the codes and

Figure 20-1 *International Plumbing Code*

the key terms to be used in the codes respectively. These provisions are very similar to those discussed in chapter two of this book for building codes. Other definitions for key terms are introduced in later relevant chapters.

Plumbing codes begin with more general, overriding requirements before dealing with requirements more specific in nature. These requirements are applicable to most projects, and are so broad in scope that they are most appropriately located together in order to establish the general principles by which one must abide when designing and constructing plumbing systems. The following is an oversimplified list of typical general plumbing requirements:

1. Plumbing systems are required to be installed in a manner that preserves the integrity of the structural system, and they must connect to the applicable services within the infrastructure (e.g., water supply system, sanitary sewer or septic tank);

2. Materials which can be detrimental to sewer systems are not allowed to be introduced into the drainage and sewer system;

3. Plumbing materials must be approved, listed, and labeled for their use. These materials are subject to third-party inspection and testing;

4. Plumbing systems must be installed in a manner which affords rodent-proofing;

5. Pipes must be protected against damage from structural loading, adverse weather conditions, and physical damage;

6. Trenching, excavation, and backfilling must be done in a manner that will support piping and will not damage it;

7. Piping must be properly supported;

8. Plumbing systems and equipment must be constructed in a floodproof manner;

9. Washrooms and toilet rooms must be provided with proper light and ventilation and with proper interior finishes. Plumbing fixtures and piping must not interfere with the means of egress from the space, and water closets must afford privacy to the individuals using them;

10. Construction workers must be provided with sanitary toilet facilities; and

11. Proper tests must be performed on plumbing systems in order to prove their proper installation.

Fixtures

Plumbing fixtures are the actual devices located at the end of the water supply systems and at the beginning of the drain and vent systems. Fixtures include automatic clothes washers, bathtubs, bidets, dishwashing machines, drinking fountains, emergency showers and eyewash stations, floor drains, food waste grinder units, garbage can washers, laundry trays, lavatories, showers, sinks, urinals, water closets, and whirlpool bathtubs. Plumbing codes give specific requirements for each type of fixture while disallowing the use of certain other types of fixtures. The materials used for the manufacture of fixtures are regulated by codes and are required to provide smooth impervious surfaces.

There are many architectural design issues addressed by plumbing codes. The minimum numbers of plumbing fixtures for each building are specified, as well as the distribution of those fixtures amongst men and women. In some cases the location of certain facilities, such as employee toilet facilities, are specified. Plumbing fixtures are required to maintain specific clearances from other fixtures so that they are usable. Plumbing codes also detail requirements for making plumbing facilities accessible to individuals with disabilities.

The installation of fixtures must provide for access for the cleaning of fixtures and must provide for level fixtures which are properly aligned with walls. Fixture connections must be secure while also being able to support the weight imposed on the fixtures. Faucets and flushing devices located on fixtures are regulated by plumbing codes to ensure their proper operation.

Water Heaters

General requirements of plumbing codes require all water heaters to be labeled. Each water heater must be installed in accordance with its manufacturer recommendations and must be installed in a manner that will permit one to observe, maintain, service, or replace it. Fuel-burning water heaters must not be located in a room with air-handling equipment if the room is also a return air plenum, and if water heaters are installed in garages, their ignition devices must be located at a specified height above the floor.

Plumbing codes specify maximum temperature settings for certain types of water heaters. Though not a code requirement, it is generally recommended that water heaters be set for no more than 120° Fahrenheit within buildings occupied by infants and small children. This is to avoid injury due to scalding.

Water heaters can be very dangerous if they are improperly installed. I have seen photographs of a building that was leveled because of a water heater explosion. When a water heater explodes, it releases a great deal of energy, the effects of which probably resemble a bomb explosion. There are many safety devices required by plumbing codes for water heaters which help them keep from experiencing conditions that may cause them to explode. Plumbing codes require anitisiphon devices and vacuum relief valves to prevent the siphoning of water from water heaters. Energy cutoff devices are required that will cut water heaters off when their temperature becomes excessive. Pressure relief valves and temperature relief valves must be installed in water heaters which operate above atmospheric pressure to relieve excessive pressures and temperatures. The requirements for how these valves terminate are regulated by plumbing codes. The location of a water heater may necessitate the installation of a pan to prevent any leakage from the water heater from damaging any construction.

Water Supply and Distribution

Potable (drinkable) water must be supplied to every structure occupied or inhabited by people (Figure 20-2). This water must be provided at the pressures necessary to operate the plumbing fixtures in each structure whether the water comes from a well or a water main. The potable water supply must be protected. Depending on the use of the structure, one may have to provide hot and cold water or cold water only. Water service pipes are required by plumbing codes to be of a specific minimum size, but large

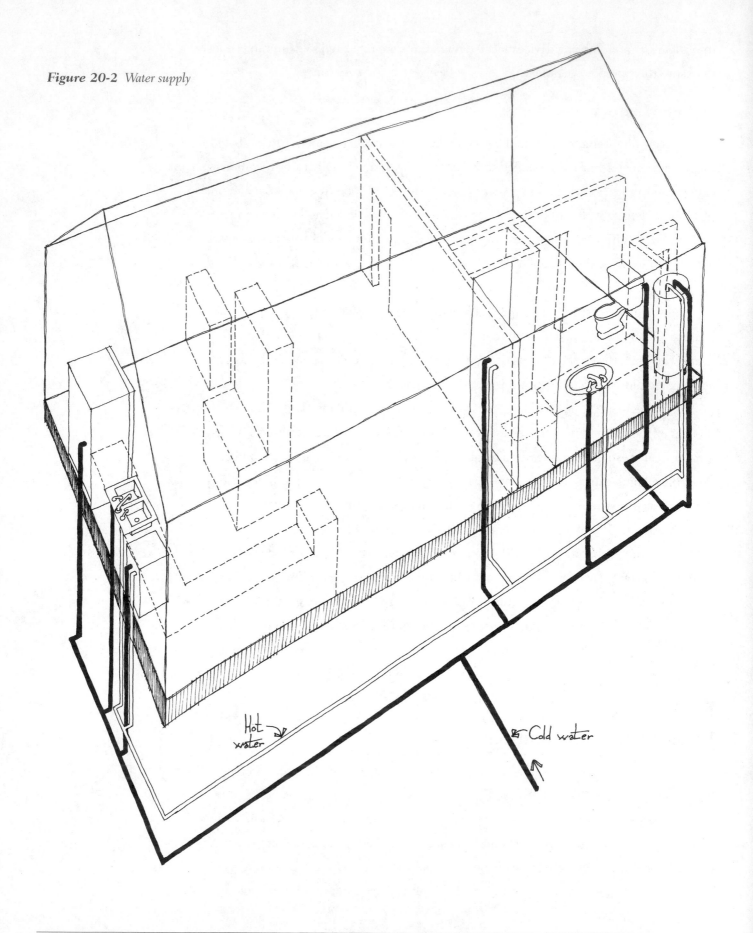

Figure 20-2 *Water supply*

Hot water

Cold water

enough to ensure adequate operating pressure at each fixture. There must be some separation between water service pipes and building sewers; moreover, water service pipes cannot be located near pollution sources. Health care occupancies require two water service pipes so that if one becomes damaged, the other will ensure a supply of water to the facility.

The design of the water distribution system is based on the types, number, and locations of fixtures, as well as on the required water flow rates and water flow pressures at each fixture. Plumbing codes specify minimum pipe sizes for each type of plumbing fixture. These are minimums, however, and often a particular plumbing fixture, because of its design, may require a pipe size larger than the minimum size mandated by codes. Furthermore, maintaining the required flow rate and flow pressure at a particular fixture may require the use of a water supply pipe larger than the minimum size mandated by codes.

Water distribution design must also account for pressure at the water service, and compensate for inadequate or erratic pressure. If the water service pressure is inadequate, one must incorporate a booster pump and pressure tank into the design. Should the water service pressure be erratic, one must design the water distribution system for the minimum pressure available. A water service pressure in excess of 80 pounds per square inch (psi) will require the use of some sort of device such as a water reducing valve to reduce the water distribution pressure to no more than 80 psi.

The materials used for water distribution systems are regulated by plumbing codes. The pipes, tubing, and fittings must be made of lead-free pipes which are corrosion and degradation resistant. Water service pipe, water distribution pipe, pipe fittings, and all other water distribution elements must comply with the nationally recognized standards referenced by plumbing codes for such elements. The joints for pipes and tubing are required to meet code requirements for allowable types and for methods of installation. Plumbing code joint requirements are extensive and vary based on the type of joint and the type of pipe or tubing.

Sanitary Drainage

All buildings with plumbing fixtures must be connected to some sort of sewer system (Figure 20-3), be it a public sewer system or a private sewage disposal system. Private sewage disposal systems are regulated by The International Private Sewage Disposal Code (IPSDC) as published by the International Code Council, Inc. (ICC). Materials used for sanitary drainage must be listed for such use in accordance with standards referenced by plumbing codes. Referenced standards are given for above-

Figure 20-3 *Drainage*

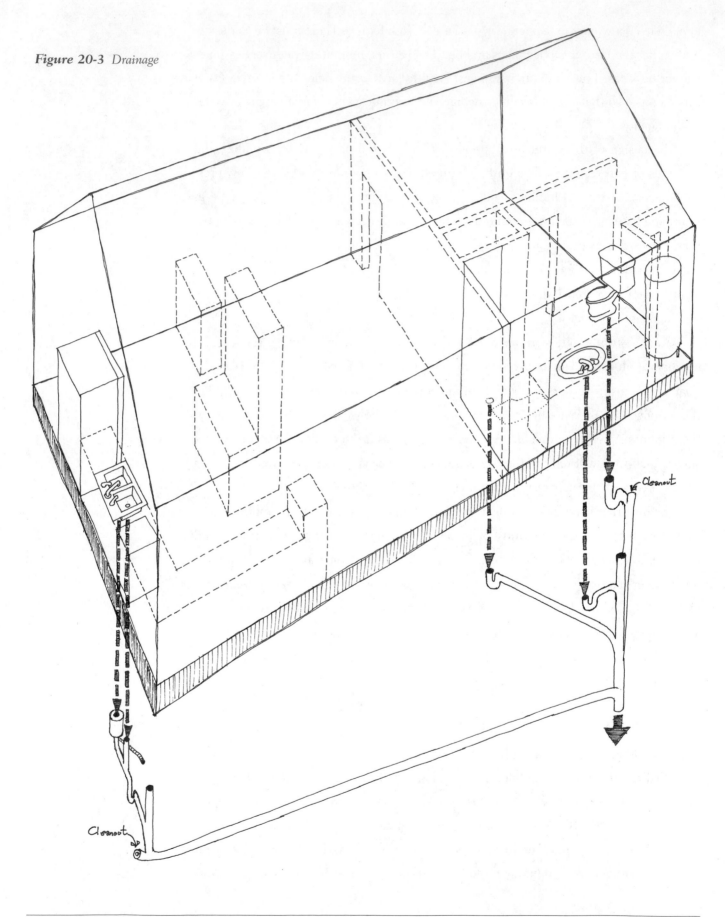

Cleanout

Cleanout

Figure 20-4 *Cleanout*

ground drainage and vent pipe, underground building drainage and vent pipe, building sewer pipe, and pipe fittings.

Building sewers must maintain a specified distance from water service pipes, but may be installed side by side in the same trench with storm sewers. When existing building sewers connect to new building sewers, the code official can require the existing sewers to be brought up to the standards of the new sewers. Plumbing codes specify minimum sizes for building sewers and require them to be fitted with cleanouts.

Horizontal drainage piping must be installed at the slopes specified in plumbing codes. Reductions in the size of the piping must not occur in the direction of flow and drainage piping must not terminate in dead ends. Plumbing codes allow some exceptions to these rules where such exceptions will not adversely affect the drainage system.

As with supply piping, joints in drainage piping are heavily regulated by plumbing codes. And as with supply piping, the requirements for joints in drainage piping vary based on the type of piping and the type of joint. Plumbing codes also regulate the joints between drainage piping and fixtures, and list prohibited types of joints and connections as well.

Cleanouts are plugged openings in drainage systems which allow one, when the plug is removed, to clean the drain with chemicals or by mechanical means (Figure 20-

4). Cleanouts must run with the direction of the drainage flow and are required at the following locations: horizontal drains with buildings, building sewers, changes of direction in the drainage piping, bases of stacks, and the connections of building drains and building sewers. Plumbing codes specify the requirements for cleanouts at each of these locations. Cleanout clearances and sizes are also specified by plumbing codes, and in larger pipes, manholes are required to be provided instead of cleanouts.

Fixture units are used to help determine the minimum sizes of drainage piping. One must determine the number of fixture units generated by plumbing fixtures and then size the drains based on the fixtures they serve. Fixture units are a means of expressing the probable discharge of waste into fixtures and the drainage system. Trap sizes also affect the minimum size of the drain and no trap is less than 1¼ inches in size. Plumbing codes provide the designer with all the tables necessary to calculate minimum fixture units. Computerized drainage system design can be employed if approved by the code official and implemented in accordance with plumbing codes.

There are some special plumbing code requirements pertaining to drainage systems. When building drains are lower than the sewer, they must rely on sumps and ejectors to lift and discharge the sewage into the sewer system. Plumbing codes regulate sumps and ejectors so that their operation will be safe and effective. Health care occupancies have many special code requirements they must adhere to concerning drainage, as they have many unique processes occurring within them, such as sterilization of equipment, fluid disposal, and bedpan washing. Many fixtures are required by plumbing codes to discharge through indirect waste pipes. Indirect waste pipes lead to traps, other fixtures, receptors, or interceptors, but are separated from them by air spaces.

Vents

Vents are required with all plumbing systems so that air can exhaust the system and can stabilize the pressure in the system, preventing the emptying of traps due to excessive pneumatic pressure differentials. If a trap's seal is broken because of water siphoning out of the trap, then the trap will no longer protect building occupants from odors and gases built up in the drainage system (Figures 20-5a and b). Vents introduce air flow to the drainage system and equalize the pressure on both sides of the trap seal, thus preventing such siphoning. Plumbing codes require each trap to be vented. As with all plumbing systems, vent systems must be constructed with pipes, tubing, fittings, and flashing which comply with nationally recognized standards as referenced in plumbing codes.

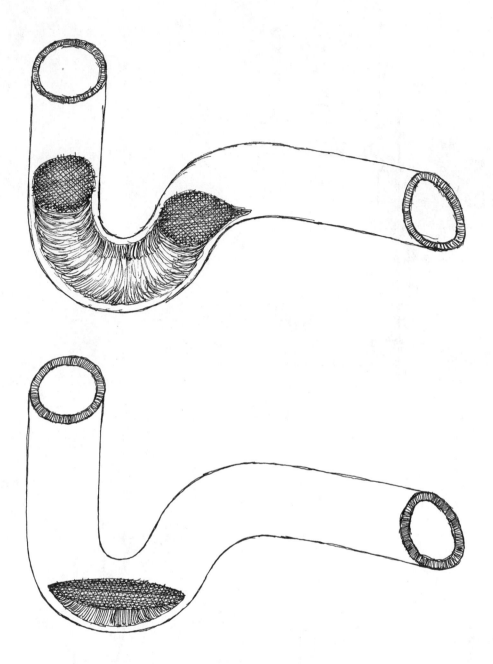

Figure 20-5a *Trap seal intact*

Figure 20-5b *Trap seal broken*

A vent stack is a vent which serves the purpose of providing a venting terminus for other branch vents (Figure 20-6a). A stack vent is a vent that sits on top of a vertical drain for the purposes of venting that drain (Figure 20-6b). Vent stacks and stack vents are required to terminate above roofs, and plumbing codes regulate how they terminate. They must terminate at a specified height above the roof, but they cannot terminate directly below doors, windows, or other air intake openings; they are required to be sized to prevent closure from frost in colder climates; they must be properly flashed; and they cannot be used for other purposes than venting (e.g., flag poles, TV antennas, etc.) unless they are specifically designed to be used for such purposes.

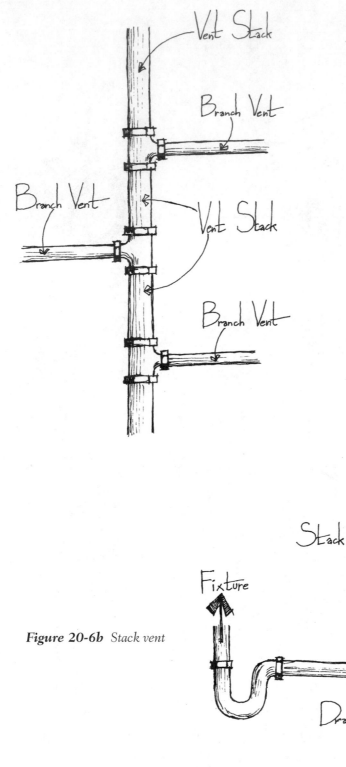

Figure 20-6a Vent stack

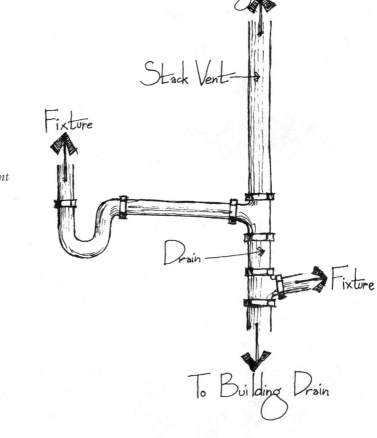

Figure 20-6b Stack vent

Vents must be sloped in a manner that will allow them to drain back into the drainage system. They must maintain heights above fixtures as required by plumbing codes in order to adequately prevent siphoning. Plumbing codes provide specific requirements for various types of vents based on their individual functions. These various types of vents include fixture vents, common vents, wet vents, waste stack vents, circuit vents, and combination drain and vent systems. Island fixture vents require special code requirements as they have no means of venting vertically through the roof directly adjacent to the fixtures. Many vents which serve other vents may require additional venting to ensure enough air movement through the venting system.

Sizing of vent stacks and stack vents is determined by at least three criteria. First, they must be at least 1¼ inches in diameter. Second, their diameter must be at least one half the diameter of the drain they serve. Third, they must be sized according to tables provided in plumbing codes. These tables account for the developed length of the vents and the number of fixture units connected to the vents.

Traps

Plumbing codes require each plumbing fixture to be trapped by a water seal trap, unless a specific exception is made (see figure 20-5a). The water seals in these traps must be two to four inches and may need to be primed if the water in the trap is susceptible to evaporation. This ensures enough water pressure to seal the trap effectively and to discourage the "blowing out" of the seal due to high water pressure entering the trap from the fixture. One may need to prevent substances harmful to the drainage system, such as oil or grease, from entering that system by using interceptors or separators.

Storm Drainage

Storm drainage is required to drain all roofs, paved areas, yards, courts, and courtyards into a drainage system that will carry the water away from all structures. If approved by the code official, one- and two-family dwellings can drain to their site if the water runs away from the dwellings. If ponding will occur on roofs because of the design of the storm drainage system, then the maximum amount of ponding that can occur must be accounted for in the design of those roofs. As with building drainage systems, the materials used for storm drainage systems must comply with nationally recognized standards as referenced by plumbing codes.

The storm drainage system for a roof begins with sloping the roof to route water off of the roof or to route water to gutters and leaders (downspouts) which carry the water

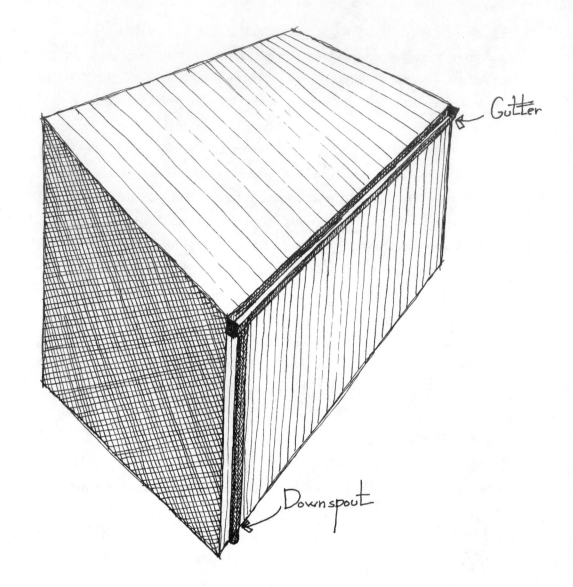

Gutter

Downspout

Figure **20-7** *Gutters, leaders, and downspouts*

to the ground level or to a storm sewer (Figure 20-7). In the case of flat roofs, the storm drainage system begins with sloping the roof towards roof drains or towards scuppers. The roof drains are covered with strainers and lead to conductors which are interior pipes that carry the water to a storm drain (Figure 20-8). Scuppers are openings in the parapets of the exterior walls used as storm drains and overflow devices and may lead to a vertical leader (scuppers are also discussed in Chapter 15 of this book).

Plumbing codes specify the requirements for installing storm drainage. They require secondary drains or scuppers for overflow drainage. They prohibit floor drains from connecting to storm drains, and prohibit the connection of storm drainage systems with sanitary sewer systems unless they are part of an approved combined sanitary and storm sewer system. The sizes of conductors, leaders, and storm drains are specified in plumbing codes as are the sizes of strainers. Backwater valves are required in many instances to halt the backflow of storm water into the drainage system. Sumps may also

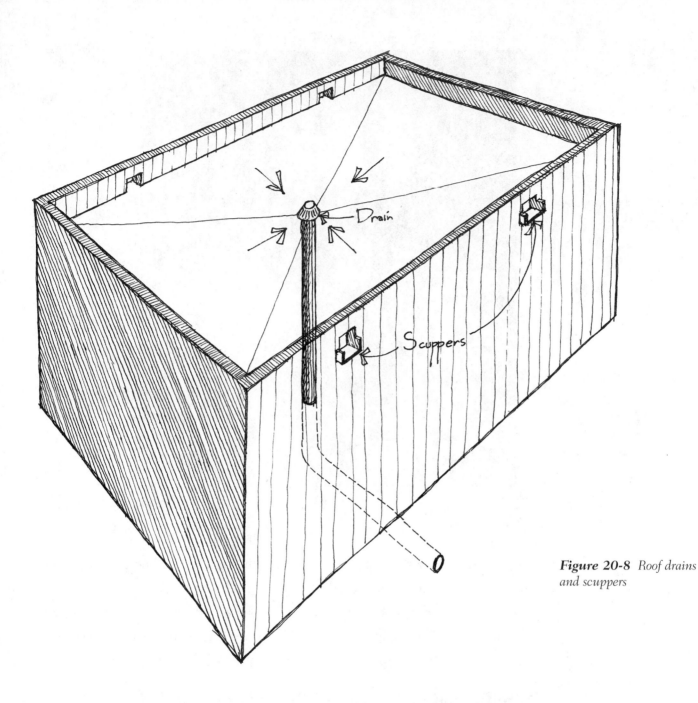

Drain

Scuppers

Figure 20-8 *Roof drains and scuppers*

be required by plumbing codes where building drains are located below the public sewer.

MECHANICAL/GAS

Building codes refer to nationally recognized mechanical and gas codes for requirements pertaining to mechanical systems. Though many of the model code organizations publish codes covering requirements for mechanical and gas systems, it is clear that the most recognized mechanical code nationally will eventually be the International Mechanical Code (IMC) as published by all three building code organizations acting

Figure 20-9 *International Mechanical Code*

jointly as the International Code Council, Inc. (ICC) (Figure 20-9). The requirements in the IMC are very similar to those found in other mechanical and gas codes; therefore, this section is based on the provisions of the IMC. The discussion in this section is very general, and attempts only to familiarize one with the sorts of things covered by mechanical (mechanical and gas) codes. There are other requirements in mechanical codes which are not discussed in this chapter.

Administration and General Regulations

As with any code, mechanical codes begin with administrative provisions and definitions which establish the rules necessary for the enforcement of the codes and the key terms to be used in the codes. These provisions are very similar to those discussed in chapter two of this book for building codes. For key terms, definitions are introduced in later chapters of the IMC.

There are many general overriding regulations in mechanical codes. Mechanical codes require the design and installation of mechanical systems to recognize the principles of energy conservation. All equipment and appliances that make up the mechanical system must be tested, listed, and labeled (Figure 20-10), and mechanical codes

Figure 20-10 *Labeled appliance*

specify the requirements for that testing and listing process, as well as specify what information must be included in the labeling. Fuel equipment must only use the fuel it was designed to use unless it can be proven that fuel conversion can be achieved safely and in accordance with manufacturers' instructions. The installation of mechanical systems must be achieved in a manner that will not reduce the structural integrity of the building. Mechanical codes regulate the amounts of notching, cutting, and boring of holes that can occur during installation. Piping must be properly supported and the supports must be structurally sound.

Mechanical equipment must be installed in locations which provide for servicing and for protection from damage, while also providing fuel-burning appliances with enough volume of intake air to operate safely. As in the plumbing code, fuel-burning equipment must be installed at specified heights above certain floors, such as garage floors. Mechanical equipment must also maintain required clearances from combustible materials. Certain mechanical equipment will require condensate disposal, the details of which are specified by codes.

Ventilation

Spaces within buildings are required to be ventilated by mechanical codes (see chapter twelve of this book for related discussion). Rules are specified for mechanical ventilation and natural ventilation. There are requirements for the amount of outside air which must be introduced into the spaces based on the uses of the spaces and on the occupancies of the buildings. Many of the requirements in the IMC for ventilation of interior spaces are similar if not identical to those required by other codes, but the IMC is more thorough in what it requires.

Exhaust Systems

Exhaust systems are required for many reasons. In commercial kitchens, exhaust systems remove smoke and grease from cooking equipment (Figure 20-11). In bathrooms and toilet rooms, exhaust systems remove odors and help keep the air fresh. Many processes within buildings require exhaust systems, such as some dry-cleaning processes, motion picture projection, spray painting, and many other processes where certain chemicals must be removed from the spaces where the processes occur. Mechanical codes regulate the many aspects of providing exhaust systems for buildings. The regulations address the different types of exhaust systems required for each situation, the motors and fans utilized by these exhaust systems, the air requirements for these systems, and the fire suppression systems that are required for certain exhaust systems.

Duct Systems

Duct systems are air passageways for air conditioning systems (both supply and return air), ventilation systems, and exhaust systems (Figure 20-12). Ducts may be metallic, nonmetallic, or a combination of several different materials as in the case of plenums. Plenums are enclosed spaces which are used as air passageways, and which meet mechanical code requirements for such use. They include uninhabited crawl spaces, attics, spaces above ceilings, spaces below floors, and mechanical equipment rooms. Duct systems cannot be installed in a manner that impedes the performance of

Figure 20-11 *Exhaust hood*

the fire protection aspects of a facility. Many ducts require the use of smoke dampers or fire dampers because of their passage through rated assemblies, or because of other fire protection measures required in building codes. These dampers must be installed in accordance with mechanical codes and any nationally recognized standards referenced by mechanical codes.

Smoke detectors are required in many ducts as a means of providing early detection of fire. Smoke detectors trigger the shutdown of the air distribution system in order to stop the spread of smoke throughout a building. In many cases, smoke detectors in ducts are required to be connected to fire-protective-signaling systems.

The construction and installation of ducts are regulated by mechanical codes, with the requirements varying based on the type of ducts employed. The properties of the materials used are regulated as are the connections of those materials. There are also mandates for duct materials and construction to conform to the requirements of different nationally recognized standards.

Figure 20-12 Duct systems

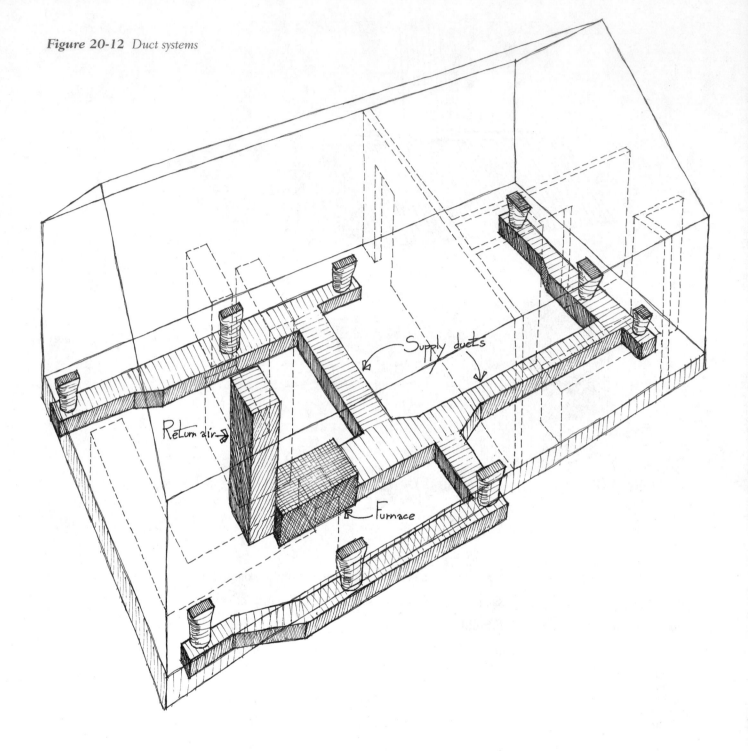

Plenums also have material requirements, but in the case of plenums those materials requirements are primarily specified in mechanical codes. Fuel-fired mechanical equipment is not allowed to be installed in plenums. Plenums must not communicate between two or more fire areas of a building. Exits and exit access are not allowed to serve as plenums, as they must remain safe egress routes, free of smoke and fire.

The insulating of ducts can create hazardous conditions where highly combustible materials may be introduced into a structure's air systems. Mechanical codes regulate the materials and installation of insulation in order to protect ducts. Codes, in regulating duct insulation, also address other fire protection concerns, like the penetration of fire-rated assemblies with combustible products.

Combustion Air

Combustion and dilution air are needed for fuel-burning appliances and equipment, so that the process of combustion can take place. The IMC defines dilution air as, "Air that is introduced into a draft hood and is mixed with flue gases (International Code Council, 1996)." The IMC defines combustion air as, "Air necessary for complete combustion of a fuel, including theoretical air and excess air (International Code Council, 1996)." Mechanical codes regulate when combustion and dilution air can be made up from inside air and when they must be made up of outdoor air. The IMC provides different options for using outdoor air and different options for the use of both inside air and outdoor air for combustion and dilution air. Some mechanical appliances and equipment may require the use of direct combustion air (air taken directly from outdoors). Codes establish rules for how to supply that direct air, as well as how to construct the ducts supplying that air.

Chimneys and Vents

Chimneys and vents are regulated by their listings when they are factory-built products. When they are not factory-built products, chimneys and vents must meet the requirements of mechanical codes. Many of the requirements in mechanical codes for masonry chimneys are similar to those in building codes (see Chapter 18 for related discussion).

Mechanical codes classify vents according to their types and then specify requirements for each different type of vent. Typical vent requirements include their allowable sizes, how they are connected to appliances and equipment, when they can be connected to other vents, and other installation requirements. The distances that vents terminate above roofs are also regulated.

Appliances and equipment are often connected to vents by connectors. Connectors are, more or less, horizontal vents (Figure 20-13). Their installation is regulated by mechanical codes, along with their thickness, size, and length. Furthermore, connectors are regulated as to what types of construction assemblies they can penetrate.

Figure 20-13 *Connector*

Specific Appliances, Fireplaces, and Solid Fuel-Burning Equipment

Mechanical appliances and equipment are regulated by mechanical codes with the requirements varying based on the particular appliance in question. Many of the requirements are references to nationally recognized standards governing the manufacture and installation of each appliance. For some appliances, there are also specific requirements for the proper use or installation of the appliance. The types of appliances regulated by the IMC are factory-built fireplaces, pellet fuel-burning appliances, fireplace stoves and room heaters, factory-built barbecue appliances, decorative gas-fired appliances for installation in vented fireplaces, gas-fired log lighters, vented gas-fired decorative appliances, incinerators and crematories, cooling towers, evaporative condensers, fluid coolers, vented wall furnaces, floor furnaces, duct furnaces, direct-fired air-heating equipment, infrared radiant heaters, clothes dryers, illuminating appliances, sauna heaters, engine and gas turbine-powered equipment, pool and spa heaters, cooking appliances, forced-air warm-air furnaces, conversion burners, unit heaters, unvented room heaters, and vented room heaters.

Boilers, Water Heaters, and Pressure Vessels

Boilers, water heaters, and pressure vessels concern code officials in that their potential explosions could destroy a building and prove to be fatal to the occupants of buildings (see the plumbing code section of this chapter). Mechanical codes require boilers, water heaters, and pressure vessels to meet nationally recognized standards for manufacture and installation. The clearances around them are specified as are their protection through the use of safety and pressure relief valves and controls. As with other mechanical equipment, the requirements in mechanical codes for installation of boilers, water heaters, and pressure vessels vary depending on the equipment being regulated.

Fuel-Gas Piping

Fuel-gas pipes must be sized according to the demand placed on them by the appliances they serve. They are required to be identified along with their meters. Mechanical codes require gas piping to be sized in accordance with code tables that give the Btus per hour (Btu/h) of different appliances, and that give the capacities that can be handled by different types of pipes and tubing. Nationally recognized standards are also referenced for the manufacture and quality of fuel-gas pipe.

Piping installation requirements in mechanical codes cover such things as how to treat the piping when it penetrates various types of construction assemblies (e.g., foundation walls, solid floors, etc). Locations for gas shutoff valves are specified and applicable referenced standards for gas shutoff valves are specified in mechanical codes as are requirements for gas flow controls. Undiluted liquid petroleum gases (LPG) have their own sets of requirements as they have a higher heating value than natural gas. Undiluted petroleum gases consist of butane and propane.

Mechanical codes regulate appliance connections to fuel-gas piping. Appliances are required to have individual shutoff valves. Flexible connectors are required on appliances which are subject to movement because of cleaning or other purposes. All connections must be protected from damage.

Fuel Oil Piping and Storage

Fuel oil systems require piping as well as storage facilities. Mechanical codes regulate the materials and storage tanks for quality and proper installation. Referenced nationally recognized standards are used to ensure the quality of the piping and of the storage tanks. Joints and connections, piping support, fuel oil system installation, oil gauging, and fuel oil valves are all regulated by mechanical codes in order to maintain safe fuel oil systems.

Solar Systems

Solar systems are regulated by mechanical codes to ensure amongst other things, that their installation does not hinder the integrity of any other building systems. They must be installed so that they do not damage roof systems because of their mounting or because of roof penetrations for their piping. Attics must be protected from potential condensation from solar systems. When solar systems provide potable water, safeguards are required to be taken to ensure that the water remains safe to drink.

Conclusion

This book has attempted to demystify the complex language of construction regulations and the confusion created by the promulgation and adoption of so many different regulatory documents. Though the book's text cannot be used as the substitute for a code, it is hoped that it can be used as a reference to help one understand more fully the provisions of the codes, standards, and other regulations that one must adhere to when designing and constructing buildings. There are some principles that one should consider when implementing construction regulation provisions.

Codes, standards, and other construction regulations are necessary, as they perform a valuable service to all. Though these codes may be cumbersome to use, their language is a mere reflection of the difficult writing contained in a document that clearly states the requirements necessary when designing and constructing buildings and other facilities to protect the public's health, safety, and welfare. The absence of construction regulations would prove to be a disastrous affair, due to the unsafe construction quality that might prevail, and the increased litigation that would almost certainly occur, clogging our already overburdened courtrooms. The single greatest improvement that can be made to construction regulations would be to reduce the number of different regulatory documents addressing the same issues so that everyone involved with the design and construction process could become more familiar with the regulations they must know, and therefore use them with greater care and confidence. After all, the ultimate goal of all construction regulation is to provide us with structures that are safe to use, easy to access, and not hinder the measures of protection provided in neighboring structures.

There are many different codes, standards, and other regulations which govern building design and construction. Those involved in design and construction processes must become acquainted with several different regulatory documents in order to practice their professions. It is important for one to know which regulations are the proper ones to apply when dealing with a specific project. One must know not only which regulations are relevant, but also which editions of these regulations are the appropriate ones to use. Furthermore, one must have an understanding of which regulations supersede other regulations when a conflict occurs, and which provisions are more stringent than others, so that the correct standards are followed. Lack of familiarity with all applicable construction regulations may lead to one's following the requirements of the wrong set of regulations.

As professionals, designers and builders must comply with construction regulations. Construction regulations are law in the jurisdictions where they are applicable, whether those jurisdictions are cities, counties, states, or the entire United States. A lack of compliance with any relevant construction code, requirement, standard, or other law is a legal violation. Designers and builders should defend fire safety provisions and accessibility provisions as much as they do structural provisions. Most clients expect designers and builders to be familiar with and to adhere to all applicable construction regulations as a matter of professional conduct. When a client wishes to circumvent the requirements of construction regulations however, the designer and builder should remind that client of their obligation to comply with such regulations. There are few better ways to separate professionals from nonprofessionals than by proper adherence to applicable construction regulations.

The more one knows about the construction regulations one must use, the more able one will be at performing his or her duties. Certain construction regulations will apply to any project whether the designer is familiar with them or not. If the designer is very familiar with all the regulations he or she must meet, then that designer can control the design and will have the best opportunity to achieve a superior design aesthetically, symbolically, and practically. However, should a designer not be familiar with the regulations governing his or her design, others will probably step in and control the outcome of the design. The result may be a building that appears as though no cohesive thought was given to the design.

Construction regulations do not address every single concern about design and construction. Every building is unique, and most buildings will require some unique consideration in order to achieve the proper level of fire, structural, and health safety. Construction regulations should be used as guidelines for good design and construction, and not as the answers for all of one's code-related questions. Buildings are much too complicated to be addressed entirely by construction regulations, no matter how voluminous the regulations are. Codes and standards do, however, provide a basis for constructing intelligent ideas for designing, building, and inspecting buildings which provide for a proper level of fire, structural, and health safety. Often, a code official and a designer will work together to generate a solution to a problem which is superior to any of the solutions available in all of the applicable codes and standards.

Designers and builders should become more involved in the promulgation of construction regulations. The voice of those who implement design and construction is, for the most part, missing from the codes and standards writing process. Each individual involved in building design and construction has a unique way of assessing construction procedures, which codes and standards should reflect. There are limits to what can actually be achieved by any construction method, and no one knows this better than the very people charged with the responsibility of designing and constructing buildings. Their opinions, balanced with the industry representatives' opinions and those of code and fire officials, can help ensure the best possible construction regulations(that is, regulations which provide a proper amount of life, safety, and property protection while not creating excessive and unnecessary expenses.

Appendix A
Resources

The following organizations enforce, interpret, or publish codes, standards, technical documents, or laws which regulate the construction industry. Though this list certainly is not exhaustive, it is a sampling of the major resources for construction regulations and technical guidelines.

Organization:	**AA The Aluminum Association, Inc.**
Address:	900 19th Street, NW, Suite 300
	Washington, DC 20006
Phone:	(202) 862-5100
Web Site (URL):	http://www.aluminum.org

Organization:	**AAMA American Architectural Manufacturers Association**
Address:	1827 Walden Office Square
	Schaumburg, IL 60173
Phone:	(847) 303-5664

Organization:	**ACI American Concrete Institute**
Address:	PO Box 9094
	Farmington Hills, MI 48333
Phone:	(810) 848-3700

Organization:	**AF&PA American Forest and Paper Association**
Address:	1111 19th Street NW, Suite 800
	Washington, DC 20036
Phone:	(202) 463-2700
Web Site (URL):	http://www.awc.org

Organization:	**AHA American Hardboard Association**
Address:	1210 West Northwest Highway
	Palatine, IL 60067
Phone:	(847) 934-8800
Organization:	**AISC American Institute of Steel Construction, Inc.**
Address:	One East Wacker Drive, Suite 3100
	Chicago, IL 60601-2001
Phone:	(312) 670-2400
Web Site (URL):	http://www.aiscweb.com
Organization:	**AISI American Iron and Steel Institute**
Address:	1101 17th Street, NW, Suite 1300
	Washington, DC 20036-4700
Phone:	(202) 452-7100
Web Site (URL):	http://www.steel.org
Organization:	**AITC American Institute of Timber Construction**
Address:	7012 South Revere Parkway, Suite 140
	Englewood, CO 80112
Phone:	(303) 792-9559
Web Site (URL):	http://www.aitc-glulam.org
Organization:	**ANSI American National Standards Institute**
Address:	11 West 42nd Street, 13th Floor
	New York, NY 10036
Phone:	(212) 642-4900
Web Site (URL):	http://www.ansi.org
Organization:	**APA The Engineered Wood Association**
Address:	PO Box 11700
	Tacoma, WA 98411-0700
Phone:	(206) 565-6600
Web Site (URL):	http://www.apawood.org
Organization:	**ASCE American Society of Civil Engineers**
Address:	1801 Alexander Bell Drive
	Reston, VA 20191-4400
Phone:	(800) 548-2723
Web Site (URL):	http://www.asce.org

Organization:	**ASME American Society of Mechanical Engineers**
Address:	345 East 47th Street
	New York, NY 10017-2392
Phone:	(212) 705-7722
Web Site (URL):	http://www.asme.org

Organization:	**ASTM American Society for Testing and Materials**
Address:	100 Barr Harbor Drive
	West Conshocken, PA 19428-2959
Phone:	(610) 832-9585
Web Site (URL):	http://www.astm.org

Organization:	**ATBCB United States Architectural and Transportation Barriers Compliance Board (Access Board)**
Address:	1331 F Street, NW, Suite 1000
	Washington, DC 20004-1111
Phone:	(800) 872-2253
TDD:	(202) 272-5449
Web Site (URL):	http://www.access-board.gov

Organization:	**AWPA American Wood-Preservers' Association**
Address:	3246 Fall Creek Highway, Suite 190
	Granbury, TX 76049-7979
Phone:	(817) 326-6300

Organization:	**AWS American Welding Society**
Address:	550 NW LeJeune Road
	Miami, FL 33126
Phone:	(305) 443-9353
Web Site (URL):	http://www.amweld.org

Organization:	**BOCA Building Officials & Code Administrators International, Inc.**
Address:	4051 W. Flossmoor Road
	Country Club Hills, Illinois 60478-5795
Phone:	(708) 799-2300
Web Site (URL):	http://www.bocai.org

Organization:	**CABO Council of American Building Officials**
Address:	5203 Leesburg Pike, Suite 708
	Falls Church, VA 22041
Phone:	(703) 931-4533
Web Site (URL):	http://www.cabo.org
Organization:	**CPSC Consumer Product Safety Commission**
Address:	Office of the Secretary
	Washington, DC 20207
Phone:	(301) 504-0500
Organization:	**DBTAC Disability Business and Technical Assistance Centers**
Phone:	(800) 949-4232
Organization:	**DOJ United States Department of Justice**
Address:	Office on the Americans with Disabilities Act, Civil Rights Division
	Washington, DC 20530
Phone:	(202) 514-0301
TDD:	(202) 514-0381
Web Site (URL):	http://www.usdoj.gov/
Organization:	**DOT United States Department of Transportation**
Address:	400 7th Street, SW., Room 10424
	Washington, DC 20590
Phone:	(202) 366-9306
TDD:	(202) 755-7687
Organization:	**EIA Electronics Industries Association**
Address:	2500 Wilson Boulevard
	Arlington, VA 22201-3834
Phone:	(703) 907-7500
Web Site (URL):	http://www.eia.org
Organization:	**FM Factory Mutual**
Address:	Standards Laboratories Department
	1151 Boston Providence Turnpike
	Norwood, MA 02062

Phone:	(617) 762-4300
Web Site (URL):	http://www.factorymutual.com

Organization:	**GA Gypsum Association**
Address:	810 First Street NE, #510
	Washington, DC 20002
Phone:	(202) 289-5440

Organization:	**HPVA Hardwood Plywood Veneer Association**
Address:	PO Box 2789
	Reston, VA 20195-0789
Phone:	(703) 435-2900
Web Site (URL):	http://www.hpva.org

Organization:	**ICBO International Conference of Building Officials**
Address:	5360 Workman Mill Road
	Whittier, California 90601-2298
Phone:	(310) 699-0541
Web Site (URL):	http://www.icbo.org

Organization:	**ICC International Code Council**
Web Site (URL):	http://www.intlcode.org

Organization:	**NAAMM National Association of Architectural Metal Manufacturers**
Address:	8 South Michigan Avenue, Suite 1000
	Chicago, IL 60603
Phone:	(312) 332-0405
Web Site (URL):	http://www.gss.net/naamm.htm

Organization:	**NBS National Bureau of Standards**
Address:	United States Department of Commerce
	Superintendent of Documents
	Government Printing Office
	Washington, DC 20401

Organization:	**NCMA National Concrete Masonry Association**
Address:	2302 Horse Pen Road
	Herndon, VA 20171-3499
Phone:	(703) 713-1900
Web Site (URL):	http://www.ncma.org
Organization:	**NFPA National Fire Protection Association**
Address:	1 Batterymarch Park
	Quincy, Massachusetts 12269-9101
Phone:	(617) 770-3000
Web Site (URL):	http://www.nfpa.org
Organization:	**NIOSH National Institute for Occupational Safety and Health**
Address:	5600 Fishers Lane
	Rockville, MD 20857
Phone:	(301) 496-9228
Organization:	**NOFMA National Oak Flooring Manufacturers Association**
Address:	Falls Building, Suite 660
	22 North Front Street
	Memphis, TN 38173-0009
Phone:	(901) 526-5016
Web Site (URL):	http://www.buidernet.com/nofma
Organization:	**NPA National Particleboard Association**
Address:	18928 Premiere Court
	Gaithersburg, MD 20879-1569
Phone:	(301) 670-0604
Web Site (URL):	http://www.pbmds.com
Organization:	**OSHA Occupational Safety and Health Administration**
Address:	Francis Perkins Department of Labor Building
	200 Constitution Avenue, NW
	Washington, DC 20210
Phone:	(202) 523-1452

Organization:	**PCA Portland Cement Association**
Address:	5420 Old Orchard Road
	Skokie, IL 60077-1083
Phone:	(847) 966-6200
Web Site (URL):	http://www.portcement.org

Organization:	**PCI Prestressed Concrete Institute**
Address:	175 West Jackson Boulevard, Suite 1859
	Chicago, IL 60604-2601
Phone:	(312) 786-0300
Web Site (URL):	http://www.pci.org

Organization:	**PS Product Standards**
Address:	National Institute of Standards & Technology
	United States Department of Commerce
	A625 Administration
	Gaithersburg, MD 20899
Phone:	(301) 975-2000

Organization:	**PTI Post-Tensioning Institute**
Address:	1717 West Northern Avenue, Suite 114
	Pheonix, AZ 85021
Phone:	(602) 870-7540

Organization:	**RCSC Research Council on Structural Connections**
Address:	see AISC

Organization:	**RMA Rubber Manufacturers Association**
Address:	1400 K Street, NW, Suite 900
	Washington, DC 20005
Phone:	(202) 682-4800

Organization:	**SBCCI Southern Building Code Congress International, Inc.**
Address:	900 Montclair Road
	Birmingham, Alabama 35213-1206
Phone:	(205) 591-1853
Web Site (URL):	http://www.sbcci.org

Organization:	**SBCCI PST & ESI SBCCI Public Safety Testing and Evaluation Services, Inc.**
Address:	900 Montclair Road, Suite A
	Birmingham, AL 35213-1206
Phone:	(205) 591-1853
Web Site (URL):	http://sbcci.org
Organization:	**SJI Steel Joist Institute**
Address:	3127 10th Avenue North Extension
	Myrtle Beach, SC 29577
Phone:	(803) 626-1995
Organization:	**TMS The Masonry Society**
Address:	3775 Iris Avenue
	Boulder, CO 80301-2043
Phone:	(303) 939-9700
Organization:	**TPI Truss Plate Institute**
Address:	583 D'Onofrio Drive, Suite 200
	Madison, WI 53719
Phone:	(608) 833-5900
Organization:	**UL Underwriters Laboratories, Inc.**
Address:	333 Pfingsten Road
	Northbrook, IL 60062-2096
Phone:	(847) 272-8800
Organization:	**USDOC United States Department of Commerce**
Address:	National Technical Information Service
	5285 Port Royal Road
	Springfield, VA 22161
Phone:	(703) 487-4600

Bibliography

Barrier Free Environments. 1993. *UFAS Retrofit Guide: Accessibility Modifications for Existing Buildings.* New York: Van Nostrand Reinhold.

Building Officials & Code Administrators International, Inc. 1993. *The BOCA National Building Code.* Country Club Hills, Illinois: Building Officials & Code Administrators International, Inc.

Council of American Building Officials. 1995. *CABO One and Two Family Dwelling Code.* Falls Church, Virginia: Council of American Building Officials.

Council of American Building Officials. 1995. *The Model Energy Code.* Falls Church, Virginia: Council of American Building Officials.

Revised by Fitzgerald, Dr. Robert W. 1991. Fundamentals of Firesafe Building Design. In *Fire Protection Handbook,* Seventeenth Edition. Arthur E. Cote, P.E. and Jim L. Linville, Quincy, Massachusetts: National Fire Protection Association.

Hall, John R., Jr. and Cote, Authur E. 1991. America's Fire Problem and Fire Protection. In *Fire Protection Handbook,* Seventeenth Edition. Arthur E. Cote, P.E. and Jim L. Linville, Quincy, Massachusetts: National Fire Protection Association.

International Code Council, Inc. 1996. *The International Mechanical Code.* Country Club Hills, Illinois: International Code Council, Inc.

International Code Council, Inc. 1995. *The International Plumbing Code.* Country Club Hills, Illinois: International Code Council, Inc.

International Conference of Building Officials. 1994. *The Uniform Building Code.* Vol. 1, *Administrative, Fire- and Life-Safety, and Field Inspection Provisions.* Whittier, California: International Conference of Building Officials.

International Conference of Building Officials. 1994. *The Uniform Building Code.* Vol. 2, *Structural Engineering Design Provisions.* Whittier, California: International Conference of Building Officials.

National Fire Protection Association. 1994. *NFPA 101 Code for Safety to Life from Fire in Buildings and Structures.* Quincy, Massachusetts: National Fire Protection Association.

National Fire Protection Association. 1996. *NFPA 14 Installation of Standpipe and Hose Systems.* Quincy, Massachusetts: National Fire Protection Association.

National Fire Protection Association. 1995. *NFPA 252 Standard Methods of Fire Tests of Door Assemblies.* Quincy, Massachusetts: National Fire Protection Association.

National Fire Protection Association. 1992. *NFPA 220 Standard on Types of Building Construction.* Quincy, Massachusetts: National Fire Protection Association.

Office of the Attorney General, 1991. U.S. Department of Justice. *Nondiscrimination on the Basis of Disability in State and Local Government Services; Final Rule.* Washington, D.C.: Government Printing Office.

Olin, Harold B., John L. Schmidt, and Walter H. Lewis. 1995. *"Construction": Principles, Materials & Methods.* Revised by H. Leslie Simmons. New York: Van Nostrand Reinhold.

The Scranton Fire Test. New York: American Iron and Street Institute. October 1972.

Southern Building Code Congress International, Inc. 1996. *The Standard Building Code.* Birmingham, Alabama: Southern Building Code Congress International, Inc.

Stephenson, Elliott O. 1993. "The Elimination of Unsafe Guardrails—A Progress Report," *Southern Building* May/June: 6-10.

Templer, John. 1994. *"The Staircase": Studies of Hazards, Falls, and Safer Design.* Chicago: The Institute of Financial Education and the Interstate Printers and Publishers.

U.S. Department of Justice. Office of the Attorney General. 1991. *Nondiscrimination on the Basis of Disability by Public Accommodations and in Commercial Facilities; Final Rule.* Washington, D.C.: Government Printing Office.

Index

using glass blocks, 390–391
Masonry construction
  cavity wall, 384
  design standards for, 385–386
  grouted hollow unit, 380–381, 383
  reinforced grouted multiple-wythe, 384–385
  reinforced hollow unit, 380–381, 383
Masonry veneer, 314–317, 380
Materials. *See also* Building materials; Insulating materials
  alternate, 41–44
  construction types and, 126–128
  duct, 443
  fire-resistant, 133–135, 161
  for footings, 355–357
  hazardous, 78
  plumbing, 427
  regulation of, 7, 376
  safety of, 13
  for sanitary drainage, 431
  for storm drainage systems, 437
  for water distribution systems, 431
Maximum occupant content, 190–191
Means of egress, 8, 177–225. *See also* Egress; Exits
  accessible, 196–199
  arrangement of exits, 191–199
  for disabled persons, 196–197
  doors, 220–221
  emergency, 293
  exit discharge, 215–218
  fire escapes, 218–219
  guardrails, 222–224
  identifying, 224–225
  maximum occupant content, 190–191
  number of exits, 182–186
  occupant load and, 178–182
  ramps, 221
  stairways, 202–212
Means of egress design, 19
Mechanical codes, 439–442
Mechanical equipment, 446
  fuel-fired, 444
  installing, 441–442
Mechanical inspections, 50
Mechanical permits, 48
Mechanical systems, 425, 439–448
Mechanical ventilation, 301
Medical care facilities under the Americans with Disabilities Act Accessibility Guidelines (ADAAG), 292
  mixed construction and, 129–130
Mental impairment, 238
Mercantile occupancies, 86-88, 100
Metal reinforcement, of concrete, 376, 380
Metals, use in construction, 406–407
Metal veneers, 317–318

Method for Fire Tests of Roof Coverings, 41–42
Mezzanines, 117–118
  means of egress for, 183, 184, 186
Minimum Guidelines and Requirements for Accessible Design (MGRAD), 228
Minimum occupant load, 180, 191
Mixed occupancies, 68, 94
  fire rating, 137
  height and area limitations for, 111–114
Mobility
  in correctional facilities, 84
  of health care occupants, 82
  of occupants, 63–65
Model code organizations, 42, 43
Model codes, 296
Model Energy Code (MEC), 307, 308–309, 310
Mortar, for glass blocks, 391
Mortar installation, 388
Mortar joints, 315
Motels, 88–89
Multifamily residential occupancies, 88–89, 90
Multiple occupancies, code limitations on, 111–114

National Building Code, 20, 21, 25, 113, 129
  height and area modifications and, 110–111
National Fire Codes, Standards, and Recommended Practices and Guides, 20
National Fire Protection Association (NFPA), xiv, xix, 20, 161. *See also* NFPA 101
  Life Safety Code code promulgation process of, 28
Natural light sources, 298–299
Natural ventilation, 299, 301
Net area, 118–119, 120
Net square footage, 180
New construction
  under the Americans with Disabilities Act (ADA), 234, 273–280
  assumed property lines and, 146–147
NFPA 14 Standard for the Installation of Standpipe and Hose Systems, 173
NFPA 72E Automatic Fire Detectors, 175
NFPA 72 Installation, Maintenance, and Use of Protective Signaling Systems, 175
NFPA 74 Household Fire Warning Equipment, 176
NFPA 101 Life Safety Code, xix, 14, 21, 22, 53, 65, 77–78, 88, 109, 114, 116, 118, 129, 144, 145, 415

fire walls and, 148
  sprinkler systems and, 172
NFPA 220 Standard on Types of Building Construction, 129
NFPA 252 Fire Tests of Door Assemblies, 152–153
Nonambulatory health care occupancies, 80
Noncombustible construction
  for chimneys, 391
  types of, 129
  in underground buildings, 103
Noncombustible materials, 126–128
Noncombustible metals, 406
Nonrated partitions, 143
Nonstructural partitions, 129
Notice requirements, of the Americans with Disabilities Act (ADA), 270
Nursing home occupancies, 63
Nursing stations, 82

Occupancy. *See also* Special occupancy
  assembly, 66–69
  business, 69–72
  certificates of, 50–51
  detention and correctional, 83–86
  educational, 72–74
  factory industrial, 74–76
  hazardous, 76–80
  health care, 80–83
  institutional restrained, 83–86
  institutional unrestrained, 80–83
  mercantile, 86–88
  mixing, 113–114
  partition requirements by, 143
  residential, 88–90
  storage, 91–93
  utility, 93–94
Occupancy classifications, 14–16, 29-30, 55, 56-65
  changes in, 36
  choosing, 94
  fire rating and, 134
  height and area limitations and, 108–109
  mixing, 30
Occupancy/construction matrix, 15–16
Occupancy groups, 65–94
Occupancy separation, 111, 113
  fire-resistance and, 137–139
Occupant alertness, 89
Occupant content, maximum, 190–191
Occupant density, 59–60
Occupant load, 178–182
Occupant load calculation, 17–18
Occupants
  alertness of, 62–63
  familiarity with building, 60–62
  mobility of, 63–65
Offices, incidental, 139

height and area modifications and, 110

Standard of care, 25, 230
  under the Americans with Disabilities Act (ADA), 235, 255
  in retroactive codes, 37
Standard of protection, 36
Standards. *See also* Codes, standards, and regulations
  defined, 2–3
  relationship to codes, 4
Standards for Accessible Design, 258
Standby power, 102, 103, 105, 416
  in underground buildings, 103
Standing space, in horizontal exits, 214
Standpipes, 9, 173–174
State accessibility codes, 229, 230-231, 295–296
State accessibility standards, 235–236
State building codes, 2, 22
State code officials, 80
State Historic Preservation Officer, 291
Steel construction, 406–407
Steel piles, 373
Steel pipe and tube piles, 373
Stop-work order, 39–40, 52
Storage areas
  in businesses, 69
  incidental, 137–139
Storage facilities, 76–77
Storage occupancies, 79, 91-93
Stores, accessibility of, 259
Structural diaphragms, 404–405
Storm drainage, 437–439
  installing, 438–439
Structural engineering, 337–338
Structural impracticability, under the Americans with Disabilities Act (ADA), 278
Structural independence requirement, 150
Structural loads, 335–337. *See also* Loads
Structural members, deflection in, 347–348
Structural regulations, writing, 337
Structural shape, wind load and, 345
Structural strength, 13
Structures, unsafe, 40. *See also* Safety
Studs, for vertical framing, 399–400
Subfloors, 398, 399
"Substantial alteration" concept, 280
Sumps, 434
Surface burning characteristics, 166
Survey reports, of inaccessible features, 272

"Technical infeasibility" limitation, 290
Telecommunications devices for the deaf (TDDs), 273
Tempered glass, 407
Tenant fire separation, 139–140

Tenant responsibilities, under the Americans with Disabilities Act (ADA), 262–263
Termite infestation, 395
  footings and, 357
Terms of art. *See* Americans with Disabilities Act (ADA)
Terrace walls, 363
Testing, 348
  of concrete, 378
  of mechanical systems, 440–441
Testing laboratories, 42–43
Testing organizations, 41, 44
Test Methods for Fire Tests of Building Construction and Materials, 127
Test reports, 51
Theaters, 68–69
Thermal barriers, 413
Thermal insulating materials, 160
Tile roofs, 333
Timber piles, 373
Time-share condominiums, 253, 292
Time-temperature curve, 153
Toilet rooms, 305
  accessible, 260
Toxic contents, 56, 58, 75–76
Toxic smoke, 413
Transient lodging, accessible, 292
Transient occupancies, 88–89
Transition plans, under the Americans with Disabilities Act (ADA), 271
Transportation barriers, removal of, 259
Traps, 437
Trap seals, 435
Trap sizes, 434
Travel paths, common, 196
Trim items, 169
Trusses, 402

Underground buildings, 96, 103–105
"Undue burden" limitation, 263–265
  under Title II (ADA), 268
Uniform Building Code, xviii–xix, 20, 21, 113, 114, 129
  height and area modifications and, 110–111
Uniform Federal Accessibility Standards (UFAS), 21, 228, 229, 235, 274, 280
Uniform loads, 394
Unsafe buildings, code sections concerning, 40. *See also* Safety
Unsafe structures, 38
Urban areas, fire districts and, 122–123
Utility occupancy, 93–94

Validity concept, 52
Vapor barriers
  under concrete slabs, 377–378
  in crawl spaces, 366
Veneered walls, 314–320

Veneers
  exterior, 311
  typical, 313
Ventilation. *See also* Openings
  attic, 332, 333
  of crawl spaces, 364–366
  of elevators, 418–420
  health concerns for, 299–301
  mechanical, 442
  in repair garages, 93
  in smokeproof enclosures, 201–202
Vents
  mechanical codes and, 445
  in plumbing systems, 434–437
Vent stack, 435–437
Vertical egress, in underground buildings, 103
Vertical framing, 399–402
Vertical loads, 315, 316
Vertical openings
  fire protection for, 154–155
  restrictions on, 8
Vertical passage, in high-rises, 102
Vertical shafts, 155–156, 158
Vestibules, 215
  exit, 218
Vinyl siding, 320
Violation notice, 53
Voice alarm signaling systems, 102, 103, 105

Wall coverings, exterior, 311–320
Wall finishes, 166–168
Wall framing, penetrating, 399-400. *See also* Vertical framing
Wall openings, 400–402
  exterior, 145
  fire protection for, 150–154
Walls. *See also* Fire walls
  carpeted, 168–169
  exterior, 143–147
  fire protection for, 150–154
  fire-rated, 137
  fire-resistant interior, 137–139
  foundation, 357–364
  parapet, 147
  veneered, 314–320
Waste pipes, indirect, 434
Water damage, in roofs, 376
Water distribution systems, 429–431
Water heaters, 429, 447
Water pipes, 431
Water pressure, 431
Waterproofing, 366–367
  for high-water-table areas, 354
Water service pipes, 429–431
Weather protection, 312. *See also* Exterior wall coverings; Roofs
  masonry construction and, 389-390
Weep holes, 388